FOUNDATIONS OF INTERNATIONAL COMMERCIAL LAW

Foundations of International Commercial Law provides a fresh analysis of both the contextual features of International Commercial Law and a range of different International Commercial Law instruments. This text covers the various elements which comprise International Commercial Law, the academic debates about the *lex mercatoria* and harmonisation, as well as a discussion of selected conventions and other instruments.

International Commercial Law is concerned with commercial transactions which have an international dimension, for example contracts between parties from multiple jurisdictions. As an area of study, it is characterised by the interaction of a wide range of national and international legal sources which all shape the overall context within which international commercial contracts are made and performed. This book focuses on the international legal sources in particular. It first explores all the different elements which together comprise the context of international commercial transactions, before examining the process of making International Commercial Law. Specific instruments of International Commercial Law discussed in the book include the conventions on the international sale of goods, agency, financial leasing, factoring, receivables financing and secured interests in mobile equipment, together with the UNIDROIT Principles of International Commercial Contracts and documentary credits. There are separate chapters on private international law and international commercial arbitration, and a final chapter exploring the existing and potential impact of the digital economy on International Commercial Law.

Offering a detailed overview of the main themes and key aspects of International Commercial Law, this book is for readers who are new to the subject, whether undergraduate or postgraduate students, legal scholars, practitioners or policymakers.

Christian Twigg-Flesner is Professor of International Commercial Law at the University of Warwick, UK.

FOUNDATIONS OF INTERNATIONAL COMMERCIAL LAW

Christian Twigg-Flesner

Routledge
Taylor & Francis Group

LONDON AND NEW YORK

First published 2022
by Routledge
2 Park Square, Milton Park, Abingdon, Oxon OX14 4RN

and by Routledge
605 Third Avenue, New York, NY 10158

Routledge is an imprint of the Taylor & Francis Group, an informa business

© 2022 Christian Twigg-Flesner

British Library Cataloguing in Publication Data
A catalogue record for this book is available from the British Library

Library of Congress Cataloging-in-Publication Data
A catalog record has been requested for this book

ISBN: 978-1-138-91132-1 (hbk)
ISBN: 978-1-138-91133-8 (pbk)
ISBN: 978-1-315-69280-7 (ebk)

DOI: 10.4324/9781315692807

Typeset in Bembo
by Taylor & Francis Books

CONTENTS

FIGURES

PREFACE

A few years ago, I was approached by Routledge to write a new textbook on International Commercial Law. Having taught the subject at both undergraduate and postgraduate level for what is now more than 15 years, I was glad to be given this opportunity. I had a particular type of text in mind which would offer a distinct perspective on the subject and would allow students new to the topic to gain a sound understanding of the essential conceptual aspects and the substance of some of the main elements of International Commercial Law.

International Commercial Law is a fascinating, challenging and rewarding subject to study. Not only does it deal with the study of various international texts on many types of international commercial contracts, it also requires some knowledge of private international law and international commercial arbitration as a dispute resolution mechanism. Alongside the doctrinal dimension, there is a rich and growing contextual literature in this area, particularly on the perennial debates around harmonisation on the one hand, and the *lex mercatoria* on the other.

I have endeavoured to keep this book to a manageable length. I could have written a lot more about many of the topics; indeed, some could easily be (and are) subjects of separate books. I hope that I have struck a reasonable balance in charting the different elements of the individual topics of this book without being too superficial, or too complex for a reader new to the subject.

This book is intended mainly for students about to embark on a postgraduate programme in International Commercial Law, who would like to gain some knowledge of the broader picture before delving deeper into specific topics. It is also suitable for use as a text for a stand-alone undergraduate or postgraduate module on International Commercial Law – indeed, much of the book reflects the way I have taught the subject as a module both at the University of Warwick, and in earlier years at the University of Hull.

I have enjoyed working on this book, although a number of unpredictable and rather disruptive events over the last five years have made this a longer process than I had planned. I am grateful to Routledge and Siobhan Poole in particular for their patience and support. My thanks also go to my colleagues on the LLM programmes at the University of Warwick, and other fellow scholars of International Commercial Law. However, my biggest thanks go to the one person who has always managed to ensure, despite the enormous pressures of academic life (particularly during the pandemic), that I would rest and eat: my husband, Paul Kilford.

Christian Twigg-Flesner

1

THE FEATURES OF INTERNATIONAL COMMERCIAL LAW

1. Introduction

This chapter explores the features of International Commercial Law. If one were to look for a single International Commercial Law applicable throughout the world, then one would seek in vain: unlike domestic areas of law such as contract law, tort law, property law or commercial law, there is no box in which all the rules and principles of International Commercial Law can be found. Rather, International Commercial Law comprises elements from a wide range of international and national sources, along with international trade usages, self-regulation and standard forms developed for international contracts. Which of these sources will apply to any particular international commercial transaction will depend on a variety of factors, partly determined by the rules of the applicable law,[1] partly determined by the choices made by the parties to the transaction, and partly on any relevant trade usages. This chapter will explain the role of all of these components and how they interact to provide the legal context for any international commercial transaction.

2 The role of commercial law

2.1 What is "commercial law"?

Before turning to the specific features of International Commercial Law, it is necessary to consider what is meant by "commercial law", and what the main objectives of commercial law are. Commercial law, in essence, is concerned with transactions between private parties who are involved in commercial activity. At the heart of commercial law are therefore the many different types of contracts and

---

1   This is discussed in more detail in Chapter 2.

DOI: 10.4324/9781315692807-1

related transactions, and the focus of commercial law is primarily on contracts. In this sense, it can be distinguished from company law, which is the law concerned with business structures and organisations, and trade law, which focuses on the way in which States facilitate or restrict trade. Commercial law is about more than just contracts and the various legal rules and principles which directly apply to contracts. Most commercial contracts are entered into in a context which includes regulatory regimes of different kinds, and such regimes can have an influence on the way in which contracts are made and performed. Commercial law therefore includes all the different types of legal principles and legal rules which shape the rights of the parties to a commercial transaction. One of the UK's most eminent legal scholars described commercial law as "the totality of the law's response to the needs and practices of the mercantile community".[2]

Commercial law can take a variety of forms. A helpful typology is provided by Block-Lieb, who distinguishes between commercial common law, commercial code and commercial regulation.[3] In her typology, commercial common law arises from the contracts between commercial parties which result in litigation and at which point a court determines the relevant law based on contracting practices and judicial precedents. A commercial code is a legislative recasting of past contracting practices and existing judgments, as well as provisions on emerging issues. Both of these interact with contracts; in particular, commercial code rules can usually be displaced by the terms of the contract. In contrast, commercial regulation concerns binding obligations for commercial parties which are mandatory and therefore cannot be contracted out of, and which can be enforced by public bodies as well as private parties. As we will see, in the areas of International Commercial Law we focus on in this book, there is hardly any commercial regulation; this is primarily found in the context of financial services regulation and intellectual property law.

2.2 Guiding principles

The main purpose of commercial law is to facilitate commercial activity, i.e., to enable commercial transactions to occur. In doing so, there are two core guiding principles.[4] The first is predictability, both with regard to the legal rules affecting commercial transactions, and the security of transactions so commercial parties can be confident that their transactions will be given effect to by the law. In the context of English Law, Lord Hoffmann once famously noted that "in a case in which there is no threat to the consistency of the law or objection of public policy, the courts should be very slow to declare a practice of the commercial community to be conceptually impossible ... . Rules of law must obviously be consistent and not

---

2   E. McKendrick, *Goode on Commercial Law*, 5th ed. (Penguin, 2017), p.1299.
3   S. Block-Lieb, "Soft and hard strategies: the role of business in the crafting of international commercial law" (2019) 40 *Michigan Journal of International Law* 433, pp.444–448.
4   A comprehensive list of commercial law principles can be found in R. Goode, "The codification of commercial law" (1988) 14 *Monash University Law Review* 135, pp.148–155.

self-contradictory ... But the law is fashioned to suit the practicalities of life."[5] This emphasises the fact that commercial law should favour recognising and giving effect to the arrangements made by commercial parties rather than be too strict in applying existing law, except where there are reasons of public policy or where doing so would undermine the consistency of the law.

The second is flexibility, which reflects the fact that commercial law has to be suitable for a wide range of different commercial transactions; furthermore, as commercial practices evolve, commercial law has to be able to adapt to such changes so as not to stifle commercial activities. In the words of Lord Devlin, "the function of commercial law is to allow, so far as it can, commercial men to do business in the way they want to do it and not to require them to stick to forms that they may think to be outmoded".[6] In other words, rather than preventing the development of new business practices by commercial parties and their recognition by the law, commercial law needs to have a sufficient degree of agility to adjust in the light of changing business practices.

Alongside these two core principles, party autonomy and freedom of contract are just as important. Freedom of contract means that commercial parties are free to decide which contracts to enter into, and to determine the terms of their contracts. In the words of Lord Toulson, a former justice of the UK's Supreme Court, "parties are ordinarily free to contract on whatever terms they choose, and the court's role is to enforce them".[7] However, this entails an added responsibility for the parties to a contract to take care in negotiating and drafting the terms of their contracts so as not to enter into a contract which may turn out rather differently from what the parties might have expected. Associated with freedom of contract is the principle of party autonomy, which covers not only the parties' freedom of contract, but also their right to determine, with few limitations, the law which will apply to their contract.

3 What is International Commercial Law?

3.1 Transnational or International Commercial Law?

It is first important to address a fundamental question of terminology, and to draw a distinction between "Transnational Commercial Law" and "International Commercial Law". Both are used in the academic literature, and it is not always clear whether, and how, the two might be distinguished.

The term "transnational law" does not have a single meaning, and the academic literature reveals a variety of different uses.[8] According to Jessup, transnational law includes "all law which regulates actions or events that transcend national frontiers.

---

5   Lord Hoffmann in *Re BCCI (No. 8)* [1997] 4 All ER 568 at 578.
6   *Kum v Wah Tat Bank Ltd* [1971] 1 Lloyd's Rep 439 at 444.
7   *Prime Sight Limited (A company Registered in Gibraltar) v Edgar Charles Lavarello (Official Trustee of Benjamin Marrache a Bankrupt)* [2013] UKPC 22, para. [47].
8   See, e.g., G. Bamodu, "Extra-national legal principles in the global village: a conception examination of transnational law" (2001) 4 *International Arbitration Law Review* 6.

Both public and private international law are included, as are other rules which do not wholly fit into such standard categories."[9] Jessup's focus was not limited to commercial law, but his broad definition can be translated into commercial context as "all law which regulates commercial activity which transcends national frontiers". It denotes the totality of sources constituting the legal context for cross-border commercial transactions. Horn observed that this is one of three possible ways of understanding transnational commercial law,[10] the other two being the factual uniformity of the law and contractual patterns, and international sources of law such as conventions or customs.

In this book, the term "transnational commercial law" is understood as the entire range of legal sources which, in one way or another, deal with the legal issues which arise in the context of commercial transactions which have a cross-border, or international, dimension. This broadly follows Jessup's conception of transnational law and aligns with Horn's first understanding of transnational commercial law. There are at least seven different categories of source which provide the legal rules, other rules and guiding principles which can govern such cross-border commercial transactions. They are summarised in Figure 1.1. Several of these categories refer to sources which have their origin at the international level, i.e., they are created by international organisations or bodies and are designed for international commercial transactions. These categories are of primary interest for this book, and therefore the focus is on the foundations of International Commercial Law, rather than on all the elements of transnational commercial law. Other scholars would not make such a distinction and either apply the label "transnational commercial law" to any commercial law which is transnational in origin, and therefore cover much of the same ground,[11] or reserve the label "international" for actions taken at the inter-governmental level.[12]

For present purposes, the distinction between international and transnational commercial law made here serves to define the substantive scope of the discussion in this book. International Commercial Law is essentially a sub-category of transnational commercial law. Indeed, it will be seen in this book that the various legal sources emanating from the international sphere do not operate in isolation and interlink with the other categories comprising transnational commercial law. It is crucial for understanding International Commercial Law to recognise that its immediate context is the wider transnational legal regime relevant to international

---

9   P. Jessup, *Transnational Law* (Yale University Press, 1956), p.1.

10   N. Horn, "Uniformity and diversity in the law of international commercial contracts" in N. Horn and C. Schmitthoff, *The Transnational Law of International Commercial Transactions* (Kluwer, 1982), pp.12–13.

11   G. Bamodu, "Extra-national legal principles in the global village: a conception examination of transnational law" (2001) 4 *International Arbitration Law Review* 6, p.9. Bamodu concludes that transnational (commercial) law has the following characteristics: "(a) its sources are extra-national; (b) its rules and principles have extensive or near-universal geographical recognition and acceptance; (c) it relates primarily to transactions of a private nature; and (d) it relates primarily to transactions involving a foreign element" (p.16).

12   M. Heidemann, *Transnational Commercial Law* (Red Globe Press, 2019), p.6.

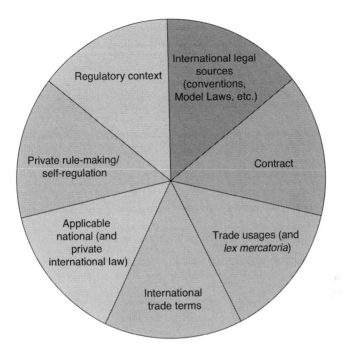

FIGURE 1.1. Sources of law for international commercial transactions

(i.e., cross-border) commercial transactions. Although much of this book focuses on the internationally made legal sources, some space must be given to explaining the wider transnational law for commercial transactions.

Some of these categories will be examined more fully in this book. Here, it will be useful to explain briefly what each of these categories are and how they comprise the transnational regime for commercial transactions.

Contract: Each commercial transaction (whether domestic or international) is based on a contract between the parties to the transaction. Contracts may be carefully and extensively negotiated by the parties and their lawyers, particularly for high-value and low-frequency transactions. Regular and recurring transactions are more likely to be conducted on the basis of pre-drafted standard form contracts, i.e., the terms of the contract will be a set of pre-prepared standard terms put forward by one of the parties. As we will see in this book, parties to an international commercial contract have a high degree of freedom in setting the terms of their contract, selecting the applicable legal regime, and in how any disputes which might arise should be resolved. For some types of international commercial contracts, standard terms have been developed by industry organisations which facilitate the conclusion of international commercial contracts by removing the need for detailed negotiation.

Applicable national law: Each contract will be subject to a national contract law regime. This is essential for requirements of contract formation and validity, in particular, i.e., the factors which must be present for a contract to be recognised in law. The applicable national law will also provide both background (or default) rules in case the parties have failed to deal with a particular matter expressly, as well as some rules which are fundamental and cannot be contracted out of (so-called mandatory rules). Parties to an international commercial contract are mostly free to choose the national law which will apply, or govern, their contract, although there are some limitations which may be set by the respective national laws where the parties have their place of business.[13] If the parties omit to choose the applicable law, the rules of private international law (discussed in Chapter 2) are used to determine the applicable law as well as the recognition of any relevant mandatory rules or other limitations. The applicable law will also determine which of the international legal sources apply to the transaction. This is because any of the international legal sources depend on the decision of national legislatures to adopt or ratify such international sources for their application.

International legal sources: As noted at the start of this chapter, there is no such thing as one International Commercial Law. However, there are a significant number of international legal sources of relevance to international commercial contracts. First and foremost, a number of conventions (essentially a type of international treaty) provide rules on aspects of certain types of international commercial transactions. Individual countries can choose to ratify these and make them part of their legal system. Contracts governed by the law of a country which has ratified a relevant convention will be subject to the international rules, rather than the otherwise applicable rules of national law. The more countries ratify a convention, the wider its reach will be. We will examine a number of conventions in more depth in some of the chapters of this book. In addition, there are a number of Model Laws, which are essentially a template offered to national governments for reforming or developing their national laws on particular areas of law relevant to international commercial transactions. These international legal sources are usually developed under the auspices of one of the two main international bodies in this field: the United Nations Commission on International Trade Law (UNCITRAL)[14] and the International Institute for the Unification of Private Law (UNIDROIT).[15] Other international legal sources are international trade terms put forward by international organisations such as the International Chamber of Commerce (ICC) or industry-specific organisations such as the Grain and Feed Trade Association (GAFTA).

Trade usages: In some trade sectors or industries, certain "rules" relevant to particular transactions, or the manner in which the parties are expected to act, may be based on the usages of that trade. We will see below that usages are regarded as *de facto* rules which are generally followed in a particular trade, despite the absence

13 See Chapter 2.
14 See www.unictral.un.org [accessed December 2020]. For an account of UNCITRAL's role, see C. Nicholas, "UNCITRAL's role in commercial law reform: history and future prospects" in O. Akseli and J. Linarelli, *The Future of Commercial Law* (Hart, 2020).
15 See www.unidroit.org [accessed December 2020].

of a legal rule requiring this. There is an extensive debate in the academic literature as to whether trade customs are of such a density that they constitute an unwritten global *lex mercatoria* (law merchant), which is presented as an alternative to the legal rules derived from national law and international sources.

International trade terms: As already noted, for some types of international commercial transactions, various international bodies have developed sets of trade terms to be used for these transactions. Although trade terms are in the form of standard form templates and usually need to be selected by the parties to an international commercial contract, they are often regarded as having a more normative status in the context of International Commercial Law than "ordinary" standard terms. In part, this may be because these trade terms have been derived from established usage, e.g., the Uniform Customs and Practices for Documentary Credits (UCP) issued by the ICC.[16]

Private rule-making (Self-regulation): A further component of International Commercial Law is private rule-making, or self-regulation. In many business and trade sectors, the relevant industry organisation operates a code of conduct for its industry, monitors compliance with the code and provides dispute resolution procedures. A different form of private rule-making is the development and adoption of technical standards, particularly by the International Organization for Standardization (ISO).[17] Technical standards are widely used to determine common criteria for, e.g., the quality and safety of goods, and the environmental impact of products and services.

Regulatory context: Finally, there are a range of regulatory measures that might be engaged by an international commercial contract. These could be matters such as tax obligations, licencing requirements in order to import or market goods in a jurisdiction other than the one where the supplier is located, or other forms of compliance requirements. Furthermore, it can also include relations between private parties and States, as well as between States in the field of international economic law. Relevant here are the decisions by the World Trade Organization, but also the many international investment treaties. The detail of all of this is beyond the scope of this book.

International Commercial Law has the same objectives and guiding principles as domestic commercial law, although its focus is on commercial transactions that have an international dimension. A commercial transaction will have an international dimension because the transaction is not limited to one jurisdiction. This would be the case, e.g., where the parties to the transaction are located in different jurisdictions, where goods are sold from one jurisdiction into another, where a bank or other financial organisation is in a different jurisdiction from the contracting parties and so on. At this point, the precise method of distinguishing between international and national transactions does not matter – this is something that will be considered in subsequent chapters when examining specific areas of International Commercial Law.

---

16   See Chapter 9.
17   See www.iso.org [accessed December 2020].

All of these components make up the overall legal context for international commercial transactions. The focus of this book is primarily on the international legal sources: the main international conventions, as well as the role of private international law and the UNIDROIT Principles of International Commercial Law. The growth of international texts since the 1960s has been considerable. Cranston has argued[18] that a key driver behind this is globalisation,[19] which has promoted the increasing internationalisation of commercial activity and resulted in a drive to harmonise relevant legal rules to facilitate such dealings. A particular feature is the shift towards international rather than national rules and the reliance on international arbitration as a preferred method of dispute resolution. As well as establishing international rules, Cranston has suggested that this has also prompted domestic law reform to enhance the flow of commercial activity,[20] not least by promoting commercial law systems which prioritise the interests of creditors over those of debtors in order to encourage international investment.[21] As part of our study of a range of International Commercial Law initiatives, we will see illustrations of all of these points.

In the remainder of this chapter, a closer look will be taken at the role of contracts in international commercial transactions, international trade terms and the role of trade customs, particularly in relation to the debate about the *lex mercatoria*.

4 The contract

A contract is the basis of any international commercial transaction. There are many different types of international commercial contract. Perhaps the most common one is a contract for the sale of goods, under which a seller agrees to supply a buyer with goods and transfer ownership of those goods to the buyer. Alongside the contract of sale, there will frequently be a contract for the carriage of goods by a third-party carrier. Many international commercial contracts are concerned with financial arrangements, such as a contract of leasing, the assignment of receivables or the use of documentary credits as a means of arranging payment in respect of a contract for the sale of goods. Some contracts involve the creation of a security interest in an asset in the context of a loan or under a reservation of title provision in a sales contract.

Some contracts are the result of complex and lengthy negotiation, with (almost) every clause drafted and redrafted by lawyers. Many contracts will, however, be based on pre-drafted sets of standard terms, particularly where the kind of transaction in issue is a recurring one. One advantage of using pre-drafted standard terms is that negotiations between the parties will primarily be about the key features of

---

18   R. Cranston, "Theorizing transnational commercial law" (2007) 45 *Texas International Law Journal* 597, pp.600–607.
19   See also J.H. Dalhuisen, "Globalisation and the transnationalisation of commercial and financial law" (2015) 67 *Rutgers University Law Review* 19.
20   R. Cranston, "Theorizing transnational commercial law" (2007) 45 *Texas International Law Journal* 597, p.608.
21   *Ibid.*, p.610.

the deal, i.e., what will be supplied by one party, and how much will the other party pay in return.

Contracts are therefore an essential ingredient of any international commercial transaction, and such contracts will do much of the work in determining the parties' respective rights and obligations in respect of that transaction. Crucially, the functions of a contract go beyond the contents of the transaction between the parties: it also engages the wider legal context through the incorporation of trade terms or industry-standard terms, the opting-out of an otherwise applicable international convention, the choice of the applicable law and the choice of the dispute resolution mechanism. It does not, however, capture the wider commercial (rather than the legal) relationship between the parties, but this "real deal"[22] can be a crucial aspect of the overall relationship between the parties to an international commercial transaction.

4.1 Role of private international law/conflict of laws

We have already noted the importance of the applicable law in providing the legal regime governing an international commercial contract. The relevance of private international law for determining the applicable law, and the extent to which the parties are free to select the applicable law as a matter of party autonomy, will be discussed in Chapter 2. However, one issue merits closer attention here. This concerns the drafting of standard form contracts which are then used frequently for similar transactions. Often, such terms will have been drafted by lawyers, and will then be used by a business for most, if not all, of the contracts it enters into. Invariably, the terms of the standard form contract will have been drafted in the context of a particular jurisdiction and will be designed to work in the context of that jurisdiction. If drafted carefully, a choice-of-law clause will be included to select the law of that jurisdiction as the law governing the contract. However, if, for some reason, there is no choice-of-law clause, or if this was amended during contract negotiations, then this could create the risk that the contract terms will not be interpreted as intended, should a dispute arise and be litigated on the basis of a different national law.[23] Legal drafting styles differ between different legal families. Generally speaking, contracts drafted against the backdrop of the common law are more likely to be detailed, because the common law is generally non-interventionist and puts the onus on the parties to make appropriate provision for most things in their contracts. In contrast, civil law jurisdictions provide background rules in their civil codes which operate to fill any gaps in a contract. As a result, contracts may be less detailed in those circumstances. If insufficient attention is given to the applicable law when drafting a contract, it is possible that the legal effects of a contract drafted in a way common in one jurisdiction could be quite

---

22 S. Macaulay, "The real and the paper deal" (2003) 66 *Modern Law Review* 44.
23 See G. Cordero-Moss, *International Commercial Contracts* (Cambridge University Press, 2014), for a detailed discussion.

different and unexpected when interpreted against the domestic law of another jurisdiction.

4.2 Templates for standard terms

Many international organisations issue model contracts which can be selected by the parties to a relevant contract as a ready-made set of standard terms. Parties are free to decide whether they wish to use them either as they are or with some modifications. For instance, GAFTA has published many different types of model contracts. These model contracts are utilised for a large number of contracts in the grain trade.[24] GAFTA standard form contracts contain a choice-of-law clause designating English Law as the applicable law, and the contracts are drafted against the backdrop of English contract law. The advantage of using a model contract lies in the fact that it reduces the need for negotiation of contract terms, particularly for types of contract which are concluded frequently and which can follow a standard pattern. As well as the saving in time and cost, it also provides a high degree of predictability in that the parties will be familiar with their respective obligations under such model contracts and will know that the model contract is suitable for the particular international transaction.

In addition to model contracts for particular transactions, there are also model clauses for particular types of contract term. The ICC has published both model contracts (e.g., on distributorship, commercial agency or the international sale of manufactured goods) and model clauses (e.g., clauses on *force majeure* and hardship,[25] or arbitration). Such templates are intended to reflect the particular requirements of international commercial contracts, and are intended both to simplify the process of contract formation and to offer a common international standard for key contract types or contract terms.

4.3 Contract as a regulatory/governance process in global value chains

In international commerce, contracts are often not just discrete transactions between two parties, but are an element in a longer supply chain. Such supply chains are themselves an interesting development in international commerce: instead of keeping all the stages of production in-house, many businesses have effectively unbundled the different stages of production and have outsourced these to businesses around the globe. This has resulted in the creation of global supply chains, or global value chains.

The primary purpose of such supply chains is ultimately to supply an end-customer, such as a major retailer, with finished products. In order to do this, a chain,

---

24 See www.gafta.com/All-Contracts [accessed December 2020], estimating the proportion at 80 per cent.
25 Issued in 2003; an updated version was issued in 2020 in light of the COVID-19 pandemic. See https://iccwbo.org/publication/general-considerations-force-majeure-clauses-in-comm ercial-contracts/ [accessed October 2020].

or a web, of contracts is established, which starts with suppliers of raw materials, component manufacturers, product designers, and eventually the final assembly of the finished product. Such global value chains are usually arranged by the business which is the supplier of the finished item to the end-customer. The buyer of the finished item is often referred to as the "chain-leader". The buyer will have made stipulations such as regarding the quality of the materials to be used, which are then imposed on each party along the supply chain through the terms of the respective sub-contracts. However, increasingly, chain-leaders will not only set out their requirements with regard to the products themselves, but also include provisions mandating that each chain member adhere to requirements in respect of human rights, sustainability, compliance with environmental requirements or labour standards.[26] The contracts in a supply chain are therefore not only concerned with the finished product, but are also key elements of the process leading to the finished product, taking into account matters which go beyond the typical focus of a commercial contract, i.e., the deal itself, and which reflect wider public policy concerns, or public values. Indeed, these are typically the kind of provisions which would, ordinarily, be imposed through State regulation. However, in the absence of international co-operation in ensuring compliance with public policy requirements and limited scope for enforcement beyond individual State borders, the utilisation of global value chains as an alternative vehicle for promoting and ultimately securing compliance with public policy concerns is a significant development.

The expectations, or requirements, relating to such public policy/value concerns may be laid down in international agreements (e.g., the United Nation's Sustainable Development Goals[27] or the conventions and recommendations by the International Labour Organization[28]), or through international NGOs (such as the World Fair Trade Organization), as well as technical standards (e.g., by the ISO). They are therefore determined externally and not by the chain-leader; instead, the chain-leader will require compliance with these as a matter of contractual obligation. In this way, each member of the supply chain undertakes to comply with these expectations/requirements, and members will have an interest in monitoring compliance of others to ensure that the supply chain as a whole complies with the stipulations made by the chain-leader.

In addition to in-chain compliance monitoring, compliance can also be monitored externally, e.g., by an agency or NGO which has issued the criteria each chain member is bound to adhere to. A failure to comply with these requirements will simultaneously be a breach of the contracts to which the infringing business is

---

26 For a detailed account, see F. Cafaggi, "The regulatory functions of transnational commercial contracts: new architectures" (2013) 36 *Fordham International Law Journal* 1557.

27 Resolution on "Transforming our world: the 2030 Agenda for Sustainable Development", 25 September 2015.

28 See ILO, *Conventions and Recommendations*, https://www.ilo.org/global/standards/introduction-to-international-labour-standards/conventions-and-recommendations/lang–en/index.htm [accessed December 2020].

a party, and a violation of the external requirements, which could attract additional sanctions such as de-certification of a sub-contractor or even of the chain as a whole.

An umbrella term for the clauses reflecting public values or concerns included in supply chain contracts is "ethical clauses",[29] to distinguish their substance from the clauses which relate to the commercial deal itself. Despite their particular purpose, such ethical clauses are still terms of the contract itself and a failure to comply by a party in the supply chain will be a breach of their respective contract. However, it may be questioned whether the contractual route is sufficient to ensure compliance with the obligations enshrined in such "ethical clauses", and further whether contract law can provide appropriate remedies in respect of such breaches.

In its typical form, a supply chain is just that: a chain of contracts between two contract parties at different levels in the supply chain. This could be an entirely linear chain, or the chain could fan out at the levels further along from the chain-leader. Despite the collective interest of all the chain members, the respective legal relationships will generally only be between the two immediate contracting parties. This means that a breach by one chain member of an ethical clause would only directly concern that member's immediate contractual opposite. The latter may have neither the resources nor the interest in pursuing that breach of contract for a variety of reasons. The two parties with the greatest interest in ensuring compliance throughout the chain will be the chain-leader and the chain-leader's immediate contractual supplier. As neither will be a party to all the various sub-contracts, they would not necessarily have a right to take action in respect of a breach of one of the sub-contracts along the supply chain.

There are ways around this. Some legal systems now recognise a right of third parties, i.e., non-contracting parties, to enforce particular terms of a contract if they are intended to be of direct benefit to them, or where the contract provides that such a third party should have a right of enforcement.[30] Where the relevant applicable law recognises such a right, and provided that the terms of the relevant contract do not exclude the rights of third parties to intervene, this might allow a chain-leader or final supplier to take action in respect of a breach of an ethical clause in a sub-contract. An alternative solution might be to require the party not in breach to assign its right of action for breach of the relevant sub-contract to the final supplier or chain-leader.[31]

Furthermore, the chain-leader may be able to reject any goods which have been produced in violation of the ethical clauses it has stipulated, either under the terms

---

29 See L. Miller, "'Ethical clauses' in global value chain contracts: exploring the limits of freedom of contract" in P.S. Davies and M. Raczynska, *Contents of Commercial Contracts – Terms Affecting Freedoms* (Hart, 2020).

30 F. Cafaggi, "The regulatory functions of transnational commercial contracts: new architectures" (2013) 36 *Fordham International Law Journal* 1557, pp.1591–1595.

31 K. Sobel-Read, G. Anderson and J. Salminen, "Recalibrating contract law: choses in action, global value chains, and the enforcement of obligations outside of privity" (2018) 93 *Tulane Law Review* 1.

of its contract with the final supplier, or on the basis that the goods may not be in conformity with the contract.

However, even where it is possible to take action in respect of a breach of contract, there may still be a question as to whether an appropriate remedy would be available to address that breach.[32] If goods have been produced without complying with ethical clauses throughout, it could be very difficult to rectify this. There may the economic loss in that the goods will be rejected by the chain-leader, but passing that loss along the chain would be of limited effect as the parties further along the chain may not have the economic resources to pay any compensation. Furthermore, where a duty to mitigate losses exists, the goods may yet find their way onto the market, particularly if they are mass-produced generic items. Were this to happen, the chain-leader's desire to ensure compliance with ethical clauses and thereby to contribute to eliminating production practices which fail to comply with the values and standards reflected in those ethical clauses would be undermined.

Some of the interests which the chain leader may seek to protect through ethics clauses are the rights of employees to fair working conditions and pay, or to ensure that high standards of environmental protection are followed. A breach of an ethical clause by a sub-contractor may harm such third parties. Whether they would be able to enforce those rights under the relevant sub-contract would, again, depend on whether this is permitted under both the applicable law and the terms of the relevant sub-contract. Even where this is possible, though, such third parties will often lack the financial resources needed to take the necessary action to enforce their rights.

Relying on contractual enforcement of ethical clauses alone therefore may not do enough to secure compliance with ethical clauses throughout the chain. The chain-leader may wish to monitor the conduct of every party along the supply chain; indeed, there may be instances when this is required from a corporate social responsibility perspective. More importantly, those NGOs and other bodies who set the relevant requirements and standards which are reflected in ethical clauses will often be able to monitor compliance separately and may have other legal and non-legal tools for sanctioning breaches at their disposal.[33] For instance, where there is a failure to adhere to fair trade requirements, the right to use a "Fair Trade" label or symbol could be revoked.

The use of ethical clauses in global value chains is attracting increasing scholarly attention, not least as this practice further blurs the dividing line between the public-regulatory sphere and the private-commercial sphere. Thus, it has been suggested that the inclusion of ethical clauses reflecting international standards or

---

32 Cf. J.C. Lipson, "Promising justice: contract (as) social responsibility" (2019) *Wisconsin Law Review* 1109, pp.1123–1129.

33 See the case-studies in F. Cafaggi and P. Iamiceli, "Private regulation and industrial organization: contractual governance and the network approach" in S. Grundmann, F. Möslein and K. Riesenhuber, *Contract Governance* (Oxford University Press, 2015), pp.361–372.

public values, as well as high(er) national standards under the law of the lead party (buyer), in the contracts within a global value chain could have a "transplant" effect in those countries where the various suppliers are located, in that the practical effect of such obligations is to influence local behaviour of suppliers in accordance with rules and standards set elsewhere.[34] Furthermore, the commitment to ethical obligations, determined by external standards setters and monitored/enforced through third-party certification, entails variations in the contractual design of global value chains, and whilst some may continue to be based on a chain of bilateral contracts, other global value chains may utilise multi-party contracts or develop into contractual networks.[35]

The growth of ethical clauses in global value chains reflects a progressive adjustment in the nature of international commercial contracts. Although much of International Commercial Law focuses on the commercial features of such contracts, it is important to recognise that international commercial contracts are often used as vehicles for promoting such wider ethical concerns and public values. That said, unless there is a transformation in the way contract law can respond to breaches of these types of clauses with a more targeted remedy, the reliance on contracts alone might not be sufficiently effective in ensuring compliance with ethical clauses throughout global value chains.

4.4 International trade terms

We saw above that trade terms are a particular form of standard terms which are drawn up by international organisations or industry associations for particular types of contracts. They are usually derived from existing trade practices or trade usages, and are therefore often treated as *de facto* rules governing certain contracts, or aspects thereof. In this regard, they differ from standard form contracts or model contracts, which generally do not derive from existing trade practices or usages, although the use of such model contracts could eventually become a usage itself. For example, the Uniform Customs and Practices for Documentary Credits (UCP), covered in Chapter 9, set out the rights and obligations of banks as well as those of a buyer and seller of goods in arranging and operating a documentary credit. This is an arrangement for payment used for international contracts, particularly for high-value contracts or for contracts where buyer and seller do not have an established commercial relationship. Rather than providing the relevant legal rules through a convention, they are set out in the UCP instead.

The UCP are issued by the ICC, which is also responsible for another set of commonly used trade terms, the so-called INCOTERMS®. The INCOTERMS deal with the respective obligations of seller and buyer under a contract of sale with

---

34 L.-W. Lin, "Legal transplants through private contracting: codes of vendor conduct in global supply chains as an example" (2009) 57 *American Journal of Comparative Law* 711.
35 F. Cafaggi and P. Iamiceli, "Private regulation and industrial organization: contractual governance and the network approach" in S. Grundmann, F. Möslein and K. Riesenhuber, *Contract Governance* (Oxford University Press, 2015).

regard to the delivery of the goods and related aspects. The first version of the INCOTERMS® was issued in 1936, and the current version is the INCO-TERMS® 2020. The INCOTERMS® are reviewed and updated periodically. Before the current 2020 version, revisions were issued in 2010 and 2000. Crucially, the INCOTERMS® are not a standard form contract for all aspects of a contract for the sale of goods, although they operate in the context of such contracts. They provide trade terms which deal with the point of delivery and the passing of risk, the allocation of responsibilities between seller and buyer (for organising carriage, insurance, obtaining documents and dealing with export/import licences), and the division of costs between the parties. The parties must choose to incorporate the relevant provisions of the INCOTERMS® into their contract. The effect of their incorporation is that the parties' obligations regarding delivery, transfer of risk and related obligations stipulated in the chosen INCOTERM® become part of the contract of sale and will displace the default rules on these aspects under national sales law and/or the UN Convention on the International Sale of Goods (CISG)[36] on these points. The INCOTERMS® provide standardised rules on delivery and transfer of risk, i.e., the point at which delivery occurs and risk is transferred depends on the type of INCOTERM® selected for the particular transaction. There are 11 INCOTERMS® in the current version, each referred to by a three-letter acronym. In the current version of the INCOTERMS®, they are as follows:

EXW [named place] – Ex works
FCA [named place] – Free carrier
CPT [named place] – Carriage paid to
CIP [named place] – Carriage and insurance paid to
DAP [named place] – Delivered at place
DPU [named place] – Delivered at place unloaded
DDP [named place] – Delivered duty paid
FAS [named place] – Free alongside ship
FOB [named place] – Free on board
CFR [named place] – Cost and Freight
CIF [named place] – Cost, Insurance and Freight

This means that parties to an international sales contract can settle their respective obligations with regard to delivery, carriage and insurance with reference to these common arrangements, and incorporate them into their contracts easily. The importance of the INCOTERMS® for international commerce was noted by the Court of Justice of the European Union (CJEU) in *Electrosteel*:[37]

Usages – especially if they are collected, explained and published by recognised professional organisations and widely followed in practice by traders –

---

36 See Chapter 4.
37 C-87/10 *Electrosteel Europe SA v Edil Cenro SpA* ECLI:EU:C:2011:375.

play an important role in the non-governmental regulation of international trade or commerce. They make it easier for traders to draft contracts because, through the use of short and simple terms, they can define many aspects of their business relations. The Incoterms drawn up by the International Chamber of Commerce, which define and codify the content of certain terms and clauses commonly used in international trade or commerce, are particularly widely recognised and used.[38]

The Court stressed the origins of the INCOTERMS® in trade usages and recognised their hybrid role as a form of "non-governmental regulation" via standard terms for incorporation into a contract. This aligns with the ICC's view that the INCOTERMS® consolidate existing commercial practice and therefore reflect what commercial parties actually do. That said, it is not universally accepted that the INCOTERMS® merely consolidate current practice; some changes, particularly since the 2010 revision, seem to be going further.[39] To some extent, this might be the consequence of capturing evolving commercial practice at a given point in time in written form.

There is one potential difficulty with trade terms, arising from their hybrid nature: on the one hand, they are incorporated by the parties into their contract and take legal effect via that route. One the other hand, the rules set out in these trade terms might not align with the legal rules of the applicable law, especially because they are not drafted on the basis of a particular national law. They might also collide with any mandatory rules of the national law applicable to the contract. However, on the whole, courts have recognised the role these trade terms play in facilitating international commerce and have been willing to uphold them on the basis that they reflect trade usages.[40]

5 Private norms/self-regulation

In addition to national and international legal rules for international commercial contracts, and the trade terms for particular contract types developed by international organisations and industry associations, there are also a range of measures in place which can broadly be described as forms of private norm creation or self-regulation. These two categories are not synonymous but have the common feature that they are determined by private actors rather than public agencies. One common form of private norm creation is the development of international standards which set out technical and safety specifications for goods, quality standards, data protection and cybersecurity standards, or service standards.

---

38 *Ibid.*, para. [21].
39 J. Coetzee, "INCOTERMS® 2010: codified mercantile custom or standard contract terms?" (2012) 23 *Stellenbosch Law Review* 564.
40 Most overtly by the UK Supreme Court in *Taurus Petroleum Ltd v State Oil Marketing Company of the Ministry of Oil, Republic of Iraq* [2017] UKSC 64.

A different form of private norm creation[41] is the self-regulatory role performed by trade or industry associations. Those operating in those trades or industries can become members of such associations. A trade association can represent its members externally, e.g., when international bodies such as UNCITRAL or UNIDROIT are developing a new international measure on a particular aspect of International Commercial Law which is of relevance to a particular trade/industry. Additionally, a trade association can perform a regulatory function for its members, in particular through a code of conduct or similar which lays down various rights and obligations for the members of the trade association when dealing with one another, their customers and any third parties.[42] A trade association may also establish their own dispute resolution mechanisms in order to deal with any disputes involving one of its members.

6 International trade usage

In many trade and industry sectors, trade usages have emerged, and continue to emerge, which are regarded as *de facto* binding rules and obligations on the parties active in that trade, despite the absence of any formal legal recognition. They are effectively akin to legal rules, albeit that trade usages have grown from business practice rather than through an enactment by a national or international legislator. Trade usages are an important, if difficult, feature of International Commercial Law, and their existence is integral to the long-running debate about the existence of a *lex mercatoria*, or law merchant, which is claimed to encompass the variety of trade customs which have emerged.

6.1 What are trade usages?

As a preliminary issue, it is necessary to distinguish between "contracting practice", "trade practices" and "trade usages". Contracting practice originate in a business relationship between two parties who over time enter into repeat contracts, and who develop business practices between them. Where these dealings occur regularly and in a consistent manner, their practices are recognised as an integral element of their particular relationship, and can, where appropriate, be implied into future contracts between them. Crucially, whatever practices have become established between these two parties are only relevant to the transactions which occur between these parties, and have no wider application beyond the specific relationship.

However, some practices may be common to many different contractual relationships in a particular trade or industry, and may consistently and frequently be

---

41 See also J. Black and D. Rouch, "The development of the global markets as rule-makers: engagement and legitimacy" (2008) 2 *Law & Financial Markets Review* 218.

42 See generally, F. Cafaggi, "The many features of transnational private rule-making: unexplored relationships between custom, jura mercatorum and global private regulation" (2015) 36 *University of Pennsylvania Journal of International Law* 875.

used. This will happen as a matter of convenience or courtesy, without there being a sense of obligation to follow the practice. It is something which emerges over time as a particular practice in a trade, but parties who decide not to follow that practice will not encounter any obstacles as a consequence.

One step up from trade practice are trade usages, or trade customs. Before we examine the trade usages more closely, it must be pointed out that whilst the terms "trade usage" and "trade custom" are often used interchangeably, some jurisdictions draw a clear distinction between usages and customs respectively. In the context of International Commercial Law, this distinction is less pronounced, if it is made at all. For the present purpose, no specific distinction is drawn between trade customs and trade usages, and both can be understood in the same way. Despite the prevalence of trade usages, it is not easy to find a definition. Dalhuisen (who uses customs and trade usage interchangeably) defines it simply as "a practice which is universal in the trade or a segment thereof".[43] The starting point therefore is a trade practice which has taken on a further quality to give it a stronger and binding character. A more nuanced definition of "trade usage" is offered by Coetzee:[44]

> Trade usage constitutes unwritten practices or patterns of behaviour that have originated in a particular trade or industry, have been in existence for a long time, are well known and are widely and regularly observed by merchants who engage in that trade or industry.

Coetzee goes on to note that knowledge of the trade usage by a party in the relevant trade or industry is not always necessary; those operating in a particular trade or industry are usually deemed to know of relevant trade usages. This knowledge is unlikely to be presented to anyone new to the trade or industry; rather, it is obtained through observing and experiencing how transactions are conducted, or from those who have been active in the trade or industry for longer.

One key feature of a trade usage is that it has a normative character, i.e., those in the relevant trade adhere to the trade usage because they perceive it to have a binding character. This may be classified as a *de facto* binding character because trade usages are not necessarily legally binding in a universal sense (although they can become legally binding through individual contracts concluded by parties in the relevant trade). As a trade usage is perceived to be binding, there is a general expectation that trade usages will be followed by everyone in the relevant trade, and that this will be done out of a sense of obligation rather than merely as a matter of convenience or expedience. In this sense, the binding nature of a trade custom is based on the collective subjective beliefs of those active in the relevant trade or industry as to the existence, and meaning, of a trade usage.

---

43 J.H. Dalhuisen, "Custom and its revival in transnational private law" (2008) 18 *Duke Journal of Comparative & International Law* 339, p.362.
44 J. Coetzee, "The role and function of trade usage in modern international sales law" (2015) 20 *Uniform Law Review* 243, p.249.

Although it is possible to draw a distinction between contracting practice, trade practices and trade usages, this does not mean that these are entirely distinct; rather, trade usages will, over time, have emerged from practices established between commercial parties in a particular trade or industry, and will eventually have become seen as *de facto* binding. Quite which aspects of an observable uniform and regular pattern of behaviour would qualify as a trade usage will be a matter of debate – some uniform patterns may be coincidental and not intended to entail some normative status,[45] and might be less-than-optimal with regard to risk allocation between the parties.[46] The fact that trade usages have taken on this normative character does not mean that they are rigid and have ceased to develop; rather, trade usages are fluid and continue to evolve, just as trade practices evolve. Changing business contexts and technological developments often influence the development of trade practices and, eventually, trade usages.

Trade usages have their roots in the practices of a particular trade or industry, i.e., they are not imposed externally by a legislator. They originate from within the trade or industry. In this sense, they share one of the characteristics of private rule-making, i.e., self-regulation. However, private rule-making and trade usages are distinct and should not be conflated. A closer examination of private rule-making regimes has revealed that these are generally much more structured and organised, follow set procedures, develop their rules centrally and will often have clearly defined enforcement mechanisms.[47] The rules made in this process focus on specific concerns, including those where the interests of members of that trade may conflict or those affecting third-party interests. This process is therefore very different from the emergence of a trade usage, which arises from practices established consensually between parties in the particular trade or industry.

6.1.1 Recognition of trade usages in law

Although trade usages have their origin in commercial practice and are regarded as binding without there being an enacted legal rule to that effect, this does not mean that trade usages and legal rules operate in separate, parallel contexts. Rather, trade usages can be recognised in law as being an element of the parties' obligations towards one another.[48] A trade usage will exist independently from legal recognition and does not require legal recognition as a pre-condition for its normative status. A failure to comply with a trade usage does not have to be met with a legal

---

45 R. Craswell, "Do trade customs exist?" in J.S. Kraus and S.D. Walt, *The Jurisprudential Foundations of Corporate and Commercial Law* (Cambridge University Press, 2000).

46 C.P. Gillette, "Harmony and stasis in trade usages for international sales" (1999) 39 *Virginia Journal of International Law* 707, p.709.

47 F. Cafaggi, "The many features of transnational private rule-making: unexplored relationships between custom, jura mercatorum and global private regulation" (2015) 36 *University of Pennsylvania Journal of International Law* 875.

48 See the analysis by D. Saidov, "Trade usages in international sales law" in D. Saidov (ed.), *Research Handbook on International and Comparative Sale of Goods Law* (Elgar, 2019).

response; instead, commercial sanctions (e.g., higher prices, or ultimately refusal to contract with a party persistently ignoring a trade usage) will often suffice to ensure that parties in a given trade act in accordance with the relevant trade usages.

Nevertheless, before a trade usage can have legal effects, it needs to be recognised in law. Broadly, legal recognition could be determined on a subjective or objective basis. From a subject perspective, a trade usage would be treated as legally binding if both parties had actual knowledge of the existence of the trade usage. In contrast, if determined objectively, the parties would be deemed to have constructive knowledge of a trade usage which is regularly followed and observed in the relevant trade, even if the parties did not have actual knowledge of that usage.

Furthermore, legal recognition of a trade usage may occur indirectly as well as directly. Indirect recognition might occur e.g., in interpreting a flexible legal standard by taking into account a relevant trade usage. For instance, the application of a "reasonableness" criterion could be aided by relying on a relevant trade usage, e.g., a trade usage regarding the time for delivery which could help with the application of a legal rule that delivery should occur within a reasonable period of time.

The direct recognition of a trade usage is usually achieved by making the relevant trade usage part of the contractual obligations of the parties to a contract. For instance, Art. 9 of the UN Convention on the International Sale of Goods (CISG)[49] sets out how trade usages relevant to contracts for the international sale of goods are recognised and applied to a contract.[50] According to Art. 9(1) CISG, the parties will be bound by any usages to which they have agreed. This suggests that the parties can expressly include usages in their contract, even if a usage so included would not normally apply to the specific contract between those parties.[51] More importantly, Art. 9(2) CISG provides that the parties are deemed "to have impliedly made applicable to their contract or its formation a usage of which the parties knew or ought to have known and which in international trade is widely known to, and regularly observed by, parties to contracts of the type involved in the particular trade concerned". There are two requirements in this provision. The crucial one is that the usage is one which is both widely known to and regularly observed by parties to contracts in the particular trade in the type of contracts entered into in that trade. It is also important that the usage is recognised in international dealings, and not merely in a domestic context. For example, in the case of a contract for the sale of cardboard, there may be an established usage about the way in which different grades of cardboard are classified. If this usage is generally known to those involved in buying and selling cardboard, and regularly followed, then the usage is binding on the parties to a contract for the sale of cardboard not only

---

49 The CISG is considered in detail in Chapter 4.

50 This provision is the basis for Art. 1.9 of the UNIDROIT Principles of International Commercial Contracts. See Chapter 10.

51 Art. 9(1) CISG also includes any practices which the parties have established between themselves within their binding obligations. As discussed above, these are practices limited to the particular commercial relationship, rather than of general application.

through its status as a usage, but also through the operation of Art. 9(2) CISG as a legally binding obligation under that contract. The usage in question must be one that is known and observed by parties to contracts in the same trade or industry sector as the parties to the specific contract in issue. The other requirement is that the parties to the specific contract must have known of the usage, or at least that they ought to have known about it. Once both requirements are met, Art. 9(2) CISG makes that usage an element of the contract between the parties, and a failure to comply with the usage would amount to a breach of the contract itself. The parties are, however, permitted to exclude the application of usages to their contract; similarly, if express terms in the contract conflict with a usage, then the usage is excluded as a result.

One thing Art. 9(2) CISG does not consider is the reason why the usage in question is widely observed by parties in the trade: the reason may simply be "a matter of habit, courtesy or convenience"[52] rather than because the usage is regarded as binding in some way. However, this distinction is important for separating frequent trade practices followed out of convenience from those trade practices which are regarded as so essential that they are treated as binding – only the latter practices should be treated as trade usages.[53]

The effect of Art. 9 CISG is to give a usage contractual force, and the non-compliance by a party with such a usage would attract the remedies for non-performance provided under the CISG.[54] Whether the effect of Art. 9 CISG is to determine the basis for the binding nature of a trade usage more generally is contested; some prefer a view which would recognise the binding nature of a usage solely as a matter of contractual agreement, whereas others attribute a normative value to a usage independent of contractual incorporation.[55] As indicated above, the normative view of trade usages is assumed in the present context, although the availability of legal redress will, of necessity, require the legal recognition of the trade usage. Thus, if a breach of a trade usage is to be sanctioned with remedies in respect of a non-performance of a contractual obligation, then the trade usage has to be recognised as being part of the contract between the parties. However, trade usages do not always require legal sanctions, and commercial sanctions, in the same way as social sanctions for violating a social norm, are equally important.[56]

---

52 R. Goode, "Usage and its reception in transnational commercial law" (1997) 46 *International and Comparative Law Quarterly* 1, p.10.

53 On the difficult question of whether the INCOTERMS® qualify as trade usage, see J. Coetzee, "INCOTERMS® 2010: codified mercantile custom or standard contract terms?" (2012) 23 *Stellenbosch Law Review* 564, pp.572–577.

54 See Chapter 4, section 5

55 For an account of these views, see P. Hellwege, "Understanding usage in international contract law harmonization" (2018) 66 *American Journal of Comparative Law* 127, pp.131–140. In his article, Hellwege seeks to mount a strong defence of the contractual view against the normative view of trade usages.

56 Cf. B. Yuan, "A law and economics approach to norms in transnational commercial transactions: incorporation and internalisation" (2016) 9 *Erasmus Law Review* 5.

6.1.2 Determining the substance of a trade usage

We now come to a crucial aspect of trade usages. Thus far, the nature of a trade usage and its recognition in law have been considered. Trade usages can be normative within the relevant trade or industry, and can also be treated as legally enforceable through contracts between parties from the relevant trade or industry. However, when it is said that a trade usage is binding, this does not explain what exactly the parties are obliged to do in order to observe a trade usage. Indeed, determining the substance, or content, of a trade usage can be difficult because of the way it has emerged gradually through observance in the context of contracts entered into by those involved in a particular trade or industry. It is, however, generally difficult (if not impossible) to determine the substance of a trade usage in advance of a particular transaction. In fact, the existence and substance of a trade usage are often only confirmed where this has become an issue in the context of a commercial dispute, and an arbitration panel or court has been asked to consider the existence and substance of a trade usage. This does not mean that the parties active in the relevant trade are entirely unaware of the relevant trade usages; their involvement in and familiarity with the trade will mean that they become aware of the way certain matters are expected to be done, and will consequently follow these expectations. However, this does not give the trade usage the same clarity and predictability as a legal provision found in a legal text such as a statute or declared by a court.

Observing patterns of behaviour in a particular trade or industry might be a good starting point in determining what the substance of a trade usage might be. However, this is unlikely to lead to the identification of a clear, bright-line rule; rather, the observed behaviour can be indicative of a range of possible underlying rules, and generalisation may be difficult.[57] If the issue arises before a court, there will usually be participants from the relevant trade or industry who will testify as to the existence of the trade usage in issue, but such evidence might not be conclusive either. There might be fundamental disagreement as to the existence or substance of the trade usage; even if there is agreement as to its existence and how it might be applied in specific instances, there might still be disagreement as to how one might capture this in a clear rule that could be treated as the trade usage.[58] Any consensus might only be found at a very general level, making the trade usage unsuitable for application in concrete cases.[59]

Unsurprisingly, there have been attempts to record trade usages in order to increase transparency and knowledge of such trade usages. However, such records are often of limited relevance for two reasons: first, any attempt to record a trade usage may not be an accurate reflection of how the trade usage is understood in

---

57 See further, R. Craswell, "Do trade customs exist?" in J.S. Kraus and S.D. Walt, *The Jurisprudential Foundations of Corporate and Commercial Law* (Cambridge University Press, 2000), pp.121–125.

58 *Ibid.*, p.127.

59 *Ibid.*, p.134.

the relevant trade or industry. The recorded meaning of the trade usage may therefore be inaccurate. Secondly, it is in the nature of trade usages that they evolve over time, and so any effort to record the existence and meaning of a trade usage will often be no more than a snapshot of a moving target taken at a particular point in time.

Furthermore, trade usages are sometimes used as a basis for providing trade terms, such as the UCP[60] or the INCOTERMS®.[61] However, even trade terms can only be a reflection of trade usages at the point at which they were drafted or revised. Subsequent changes in the way trade usages are understood will not be reflected in the trade terms until they are revised to reflect such developments at some future point.

In short, there is no doubt that trade usages exist and that they have a normative, i.e., binding, status in the relevant trade or industry. However, their existence and substance are only established once confirmed by an arbitration panel or court in the context of a particular dispute. Even then, the findings of the arbitration panel or court might not be a true reflection of the trade usage but merely the finding of the panel/court based on the evidence put forward by the parties, but the outcome of such judicial interpretation is just as liable to be an inaccurate determination of the substance of the trade usage, tainted by the view of the adjudicator as to the appropriate resolution of the case before it.[62] Trade usages are therefore inherently vague and uncertain, and of limited value when it comes to risk allocation and planning during negotiations towards an international commercial contract.

Nevertheless, as we will see in the next section, the fact that trade usages exist and that they are regarded as binding in the relevant trade or industry has resulted in an intensive debate about the existence and relevance of some alternative legal regime based on the sum of the various trade usages which might exist both within a particular trade or industry and those which are common to multiple trades or industries. The label attached to this alternative legal regime is the *lex mercatoria*, which suffers from some degree of vagueness as to its precise scope itself.

6.2 *Trade usages and the* lex mercatoria

In the previous section, we have focused on the role of trade usages in the context of International Commercial Law. In this section, we turn to a different aspect of trade usages: their potential relevance in comprising a comprehensive, a-national, global law for international commercial transactions. In 1961, Aleksander Goldstajn declared that

---

60 See Chapter 9.
61 See above at 4.4.
62 C.P. Gillette, "Harmony and stasis in trade usages for international sales" (1999) 39 *Virginia Journal of International Law* 707.

... a new law merchant is rapidly developing in the word of international trade. It is time that recognition be given to the existence of an autonomous commercial law that has grown independent of the national systems of law.[63]

This development was driven by the combined effects of party autonomy and the increasing use of arbitration for the resolution of disputes, with arbitrators "taking into account customs, usage and business practice".[64] Within the literature on International Commercial Law, there has been considerable focus on the idea that there is a body of trade usages which constitutes a viable alternative to national law and international legal sources, and, as we will see, it has become particularly popular in the context of international commercial arbitration.[65] This idea is anything but uncontroversial, and there is an extensive debate among scholars about the very idea of the *lex mercatoria*, as well as its practical usefulness. One particularly interesting feature of this debate is the attempt to see the contemporary version of the *lex mercatoria* as continuing a medieval, pre-nation state form which some claim existed then to support mercantile dealings.

6.2.1 The historical context of the lex mercatoria

We will turn to the debate about the modern-day *lex mercatoria* in the next section, but first, it will be helpful to consider the historical context of that debate. Scholars have drawn a link between the historic *lex mercatoria* and its modern-day incarnation, often to strengthen their case for recognising the modern *lex mercatoria* as a viable alternative to national and international legal rules for international commercial contracts. Often, a particular historical narrative is assumed,[66] although there is significant evidence unearthed by legal historians which suggests that much of this historical narrative is unsupported by the available evidence. The gist of this historical account was expressed by Schmitthoff as follows:

It arose in the Middle Ages in the form of the law merchant, a body of truly international customary rules governing the cosmopolitan community of international merchants who travelled through the civilised world from port to port and fair to fair.[67]

---

63 A. Goldstajn, "The new law merchant" (1961) *Journal of Business Law* 12.
64 *Ibid.*
65 See Chapter 11.
66 See, e.g., M.T. Medwig, "The new law merchant: legal rhetoric and commercial reality" (1992) 24 *Law and Policy of International Business* 589, pp.590–596; L.E. Trakman, "From the medieval law merchant to e-merchant law" (2003) 53 *University of Toronto Law Journal* 265, pp.270–283; F.K. Juenger, "The lex mercatoria and private international law" (2000) 60 *Louisiana Law Review* 1133, pp.1134–1136; R.J. Howarth, "Lex mercatoria: can general principles of law govern international commercial contracts?" (2004) 10 *Canterbury Law Review* 36, p.40.
67 C.M. Schmitthoff, "The unification of the international law of trade" (1968) *Journal of Business Law* 105.

Schmitthoff goes on to explain that the medieval law merchant was characterised by the fact that the law of the fairs was universal, as was the law of the sea, and that this was combined with special courts dealing with commercial disputes.[68]

This is just one example of how the medieval *lex mercatoria* has been presented. At the core of this disputed historical narrative is the idea that, in medieval times, commercial activity was not confined to "national" territories but was conducted across territorial boundaries. It is important to appreciate that, in medieval times, there were far more separate political territories than there are today. The large European nation states with which we are familiar today are largely a product of the 18th and 19th centuries, for example – before then, there was a much larger number of smaller kingdoms, principalities and city states. Trade crossed those boundaries, often with merchants travelling from market to market to buy and sell goods. Within this narrative, there is an assumption that the rules by which such trade was conducted were not territorial but rather based on rules common to merchants. Moreover, dispute resolution was said to occur mostly through mercantile courts, where disputes were adjudicated by experts and dealt with speedily. For proponents of a modern-day *lex mercatoria*, this particular narrative provides the necessary historical context, based on "international" mercantile rules applied by mercantile dispute resolution procedures.[69] In the modern context, this is equated with the application of the *lex mercatoria* in the context of international commercial arbitration.[70] The historical account concludes with the replacement of the law merchant by the codifications of the law in the 18th and 19th centuries on the European continent, and the "absorption" of the law merchant by the common law courts.

However, as attractive as this account may be, it does not seem to withstand rigorous historical scrutiny. Whilst there is an indication from 17th-century sources that both lawyers and merchants seemed to think that there was something like a *lex mercatoria*, tracing back further to the Middle Ages does not reveal any signs of some kind of international body of mercantile law.[71] Emily Kadens has researched the history of the medieval *lex mercatoria* extensively,[72] and her findings indicate that very little of the standard historical account is supported by historical evidence. Yet, it seems that all too often, scholars writing about the *lex mercatoria* gloss over the writings of legal historians which show that the widely recounted account of the medieval *lex mercatoria* is flawed.[73] In summary, Kaden's main findings show

---

68   *Ibid.*, p.106.
69   See, e.g., L.E. Trakman, "From the medieval law merchant to e-merchant law" (2003) 53 *University of Toronto Law Journal* 265, pp.270–283.
70   See Chapter 11.
71   C. Donahue Jr, "Medieval and early modern lex mercatoria: an attempt at the probatio diabolica" (2004) 5 *Chicago Journal of International Law* 21, p.26.
72   See, e.g., E. Kadens, "Order within law, variety within custom: the character of the medieval merchant law" (2004) 5 *Chicago Journal of International Law* 39; E. Kadens, "The myth of the customary law merchant" (2012) 90 *Texas Law Review* 1153; or E. Kadens, "The medieval law merchant: the tyranny of a construct" (2015) 7 *Journal of Legal Analysis* 251.
73   "Historians have for decades now been sounding the warning that the law merchant emperor has no clothes, but to little avail": E. Kadens, "The medieval law merchant: the tyranny of a construct" (2015) 7 *Journal of Legal Analysis* 251, p.252.

that not only did a comprehensive medieval *lex mercatoria* not exist, but also that medieval merchants did not need a uniform commercial law to trade successfully.[74] According to her research, much of medieval trade happened at fairs and markets in various towns across Europe, and predominantly involved local merchants, although some "international" merchants also attended these fairs. Trade at these fairs was mostly conducted on the basis of local customs, rules of the individual fairs, as well as local laws and the rules set by local guilds for the conduct of particular trades. Dispute resolution was not conducted in separate merchant courts; the merchant courts that did exist had been established by towns or local rulers.[75] Mercantile customs were mostly local and did not have wider application.[76]

There is evidence of some more widely generalised practices, such as the use of bills of exchange,[77] and in respect of insurance, banking and maritime law, as well as the role of agents. Insofar as there are contemporary sources which make reference to the *lex mercatoria*, they are limited to procedural variations[78] to the English common law in medieval times, rather than substantive rules,[79] and similar findings have also been made in respect of mercantile courts elsewhere in Europe.[80] Moreover, there is no evidence of the *lex mercatoria* being taken over by the common law; in fact, the common law had always provided for the resolution of commercial disputes.[81] There was no separate coherent law merchant comprising substantive rules, but only provision for speedier resolution of commercial disputes.[82]

In addition to the limited historical evidence for a medieval *lex mercatoria*, Gbenga Oduntan raises a different concern about the historical account of the *lex mercatoria*.[83] In essence, he points out that the contemporary *lex mercatoria* debate is

---

74 E.g., *Ibid.*, pp.271–281.
75 E. Kadens, "Order within law, variety within custom: the character of the medieval merchant law" (2004) 5 *Chicago Journal of International Law* 39, p.52.
76 E. Kadens, "The myth of the customary law merchant" (2012) 90 *Texas Law Review* 1153, p.1158, pp.1181–1196.
77 Baker notes that bills of exchange may have been an instance of commercial usage rather than something recognised in law because of the pleadings once permitted before the common law courts, although commercial bills could be produced as evidence: J.H. Baker, "The law merchant and the common law before 1700" (1979) 38 *Cambridge Law Journal* 295, p.304. When the bill of exchange was recognised at common law, this happened without express invocation of the law merchant, p.310.
78 C. Wasserstein Fassberg, "Lex mercatoria – hoist with its own petard?" (2004) 5 *Chicago Journal of International Law* 67, p.68.
79 J.H. Baker, "The law merchant and the common law before 1700" (1979) 38 *Cambridge Law Journal* 295, p.300.
80 C. Donahue Jr, "Medieval and early modern lex mercatoria: an attempt at the probatio diabolica" (2004) 5 *Chicago Journal of International Law* 21, pp.35–36.
81 J.H. Baker, "The law merchant and the common law before 1700" (1979) 38 *Cambridge Law Journal* 295, p.321.
82 *Ibid.*
83 G. Oduntan, "The 'reimaginarium' of *lex mercatoria*: critique of the geocentric theory about the origins and episteme of the *lex mercatoria*" (2016) 13 *Manchester Journal of International Economic Law* 63.

premised on a Eurocentric conceptualisation of the *lex mercatoria*.[84] This echoes Samson Sempasa's point that

> The common principles that are said to make up the lex mercatoria were themselves largely developed at a point in time when trading relationships with Africans were undertaken mainly for the benefit of Europeans in the context of a colonial political structure. The African could take no part in those relationships. African lawyers do not necessarily share those principles on all points.[85]

Oduntan explains that the historical account fails to recognise that any historical origins of the *lex mercatoria* would go beyond medieval Europe, in terms of both geography and time.[86] The role of Persian, Arab or Chinese traders and the impact of trade along the Silk Road in shaping the *lex mercatoria* are often ignored, but these are no less relevant. Consequently, the investigation of mercantile customs and practices has to go back much further in time and geography – a more comprehensive attempt at providing a historical account of the *lex mercatoria* therefore needs to extend both geographically and in terms of time beyond medieval Europe.

This summary of the historical context of the *lex mercatoria* shows that there is a mismatch between the historical account often relied on by those writing about the *lex mercatoria* and the research of legal historians. It seems clear that the idea of an international law merchant based on trade usages/customs common to all merchants is not supported by the historical evidence, and consequently is likely to be incorrect.[87] Moreover, it suffers from being an essential Eurocentric conception, underscored by the way in which the flawed historical account is relied upon to support the idea of a contemporary a-national *lex mercatoria*.

6.2.2 Debates surrounding the modern lex mercatoria

In a sense, whether the historical account of the *lex mercatoria* is accurate or not is only of limited relevance to the debate about its modern incarnation, save to the extent that some scholars seek to derive a continuity from this that leads to the present-day efforts to recognise the modern *lex mercatoria*. Much has been written about this modern *lex mercatoria*.[88] Much of the debate seems to centre around three key questions: (i) What is the *lex mercatoria*? (ii) Does the *lex mercatoria* exist at

---

84   Cf. M. Douglas, "The lex mercatoria and the culture of transnational industry" (2005) 13 *University of Miami International and Comparative Law Review* 367, p.380.

85   S.L. Sempasa, "Obstacles to international commercial arbitration in African countries" (1992) 41 *International and Comparative Law Quarterly* 387, p.410.

86   A similar observation in earlier accounts of the *lex mercatoria* is noted by C. Donahue Jr, "Medieval and early modern lex mercatoria: an attempt at the probatio diabolica" (2004) 5 *Chicago Journal of International Law* 21.

87   Donahue noted that the lack of any evidence for something does not conclusively show that it did/does not exist, of course: *Ibid.*, p.27.

88   See, e.g., O. Toth, *The Lex Mercatoria in Theory and Practice* (Oxford University Press, 2017).

all? and (iii) What use does the *lex mercatoria* have in the context of modern international commercial dealings?

6.2.2.1 What is the *lex mercatoria*?

A fundamental problem with the entire debate about the *lex mercatoria* is the huge variety of conceptions and definitions which are given to it,[89] along a spectrum which has trade usages at one end, and the entirety of national and international sources of commercial law at the other. Indeed, two early proponents of the modern conception of the *lex mercatoria* had different views as to its nature: Clive Schmitthoff (initially) equated it with treaties and model contracts,[90] whereas Berthold Goldman treated the *lex mercatoria* as based on customs.[91] Such contrasting views of the *lex mercatoria* persist. For instance, Roy Goode characterises the *lex mercatoria* as based entirely on international trade practice and usages and juxtaposes it with the adoption of legal rules through instruments such as conventions and Model Laws. In essence, it is an autonomous system based entirely on customs and usages which have developed spontaneously from commercial practice. It is entirely uncodified, which inevitably results in the difficulty of determining its substance. It is binding on commercial parties because usages are widely regarded as *de facto* binding. Goode acknowledges that this conception of the *lex mercatoria* makes it difficult to operate as the law governing a contract because of its a-national and indeterminate nature, but it can play a role in dispute resolution, particularly in international commercial arbitration.

In his seminal account of the *lex mercatoria*,[92] Lord Mustill adopted a definition which is similar to Goode's. Thus, the *lex mercatoria* is based on usage, although Mustill saw nothing remarkable in this as the law already takes usages into account.[93] The *lex mercatoria* is a-national, in that it provides rules applicable to international commercial contracts which are not directly derived from a body of national substantive law. It is autonomous in that its rules have a normative value which is independent of any national legal system. It is also distinct from rules of commercial law which may have been developed on the basis of recognised trade

---

89 R.J. Howarth, "Lex mercatoria: can general principles of law govern international commercial contracts?" (2004) 10 *Canterbury Law Review* 36, pp.43–44.

90 C.M. Schmitthoff, "The unification of the international law of trade" (1968) *Journal of Business Law* 105; "The codification of the law of international trade" (1985) *Journal of Business Law* 34.

91 K.P. Berger, "The new law merchant and the global market: a 21st century view of transnational commercial law" (2000) 3 *International Arbitration Law Review* 91; for a recent analysis of Schmitthoff's and Goldman's writings on the *lex mercatoria*, see D. de Ruysscher, "Conceptualizing lex mercatoria: Malynes, Schmitthoff and Goldman compared" (2020) 27 *Maastricht Journal of European and Comparative Law* 465.

92 M. Mustill, "The new *lex mercatoria*: the first twenty-five years" in M. Bos and I. Brownlie (eds.), *Liber Amicorum for Lord Wilberforce* (Clarendon Press, 1987); also published in (1988) 4 *Arbitration International* 86.

93 See above.

customs and usages. Unlike commercial law, the *lex mercatoria* is not created: "it springs up spontaneously in the soil of international trade. It is a growth, not a creation."[94]

In contrast, Jan Dalhuisen[95] developed a much more expansive notion of the *lex mercatoria*, based on a hierarchy of different legal sources. At the top are fundamental basic principles such as *pacta sunt servanda*, followed by various legal sources, including usages, which have a mandatory character. Further down are the terms of the contract, followed by various legal sources which are of a dispositive character, i.e., those which can be displaced by the terms of the contract. National law is at the bottom of this hierarchy.

There are many more definitions of the *lex mercatoria*, but this selective overview suffices to establish that there is no consistent view of what the *lex mercatoria* is. It is possible to distinguish broadly between a narrow and a wide conception of the *lex mercatoria*. The narrow conception limits the *lex mercatoria* to the body of trade usages, whereas the wide conception draws on other legal sources, such as international treaties. However, it seems that the wide notion of the *lex mercatoria* is a characterisation of International Commercial Law as a whole. The narrow conception of the *lex mercatoria* is preferable so as to distinguish it from the various international and national initiatives to develop legal rules for international commercial transactions.

6.2.2.2 Is there a *lex mercatoria*?

The proponents of the modern *lex mercatoria* argue that there is a sufficient volume of trade usages for these to constitute a separate body of a-national law that can be a viable alternative to the complex interaction of different legal sources which comprise International Commercial Law. However, not everyone agrees. For instance, Highet[96] has expressed scepticism about the possibility that there is an "undiscovered legal system" we can call the *lex mercatoria*, not least because it is not possible to have a law without the context of a legal system. At best, therefore, the trade usages reflect underlying commercial principles, or *principia mercatoria*, which might be applied by arbitrators to guide them in resolving the disputes before them, but which offer no guidance to the parties in concluding and performing their contracts.[97] Highet is concerned, in particular, about the difficulty of determining the substance of the *lex mercatoria*, noting that it is "not even possible to supply more than a meagre inventory, loaded with vagueness and charged with logical or analytical legal error".[98] Indeed, we saw above that one of the greatest difficulties with individual trade usages is in determining their substance. This problem is exacerbated in the context of the *lex mercatoria*, because the *lex mercatoria* is said to comprise a large number of trade usages. Attempts

94 M. Mustill, "The new *lex mercatoria*: the first twenty-five years" (1988) 4 *Arbitration International* 86, p.90.
95 J. Dalhuisen, *Dalhuisen on Transnational, Comparative, Commercial, Financial and Trade Law*, 7th ed. (Hart, 2019).
96 K. Highet, "The enigma of the lex mercatoria" (1989) 63 *Tulane Law Review* 613.
97 *Ibid.*, p.628.
98 *Ibid.*, p.623.

have been made to identify the substance of the *lex mercatoria* by compiling lists of principles or rules which are claimed to be part of the *lex mercatoria*.[99] The very attempt to restate the *lex mercatoria* in list form, i.e., as a type of codification, seems to conflict with its nature as an a-national system based on trade usages: not only do these efforts not seem to include any rules which are specific to the *lex mercatoria* and not found in any national law, but codification seems to be an inherently legal exercise undertaken by lawyers.[100]

Douglas[101] has attempted to meet concerns about the alleged universality of the *lex mercatoria* as relevant to all international commercial transactions by arguing for a refined conception of the *lex mercatoria*. Instead of a single, international, universally applicable system, the *lex mercatoria* should be linked to industries with an international reach (e.g., the construction industry) and where participants share a common culture.[102] Accordingly, each industry will have its own *lex mercatoria*, based on the culture and custom of that industry.[103] Whilst this suggestion might address concerns regarding the universal reach of the *lex mercatoria*, it does not resolve the more fundamental concerns about the *lex mercatoria*, in particular the difficulty in determining its substance.

6.2.2.3 Relevance for international commercial dealings

For commercial parties, the debate about the *lex mercatoria* might well be little more than academic eccentricity. The idea of relying exclusively on unwritten trade usages and no legal rules at all would make it almost impossible to use contracts as a reliable means of risk allocation and transaction planning, unless such contracts were drafted in a very detailed fashion,[104] not least because of the inherent vagueness of the *lex mercatoria*.[105] One of the first things any student of commercial law is told about the nature of the subject is that its primary focus is to facilitate commercial dealings and to provide legal rules which are as predictable as possible, offset only by the need for some flexibility to ensure the law remains adaptable and capable of accommodating as broad a range of commercial transactions as possible. The possibility of permitting arbitrators to decide a dispute on the basis of the *lex*

99 Seminally, M. Mustill, "The new *lex mercatoria*: the first twenty-five years" in M. Bos and I. Brownlie, (eds.), *Liber Amicorum for Lord Wilberforce* (Clarendon, 1987); K.P. Berger, *The Creeping Codification of the Lex Mercatoria*, 2nd ed. (Wolters Kluwer, 2010).

100 C. Wasserstein Fassberg, "Lex mercatoria – hoist with its own petard?" (2004) 5 *Chicago Journal of International Law* 67.

101 M. Douglas, "The lex mercatoria and the culture of transnational industry" (2005) 13 *University of Miami International and Comparative Law Review* 367.

102 *Ibid.*, p.383.

103 *Ibid.*, pp.394–395.

104 There is some evidence that 20th-century contracts between States and commercial parties gave preference to something like the *lex mercatoria* rather than any national law for the resolution of disputes, but even in this context, the *lex mercatoria* is of no value: G.R. Delaume, "Comparative analysis as a basis of law in state contracts: the myth of the lex mercatoria" (1989) 63 *Tulane Law Review* 575.

105 C.R. Drahozal, "Contracting out of national law: an empirical look at the new law merchant" (2004) 80 *Notre Dame Law Review* 523, pp.546–547.

mercatoria[106] might occasionally be preferred by the parties in the context of a particular dispute but is certainly not something which seems to be happening on a wide-spread basis.[107] It is also no guarantee of predictability as to how the dispute might be resolved: opting for the *lex mercatoria* surrenders "the ultimate determination of substantive rules to transnational arbitrators whose views on the subject may not always be as concordant as might have been expected".[108] The *lex mercatoria* seems to have had its heyday in the context of investment dispute arbitration between commercial parties and States in the global south, particularly during the middle part of the 20th century.[109] Initially, this was dominated by legal scholars because of their claimed expertise about the *lex mercatoria* through their academic writings, with the effect that such disputes were not resolved on the basis of any law. However, the role of the *lex mercatoria* in this regard soon declined.[110] Nevertheless, it seems that both practitioners and legal scholars have continued to extol the virtues of the *lex mercatoria* in jostling for position in the increasingly competitive market for arbitration.[111] Arbitration based on the *lex mercatoria* for international commercial transactions is promoted over reliance on national law.[112]

Yet, the literature on the *lex mercatoria* and its alleged significance for international commercial transactions continues to grow, arguably driven by "matters of faith rather than of academic rigor".[113] If there is a theoretical driver behind this, it is the desire that international commercial transactions should be governed by an a-national commercial law, but, practical difficulties aside, there is no convincing empirical support for such an a-national commercial law: instead, insofar as there is a specific International Commercial Law, it combines elements of national law and non-national and international legal sources.[114]

Cuniberti offers three explanations for the continuing popularity of the *lex mercatoria* idea.[115] First, he adopts Drahozal's view[116] that much scholarly writing on the *lex mercatoria* may be driven by the market for arbitration service, i.e., the desire

---

106 See Chapter 11 at section 6.
107 C.R. Drahozal, "Contracting out of national law: an empirical look at the new law merchant" (2004) 80 *Notre Dame Law Review* 523; G. Cuniberti, "Three theories of lex mercatoria" (2014) 52 *Columbia Journal of Transnational Law* 369, pp.396–404.
108 G.R. Delaume, "Comparative analysis as a basis of law in state contracts: the myth of the lex mercatoria" (1989) 63 *Tulane Law Review* 575, p.578.
109 Y. Dezalay and B.G. Garth, *Dealing in Virtue* (University of Chicago Press, 1996), pp.88–91.
110 *Ibid.*
111 *Ibid.*, pp.41–42.
112 E.g., T. Medwig, "The new law merchant: legal rhetoric and commercial reality" (1992) 24 *Law and Policy of International Business* 589.
113 R. Michaels, "The true lex mercatoria: law beyond the state" (2007) 13 *Indiana Journal of Global Legal Studies* 447, p.448.
114 *Ibid.*, pp.465–466.
115 G. Cuniberti, "Three theories of lex mercatoria" (2014) 52 *Columbia Journal of Transnational Law* 369.
116 C.R. Drahozal, "Contracting out of national law: an empirical look at the new law merchant" (2004) 80 *Notre Dame Law Review* 523.

of authors to be seen as knowledgeable and therefore suitable as arbitrators or counsel. Secondly, he argues that, in relying on the *lex mercatoria*, arbitrators are given the discretion to achieve a balanced result in an arbitration that might keep both parties reasonably satisfied with the outcome whilst at the same time avoiding the need to decide on the basis of a national law with which the arbitrator might not be familiar. Finally, he suggests that in drafting model contracts, some international bodies seek to avoid the need to align their terms with a particular national law by encouraging the use of arbitration or other dispute resolution mechanisms offered by the same bodies.

It certainly seems that the debate about the *lex mercatoria* will carry on for some time yet, but perhaps eventually, Lord Wilberforce's conclusions about the *lex mercatoria* will prevail:

> In the light of all these considerations one may take stock of the lex mercatoria as it stands today by asking. Does it provide the businessman with a set of rules which is sufficiently accessible and certain to permit the efficient conduct of his transactions? Is the lex manifestly superior, in its content and methodology, to establish national systems of commercial law? If so, is its superiority so obvious that it can now be said to have imposed itself, whether by the very fact of its existence or by a notion of implied consent, on the international business community as a whole, and on all transactions in which it is not expressly excluded? In short, has the lex mercatoria stolen the international commercial scene, pushing national laws into the wings? In each case, the detached observer must, I believe, be driven to answer "no". More sympathetically, he might add "… or at least not yet".[117]

Indeed, it would be better to disregard the "sympathetic" rider at the end of this quote: one inherent flaw in arguing in favour of a *lex mercatoria* is its juxtaposition to everything else. However, as we saw earlier, trade usages – and therefore, by extension, the *lex mercatoria* – are an element of the wider pluralist commercial law structure, and so it should not be seen as an alternative to, but a feature of, that structure. A recalibration of the *lex mercatoria* in light of legal pluralism[118] seems necessary for any debate about its role to continue. And if the debate is to continue, it needs to overcome the concerns that this debate remains Eurocentric[119] rather than a true global debate which takes full account of all perspectives.

---

117 M. Mustill, "The new *lex mercatoria*: the first twenty-five years" (1988) 4 *Arbitration International* 86, p.117.
118 Cf R. Wai, "The interlegality of transnational private law" (2008) 71 *Law and Contemporary Problems* 107, pp.111–112.
119 S.L. Sempasa, "Obstacles to international commercial arbitration in African countries" (1992) 41 *International and Comparative Law Quarterly* 387; G. Oduntan, "The 'reimaginarium' of *lex mercatoria*: critique of the geocentric theory about the origins and episteme of the *lex mercatoria*" (2016) 13 *Manchester Journal of International Economic Law* 63.

6.3 The relevance of trade customs in International Commercial Law

The recognition of trade customs and the debate about the *lex mercatoria* are an important reminder about the role of commercial law generally, and International Commercial Law in particular: its purpose is to facilitate commercial transactions and to allow businesses to deal in ways that work best for them. There will, of course, be matters in respect of which regulation to set constraints and to channel behaviour will be required. However, when it comes to drafting new legal rules for commercial transactions, it is important that those directly affected by such rules are involved in that process. Indeed, the starting point for reforming or for developing new legal rules in the commercial field should generally be commercial practice. In that regard, trade usages are an important indicator of what sort of rules are likely to work from a commercial perspective, and reform of commercial law might benefit from exploring trade usages. As Lord Lloyd observed in *Kleinwort Benson Ltd v Lincoln City Council*,[120] "[i]n the field of Commercial Law ... the custom of merchants has always been a fruitful source of law".[121] This is true of the common law, which has often regarded itself as being facilitative of commercial transactions and as adaptable to changing commercial practice.

In developing an instrument in International Commercial Law, whether a new convention, Model Law or statement of principles, the relevant practices and trade usages of the affected trade or industry should be given due consideration, assuming that it is possible to reach a broad consensus as to their existence and substance. However, it is unlikely that an international convention will, ultimately, be an accurate reflection of established trade usages. As we will see later,[122] conventions are usually the final product of intensive and lengthy negotiations, both during the preparatory phase and at the diplomatic conference at which agreement on a final text will be sought. Such conventions are ultimately a diplomatic text, rather than a reflection of trade practices and usages, and as such often a compromise between competing national interests. Whilst trade practices and trade usages and the wider interests of the commercial community directly affected by the convention should be, and usually will have been, taken into account, the final product will have been shaped by multiple and often competing interests. Nevertheless, the discussion of trade usages and the debate surrounding the *lex mercatoria* should be a constant reminder that commercial law should facilitate commercial transactions and not conflict with commercial expectations unless there are overriding policy reasons for doing so.

7 International Commercial Law as part of the pluralist transnational commercial law system

This chapter has provided an overview of the different elements which together constitute the legal regime for international commercial transactions. It was seen

---

120 [1998] 4 All ER 513.
121 *Ibid.*, p.549.
122 See Chapter 3 at section 5.1.

that international commercial transactions are governed by a variety of legal sources at the same time. Quite which sources will be relevant will depend on a variety of factors, not least the national law applicable to the contract concluded between the parties to an international commercial transaction. These legal sources have their origins in national law, internationally created legal rules, contract provisions, rules based on private norm creation and trade usages. Transnational commercial law is therefore best understood as a pluralist[123] system in which legal rules from different sources can be combined, in different permutations, to provide the legal context within which an international commercial transaction is arranged and performed. Many of these legal rules stem from the international level, and the remainder of this book will focus on a variety of these international sources.

Viewing the nature of transnational commercial law through the lens of legal pluralism is important so as to understand how a wide range of sources can set the legal regime which provides the context for any particular international commercial transaction, and, crucially, how they interact with one another.[124] In addition to capturing the reality of these various components, legal pluralism is also a reminder that there is no monopoly for any one actor to specify the legal context for international commercial transactions;[125] rather, national and international laws, combined with trade usages, private norm-creation and the contract itself, together determine this legal context.

123 For a concise account of legal pluralism in this context, see G.-P. Callies and I. Buchmann, "Global commercial law between unity, pluralism, and competition: the case of the CISG" (2016) 21 *Uniform Law Review* 1, pp.8–11.
124 R. Wai, "The interlegality of transnational private law" (2008) 71 *Law and Contemporary Problems* 107.
125 *Ibid.*, p.10.

2

PRIVATE INTERNATIONAL LAW

1. Introduction

In Chapter 1, we saw that International Commercial Law is not a complete system of rules adopted at the international level for international commercial transaction, but rather a complex combination of multiple sources of law which make up the legal regime applicable to international commercial transactions. Among these sources is the national law which governs the contract concluded between the parties. Every contract depends for its recognition and effectiveness on a particular national law. However, an international commercial contract by its very nature involves parties from multiple jurisdictions, but their contract can, generally speaking, only be governed by one national law. It is therefore essential to determine *which* national law will govern, or apply to, a particular contract. The applicable law will determine the requirements for the formation of a contract, its validity and any particular obligations of the parties throughout the lifetime of the contract. If the country of the law applicable to the contract is a Contracting State to any international commercial conventions, then those conventions to which it is a party will also apply to the contract.

Furthermore, if a dispute arises between the parties (e.g., because a seller has delivered faulty goods to a buyer), it will also be necessary to determine in which country a claimant should launch its legal action.[1] Once a judgment has been given in one country, it may be necessary to enforce it in another country if the losing party is located in a country other than the court where the case was heard.

In short, for every international commercial contract, there are three key questions: (i) Which national law applies to the contract? (ii) In which court can a claim in respect

---

1   Many disputes arising from international commercial contracts are resolved through arbitration, rather than litigation. This is a special feature of such contracts. The main aspects of International Commercial Law on arbitration are discussed in Chapter 11.

DOI: 10.4324/9781315692807-2

of that contract be launched; and (iii) How can a judgment be enforced in another country? These questions fall within the remit of private international law.

1.1 Private international law

Private international law, also known as the "Conflict of Laws", does not provide any substantive legal rules for international transactions; its purpose is to provide rules which can answer these questions. In other words, Private international law rules determine the law governing a contract (applicable law), as well as where litigation should take place (jurisdiction), and how a judgment can subsequently be enforced in other countries. Each national law will have its own provisions on private international law. Frequently, there may be more than one set of rules, and determining which of which these apply will depend on the countries in which the respective parties are located. For instance, all the countries of the European Union (EU) have a common set of private international law rules, some of which (particularly those on jurisdiction and recognition of judgments) only apply in respect of parties domiciled in a Member State or judgments handed down by a court of a Member State.[2] However, if a dispute involves a party not domiciled in a Member State, the EU rules do not apply to questions of jurisdiction and recognition.[3] Instead, there may be an international convention, such as the Hague Convention on Choice of Court Agreements 2005, the Mexico Inter-American Convention on the Law Applicable to International Contracts 1994 or the Hague Convention on the Recognition and Enforcement of Foreign Judgments in Civil and Commercial Matters 2019 which might apply instead, provided that the parties are domiciled, or have their habitual residence, in Contracting States. For other instances, each country will have its own national rules on private international law. There have been calls for greater harmonisation of private international law rules, particularly with regard to party autonomy (see next section), in order to encourage a market for commercial law through enabling competition between national commercial laws.[4]

1.2 Party autonomy

A common feature of most private international law regimes is the recognition that the parties may themselves wish to determine the law applicable to their contract, and the court which should have jurisdiction in respect of any litigation arising from their contract. Such "choice of law" and "choice of court" (or "choice of forum") clauses are common in international commercial contracts. Generally speaking, priority will

---

2   Regulation (EU) 1215/2012 on jurisdiction and the recognition and enforcement of judgments in civil and commercial matters ("Brussels I") (2012) OJ L35/1 only applies in respect of persons domiciled in a Member State (Art. 4(1)) and the recognition of judgments handed down by a court in a Member State (Art. 36(1)).
3   Regulation (EU) 593/2008 on the law applicable to contractual obligations ("Rome I") (2008) OJ L177/6 will recognise a law as the applicable law, irrespective of whether it is the law of a Member State or non-Member State (Art. 2).
4   J.F. Coyle, "Rethinking the commercial law treaty" (2011) 45 *Georgia Law Review* 343.

be given to the choice the parties have made, i.e., party autonomy in determining the applicable law and jurisdiction is paramount. However, party autonomy is not absolute in the context of private international law. There will be limitations in respect of certain rules of a national law of one (or both) of the parties which are regarded as so essential that a choice of law of another country should not prevent their application (simple and overriding mandatory rules), as well as of matters of public policy (*ordre public*). Subject to such limitations, the exercise of party autonomy through choice-of-law and choice-of-court clauses will usually determine the applicable law and jurisdiction. Consequently, the rules of whichever private international law regime is applicable to a particular contract will only be needed where the parties have not made provision for the applicable law and jurisdiction in their contract.

This chapter will provide a general overview of selected examples of private international law to illustrate how jurisdiction, applicable law, and cross-border recognition and enforcement are dealt with under various legal instruments. The focus will be on texts adopted by the Hague Conference on Private International Law and the EU, with some reference to the Inter-American Conventions on the Law applicable to International Contracts (Mexico, 1994) and on Extraterritorial Validity of Foreign Judgments and Arbitral Awards (Montevideo, 1979). However, it is not the intention to provide an exhaustive account – for this, readers are referred to texts specifically about private international law.[5]

2. Jurisdiction

The first issue is to determine the country whose courts would have jurisdiction in respect of a legal action brought by one of the parties to an international commercial contract.

2.1 Hague Convention on Choice of Court Agreements 2005

The Hague Convention on Choice of Court Agreements was adopted in 2005, and currently has 32 Contracting States.[6] This includes all the EU's Member States by virtue of the EU's ratification of the Convention which is binding on all the Member States,[7] with the exception of Denmark (which has ratified separately).[8]

---

5   E.g., D. McClean and V. Ruiz Abou-Nigm, *Morris: The Conflict of Laws* (Sweet and Maxwell, 2016); P. Torremans (ed.), *Cheshire, North and Fawcett on Private International Law*, 15th ed. (Oxford University Press, 2017) or T.C. Hartley, *International Commercial Litigation*, 3rd ed. (Cambridge University Press, 2020).

6   See https://www.hcch.net/en/instruments/conventions/status-table/?cid=98 [accessed 5 April 2021].

7   Art. 29 Hague Convention (2005).

8   At the time of writing, the countries which had ratified the Convention in addition to the EU are Mexico, Montenegro and Singapore. China, North Macedonia, the Ukraine and the USA have signed but not (yet) ratified the Convention. The UK acceded to the Convention after the transitional period under the EU Withdrawal Agreement ended at the end of December 2020.

However, as between the EU Member States, the Brussels I Regulation (Regulation (EU) 1215/2012) applies, so in respect of any EU Member State, the Convention will only apply in respect of non-EU Contracting States.

The Choice of Court Convention applies to exclusive choice-of-court agreements in respect of civil or commercial[9] matters, but only in international cases.[10] The criterion for determining internationality is a negative one, i.e., there is a presumption in favour of internationality unless all the parties to the agreement are resident in the same Contracting State and all other aspects are also connected only with that State.[11] This means that purely domestic contracts which do not have elements in another Contracting State are not covered by the convention, and the choice of a court in another Contracting State would not be recognised on the basis of this Convention.

Article 4(2) sets out what is meant by being resident in a State. In the case of a legal person, a person is resident in a State if it has its statutory seat there, or its central administration, or its principal place of business; also, where it was incorporated or formed under the laws of that State.

The Convention only applies to "exclusive choice of court agreements" in civil and commercial matters. A "choice of court agreement" is defined as designating "for the purpose of deciding disputes which have arisen or may arise in connection with a particular legal relationship, the courts of one Contracting State or one or more specific courts of one Contracting State to the exclusion of the jurisdiction of any other courts".[12] Thus, the agreement must identify a particular Contracting State and either allocate exclusive jurisdiction to the courts in that State, or one particular court in that State (for example, a commercial court in a particular city). Moreover, the State chosen by the parties must be a Contracting State in order for the provisions of the Convention to apply.

A choice-of-court agreement can be either a separate agreement, or it can be part of a contract in the form of a choice-of-court clause.[13] In the latter case, the clause is treated as autonomous, i.e., as separate from the rest of the contract, and its validity is not affected purely because the rest of the contract might be invalid.[14] It is a requirement that the agreement is either concluded or documented in writing or in another appropriate digital equivalent.[15]

The effect of a choice-of-court agreement is that the court designated in such an agreement is to have jurisdiction in respect of any dispute covered by the

9   Consumer contracts are excluded (Art. (2)(1)(a)), as are employment contracts (Art. 2(1)(b)).
10   Art. 1(1) Hague Convention (2005).
11   Art. 1(2) Hague Convention (2005).
12   Art. 3(a) Hague Convention (2005).
13   Art. 3(d) Hague Convention (2005).
14   *Ibid.*
15   Art. 3(c) Hague Convention (2005). If it is not in writing, it would have to be by "means of communication which renders information accessible so as to be usable for subsequent reference" (Art. 3(c)(ii)), a phrase which is increasingly used in international texts to describe a functional equivalent of "writing" (see Chapter 12).

agreement.[16] The designated court cannot refuse to accept jurisdiction if the reason for refusing is that the dispute should heard by a court in another State.[17]

If proceedings have been started in a court in another Contracting State, then that court should either stay or dismiss those proceedings.[18] There are exceptions to this, however: first, the agreement is null and void under the law of the Contracting State where the designated court is located; second, a party to the agreement did not have capacity in respect of that agreement under the law of the State where the proceedings are pending; third, respecting the agreement would either cause "manifest injustice, or be manifestly contrary to the public policy"[19] of that State; fourth, there are exceptional reasons beyond the control of the parties which have the consequence that the agreement cannot reasonably be performed; and fifth, the chosen court has declined to hear the case.

The purpose of the Convention in respect of an express choice-of-court agreement therefore is to give effect to it, and to prevent litigation from being commenced by one of the parties in the courts of another Contracting State unless one of the situations mentioned above exists. However, there are no provisions in the Convention which allocate jurisdiction to the courts of a particular Contracting State in the absence of a choice-of-court agreement, i.e., there are no default provisions on jurisdiction in this Convention.

2.2 European Union: the Brussels I Regulation

The Brussels I Regulation (Regulation (EU) 1215/2012) provides the EU's regime in respect of identifying the courts which have jurisdiction in respect of civil and commercial matters.[20] It contains provisions which recognise the parties' agreement in respect of the court which should have jurisdiction in respect of a dispute arising from their legal relationship, as well as default provisions to determine jurisdiction in the absence of such an agreement.

The current version of the Brussels I Regulation was adopted in 2012. Its predecessor was Regulation (EU) 44/2001,[21] and many of the cases mentioned in this section were decided under the earlier version of the Brussels I Regulation. Moreover, in 2007, the Lugano Convention[22] was adopted. The text of the Convention is essentially the same as that of Regulation (EU) 44/2001, but does not take into

---

16 Art. 5(1) Hague Convention (2005).
17 Art. 5(2) Hague Convention (2005).
18 Art. 6 Hague Convention (2005).
19 Art. 6(c) Hague Convention (2005).
20 The notion "civil and commercial" is broader here than in the context of the Hague Convention; in particular, the Brussels I regulation contains provisions on consumer contracts (Arts. 17–19) and contracts of employments (Arts. 20–23). Both contract categories are beyond the scope of this book.
21 Regulation (EU) 44/2001 on jurisdiction and the recognition and enforcement of judgments in civil and commercial matters (2001) OJ L 12/1.
22 Convention on jurisdiction and the recognition and enforcement of judgments in civil and commercial matters, signed at Lugano on 30 October 2007.

account the changes made in the current version of the Brussels I Regulation. It applies between the EU Member States and members of EFTA[23] (Norway, Iceland and Switzerland) as well as Denmark.[24]

A preliminary point is that one of the criteria for determining which court should have jurisdiction is the identification of a party's *domicile*. For natural persons, a court in a Member State where legal action has commenced should determine whether a party is domiciled in that State on the basis of its internal rules.[25] Where this leads to the conclusion that the party in question is not domiciled in that Member State, then the court should consider whether the party is domiciled in another Member State on the basis of the national law of the other Member State.[26] In the case of a legal person, such as a company, the domicile is determined with reference to (i) its statutory seat,[27] or (ii) its central administration, or (iii) its principal place of business.[28]

2.2.1 Party autonomy: express choice of court by the parties

In the same vein as the Hague Convention, the Brussels I Regulation permits the parties to a contract to agree that the courts of a particular Member State should have jurisdiction for any disputes arising from their contractual (or other legal) relationship.[29] A court designated in this way will then have exclusive jurisdiction in respect of such disputes,[30] which means that the courts in another Member State should decline to hear the dispute.[31] Such an agreement may be a separate agreement, but a term in the contract between the parties designating the courts of a Member State as having exclusive jurisdiction would suffice. This includes a term contained in the standard terms and conditions of one of the parties if this is contained or referred to in a contractual document signed by both parties.[32] This also applies in the case of a contract concluded electronically where the relevant term is contained in the standard terms and conditions, and the customer has to tick ("click") a box next to a link to those standard terms and conditions in order to agree to them and proceed with the transaction.[33]

---

23 The European Free Trade Association.
24 The UK had applied to sign the Lugano Convention in time for the end of the transitional period following its withdrawal from the EU on 31 January 2020, but this was rejected.
25 Art. 62(1) Brussels I.
26 Art. 62(2) Brussels I.
27 Art. 63(2) provides that in respect of Cyprus, Ireland and the United Kingdom (until the end of the post-withdrawal transitional period), the "statutory seat" is the registered office, or, where there is no such office, the place of incorporation, or, in the absence of that, the place under the law of which incorporation occurred.
28 Art. 63(1) Brussels I.
29 Art. 25(1) Brussels I.
30 *Ibid.*
31 Art. 31(2) Brussels I.
32 See, e.g., case C-222/15, *Hösig Kft. v Alstom Power Thermal Services* ECLI:EU: C:2016:525 (judgment of 7 July 2016).
33 Case C-322/14 *Jaouad El Majdoub v CarsOnTheWeb.Deutschland GmbH* ECLI:EU: C:2015:334 (judgment of 21 May 2015).

However, this will not be the case where the contract was concluded verbally and not evidenced in writing, and where the standard terms and conditions containing a jurisdiction clause were only mentioned on invoices subsequently submitted.[34] The crucial point here is that there has to be evidence of an agreement between the parties. For the same reason, a jurisdiction clause in a contract between a manufacturer of goods and a buyer does not bind any subsequent sub-buyers unless they have also agreed to the jurisdiction clause.[35]

If the choice-of-court agreement is contained in a contract, then this contract term is treated autonomously, i.e., independent of the other terms of the contract, and the validity of the choice-of-court clause cannot be challenged on the basis that the rest of the contract is invalid for some reason.[36]

Furthermore, for such a choice-of-court agreement to be recognised, there are certain form requirements. Thus, the agreement should be either in writing or evidenced in writing,[37] or in line with any practices about forming an agreement which have been established between the parties.[38] Alternatively, in the case of international trade or commerce, the choice-of-court agreement accords with an established and regularly observed usage of that trade of which the parties were, or ought to have been, aware.[39]

The validity of a choice-of-court agreement would be established by the courts in the designated Member State on the basis of that Member State's laws, which, for this purpose, include its private international law rules.[40] Thus, the validity of a choice-of-court agreement could be determined by the law applicable to that agreement, if the private international law rules of the designated Member State so provide.

Irrespective of whether the parties have agreed on a choice of court, a court of a Member State will also have jurisdiction if a claimant commences legal action in that court, and the defendant appears in that court to respond to the claim.[41] For example, if the parties have designated the Spanish courts to have exclusive jurisdiction in respect of their contract, but one of the parties commences legal action before a court in Portugal and the defendant appears to respond to the substance of that claim, then the Portuguese court will have jurisdiction.[42]

---

34 Case C-64/17 *Saey Home & Garden NV/SA v Lusavouga-Máquinas e Acessórios Industriais SA* ECLI:EU:C:2018:173 (judgment of 8 March 2018).

35 Case C-543/10 *Refcomp SpA v AcA Corporate Solutions Assurance and others* ECLI:EU:C:2013:62 (judgment of 7 February 2013).

36 Art. 25(5) Brussels I.

37 Art. 25(1)(a) Brussels I. Electronic means of communication providing a durable record of the agreement are treated as "writing". See Art. 25(2) Brussels I.

38 Art. 25(1)(b) Brussels I.

39 Art. 25(1)(c) Brussels I.

40 Cf. Recital 20, Brussels I.

41 Art. 26(1) Brussels I. This does not apply where the sole reason for the defendant's appearance is to challenge the jurisdiction of the court.

42 The opening words of Art. 31(2) make it clear that the designation of exclusive jurisdiction of the courts of a Member State through a choice-of-court agreement is without prejudice to the application of Art. 26.

2.2.2 Jurisdiction in the absence of express choice

For situations when the parties have not made a choice-of-court agreement, the Brussels I Regulation provides a number of default rules. In addition, there are several instances for which there are rules determining jurisdiction irrespective of whether the parties have made an agreement or not. These instances are matters relating to insurance,[43] consumer contracts[44] and individual contracts of employment,[45] but these are not discussed further in this chapter. It is worth noting that, in respect of disputes concerning property (*in rem*) rights in immovable property or tenancies therefore, the Brussels I Regulation allocates exclusive jurisdiction to the courts of the Member State where the property is located.[46]

In the absence of party choice, and where none of the special jurisdiction rules apply, the default rule is set out in Article 4. This states that a person domiciled in a Member State shall be sued in the courts of that Member State. If, however, the person being sued is not domiciled in a Member State, then the courts of the Member State have to determine whether they have jurisdiction based on their national laws.[47]

It has already been noted that if a person sued in a different Member State from that of their domicile appears in those proceedings as a defendant, then the court in that Member State will have jurisdiction.[48] However, if a defendant domiciled in a Member State is sued in a court of another Member State but does not appear before that court, then the court should, of its own motion, decline to hear the case, unless the court would have jurisdiction under the special provisions of the Regulation.[49]

However, there are a number of special situations (in addition to insurance, consumer contracts and individual employment contracts) when a person domiciled in one Member State can be sued in another Member State. Some of these are of particular relevance to commercial contracts.

In respect of contracts, the general rule is that jurisdiction is allocated to the courts for the "place of performance of the obligation in question".[50] There is then further clarification of where the place of performance is with regard to contracts for the sale of goods and the provision of services respectively.

2.2.2.1 Place of performance in contracts for the sale of goods

In the case of a contract of sale, the place of performance is the place where the "goods were delivered, or should have been delivered"[51] in accordance with the

---

43 Arts. 10–16 Brussels I.
44 Arts. 17–19 Brussels I.
45 Arts. 20–23 Brussels I.
46 Art. 24(1) Brussels I.
47 Art. 6(1) Brussels I.
48 Art. 26(1) Brussels I.
49 Art. 28(1) Brussels I. Special situations arise, e.g., in respect of consumer and employment contracts.
50 Art. 7(1)(a) Brussels I.
51 Art. 7(1)(b) Brussels I.

contract. Thus, in order to determine where the goods were, or should have been, delivered, the starting point is the contract between the parties. If this clearly states where the goods have to be delivered, then this is the place of performance and therefore the courts of that place, or in that Member State, have jurisdiction. If the parties have utilised one of the INCOTERMS® to determine the delivery obligation, then the place of delivery stipulated in respect of the particular INCO-TERM® applies.[52] In *Electrosteel*, the CJEU observed that

> In order to verify whether the place of delivery is determined "under the contract", the national court seised must take account of all the relevant terms and clauses of that contract which are capable of clearly identifying that place, including terms and clauses which are generally recognised and applied through the usages of international trade or commerce, such as the Incoterms drawn up by the International Chamber of Commerce...[53]

However, there may be instances when there is no indication in the contract as to where the goods should be delivered. In that case, a default criterion is needed to determine the place where the goods should be delivered. It may be tempting to refer to the default rules of the law applicable to the contract to determine where a seller of the goods has to perform its obligation to deliver the goods. This will often be at the seller's premises,[54] or the place where the goods have to be handed over to the carrier who will transport them to the buyer.[55] However, deferring to the applicable law might mean that the place of delivery will vary depending on whatever the relevant rules of the applicable law might provide. An alternative approach to avoid this outcome would be to treat the notion of "delivery" as having a particular meaning in the context of the Brussels I Regulation which is independent of the law applicable to the contract. The latter approach was adopted by the CJEU in *Car Trim*,[56] which arose from a dispute between an Italian airbag manufacturer and a German component supplier. One of the questions the CJEU had to consider was whether, in the context of a contract requiring carriage of goods to the buyer, "delivery" for the purposes of the Brussels I Regulation occurred at their final destination or where they are handed over to a carrier. The Court first said that in instances when it is not possible to determine the place of delivery from the contract, an autonomous notion of delivery had to be followed. It then held that the place of delivery is the "place where the physical transfer of the goods took place, as a result of which the purchaser obtained,

---

52 Case C-87/10 *Electrosteel Europe SA v Edil Cenro SpA* ECLI:EU:C:2011:375, concerning the "ex works" INCOTERM® rule.

53 *Ibid*. at para. 26.

54 See, e.g., Art. 31(c) of the UN Convention on the International Sale of Goods 1980, or s.29(2) of the UK's Sale of Goods Act 1979.

55 Cf., e.g., Art. 31(a) of the UN Convention on the International Sale of Goods 1980, or s.32(1) of the UK's Sale of Goods Act 1979.

56 C-381/08 *Car Trim GmbH v KeySafety Systems Srl* ECLI:EU:C:2010:90 (judgment of 25 February 2010).

or should have obtained, actual power of disposal over those goods at the final destination of the sales transaction".[57] The Court justified its interpretation of the delivery in this way on the basis that it was both a "highly predictable"[58] criterion, and went on to say that

> It also meets the objective of proximity, in so far as it ensures the existence of a close link between the contract and the court called upon to hear and determine the case. It should be pointed out, in particular, that the goods which are the subject-matter of the contract must, in principle, be in that place after performance of the contract. Furthermore, the principal aim of a contract for the sale of goods is the transfer of those goods from the seller to the purchaser, an operation which is not fully completed until the arrival of those goods at their final destination.[59]

In short, "delivery" for the purposes of the Brussels I Regulation occurs at the place where the goods ended up, or should have ended up, after full performance of the contract. Where there are several places of delivery in the same Member State, the place which can be treated as the principal place of delivery would determine the court with jurisdiction; if there is no such principal place, each place of delivery is treated in the same way and the claimant has the choice where to commence proceedings.[60]

2.2.2.2 Place of performance in contracts for the supply of services

A contract for the supply of services is covered by Art. 7(1)(b). The notion of "service" is broad, and has been held to include contracts for the storage of goods[61] and exclusive distribution agreements.[62] According to Art. 7(1)(b), the place of performance is the Member State where the services were provided, or should have been provided. This should be determined on the basis of the contract itself, but where this cannot be done, it is possible to consider where the service was in fact provided.[63] If this is also not possible, then the domicile of the person providing the service would be the place where the service is deemed to have been provided.[64]

---

57 *Ibid.*, operative part.
58 *Ibid.*, para. 61.
59 *Ibid.*
60 C-386/05 *Color Drack GmBH v Lexx International Vetriebs GmBH* ECLI:EU:C:2007:262 (judgment of 3 May 2007). This might be particularly important for countries with a federal structure such as Austria (where this case originated) or Germany.
61 Case C-469/12 *Krejci Lager & Umschlagsbetriebs GmbH v Olbrich Transport und Logistik GmbH* ECLI:EU:C:2013:788 (judgment of 14 November 2013).
62 Case C-9/12 *Corman-Collins SA v La Maison du Whisky SA* ECLI:EU:C:2013:860 (judgment of 19 December 2013).
63 Case C-19/09 *Wood Floor Solutions Andreas Domberger GmbH v Silva Trade SA.* [2010] ECR I-2121, para. 40. See also C-64/17 *Saey Home & Garden NV/SA v Lusavouga-Máquinas e Acessórios Industriais SA* ECLI:EU:C:2018:173 (judgment of 8 March 2018).
64 *Ibid.*, para. 42.

3. Applicable law

In the absence of a complete International Commercial Law system, any international commercial contract will be subject to a combination of rules which have different origins. However, fundamentally, every contract has to be linked to one particular national law. The national law to which a contract is linked is referred to as the "applicable law" or the "governing law". The applicable law tells us what is needed to conclude a valid and binding contract, what the criteria for the interpretation of such a contract are, rules regarding performance, remedies for a breach of that contract, and factors which might permit a party not to perform its obligations without being in breach of the contract. Whilst there are quite a few similarities in the different national contract law systems, there can also be significant differences. Such differences might follow the dividing line between different types of "legal family", but there are also variations between legal systems broadly within the same legal family.

It is therefore crucial to know which law governs a contract. There are multiple possibilities: it could be the substantive law of the country in which the court with jurisdiction to hear any claims arising from the contract is located (*lex fori*, or law of the forum); it could be the law chosen by the parties, or it could be the law which applies to the contract under the rules of the forum's private international law (*lex causae*). Furthermore, once the applicable law has been identified, it is also possible to determine whether the particular country or jurisdiction whose law governs the contract has ratified any relevant international conventions, which would apply to the parties' contract in tandem with the national rules of contract law.

As we will see, it is widely (although by no means universally[65]) accepted that the parties to a contract are able to exercise their autonomy by stipulating, in their contract, which particular national law will govern, or apply to, their contract. The parties might choose the law of the country where one of the parties is domiciled, or they might prefer the law of a different country. English Law, in particular, is a popular law of choice for many international commercial contracts, especially those concerned with transactions in commodities.

3.1 Hague Principles on Choice of Law in International Commercial Contracts 2015

The Hague Principles on Choice of Law in International Commercial Contracts ("Hague Principles") were adopted by the Hague Conference on Private International Law in March 2015. As a statement of principles, they are not intended to be legally binding, but rather to offer "a model for national, regional, supranational or

---

65 See, e.g., S. Symeonides, "The Hague Principles on Choice of Law for International Contracts: some preliminary comments" (2013) 61 *American Journal of Comparative Law* 873, p.876 (referring to Latin America, in particular).

international instruments".[66] In this way, the Principles serve what might be termed an "advocacy function"[67] to encourage legislatures to act.

As with other Hague instruments in this field, they "apply to choice of law in international contracts where each party is acting in the exercise of its trade or profession"[68] only and exclude consumer and employment contracts for their scope. There are a total of 12 Articles, but the key provision is Article 2, according to which the law governing a contract is the law chosen by the parties.[69] The Hague Principles only deal with the choice of the applicable law by the parties, but do not provide any default rules in the absence of party choice.

The Hague Principles are significant because of the emphasis put on choice of law by the parties. This choice is broad: there is no requirement for any kind of connection between the parties and the law they have chosen to govern their contract.[70] Their choice of law may cover the whole contract or only parts of it.[71] Moreover, the parties are free to choose different laws to apply to different parts of their contract.[72] This latter option, *dépeçage*, can raise complex questions. It can operate in two ways. First, it can have horizontal application in that different laws are chosen to apply to different aspects of the contract (which is the type of *dépeçage* envisaged in the Hague Principles); secondly, within the chosen law, there may be scope for vertical *dépeçage*, e.g., by excluding elements of an international convention that would otherwise apply in favour of the underlying national law.[73]

The law chosen by the parties will cover all aspects of the contract between the parties, including any pre-contractual obligations, the interpretation of the contract and the consequences of non-performance.[74] Somewhat strangely, Art. 9 of the Hague Principles is expressed in the singular and uses mandatory language ("The *law* chosen *shall* govern..."). This may be unproblematic where the parties have only chosen one law to apply to the entirety of the contract, but it fits rather uneasily with instance of *dépeçage*, where different laws are chosen to apply to different aspects of the contract. It also seems surprising in view of the strong emphasis on party autonomy in the Hague Principles.[75]

---

66 Preamble (2) Hague Principles.
67 S. Block-Lieb, "Soft and hard strategies: the role of business in the crafting of international commercial law" (2019) 40 *Michigan Journal of International Law* 433, p.462.
68 Art. 1(1) Hague Principles.
69 Art. 2(1) Hague Principles.
70 Art. 2(4) Hague Principles.
71 Art. 2(2)(a) Hague Principles.
72 Art. 2(2)(b) Hague Principles.
73 See further, B. Marshall, "The Hague Choice of Law Principles, CISG, and PICC: a hard look at a choice of soft law" (2018) 66 *American Journal of Comparative Law* 175, pp.196–203 (focusing in particular on the choice of non-State rules of law and the added complexity this would create in cases of *dépeçage*).
74 Art. 9 Hague Principles. Note also the provisions on assignments in Art. 10 Hague Principles.
75 Cf. S. Symeonides, "The Hague Principles on Choice of Law for International Contracts: some preliminary comments" (2013) 61 *American Journal of Comparative Law* 873, p.895.

However, designating a particular law as the law governing a contract does not include the private international law of the chosen law.[76] This is to avoid the designation of a different law than that chosen by the parties under the chosen law's rules of private international law (*renvoi*).

The parties are not confined to choosing a particular national law, but the range of laws they can choose extends to "rules of law generally accepted on an international, supranational or regional level as neutral and balanced set of rules".[77] This would make it possible for the parties to choose non-national rules such as the UNIDROIT Principles of International Commercial Contracts, or even the Convention on the International Sale of Goods (CISG) when this would not be possible otherwise. However, a choice of non-national rules of law will not be possible if the law of the forum (i.e., the court which has jurisdiction in respect of matters arising from the contract) does not so permit.[78] By permitting such choices, the Hague Principles are broader than other private international law measures dealing with the choice of law. However, there is some uncertainty as to what exactly is permitted; for example, it is unclear whether a choice of the CISG, when it would not otherwise apply because the parties to the contract have not chosen the law of a CISG Contracting State, is confined to the types of contracts within the CISG's scope or whether it can include other contract types.[79] Indeed, if the parties were to choose non-State rules of law as the sole applicable law, there could be difficulties to the extent that such rules of law may be incomplete. For instance, assume that the CISG were directly chosen as the applicable law rather than as a consequence of choosing the law of a CISG Contracting State. Any matters not dealt with in the CISG (such as questions regarding the validity of the contract) which would normally be supplemented by the relevant national law of the chosen CISG Contracting State, would be left unaddressed.

There are no form requirements for choosing the governing law.[80] The choice of law may be made expressly, e.g., through a choice-of-law clause in the contract, or appear clearly from the provisions of the contract or other circumstances.[81] The commentary to the Hague Principles suggests that the choice of a set of standard terms in a "standard form which is generally used in the context of a particular system of law"[82] points to the choice of that particular system of law as the governing law.[83] On the other hand, an agreement in respect of jurisdiction, or a choice-of-court clause in

---

76 Art. 8 Hague Principles.

77 Art. 3 Hague Principles.

78 *Ibid.*, final words.

79 B. Marshall, "The Hague Choice of Law Principles, CISG, and PICC: a hard look at a choice of soft law" (2018) 66 *American Journal of Comparative Law* 175, pp.187–196.

80 Art. 5 Hague Principles. The parties may agree otherwise and require a particular form to be used, although Symeonides queries when that might be the case: S. Symeonides, "The Hague Principles on Choice of Law for International Contracts: some preliminary comments" (2013) 61 *American Journal of Comparative Law* 873, p.891.

81 Art. 4 Hague Principles.

82 Commentary to the Hague Principles, para. 4.9.

83 Cordero Moss argues that this would be appropriate where a standard form contract is known to have been drafted against the backdrop of a specific law. However, where the drafting style of the contract is closer to, e.g., the common law style of drafting, then this does not invariably imply the choice of English Law as the applicable law: G.

the contract, does not mean that the parties have also chosen the national law of the designated court as the governing law.[84]

As is the case with choice-of-court clauses, a choice-of-law clause is treated as severable from the rest of the contract insofar as a challenge to the contract containing the choice-of-law clause will not invariably mean that the choice-of-law clause is also invalid.[85] Should there be a dispute about whether a particular law had been agreed on as the applicable law, the law designated in the choice-of-law clause or agreement will determine whether the parties have actually agreed on a choice of law.[86]

In addition to the straightforward situation where both parties agree on the choice of law as part of their contractual negotiations, the Hague Principles also address the common situation where parties are negotiating a contract on the basis of their respective standard terms. This situation is known as the "battle of the forms", and involves parties making offers and counter-offers on the basis of their respective sets of standard terms. This can often make it difficult to determine whether a contract has ultimately been concluded at all, and if so, which of the standard terms are the basis of that contract. The Hague Principles include a provision that seeks to deal specifically with a battle of the forms where the standard terms of both parties contain a choice-of-law clause, but the choice-of-law clauses in the respective standard terms designate different laws as the applicable law. In order to determine whether there has been a successful choice of law, Art. 6(1)(b) of the Hague Principles requires that the outcome of the battle of the forms under both laws has to be considered. This is potentially problematic as Art. 6(1)(b) seems to refer to the relevant rules of the respective chosen laws which deal with the battle of the forms in respect of *substantive* obligations under the contract, whereas there are distinct private international law approaches to conflicting choice-of-law clauses.[87]

For substantive "battle of the forms" instances, there are at least three different approaches: the "first shot" rule will let the standard terms which were first presented prevail, whereas conversely, the "last shot" rules will let the standard terms which were presented last at the time of contract formation prevail. A third approach is the "knock-out" rule, which requires, if there is no agreement in respect of the standard terms, that any conflicting terms in the respective sets of standard terms are disregarded. The basic operation of Art. 6(1)(b) entails that if both laws indicated in the respective standard terms lead to the conclusion that the same set of standard terms applies, then the choice-of-law clause in the "winning" standard terms determines the applicable law. However, if each law leads to a different conclusion as to the prevailing standard terms (which will invariably be the case when at least one of the

Cordero-Moss, *International Commercial Contracts* (Cambridge University Press, 2014), esp. pp.148–152.

84   Art. 4 Hague Principles.
85   Art. 7 Hague Principles.
86   Art. 6(1)(a) Hague Principles.
87   B. Marshall, "The Hague Choice of Law Principles, CISG, and PICC: a hard look at a choice of soft law" (2018) 66 *American Journal of Comparative Law* 175, pp.209–210. Marshall notes that the private international law solutions for conflicting choice-of-law clauses is to apply either the law of the forum, or the law that would apply in the absence of any choice (at p.210).

chosen laws follows the "knock-out" rule), or to no standard terms being applicable at all, then there is no choice of law either. The apparent simplicity of this approach may be deceptive, as the precise consequences of applying the battle of the forms solution under the two laws concerned may be a rather complex exercise.[88]

3.2 EU Law: Rome I Regulation

For the EU, the relevant rules are found in *Regulation 593/2008 on the law applicable to contractual obligations (Rome I) – OJ L177/6*, which replaced the Rome Convention in the EU Member States with effect from December 2009. Following its withdrawal from the European Union on 31 January 2020, the Rome I Regulation continues to apply with amendments[89] in the UK as "retained EU Law" under the European Union (Withdrawal) Act 2018.

The Rome I Regulation covers both a choice by the parties of the applicable law, and default rules in the absence of a choice of law. Irrespective of how the applicable law is determined, it will cover, in particular, the interpretation of the contract, its performance, the consequences of a breach of contract, the way in which contractual obligations can be discharged and the consequences of nullity of the contract.[90]

Reflecting the principle of party autonomy, the Rome I Regulation grants the party the right to choose[91] the law applicable to their contract.[92] This choice has to be made either expressly, or "clearly demonstrated by the terms of the contract or the circumstances of the case".[93] Although the Rome I Regulation only applies within the EU, the parties may choose any law, whether or not it is the law of a Member State. However, unlike the Hague Principles, it is not possible to choose non-State rules of law such as the UNIDROIT Principles of International Commercial Contracts, or the Principles of European Contract Law.[94]

If the parties have not chosen the applicable law, then Articles 4–8 of the Rome I Regulation provide a set of rules to determine the applicable law.[95] In many instances, the applicable law will be the law of the country where one of the

---

88 Marshall, *infra*. See also P. Winship, "The Hague Principles, the CISG and the 'battle of the forms'" (2015) 4 *Penn State Journal of Law and International Affairs* 151, p.164. Winship's paper focuses on the interaction between the relevant CISG rules (see Chapter 4) and the Hague Principles.

89 See The Law Applicable to Contractual Obligations and Non-Contractual Obligations (Amendment etc.) (EU Exit) Regulations 2019 S.I. 2019/834.

90 Art. 12(1) Rome I.

91 Note that no choice is possible in respect of certain consumer contracts, when the law of the consumer's habitual residence will apply: see Art. 6(1) Rome I.

92 Art. 3(1) Rome I.

93 *Ibid*.

94 It would be possible for the parties to incorporate such principles into their contract, where they would take effect as terms of the contract (Recital 13). This would be subject to any non-derogable rules of the applicable law.

95 In either situation, the applicable law determined on the basis of the Regulation will not include the rules of private international law of the country whose law otherwise governs the contract (Art. 20 Rome I).

parties has its habitual residence. The criterion[96] for establishing a party's habitual residence is set out in Art. 19 Rome I, which is done with reference to the time when contract was concluded.[97] Thus, in the case of a company and other bodies, the place of its central administration determines its habitual residence.[98] For natural persons acting in the course of their business activity, their principal place of business determines their habitual residence.[99]

There are detailed rules for some contract types. Thus, in respect of a contract for the carriage of goods, the applicable law would be the law of the country of the carrier's habitual residence, but only if either the place of receipt or delivery of the goods, or the consignor's habitual residence, is in the same country.[100] Otherwise, it would be the law of the country where the goods are to be delivered under the terms of the contract.[101] There are further rules determining the applicable law in respect of contracts of insurance,[102] and individual employment contracts.[103]

For other contract types, Article 4 contains a set of default rules to determine the applicable law in the absence of a choice made by the parties. In the case of a contract for the sale of goods, the applicable law would be the law of the seller's habitual residence.[104] This could produce a strange result in the case of a contract of sale containing neither a choice-of-court clause nor a choice-of-law clause. As we saw earlier, the default rule to determine which court has jurisdiction is on the basis of the place where the goods were, or should have been, delivered.[105] If the contract requires the seller to deliver the goods to a place which is not in the country of the seller's habitual residence (e.g., to the buyer's premises in another Member State), then this would mean that jurisdiction is given to the courts of one country, but that court would have to apply the laws of another country. Such an outcome could, of course, easily be avoided by ensuring that the parties have agreed a choice-of-court and a choice-of-law clause for their contract.

The applicable law for a contract involving the supply of services is the law of the country where the provider of the services has its habitual residence.[106] A contract relating to property rights (*in rem*) in immovable property, or a tenancy in such property, is governed by the law where the immovable property is situated.[107] For

---

96 For the purposes of the Rome I Regulation, a single criterion was chosen in the interest of legal certainty (Recital 39).
97 Art. 19(3) Rome I.
98 Art. 19(1), first sentence. Note the criterion for branches, agencies and similar in Art. 19 (2).
99 Art. 19(1), second sentence.
100 Art. 5(1) Rome I.
101 *Ibid.*
102 Art. 7 Rome I.
103 Art. 8 Rome I.
104 Art. 4(1)(a) Rome I.
105 Art. 7(1)(b) Brussels I.
106 Art. 4(1)(b) Rome I.
107 Art. 4(1)(c) Rome I.

franchise and distribution contracts, the applicable laws are those of the franchisee's[108] or distributor's[109] habitual residence respectively.

Where it is not possible to determine the applicable law on the basis of these default rules, e.g., because a contract involves a combination of different elements, or the contract is not one of the ones listed in Article 4(1) or dealt with in Arts. 5–8, then the applicable law should be "the law of the country where the party required to effect the characteristic performance of the contract has his habitual residence".[110] However, if the applicable law still cannot be determined, then the law of the country with which the contract is most closely connected will be the governing law.[111]

With regard to the substantive validity of the contract or any particular term, including a choice-of-law clause, within the contract, the law which would govern the contract if the contract or term were valid will apply. However, one of the parties might deny that it consented to a term in the contract, or the contract as a whole. In order to prove that it did not consent, that party can rely on the law where it is habitually resident, if it would not be reasonable to determine the effect of that party's conduct on the basis of the law otherwise applicable.[112]

In respect of validity based on compliance with formal requirements, a contract will be valid if it satisfies the formal requirements of the governing law, as determined by the rules of the Rome I Regulation. Alternatively, where both parties were present in the same country at the time of concluding the contract, it will be valid if it complies with the formal requirements of that country. If the parties were in different countries at the time of concluding the contract, alternative laws which will determine the formal validity of the contract would be the law of either country where the parties were present, or the law of the country of either party's habitual residence.

3.3 Inter-American Convention on the Law Applicable to International Contracts 1994 ("Mexico Convention")

The Mexico Convention entered into force in December 1996, but the only two countries which have ratified it are Mexico and Venezuela.[113] It only applies to international contracts, defined as contracts where the parties have their places of business or habitual residence in different Contracting States, or where the contract has connections to more than one State.[114]

---

108 Art. 4(1)(e) Rome I.
109 Art. 4(1)(f) Rome I.
110 Art. 4(2) Rome I.
111 Art. 4(4) Rome I.
112 Art. 10 Rome I.
113 In addition to these two countries, Bolivia, Brazil and Uruguay signed the Convention, but have not (yet) ratified it. See "Signatories and Ratification" at http://www.oas.org/juridico/english/sigs/b-56.html [accessed May 2021].
114 Art. 1 Mexico Convention.

The Mexico Convention also gives the parties to a contract the right to choose the applicable law.[115] This may be the law of a non-Contracting State,[116] but will not include that State's rules of private international law.[117] Such choice must be made expressly, or alternatively evident from the conduct of the parties and the terms of the contract.[118] However, a choice-of-court clause in the contract allocating jurisdiction to a particular country does not entail that the parties have also chosen to apply the substantive law of the forum.[119]

In the absence of a choice made by the parties, the default rule is that the applicable law is the law of the State with which the contract has its closest ties.[120] This will be determined on the basis of all objective and subjective elements of the contract, as well as any general principles of International Commercial Law which have been recognised by international organisations.[121] Furthermore, the requirements of justice and equity may require the application of "the guidelines, customs, and principles of international commercial law as well as commercial usage and practices generally accepted".[122]

Questions of validity of the contract or a choice-of-law clause are to be determined by the applicable law, although in order to establish whether a party has consented, the relevant rules of the law of the country where that party's habitual residence or place of business is can be applied.[123]

3.4 Limits to the application of the governing law

The purpose of private international law rules regarding the applicable law is to ensure that there is a clearly identifiable law that will govern a contract. As we have seen, the applicable law can be determined either based on the choice of the parties, or by referring to whatever default rules are applicable in respect of particular contract types.

However, there are a number of instances when the law chosen by the parties, or determined on the basis of default rules, will not apply at all or only subject to provisions of law from another country being taken account of. Both the Hague Principles and the Rome I Regulation contain provisions dealing with such instances. Generally speaking, there are three commonly found instances when the application of the governing law will be subject to constraints: first, there may be some rules of law which cannot be contracted out of ("simple mandatory rules"); the second concerns so-called "overriding mandatory rules" of a country other than that of the applicable law; and the third concerns limitations based on public policy (*ordre public*) of a country other than that of the applicable law. The key question here is to identify the law (or laws) whose limiting

---

115 Art. 7, first sentence, Mexico Convention.
116 Art. 2 Mexico Convention.
117 Art. 17 Mexico Convention.
118 Art. 7, second sentence, Mexico Convention.
119 Art. 7, final sentence, Mexico Convention.
120 Art. 9, first para., Mexico Convention.
121 Art. 9, second para., Mexico Convention.
122 Art. 10 Mexico Convention.
123 Art. 12 Mexico Convention.

factors apply. The candidates are the law of the forum (*lex fori*) and the law applicable to the contract under the rules of private international law (*lex causae*). There are different approaches in the various private international law systems: some defer exclusively to the *lex fori*, some to the *lex causae*, and others combines the limitations of the *lex fori* with those of the *lex causae* or some other relevant law.[124] The examples covered in this chapter all broadly follow the third approach, but in different ways.

3.4.1 Hague Principles

As explained earlier, the Hague Principles focus on choice-of-law agreements, and do not contain any fall-back rules in the absence of party choice. Article 11 of the Hague Principles deals with the impact of both overriding mandatory rules and public policy. First, the choice of a particular applicable law by the parties will not prevent the application of overriding mandatory provisions of the law of the forum.[125] Secondly, the law of the forum may also determine when the overriding mandatory provisions of another law must be taken into account.[126] There is no definition of "overriding mandatory provision" in the Hague Principles itself, and there is some uncertainty as to whether it covers only rules which cannot be contracted out of, or also more fundamental mandatory rules.[127] The commentary to the Hague Principles[128] explains that such provisions are provisions which are relevant to dealing with a dispute between the parties to a contract irrespective of which law has been chosen as the governing law. Their mandatory nature is due to the fact that the parties are not able to contract out of the application of those provisions, and they are overriding because these provisions continue to apply despite the choice of a different governing law. Every legal system will contain certain rules which parties cannot exclude through the terms of their contract, and any attempt to do so would be ineffective. The effect is that the law chosen by the parties will apply to their contract and the resolution of any disputes arising therefrom, but will be subject to any overriding mandatory provisions of the law of the forum, or those of another relevant law.

A similar approach is taken in respect of provisions of the governing law. If their application would be regarded as "manifestly incompatible with fundamental notions of public policy" of the forum, then those, and only those, provisions which are incompatible for this reason will be excluded.[129] Moreover, depending on the law of the forum, the public policy of the country the law of which would apply, had the parties not chosen the governing law, may also be taken into account.[130] This might be

124 S. Symeonides, "The Hague Principles on Choice of Law for International Contracts: some preliminary comments" (2013) 61 *American Journal of Comparative Law* 873, pp.882–883.

125 Art. 11(1) Hague Principles.

126 Art. 11(2) Hague Principles.

127 S. Symeonides, "The Hague Principles on Choice of Law for International Contracts: some preliminary comments" (2013) 61 *American Journal of Comparative Law* 873, p.887.

128 See para. 11.16, Commentary to the Hague Principles.

129 Art. 11(3) Hague Principles.

130 Art. 11(4) Hague Principles.

important if the *lex causae* contained restrictions not found in the *lex fori*. The notion of public policy goes beyond particular overriding mandatory provisions. It refers to "policies of the legal system of the forum (in whatever form) that are so important that they extend to contracts of an international character",[131] irrespective of the ability of the parties to choose a different applicable law. It is therefore first necessary to establish whether there are any relevant public policy concerns under the law of the forum. Then it must be considered whether applying a particular rule of the governing law would conflict with the forum's public policy, and if so, whether that conflict would render the governing law's rule *manifestly incompatible* with the forum's public policy. The threshold for disapplying a provision of the governing law chosen by the parties on public policy grounds is therefore a high one.

3.4.2 Rome I Regulation

The Rome I Regulation also contains a number of provisions which would have the effect of displacing the law chosen by the parties wholly or in part.

The first situation addressed in the Rome I Regulation essentially seeks to prevent a situation where the parties to a contract choose a governing law which has no connection to the contract itself, but where the chosen law might be more favourable to the parties, e.g., by allowing the parties greater freedom to determine their rights and obligations. In other words, the situation is one where "all other elements relevant to the situation at the time of the choice"[132] relate to one country, but the applicable law chosen by the parties is that of another country. In this situation, any provisions of the law to which all the "other elements" relate, which cannot be derogated from by the parties (i.e., simple mandatory rules), can be applied to the contract, despite the choice of a different governing law.[133] This does not mean that the choice of law by the parties is wholly ineffective; rather, it is effective subject to the applications of the relevant non-derogable rules from the other country. Similarly, if the parties have chosen the law of a non-Member State even though all aspects of the contract are connected to one or more Member States, then any relevant provisions of EU Law will apply alongside the law chosen by the parties.[134]

---

131 Para. 11.24, Commentary to the Hague Principles. The commentary gives the example of a wagering contract which a casino seeks to enforce in the country of residence of a professional gambler. As wagering contracts are contrary to public policy in the gambler's country, but legal under the law of the casino's country and the latter is applicable to the contract, the question arises whether the court in the gambler's country can refuse to treat the contract as binding (Illustration 11.4).

132 Opening words of Arts. 3(3) and 3(4) Rome I.

133 Art. 3(3) Rome I.

134 Cf. Case C-381/98 *Ingmar GB Ltd v Eaton Leonard Technologies Inc.* ECLI:EU: C:2000:605, [2000] ECR I-9305, where the CJEU held that the choice of Californian law in respect of a commercial agency contract did not preclude the application of EU rules on commercial agents (Directive 86/653/EEC) where the commercial agent's activities were conducted within the EU.

Furthermore, Art. 9 Rome I recognises the relevance of "overriding mandatory provisions" of both the country whose courts have jurisdiction in respect of a contract (*lex fori*) and such rules of the country where the contract is to be performed. Unlike the Hague Principles, overriding mandatory provisions are defined in the Rome I Regulation as "provisions the respect for which is regarded as crucial by a country for safeguarding its public interests, such as its political, social or economic organisation, to such an extent that they are applicable to any situation falling within their scope",[135] even if the parties have chosen a different governing law. The application of such provisions by the court which has jurisdiction under the law of the country where it is located (*lex fori*) is not precluded, irrespective of which law is applicable to the contract.[136] Moreover, those overriding mandatory provisions of the law of the country where the obligations under the contract are to be performed which would mean that performance of the contract is unlawful may be applied by the forum court.[137] As an exception to the general freedom of choice given to the parties under Art. 3(1) Rome I, the scope of Art. 9 has to be interpreted restrictively.[138]

Finally, with regard to public policy (*ordre public*), the court which has jurisdiction may refuse to apply any rule of the applicable law insofar as that rule would be *manifestly incompatible* with the public policy (*ordre public*) of the law of the forum.[139]

3.4.3 Inter-American Convention on the Law Applicable to International Contracts 1994 ("Mexico Convention")

The Mexico Convention provides that any mandatory requirements of the law of the forum "shall necessarily be applied".[140] Moreover, the court hearing the dispute can decide whether to apply also the mandatory rules of another State with which the contract has a close connection.[141] Furthermore, where a provision of the law applicable according to the Convention is manifestly contrary to the public order of the forum, then this provision can be excluded and not be applied.[142]

From the account above, we can see that the broad preference given to party autonomy in permitting the parties to a contract to determine the law applicable to that contract is not unlimited. None of the restrictions noted above have the effect of undoing the choice of law by the parties – the chosen law will govern most aspects of the contract between the parties. However, if there are any relevant rules in the country where the contract is located and which are mandatory in the sense that the parties cannot contract out of them, then these rules will apply notwithstanding the

---

135 Art. 9(1) Rome I.
136 Art. 9(2) Rome I.
137 Art. 9(3) Rome I.
138 Case C-135/15 *Hellenic Republic v Grigorios Nikiforidis* ECLI:EU:C:2016:774 (18 October 2016), paras. 43 and 44.
139 Art. 21 Rome I.
140 Art. 11 Mexico Convention.
141 *Ibid.*
142 Art. 18 Mexico Convention.

choice of a different applicable law. Furthermore, where the court which has jurisdiction is located in one country, but a different law is applicable to the contract, then both overriding mandatory provisions and conflicts of the applicable law with the public policy of the forum can affect the application of the law chosen by the parties.

4. Recognition and enforcement of judgments

A third strand of private international law is the way in which it facilitates the recognition of judgments in a country other than that where the court was located. In the context of international commercial contracts, the enforceability of judgments across borders is crucial, particularly for a successful claimant who might need to enforce a judgment against a defendant located in a country other than that of the court which decided the case. Various international regimes on private international law deal with the recognition and enforcement of judgments.

4.1 Hague Convention on Choice of Court Agreements 2005

We saw earlier how the Hague Convention on Choice of Court Agreements 2005 facilitates the designation of the country whose courts have jurisdiction to decide a dispute between the parties to a contract. The 2005 Hague Convention further deals with the recognition and enforcement of judgments in another Contracting State than that where the court is located, as well as setting out the grounds on which recognition and/or enforcement may be refused.

The basic rule is that a judgment[143] which was handed down by a court in one Contracting State, which is in effect and enforceable in this State,[144] must be recognised and enforced in another Contracting State.[145] The courts in the State where recognition and enforcement is sought cannot review the merits of the decision, nor question any findings of fact by the court which gave the judgment.[146]

Recognition or enforcement of a judgment may be refused on the grounds set out in Art. 9 of the Hague Convention. Thus, recognition or enforcement can be refused if the choice-of-court agreement was invalid under the law of the country of the designated court, or if a party lacked capacity under that law.[147] This will also be the case where the defendant was not notified of the claim in sufficient time to prepare their defence, except when the defendant did appear and present

---

143 This includes a settlement agreement approved by a court, or made before a court, which is enforceable in the same way as a judgment in the country where the court is located (Art. 12).

144 Art. 8(3) Hague Convention (2005). If the judgment is under review (appeal) or if the time for lodging a review has not yet passed, then recognition and enforcement may be postponed (Art. 8(4)).

145 Art. 8(1) Hague Convention (2005).

146 Art. 8(2) Hague Convention (2005). The exception to this is where the judgment was given by default.

147 Art. 9(a) and (b) Hague Convention. Invalidity will not be a bar if the court decided that the agreement was valid.

their case, or where the notification was not in accordance with the requirements for serving documents in the defendant's country.[148] Fraud in connection with procedural matters is a further ground for refusal.[149]

More significantly, recognition or enforcement can be refused where this would be "manifestly incompatible with the public policy"[150] of the Contracting State where recognition or enforcement is sought. Finally, refusal is permitted where the judgment conflicts with an earlier judgment in a dispute between the same parties, handed down either in the Contracting State where recognition and enforcement is sought,[151] or in another State if that judgment is also recognised in the State where recognition and enforcement is sought.[152]

A further ground for enforcement is concerned with the substance of the judgment: recognition and enforcement can be refused to the extent that an award of damages under the judgment at issue goes beyond compensation of a party for the losses or harm suffered.[153] This would be particularly so where damages are of an exemplary nature or are intended to be punitive.

In order to request the recognition and enforcement of a judgment, the party must provide a certified copy of the judgment, the choice-of-court agreement and documentation to confirm that the judgment is effective and enforceable in the country where it was given.[154] A certified translation into one of the official languages of the State where recognition or enforcement is sought must be provided where the judgment was handed down in a different language.[155] The procedure for recognition and enforcement is determined by the law of the State where enforcement has been requested.[156]

4.1.1 Hague Convention on the Recognition and Enforcement of Foreign Judgments in Civil and Commercial Matters 2019

The 2005 Hague Convention is limited to the recognition and enforcement of judgments which resulted from a choice-of-court agreement by the parties. In July 2019, the Hague Conference adopted the broader Hague Convention on the Recognition and Enforcement of Foreign Judgments in Civil and Commercial Matters 2019.[157] This Convention focuses on the recognition and enforcement of judgments in civil and commercial matters handed down in one Contracting State by a court in another Contracting State.[158]

---

148 Art. 9(c) Hague Convention (2005).
149 Art. 9(e) Hague Convention (2005).
150 Art. 9(d) Hague Convention (2005).
151 Art. 9(f) Hague Convention (2005).
152 Art. 9(g) Hague Convention (2005).
153 Art. 11(1) Hague Convention (2005).
154 Art. 13(1)(a)–(c) Hague Convention (2005).
155 Art. 13(4) Hague Convention (2005).
156 Art. 14 Hague Convention (2005).
157 At the time of writing, there were no ratifications, and only Israel, Ukraine and Uruguay had signed the Convention.
158 Art. 1 Hague Convention (2019).

The basic rule is that a judgment handed down in one Contracting State must be recognised in another Contracting State,[159] provided that the judgment is effective and enforceable in the Contracting State where it was given.[160] There can be no review of the merits,[161] and recognition and enforcement may only be refused on the grounds set out in Art. 7.

As a precondition to recognition and enforceability, at least one of the requirements set out in Art. 5(1)(a)–(m) must be satisfied. This is not the place to go through all of these. The assumption underpinning the recognition and enforcement regime is that the person against whom enforcement is sought ("Person A") is present in the Contracting State where enforcement or recognition has been requested. Some of the criteria for eligibility listed in Art. 5 are linked to the fact that Person A was habitually resident,[162] or had its place of business,[163] in the country where the judgment originated. Another ground to be mentioned by way of example is that the judgment relates to a contractual obligation given by the court of the State where that obligation was, or should have been, performed, either in accordance with the parties' agreement, or under the governing law if the parties have not agreed on a place of performance.[164] The key point to note here is that the 2019 Convention largely complements the 2005 Convention, although it is not a fully comprehensive system for the recognition and enforcement of judgments as between the Contracting States.

4.2 European Union: the Brussels I Regulation

The Brussels I Regulation also provides for the recognition and enforcement of judgments. The basic rule is that a judgment handed down by a court in one Member State must be recognised by a court in another Member State without any special procedure for its recognition having to be followed.[165] A party seeking to rely on a judgment given in one Member State in another Member State has to produce a copy of the judgment which is sufficient to ensure its authenticity, together with a certificate[166] following the format specified in Annex I to the Brussels I Regulation.[167] A translation or transliteration of either the certificate or the judgment may be requested by the court in the Member State where the judgment is

---

159 Art. 4(1) Hague Convention (2019).
160 Art. 4(3) Hague Convention (2019).
161 Art. 4(2) Hague Convention (2019).
162 Art. 5(1)(a) Hague Convention (2019). The habitual resident of a legal person is determined on the basis of one of its statutory seats, the country of its law of incorporation/ formation, its central administration or its place of business (Art. 3(2) Hague Convention (2019)).
163 Art. 5(1)(b) Hague Convention (2019).
164 Art. 5(1)(g) Hague Convention (2019).
165 Art. 36(1) Brussels I.
166 This certificate must be issued by the court which handed down the judgment on request: Art. 53 Brussels I.
167 Art. 37(1) Brussels I.

sought to be recognised and enforced.[168] Recognition may be refused, *int. al.*, where this would be contrary to the public policy of the Member State where recognition is sought,[169] where the judgment conflicts with a judgment between the same parties handed down in that Member State or in another Member State or third State,[170] or where the judgment was handed down in violation of the jurisdiction rules of the Brussels I Regulation.[171]

Furthermore, judgments handed down in one Member State can be enforced in another Member State, without any further declaration of enforceability required.[172] The party seeking enforcement has to provide the copy and certificate in the same way as required in respect of recognition of a judgment.[173] Enforcement may be refused on the same grounds on which recognition may be refused.[174]

4.3 Inter-American Convention on Extraterritorial Validity of Foreign Judgments and Arbitral Awards 1984 ("Montevideo Convention")

The Montevideo Convention is a short convention dealing with the recognition of judgments (and arbitral awards) handed down in civil, commercial or labour proceedings in one of the Contracting States[175] in one of the other Contracting States. The conditions for such recognition are set out in Article 2 of the Convention. This Article combines both substantive and procedural aspects. In terms of the substantive conditions for recognition, the judgment must be authentic in the State of origin; it must have been handed down by a judge or tribunal competent in the international sphere (i.e., have jurisdiction in the private international law sense) to adjudicate in the State of origin; the parties must have had an opportunity to present their defence; and the judgment is final and has the force of *res judicata* in the State of origin.[176] Furthermore, the judgment must not be "manifestly contrary" to the public policy (*ordre public*) of the State of enforcement.[177] Procedural requirements are that the judgment and other relevant documents have been translated into the official language of the State of enforcement, and that they are authenticated in accordance with the law of the State of enforcement.[178]

To complement the scope of Art. 2(d) on the meaning of "competent in the international sphere", the La Paz Convention on Jurisdiction in the International

---

168 Art. 37(2) Brussels I.
169 Art. 45(1)(a) Brussels I.
170 Art. 45(1)(c) and (d) Brussels I.
171 Art. 45(1)(e) Brussels I.
172 Art. 39 Brussels I.
173 Art. 42 Brussels I.
174 Art. 46 Brussels I, referring back to Art. 45(1).
175 There are 10 Contracting States: Argentina, Bolivia, Brazil, Colombia, Ecuador, Mexico, Paraguay, Peru, Uruguay and Venezuela. See http://www.oas.org/juridico/english/sigs/b-41.html [accessed May 2021].
176 Art. 2, paras. (a), (d), (f) and (g) Montevideo Convention.
177 Art. 2(h) Montevideo Convention.
178 Art. 2(b) and (c) Montevideo Convention.

Sphere for the Extraterritorial Validity of Foreign Judgments 1984 was adopted. It entered into force in December 2004 but applies only to Uruguay and Mexico.[179] Article 1 of the La Paz Convention sets out several criteria by which the competence of a court "in the international sphere" is determined, depending on the type of action. This includes the possibility of a choice-of-court agreement in an international business contract, provided that such an agreement was in writing, the parties agreed to submit to the jurisdiction of a Contracting State, and that State had a reasonable connection with the subject-matter of the dispute between the parties.[180] Otherwise, the defendant must have had its domicile or habitual residence (in the case of natural persons) or its principal place of business (in the case of legal persons) in the territory of the State where the judgment was given. Similarly, a court will be competent in the international sphere if an unincorporated business enterprise or a branch, agency or affiliate of the same had its place of business in the territory of the State where the judgment was handed down.[181] In the case of tangible movable property, the property must have been in the State where the judgment was given, or one of the conditions mentioned previously must have been satisfied.[182] Immovable property must be located in the country where the judgment was given.[183]

5. Conclusions

The purpose of this chapter has been to stress the importance of private international law in the context of international commercial transactions, because the contract at the heart of any such transaction has its roots in a national law, and depends for its enforcement on both the determination of any disputes in a national court, but also the subsequent recognition and enforcement of such judgments. Whilst there are various regional and international initiatives to facilitate both the choice of court and applicable law by the parties, as well as default determinations of either in the absence of party choice, the present picture is far from comprehensive.[184] Within the confines of this chapter, a broad overview and a selection of some points of difficulty suffice to highlight the complexities involved in dealing with questions of both jurisdiction and determination of the applicable law. Party autonomy is increasingly becoming the norm for the choice of both forum and governing law, but the high degree of leeway given to party autonomy (especially under the Hague Principles and the Rome I Regulation) is not unfettered. In the chapters which follow, the focus will be primarily on the legal rules emanating from the international level, but their application to any

---

179 Eleven other countries have signed the Convention but not ratified it as yet. See "Signatories and Ratification" at http://www.oas.org/juridico/english/sigs/b-50.html [accessed May 2021].
180 Art. 1(D) La Paz Convention.
181 Art. 1(A) La Paz Convention.
182 Art. 1(B) La Paz Convention.
183 Art. 1(C) La Paz Convention.
184 This can be contrasted with the international framework for international commercial arbitration, discussed in Chapter 11.

international commercial contract will be in tandem with a particular national law (or potentially multiple national laws, where the parties have made such a choice).

It is surprising that, apart from the EU measures, the number of ratifications of conventions dealing with the private international law aspects of commercial agreements has generally been low. Block-Lieb argued that regional agreements have tended to be more successful,[185] but that seems only true of the EU, not in the Americas.

---

185 S. Block-Lieb, "Soft and hard strategies: the role of business in the crafting of international commercial law" (2019) 40 *Michigan Journal of International Law* 433, p.458.

3

MAKING INTERNATIONAL COMMERCIAL LAW

Harmonisation – process and methods

1. Introduction

We have examined the legal challenges arising in the context of international commercial transactions, and the extent to which private international law alleviates some of these. However, identifying which particular national law governs an international commercial transaction does not remove all of the legal difficulties, not least the uncertainty about what precisely the requirements and constraints of that national law might be. Moreover, national laws have largely evolved in a domestic context and will not necessarily be able to address all the issues associated with international commercial transactions.

It might seem, at first glance, that a solution to this would be the adoption of a legal regime for international commercial transactions common to many countries, which supplements – or even replaces – the otherwise applicable rules of national law. The advantage of this approach would be that it could enhance legal predictability for the parties to an international transaction, in so far as the common regime would apply to their transaction, as it would obviate the need to identify or agree on the national law that will govern the transaction. It would also reduce the consequences of a particular law being determined as the law applicable to the transaction if that particular national law includes the common legal regime for international transactions.

The process of creating such legal regimes for international transaction is commonly referred to as "harmonisation". In essence, harmonisation is a process of approximating the laws of several countries. This can be done (i) by *replacing* existing domestic rules with an internationally agreed rule or (ii) by *supplementing* domestic law with an internationally agreed rule applicable only to international dealings. In the field of International Commercial Law, the second of these

DOI: 10.4324/9781315692807-3

approaches is followed. An example in the former category is the harmonisation programme carried out by the EU in the field of consumer contract law.[1]

In the field of International Commercial Law, there are a number of such common legal regimes specifically for international transactions, such as the United Nations Convention on the International Sale of Goods, or the UNIDROIT Convention on Security Interests in Mobile Equipment. These and others will be examined more closely in later chapters. In this chapter, we will first explore the concept of harmonisation, before turning to the specific ways in which International Commercial Law is made through a process of harmonisation using a range of different legal instruments.

One important point should be noted from the outset, however: although harmonisation and the making of International Commercial Law often go hand-in-hand, the concept of harmonisation can be understood in different ways. The pursuit of harmonisation of commercial law as an end in itself has given way to a modified view that harmonisation should be pursued where this would result in a reduction of legal risk and the costs associated with transaction in the international context.[2] As we will see, the focus has narrowed further on specific problems (going beyond the mere fact that national commercial laws differ) affecting international commercial transactions which can best be resolved through action at the international level. Therefore, instead of seeing harmonisation as a tool for overcoming the variety of potential legal sources for an international commercial transaction, it is better to see harmonisation of selected areas of commercial law as an element of the pluralist nature of International (and transnational) Commercial Law.

2. Defining harmonisation

One of the first hurdles one meets when examining the concept of "harmonisation" is that there is a lack of agreement on how best to define it.[3] In the scholarly literature on harmonisation, numerous suggestions for how one might define harmonisation are made. For example, Leebron[4] offers a very broad definition:

> Harmonization can be loosely defined as making the regulatory requirements or government policies of different jurisdictions identical or at least more similar.

This definition captures both the *focus* of harmonisation, and the *objective* pursued by it. Thus, the focus of harmonisation could be regulatory requirements, i.e., legal

---

1 Developments are the EU level are not considered further in this book. The EU's activities in the field of consumer law are analysed in G. Howells, C. Twigg-Flesner and T. Wilhelmsson, *Rethinking EU Consumer Law* (Routledge, 2017).
2 Cf. G.-P. Callies and I. Buchmann, "Global commercial law between unity, pluralism, and competition: the case of the CISG" (2016) 21 *Uniform Law Review* 1, pp.3–5.
3 See S. Gopalan, "New trends in the making of international commercial law" (2004) 23 *Journal of Law and Commerce* 117, pp.120–121.
4 D.W. Leebron, "Claims for harmonization: a theoretical framework" (1996) 27 *Canadian Business Law Journal* 63.

rules, or policies in respect of specific matters. A related element is that harmonisation relates to several jurisdictions. The minimum objective is to make such regulations or policies more similar, i.e., the divergences between them is to be reduced as much as possible, with the ultimate ideal being uniformity ("identical").

A similarly broad definition is suggested by Boodman:[5]

> Harmonization is a process in which diverse elements are combined or adapted to each other so as to form a coherent whole while retaining their individuality.

Like Leebron's definition, this definition also focuses on the desire to take diverse elements and to align them to ensure that there is coherence, although he also notes that the individuality of the combined elements is retained. In the context of International Commercial Law, this could be interpreted as adapting diverse national laws towards a coherent approach towards international transactions without losing the characteristic features of their respective jurisdiction. Understood in this way, this definition is not that different from the one put forward by Goode:[6]

> The particular characteristic of … harmonisation lies in its motivation, which is to reduce the impact of national boundaries [by creating] a special regime for international transactions whilst preserving the identity of national laws for domestic transactions.

Once more, it can be seen that the desire is not the full replacement of existing national laws with a single uniform regime, but rather to lessen the significance of variations between national laws by establishing special rules for international transactions. That way, the identity of national laws remains unaffected and will continue to apply to domestic transactions. The emphasis on international transactions is also evident in Gopalan's definition,[7] which regards harmonisation as

> any attempt, by whatever instrument … to minimize or eliminate discord between national commercial laws as they apply to international commercial transactions.

Again, the scope of the harmonising instrument is confined to international commercial transactions, although the target is the "discord" which exists between national commercial laws as a result of the differences between those laws. Gopalan also suggests that there are degrees of harmonisation, ranging from minimising discord to eliminating it altogether – the latter would be a uniform legal regime for international transactions.

5   M. Boodman, "The myth of harmonization of laws" (1991) 39 *American Journal of Comparative Law* 699.
6   R. Goode, "Reflections on the harmonisation of commercial law" (1991) *Uniform Law Review* 54.
7   S. Gopalan, "The creation of international commercial law: sovereignty felled?" (2004) 5 *San Diego International Law Journal* 267, p.276.

There are common features to all of these definitions. Most are expressly confined to the harmonisation of laws as they relate to international transactions. Doing so would have multiple benefits. First, it would make it easier to develop international rules which address the specific issues which might affect international transactions, without having to adjust national laws insofar as they apply to transactions within one jurisdiction. Secondly, limiting harmonisation to the international sphere might make it more palatable to individual countries to sign up to harmonising measures because it would not interfere with each country's ability to continue to develop laws for domestic transactions which differ from those of the harmonising instrument. A possible drawback, however, is the fact that this approach would result in two distinct regimes for commercial transactions, one for domestic and another for international ones. Indeed, as few harmonising instruments have managed to gain the support of a large number of countries, a business in a particular jurisdiction will face not only its domestic regime and whatever international rules its country applies, but also the national laws of the countries where the other parties to its transactions are located and in respect of which the international rules do not apply.

In addition, most of the definitions considered above combine a sense of realism with idealism. The idealist outcome, at least to some, would be the creation of a global uniform law on (International) Commercial Law. However, realistically, this is not something that will ever truly be attainable. Recognising that the most likely outcome of any harmonisation initiative is going to be a reduction or minimisation of differences between laws as they apply to international transactions is indicative of the fact that this is the best-case outcome of any harmonisation endeavour. This is not to be understood as a reason for not pursuing harmonisation initiatives: even the reduction of legal obstacles, whatever they might be, is going to facilitate international commercial transactions, not least by providing a greater degree of certainty and clarity as to the relevant legal requirements which arise in respect of a particular international transaction.

3. Harmonisation: advantages and objections

Having considered the concept of harmonisation and the tools for making International Commercial Law, we can now consider common advantages of, and objections to, the process of law-making in this way.

Proponents of harmonisation have identified numerous benefits.[8] The most fundamental advantage is that harmonisation can reduce the impact of divergent national commercial laws and the challenge of selecting the applicable law. Broadly speaking, the need to investigate different national laws and the potential choice of an applicable law for an international commercial transaction will result in additional costs, and such costs might make the transaction itself too expensive.

8   E.g., R. Goode, "Reflections on the harmonisation of commercial law (1991) *Uniform Law Review* 54; S. Gopalan, "The creation of international commercial law: sovereignty felled?" (2004) 5 *San Diego International Law Journal* 267, pp.278–297.

Reducing such transaction costs would facilitate international commercial transactions, and one way of doing so is to reduce the differences between national commercial laws to such an extent that it will no longer matter which law applies.[9]

Furthermore, to the extent that international commercial activity raises distinct legal issues from those arising in a purely national context, the development of targeted international rules specifically for international transactions can support commercial dealings. Also, a harmonising measure which applies across multiple jurisdictions, irrespective of legal family and substantive national law regimes for commercial transactions, can provide a neutral and therefore common regime to facilitate international commercial transactions. A further positive aspect is that some harmonisation initiatives address aspects on which there may not yet be clearly developed national legislation. It can thereby prevent the emergence of new legal obstacles which might otherwise happen as national legislatures develop separate, and possibly conflicting, approaches.

On the other hand, there are also drawbacks to harmonisation. As any international harmonisation effort ultimately requires a carefully negotiated compromise, there is a likelihood that the measure which is finally agreed is more restricted in its scope and fails to tackle adequately the key issues affecting international commercial transactions. Many conventions illustrate that the drafting of legal rules, particularly when they are intended to be binding, can be difficult and may result in open-ended terminology which is liable to be interpreted differently by different national courts or arbitrators. Furthermore, in some instances, it may be preferable to rely on an existing national law rather than a harmonising measure, because national law may provider greater coherence and be more comprehensive. In addition, there will be a body of lawyers trained in their national law and therefore be familiar with the relevant law and its interpretation by the national courts.

There are wider concerns about the process of harmonisation. Boodman has stressed that harmonisation in a broader, non-legal sense involves "recognizing and reconciling differences",[10] but that harmonisation in a legal sense seeks the opposite, i.e., the elimination of diversity[11] in favour of uniformity. He has argued that before any attempt at harmonisation is made, the case for doing so has to be made out. Whilst Boodman does not reject harmonisation outright, he sees no value in harmonisation projects which are pursued just for the sake of harmonisation. Any harmonising measure would have the effect of superimposing harmonised rules on the national legal systems concerned, but this could collide with each jurisdiction's desire to preserve the internal consistency of the interpretation and application of the law.[12] His conclusion is that harmonisation in a legal sense should only be deployed when there is a particular problem to be solved, and that "harmonization of the law *per se*

---

9 See, e.g., D.W. Leebron, "Claims for harmonization: a theoretical framework (1996) 27 *Canadian Business Law Journal* 63, pp.76–77.

10 M. Boodman, "The myth of harmonization of laws" (1991) 39 *American Journal of Comparative Law* 699, p.702.

11 *Ibid.*, p.707.

12 *Ibid.*, p.703.

has no general meaning".[13] As we will see below, the importance of defining the problem at which an initiative is targeted is a crucial step in the process of harmonisation; however, there are examples of harmonising instruments in respect of which this process may not have been conducted with sufficient care.[14]

Similar restraint has been argued for by Stephan. His general concern is that there might have been too much focus on drafting legal rules rather than facilitating international contracting.[15] In his view, harmonisation of International Commercial Law should only be deployed where this can reduce legal risk, i.e., the levels of unpredictability in international commercial transactions.[16] Diversity between national laws can increase legal risk and consequently affect the value of transactions, but efforts to reduce legal risk will not invariably result in lower costs. If one were to focus on increasing predictability, one would be driven towards more and more precise rules to cover a wide range of circumstances, but that would upset the balance which commercial law seeks between flexibility and certainty. The fact that most commercial law rules operate as dispositive provisions, which can be adjusted or disapplied altogether by the terms of the contract between the parties to an international commercial transaction, would not remove the additional cost such contractual modifications would entail.[17] There are some benefits of harmonisation in that it can lead to the adoption of legal rules which are better suited to international commercial transactions, and which might not be developed at a national level because of the distinctive features of international commerce.[18] Nevertheless, Stephan remains unpersuaded that many of the efforts which had been made at the time were worth the trouble:

> Much of the effort directed at unifying [commercial] laws is unnecessary, and some produces rules that hinder rather than promote international business.[19]

Essentially, Stephan's critique is based on two strands: first, the alleged gains for legal certainty through the introduction of a harmonised legal regime to replace divergent national ones are lost by a new lack of legal certainty arising from the fact that many harmonisation instruments are based on compromises between competing interests. The second objection is that harmonisation does not always benefit all commercial actors, but may work out better for some actors who are able to lobby for their interests more strongly. As a consequence, the harmonisation instrument may work in their favour and therefore be skewed towards the interests of one group. His conclusion is that rethinking the process of

13 *Ibid.*, p.707.
14 See Chapter 5 on agency.
15 P.B. Stephan, "The futility of unification and harmonization in international commercial law" (1999) 39 *Virginia Journal of International Law* 743, p.744.
16 *Ibid.*, p.746.
17 *Ibid.*, pp.747–748.
18 *Ibid.*, pp.748–750.
19 *Ibid.*, p.744.

harmonising aspects of International Commercial Law in light of his critique would enhance its value.[20]

The process which results in the adoption of harmonising instruments is also the key concern highlighted by Wool. He criticises the process of harmonisation which is behind most International Commercial Law conventions.[21] He characterises the prevalent approach as an "undifferentiated unification model", characterised by three features:[22] first, comparative analysis is deployed to identify a common language based on common underpinning principles which forms the basis of a proposal for addressing the problem at issue. Secondly, diplomats discussing the proposal will focus on the policy implications of the proposed rules and their wider impact within their national systems. Third, the proposed text is adjusted to meet such policy concerns, which often results in open-textured provisions and compromise wording, as well as the option to enter a reservation, and some matters may be omitted altogether if no agreement can be reached. He sums up his assessment of the process of harmonisation thus:

> [Harmonisation] is designed to produce, as a starting point in an essentially diplomatic process, a set of uniform rules. Derived from application of comparative methodology, such rules do not differentiate matters of policy from more technical common points of law … the undifferentiated unification model is forced to accommodate the policy concerns of governments by seeking text-based solutions and compromises, typically in a reactive and unsystematic manner. These text based solutions and compromises, in turn, are inconsistent with the overriding commercial objective of achieving greater levels of certainty and predictability.[23]

Based on this critique, he advances a "policy-based unification model" which seeks to prioritise the identification of potential policy issues which might trigger the need for compromises by making greater efforts to distinguish between points of law which he describes as "more technical", and matters of policy.[24] Drafting a new harmonising instrument should first seek to produce close-textured core provisions which are clear, certain and predictable and which address the primary object at issue. Ancillary policy issues are then identified to determine which of these need to be addressed in the harmonising instrument and whether a solution acceptable to a group of States could be found. States who do not accept the proposed policy can enter a reservation at the time of ratification. This might increase the number of permitted reservations under such a harmonising instrument, although States might also decide to accept a policy at that time whereas they would not have felt able to do so during the diplomatic

---

20 *Ibid.*, p.797.
21 J. Wool, "Rethinking the notion of uniformity in the drafting of international commercial law: a preliminary proposal for the development of a policy-based unification model" (1997) *Uniform Law Review* 46.
22 *Ibid.*, pp.48–49.
23 *Ibid.*, p.49.
24 *Ibid.*, pp.50–54.

conference. Such an approach might avoid instances of compromise wording and provide a text which is overall more coherent and offers greater legal predictability. However, it also depends on how clearly a distinction could be drawn between technical matters and policy issues.

Wool's primary concern therefore is that matters of policy are insufficiently identified as such during the diplomatic process through which conventions are drafted. The drafting process will invariably start with a survey of different national laws on the topic chosen for harmonisation to identify where the need for harmonisation may arise, but Wool criticises this for reducing the entire process to a question of reconciling legal rules rather than a discussion of the conflicting policy objectives which such a comparative law exercise should reveal. Without separating questions of policy from matters which can be treated as largely "technical", the process will invariably result in a text which has to compromise between the competing policy considerations. At the time Wool proposed his policy-based unification model, the Cape Town Convention on Security Interests in Mobile Equipment was under preparation, and the final text of that Convention is a useful illustration of the policy-based approach in operation.[25]

All of these counterarguments need to be taken seriously when considering whether it would be appropriate to pursue a particular harmonisation measure. We will explore this more fully in the next section. If harmonisation of substantive commercial law were rejected, then commercial parties would have to fall back on whichever national law governs their transaction. Coyle has argued[26] that this would not necessarily be a bad thing; indeed, he has argued that instead of pursuing substantive harmonisation, greater efforts should be made in developing harmonised rules of private international law and to encourage a "market for commercial law" through the freedom of the parties to choose the applicable law.[27] As we saw in Chapter 2, greater standardisation of private international law surrounding the choice of law (and forum) in international commercial contracts would be desirable, particularly because national law remains highly important for international commercial transactions even where there is a harmonising instrument in place. However, this should not be reduced to a stark choice between substantive harmonisation or harmonisation of private international law: both have a role to play, and it is important to consider when either would be better suited in facilitating international commercial transactions. Indeed, sometimes, substantive harmonisation and private international law may complement one another.[28]

---

25 See Chapter 8.

26 J.F. Coyle, "Rethinking the commercial law treaty" (2011) 45 *Georgia Law Review* 343.

27 See also G.-P. Callies and I. Buchmann, "Global commercial law between unity, pluralism, and competition: the case of the CISG" (2016) 21 *Uniform Law Review* 1, pp.11–16, on "legal pluralism".

28 F. Ferrari, "A new paradigm for international uniform substantive law conventions" (2019) 24 *Uniform Law Review* 467.

4. When, how and what to harmonise

4.1 Possible targets for harmonisation

Before turning to the process of harmonisation itself, it is necessary to be clear about what might be the target of harmonisation. It is possible to identify at least four different targets, or levels, or harmonisation.[29] Often, the focus seems to be primarily on establishing common legal rules on the assumption that this will have the desired effect in providing a common legal framework that will benefit international commerce. However, as discussed later, common legal rules alone rarely achieve this, because common legal rules agreed internationally often need to interact with rules of the underlying applicable national law. This can result in friction particularly where the common legal rules reflect underlying principles which differ from those of a national law. Moreover, as national courts are charged with the task of interpreting the common legal rules, there is a risk that national courts will interpret these rules differently.

Instead of focusing purely on establishing common legal rules, therefore, harmonisation might also, or instead, focus on the principles or values which underpin those legal rules. This might be particularly important where national laws have divergent underpinning principles in the area of law targeted by a harmonisation initiative. Focusing solely on underpinning principles may, however, have a limited chance of success, except perhaps in the context of particular regions such as the EU.[30] Rather, articulating clearly the principles which are embodied in a set of common legal rules agreed internationally may promote harmonisation, particularly where this is confined to commercial transactions with an international dimension. That said, it has been suggested that fostering a common legal culture might be a more valuable endeavour than pushing ahead with the harmonisation of legal rules.[31]

A third level would be to ensure that harmonisation ensures common outcomes in comparable factual situations. This should be the overall objective of a harmonisation initiative which pursues common rules and/or principles in any event, although it is also possible to determine in broad terms how recurring factual situations should be managed. This would not entail detailed common legal rules, but rather sufficient guidance to national laws as to what the common outcomes should be, with the onus on national legislators and courts to ensure that national law can achieve this.

Finally, harmonisation could simply focus on promoting the use of common contract terms and models throughout a number of jurisdictions. Rather than harmonising substantive commercial laws,[32] this would instead seek to ensure that

---

29 Cf. R. Brownsword, *Contract Law – Themes for the Twenty-First Century*, 2nd ed. (Oxford University Press, 2016), p.173, suggesting six forms of convergence.
30 Cf. H. Collins, *European Civil Code* (Cambridge University Press, 2008), pp.132–136.
31 A. Rosett, "Unification, harmonization, restatement, codification, and reform in international commercial law" (1992) 40 *American Journal of Comparative Law* 683, p.697.
32 Although some would argue that the best way of avoiding such consequences would be the harmonisation of contract law at a global level: I. Schwenzer, "Global unification of contract law" (2016) 21 *Uniform Law Review* 60.

for common, high-frequency, international transactions, it is possible to utilise standardised contracts without running the risk that particular terms would fall foul of the requirements of a national law, e.g., because such a term would conflict with the mandatory rules of that law.

When we come to examine specific measures of International Commercial Law, we can identify instances of all of these targets. Sometimes, the target is obvious (e.g., legal rules), but at other times, the target may be hidden, e.g., where legal rules also reflect a specific underlying principle.

4.2 The process of harmonisation

Several essential issues need to be borne in mind when considering whether to pursue the harmonisation of a particular area of commercial law. Few people would argue that harmonisation should be an end in itself in order purely to overcome legal differences.[33] The general view is that harmonisation should be pursued to deal with concrete and identified legal obstacles to international commercial transactions.[34] One might think that the mere fact that there are so many variations between the national commercial laws around the world would suffice to justify the pursuit of harmonisation. The differences between national commercial laws mean that parties (or rather, their legal advisers) to any international commercial transaction need to investigate the national commercial laws which might affect the transaction in order to identify any potential legal pitfalls. This process requires expertise in those national laws and is both time-consuming and costly. Harmonisation of large parts of commercial law could reduce or even eliminate these variations and thereby reduce the costs associated with international transactions. However, despite its superficial attractiveness, the justification of harmonising efforts purely to reduce or remove legal differences is not a sufficient reason for harmonisation,[35] not least because it does not take proper account of the reasons for the differences in national commercial law and the costs associated with large-scale harmonisation.[36]

The starting point for any harmonisation project has to be the identification of an obstacle, or problem, for international commerce,[37] followed by an analysis of whether this problem is something which requires resolution at the international level in the first place, and, if so, whether a solution which is suitable for adoption in a harmonising instrument could be developed. Harmonisation should therefore only be considered once it is clear that there is an identified obstacle which affects international

33 S. Gopalan, "New trends in the making of international commercial law" (2004) 23 *Journal of Law and Commerce* 117, pp.123–127.
34 R. Goode, "Reflections on the harmonisation of commercial law" (1991) *Uniform Law Review* 54.
35 M. Boodman, "The myth of harmonization of laws" (1991) 39 *American Journal of Comparative Law* 699, pp.702–707.
36 D.W. Leebron, "Claims for harmonization: a theoretical framework" (1996) 27 *Canadian Business Law Journal* 63, esp. pp.91–107.
37 R. Goode, "Reflections on the harmonisation of commercial law" (1991) *Uniform Law Review* 54, pp.56–57.

commercial transactions and which could be removed, or its impact lessened, by a harmonising initiative at the international level.[38] Whilst it is often the case that variations between national laws will be a significant contributing factor to the obstacle which has been identified, this does not imply that any variation between national laws necessarily creates an obstacle to international commercial transactions. Many variations can be navigated by the parties to an international commercial transaction through the terms of their contract. Others, however, may be more problematic: variations at national law with regard to the recognition and treatment of specific types of contract term (e.g., non-assignment clauses,[39] liquidated damages clauses, etc.) might be an issue, as might be conceptual discrepancies between national laws (e.g., with regard to the recognition of security interests[40]). It is therefore important to be specific about the nature of the problem and to determine its extent (both in practical and legal terms), and then to consider how a harmonising measure could alleviate this. At other times, the problem might not be that there are significant differences between national laws. Rather, national laws might be problematic, either because they do not deal with a specific issue at all,[41] or because existing national approaches are out-of-step with international commercial practice.[42]

Identification of the problem also requires determining its full extent, i.e., the legal issues relating to the problem which would have to be tackled. Once more, experience shows that a clearly defined problem concerning a limited number of legal issues is more likely to result in a harmonising instrument which will get wide-spread support.[43] An overly ambitious initiative which seeks to tackle a wide range of different issues is more likely to become difficult to progress, and will provide many reasons why individual countries might subsequently decline to endorse whatever emerges from the process.

This initial step is crucial if a harmonisation project is to have any chance of succeeding. As will be seen, many harmonisation projects take years to develop, but reaching agreement on a harmonising measure is not a guarantee that it will subsequently receive endorsement from a large enough number of countries to become widely applicable. Commercial parties will look for "a superior answer to the concrete problems"[44] which affect international commercial transactions. There

---

38 M. Boodman, "The myth of harmonization of laws" (1991) 39 *American Journal of Comparative Law* 699, p.719: "Harmonization in a legal context is problem-specific".

39 See Chapter 7.

40 See Chapter 8.

41 For instance, in the early days of e-commerce, when few national laws contained any provisions supporting electronic commercial activity (see Chapter 12).

42 The solutions provided under the Leasing Convention are one example of how an international measure could provide rules better suited to a particular commercial transaction. See Chapter 6.

43 R. Goode, "Reflections on the harmonisation of commercial law (1991) *Uniform Law Review* 54, pp.61–63.

44 A. Rosett, "Unification, harmonization, restatement, codification, and reform in international commercial law" (1992) 40 *American Journal of Comparative Law* 683, p.697.

are a lot of examples of harmonising instruments in the field of International Commercial Law which have been ratified or adopted by only a small number of countries. It seems that those measures which have targeted specific problems inviting action at the international level have tended to be more successful than those which dealt with an issue which seemed to pose less of an obstacle to international commerce.[45]

4.3 The involvement of commercial parties and organisations in the harmonisation process

The organisations and individuals which take the lead in pursuing a particular method vary as to their respective working methods, but in general terms, it is a process dominated by legal experts and diplomats.[46] This might serve to ensure that the end result of any given harmonisation project will be of good quality as a matter of legal drafting, and that it will reflect whatever diplomatic compromises had to be made to secure broad endorsement of the final version of the harmonising instrument. However, it is important not to lose sight of the fact that the focus of any harmonising initiative should first and foremost be on supporting international commercial transactions. Consequently, the interests and concerns of those directly affected by a harmonising instrument need to be taken into account before and during the drafting stage. There are a range of different options for doing so.[47] Commercial parties could lobby their national governments, either individually or through their trade associations, to take a particular stance when participating in discussions about a new harmonising instrument. Furthermore, commercial parties might be consulted directly in the early stages of the project in order to scope the various issues at stake. Further consultation might occur at the drafting stage. One might even go further and ensure that commercial parties are represented throughout the drafting phase and are able to have an active input into all stages of the drafting process, whether through observers during drafting meetings or as active participants in the process. Whatever mechanism is most appropriate will depend on the focus and type of harmonising instrument, but in all instances, the interests and concerns of commercial parties need to feed into the process – otherwise, the risk that any instrument will ultimately not be adopted and utilised will be high.[48] Block-Lieb has argued that harmonising instruments which could broadly be described as "soft law", i.e., as instruments not intended to

---

45 Contrast the area of agency (Chapter 5) with security interests in mobile equipment (Chapter 8).

46 For a rich account of the process of law-making, see S. Block-Lieb and T.C. Halliday, *Global Lawmakers* (Cambridge University Press, 2017).

47 Specifically on the contribution of business to convention, see M. Durkee, "The business of treaties" (2016) 63 *UCLA Law Review* 264.

48 S. Carbone, "Rule of law and non-state actors in the international community: are uniform law conventions still a useful tool in international commercial law?" (2016) 21 *Uniform Law Review* 177, p.179.

be immediately binding but being available for incorporation by contracting parties or for enactment through national legislation,[49] can have an important co-ordinating effect for commercial contracts, as well as fulfilling an advocacy role in encouraging national legislators to act.[50] She concluded that commercial parties can influence the development of International Commercial Law measures both indirectly through their contracting practices and dispute resolution practices, as well as more directly through lobbying.[51]

Gopalan has also suggested that commercial parties might be the main drivers behind not only the focus of a harmonising measure, but also the type of measure to be utilised.[52] Below, we will examine the main instruments used for International Commercial Law. One of these, the convention, is legally binding and requires individual countries to ratify them; other measures can be utilised through incorporation into the parties' agreement without needing State support. Gopalan suggests that strong commercial parties who require State intervention will push for a convention, whereas if there is no need for State intervention, other measures such as trade terms will suffice.[53] The paradigm example of the former is the Cape Town Convention on Security Interests in Mobile Equipment;[54] the UNIDROIT Principles of International Commercial Contracts[55] or the Uniform Customs and Practices on Documentary Credits[56] exemplify the latter.

On the other hand, there is a risk that more vocal commercial actors, able to lobby more effectively than other participants in the relevant commercial sector, might be able to influence the drafting of the harmonising instrument so as to favour their own interests over the collective interests of all the participants.[57] For example, Stephan has noted that the Hague rules on carriage of goods by sea favour the interests of carriers over those of shippers and passengers by shifting the cost of accidents to them, with some redressing of the balance in the later Hamburg rules.[58] Such concerns about the weight given to contributions from the commercial community need to be taken into account in determining how the views of affected commercial parties should be reflected in the process of drafting a new harmonising instrument.

---

49 Discussed fully below.
50 S. Block-Lieb, "Soft and hard strategies: the role of business in the crafting of international commercial law" (2019) 40 *Michigan Journal of International Law* 433.
51 *Ibid.*, p.476.
52 S. Gopalan, "A demandeur-centric approach to regime design in transnational commercial law" (2008) *Georgetown Journal of International Law* 327.
53 *Ibid.*, pp.348–350.
54 See Chapter 8.
55 See Chapter 10.
56 See Chapter 9.
57 P.B. Stephan, "The futility of unification and harmonization in international commercial law" (1999) 39 *Virginia Journal of International Law* 743.
58 *Ibid.*, pp.762–768.

5. The main instruments

In the field of International Commercial Law, there are five different types of instrument which can be used to promote the harmonisation of commercial law: conventions, model laws, international contract and trade terms, legislative guidelines, and statements of principles. The choice of the type of instrument will depend on the nature of the problem which has been identified and for which a solution is proposed. Not every problem invariably requires the adoption of binding legal rules at the international level. Farnsworth identified four alternatives to harmonisation by means of binding legal rules introduced through a convention:[59] first, the parties may work around any problems by structuring their transaction so as to apply only one legal system; secondly, many aspects of an international commercial transaction can be addressed through contract terms and thus through standard contract terms; thirdly, parties can exercise their autonomy under private international rules to choose both the law governing their transaction and the courts where disputes should be heard; and finally, parties can utilise arbitration for the resolution of disputes to side-step some of the problems which might otherwise arise. This suggests that priority for legally binding legal rules should be given to issues which cannot be resolved by the parties through the way in which they arrange their transaction. In other words, developing harmonising instruments should focus on specific, identified obstacles for international commercial transactions which require action at the international level.

Out of the various instruments used in making International Commercial Law, only a convention would have the effect of introducing binding legal rules. Other measures require either action by a national legislator or by the parties themselves, and can therefore be collectively referred to as "soft law" insofar as these instruments are not binding without implementation or adoption.[60]

5.1 Conventions

A convention is an international treaty, which has to be negotiated and adopted in accordance with the procedures for the adoption of any other type of international treaty. However, it is not like any other type of international treaty in one important way: international treaties are concluded between States and will contain either binding commitments for all the States which have signed the treaty, or at least aspirations or common policies to which all signatories subscribe. International Commercial Law treaties (i.e., conventions) are also signed by States, but rather than committing signatory States to take specific action, the provisions of such treaties are intended to provide rights and duties for commercial parties in respect of the international commercial transactions which fall within the scope of the treaty.

---

59 E.A. Farnsworth, "Unification and harmonization of private law" (1996) 27 *Canadian Business Law Review* 48, pp.52–53.

60 Cf. S. Block-Lieb, "Soft and hard strategies: the role of business in the crafting of international commercial law" (2019) 40 *Michigan Journal of International Law* 433, pp.440–444.

As an international treaty, a convention has the advantage of being an instrument that can be utilised to introduce a set of legal-binding rules, determined at the international level, which become binding as part of the law of those countries who agree to ratify a convention. The requirement of ratification[61] is a crucial element in respect of any international treaty. Each country has to take the sovereign decision whether to sign a particular international treaty, and then whether to ratify it in order to give the rules from that treaty full legal effect as part of their legal system. On ratification, the legal rules contained in a convention will be part of the laws of each country which has ratified the convention (usually referred to as "Contracting States"). As a result, legal rights and obligations can be imposed on private parties, such as those to a commercial transaction.

As a convention is an international treaty, it has a lengthy gestation period, often taking many years or even decades to negotiate. Once agreement on a final text is likely, a diplomatic conference has to be convened at which representatives of national governments agree to adopt the convention. In the case of UNCITRAL, this can be the General Assembly of the United Nations; UNIDROIT will convene a separate diplomatic conference under its auspices. Once adopted, the convention will be open for signature. However, it will not enter into force immediately, because of the need for individual countries to decide whether to ratify the convention. A convention cannot enter into force until the minimum number of ratifications has been achieved. The number required varies: the CISG required 10 ratifications,[62] the Receivables Convention requires five ratifications[63] and the Cape Town Convention required only three ratifications.[64] Some conventions have only secured a small number of ratifications above the threshold even after entering into force, whereas others have never managed to secure the minimum number of ratifications required and are consequently not in force.[65]

There are many reasons why it may be difficult to secure the requisite number of ratifications. Some of these may concern the convention itself. Due to its nature as an international treaty, it requires a complex process of negotiation, and in order to reflect the often-competing interests of the many countries involved, this process will involve a lot of compromises.[66] Whilst these may suffice to get a convention adopted, such compromises may subsequently deter countries from ratifying it because the compromise solutions may not be regarded as workable from the perspective of individual jurisdictions. A further effect of the need to compromise is that conventions will often be limited to dealing with a limited number of legal issues and may refer many matters back to national law. On the one hand, this

---

61 "Ratification" is used as a short-hand for the different ways in which a State can become a Contracting State to a convention, i.e., ratification, accession or approval.

62 Art. 99(1) CISG.

63 Art. 45 of the Receivables Convention.

64 Art. 49(1) Cape Town Convention.

65 E.g., the Agency Convention or the Receivables Convention.

66 Whether the fact that a convention offers a compromise is a good thing is, at the very least, open to debate, although some scholars seem to view compromises, e.g., between common law and civil law, as a positive outcome: I. Schwenzer, "Global unification of contract law" (2016) 21 *Uniform Law Review* 60, p.74.

increases the likelihood that agreement on a final text can be reached. On the other hand, it could mean that the convention fails to address those issues which are regarded by many countries as the real problem for international commerce. Compromises might reflect competing national interests, and in the end, no country might be satisfied with the result. A former Law Lord, Lord Hobhouse, summed up his criticism of conventions thus:

> Conventions which represent an amalgam of inconsistent rules drawn from different systems differently structured with different underlying assumptions do not make a satisfactory basis for a commercial code.[67]

Trying to balance competing national laws through a convention therefore is unlikely to result in many ratifications subsequently. Beyond this, there may be more practical, and comparatively mundane, reasons for a lack of ratifications. The process of ratification will take up some time in the calendar of any legislature. Depending on the legislative agenda of the government of the day, it may be difficult to allocate sufficient time to ratify a convention, particularly where this is not regarded as a matter of priority. It may also simply be down to the fact that business organisations in the country concerned are not pushing for ratification or are actively opposed to it.

A further aspect is that conventions mostly require ratification of the document as it stands, i.e., it is not possible for an individual country to pick only those aspects which it likes and disregard others. Some conventions permit countries not to apply certain provisions if they make a declaration or enter a reservation (where permitted) to that effect at the time of ratification, but this is only possible insofar as the text of the convention provides for the possibility of such derogations.

A final difficulty with conventions is that, once adopted, they are impossible to amend in practice. Whilst theoretically, it would be possible to agree amendments in a subsequent treaty or through a protocol to the original treaty, these amendments would only then take effect among all the existing Contracting States if they all ratified the amending treaty. As this would be akin to the process of ratifying a new treaty, it would be affected by the same problems as the ratification of the initial convention.

Conventions which do not get ratified widely or which do not manage to secure a sufficient number of ratifications to enter into force may not be without any effect, however: countries may, for whatever reason, not wish to ratify a convention but might align their domestic laws with the substantive provisions of a convention.[68] A country might not wish to ratify all of the convention (especially when there are no derogations or reservations permitted in respect of a provision a country does not like), or might wish to retain the flexibility of national legislation

---

67 John Hobhouse, "International conventions and commercial law: the pursuit of uniformity" (1990) *Law Quarterly Review* 530.

68 See, e.g., J.B. Lambert, "The UN Convention on Electronic Contracting: back from the dead?" (2017) 25 *Michigan State International Law Review* 31, discussing countries which have adopted legislation based on the UN Convention but not ratified the Convention. See Chapter 12.

both in terms of language and the possibility to amend national legislation more easily. A convention might therefore have an indirect effect of harmonising the national laws of a larger number of countries than the number of ratifications would suggest.

5.1.1 Interpretation of international conventions

A particular challenge with any conventions is the interpretation of its provisions. As conventions are generally drafted in a way that seeks to avoid following any particular national law too closely, as well as being a compromise solution to reconcile contrasting views, there is a challenge for national courts and arbitration panels to determine what a word or phrase used in a convention should mean. In some instances, there may be definitions of particular terms, but in international conventions, it is rare to find detailed definitions. In the absence of such definitions, courts and arbitrators will therefore have to use other means to interpret the meaning of particular words in a convention. For national courts, in particular, it may be tempting to rely on the interpretation given to identical or similar words or phrases found in national law, but such an approach would invariably risk the development of divergences in the way a convention is interpreted by the courts in different jurisdictions. This could, over time, seriously undermine a convention's objective of reducing the differences in the laws of the various Contracting States. Crucially, there is no international court which has the power to provide authoritative guidance on the interpretation of a convention nor to correct what might be regarded as an incorrect interpretation of an international convention by a national court.[69] There is therefore a constant risk that the efforts made in harmonising aspects of the law through an international convention are subsequently undermined through the way in which national courts interpret the convention.[70]

In order to facilitate the task of national courts and arbitrators to interpret a convention, there are several guiding provisions available in International Commercial Law. As a convention is, in essence, an intergovernmental treaty, the Vienna Convention on the Law of Treaties 1969, which contains a number of general rules regarding the interpretation of international treaties, is relevant. The general rule is set out in Article 31(1), according to which a Treaty has to be interpreted "in good faith in accordance with the ordinary meaning to be given to the terms of the treaty in their context and in the light of its object and purpose". The relevant context is first and foremost the text of the Treaty, including its Preamble and any annexes, as well as any agreements or instruments related to the Treaty and made by the parties to the Treaty.[71] A departure from the ordinary

---

69 Zeller is doubtful whether many countries would agree to such an international court because of the constraining effect on each State's sovereignty: B. Zeller, "International trade law – problems of language and concepts" (2003–04) 23 *Journal of Law and Commerce* 39, p.41.

70 Cf. S. Block-Lieb, "Soft and hard strategies: the role of business in the crafting of international commercial law" (2019) 40 *Michigan Journal of International Law* 433, p.454.

71 Art. 31(2) Vienna Convention on the Law of Treaties 1969.

meaning of a term is permitted where it is clear that the parties intended to give the term a special meaning.[72] If an interpretation on the basis of Article 31(1) produces a meaning which is "ambiguous or obscure",[73] or where this interpretation "leads to a result which is manifestly absurd or unreasonable",[74] then its permissible additionally to consider any preparatory documents (*travaux préparatoires*) and the circumstances of its conclusion.[75] Furthermore, as many Treaties are made available in several authentic languages, the presumption is that each authentic language version is equally authoritative,[76] and the terms used in the Treaty are presumed to have the same meaning in all the authentic language versions.[77] If, however, a comparison of the different authentic language versions reveals a discrepancy in the meaning of a particular term, then "the meaning which best reconciles the texts"[78] is to be chosen.[79]

In addition to these quite general criteria, it has become common practice in conventions in the field of International Commercial Law to have a specific provision with additional criteria which a national court (or arbitrators) should follow when interpreting a term in such a convention. The template which has formed the basis for many subsequent provisions can be found in Art. 7(1) of the UN Convention for the International Sale of Goods (CISG). This provides as follows:

> In the interpretation of this Convention, regard is to be had to its international character and to the need to promote uniformity in its application and the observance of good faith in international trade.

A modified version of this has been used in more recent conventions, such as the UNIDROIT Convention on International Factoring 1988:

> In the interpretation of this Convention, regard is to be had to its object and purpose as set forth in the preamble, to its international character and to the need to promote uniformity in its application and the observance of good faith in international trade.

The addition of the reference to the object and purpose of the Convention, found in its preamble, reinforces the general approach to the interpretation of treaties found in Art. 31(1) of the Vienna Convention on the Law of Treaties. In the context of commercial law conventions, words which may have an ordinary meaning are often used

---

72 Art. 31(4).
73 Art. 32(a).
74 Art. 32(b).
75 Art. 32. It is also permissible to consult preparatory documents in order to confirm the interpretation reached on the basis of Art. 31.
76 Art. 33(1).
77 Art. 33(3).
78 Art. 33(4).
79 If, however, it is agreed that one particular language version is to prevail over all others, then the meaning of a term in that language has to be adopted: Arts. 33(1) and (4).

with a specific legal meaning in mind. It is therefore important that, in interpreting a particular term in a commercial law convention, the overall object and purpose is used as a guide in determining the meaning of that term.

A crucial obligation is to have regard to a convention's "international character". This is an important reminder to national courts and arbitrators that terms in a convention should not be interpreted with reference to any particular domestic law. Instead, terms used in a convention should be interpreted *autonomously*, i.e., their meaning should derive from the context in which they are used (and bearing in mind the object and purpose of the convention). Whether this will always be an easy task is debatable, not least because of the terminology chosen in a convention.[80] Moreover, national courts follow distinct methodologies for the interpretation of legal texts and attach different weight to decisions by other courts and academic commentary.[81] Nevertheless, for a national court, "it is important to avoid an interpretation ... that is influenced by concepts used in the legal system of the forum country".[82]

A further requirement is to bear in mind "the need to promote uniformity in its application". In essence, this means that the convention should be applied consistently. In order to follow these mandates in practice, national courts might need to consider how the provision of the convention at issue has previously been interpreted by other national courts in the Contracting States, and the results produced by the application of that interpretation to the facts of such earlier cases. If possible, a court should follow earlier cases to minimise the risk that different national courts take diverging views regarding the meaning and application of a particular provision of the convention. However, this is not as easy as it may sound. For a start, it may not always be possible to discover previous judgments dealing with the interpretation or application of the provision at issue before a national court, because earlier decisions may not have been reported properly, nor will they necessarily be available in a language which the national court can understand. Moreover, even where relevant judgments are available and accessible to a national court, this does not mean that that court should invariably follow previous decisions. There is no comparable requirement to the common law doctrine of *stare decisis*, i.e., there are no binding precedents, nor is there a hierarchy as between the national courts from different jurisdictions. At best, therefore, a national court can consider what has been decided and whether it agrees with the reasoning in those earlier judgments, but it cannot be compelled slavishly to follow earlier decisions.

In the absence of some kind of international court or tribunal with the power to determine authoritatively how a provision in a convention should be interpreted, there is therefore always a likelihood that conflicting interpretations may develop.

---

80 On the difficulties arising from the language used in the CISG, see generally B. Zeller, "International trade law – problems of language and concepts" (2003–04) 23 *Journal of Law and Commerce* 39.

81 P.S. Berman, "The inevitable legal pluralism within universal harmonization regimes: the case of the CISG" (2016) 21 *Uniform Law Review* 23, p.25.

82 A.S. Komarov, "Internationality, uniformity and observance of good faith as criteria in interpretation of CISG" (2005–06) 25 *Journal of Law and Commerce* 75, p.77.

We have already noted that, unlike in the context of EU Law,[83] there is no international court with the power to give guidance on the interpretation of a provision in a convention, nor to overturn an interpretation given by a national court which might be regarded as wrong. In order to assist national courts, there are a number of initiatives which seek to facilitate access to decisions by national courts of matters involving a convention. For example, UNCITRAL has created a database (CLOUT) to record court judgments and arbitration awards involving any of its legal texts.[84] This provides both a record of such decisions and increasingly access to the full text, and UNCITRAL has published abstracts of cases recorded on CLOUT at periodic intervals. In addition, for the CISG and the Model Law on International Commercial Arbitration, UNCITRAL has also published digests of decisions in order to make information about the interpretation of these texts more accessible.[85] The digests only record decisions, but they do not provide a qualitative evaluation.[86] Nevertheless, they are a useful guide to identifying any relevant decisions on the interpretation of a provision in a convention by other national courts.

Finally, there is the requirement to have regard to the "observance of good faith in international trade". This is one of the most difficult aspects of the guidelines for interpreting a convention. Its history is somewhat unusual in that it was introduced in order to break a deadlock about the role of good faith which had caused a serious obstacle to the successful conclusions of the negotiations for the CISG.[87] Broadly, there was a difference of views between the common law countries who did not want a duty on the parties to act in accordance with good faith in the CISG,[88] and others who did want to introduce this. This clash between different legal families about good faith and the way this was dealt with in the context of the CISG is perhaps the paradigm example of the kinds of compromises which had to be found in order to secure agreement on the CISG as a whole.

However, this compromise has far from settled the issue. There continue to be conflicting views as to whether the effect of this element is to impose a duty on the parties to the contract to act in accordance with good faith, or whether it merely requires those charged with the interpretation of a provision in the convention to

---

83 The Court of Justice of the European Union has the power under Art. 267 of the Treaty on the Functioning of the European Union to give a preliminary ruling on the interpretation of a provision of EU Law. It does not have the power to overturn decisions by a national court, however.

84 Available via https://uncitral.un.org/en/case_law [accessed December 2020].

85 Available via https://uncitral.un.org/en/case_law/digests [accessed December 2020].

86 Cf. J. Lookofsky, "Walking the Art.7(2) tightrope between CISG and domestic law" (2005–06) 25 *Journal of Law and Commerce* 87, p.88.

87 See, e.g., A.S. Komarov, "Internationality, uniformity and observance of good faith as criteria in interpretation of CISG" (2005–06) 25 *Journal of Law and Commerce* 75, pp.82–83.

88 In the intervening 40 years since the CISG was ratified, there has been some shift even within the common law as to whether "good faith" should be recognised, although some common law jurisdictions, notably England, have thus far refused to consider the acceptance of a legal duty to act in accordance with good faith.

adopt an interpretation which would accord with good faith in international trade. The matter is further complicated by the lack of a defined understanding of what "good faith in international trade" might mean. Good faith is a concept known to many legal systems, primarily those in the civil law family but also increasingly among the common law jurisdictions. One thing which is clear, however, is that good faith in the context of an International Commercial Law convention will have a different meaning from any particular national meaning. It might not even be appropriate to examine whether there has been convergence in the way the national conceptions of good faith in the Contracting States have been interpreted in the context of commercial transactions. This is because such convergence would not necessarily be indicative of what meaning should be ascribed to good faith in the context of *international trade*.

National courts can apply good faith in several ways: first, a court might only refer to the notion of good faith, but not regard it as relevant to the decision in the case. Secondly, a court might refer to good faith as an alternative basis to justify an outcome which has already been established on the basis of other grounds. Thirdly, a court might use good faith as an additional supporting reason for the outcome which has already been reached on other grounds. Finally, a court might use good faith as the basis for their decision, thus using it as a positive obligation and not merely an interpretative criterion. This variation shows how the purported compromise in Art. 7(1) cannot provide consistency, but instead has caused national courts to apply "good faith" in a manner which reflects its approach under national law.

5.1.2 Filling gaps in conventions

A related matter to interpretation is the question of how a national court or arbitrator should deal with gaps in a convention. No convention can exhaustively cover every matter even in respect of the issues which it addresses, and so there will at times be a need for a national court or arbitrator to read between the lines in order to determine how the particular dispute before it should be resolved.

A preliminary distinction that needs to be drawn here is between *internal* and *external* gaps. This is a useful shorthand for distinguishing between an issue which relates to matters covered in a convention but in respect of which there is no readily applicable provision in the convention itself (internal gap), and an issue which concerns a matter outside the scope of the convention (external gap). The standard provision which deals with the issue of gaps provides as follows:

> Questions concerning matters governed by this Convention which are not expressly settled in it are to be settled in conformity with the general principles upon which it is based, or, in the absence of such principles, in conformity with the law applicable by virtue of the rules of private international law.[89]

---

89 This is taken from Art. 7(2) CISG, but this provision has also been used in many other conventions.

It is immediately apparent that this provision is only concerned with internal gaps, i.e., "matters governed by this Convention, but not expressly settled in it". So any matter which falls outside the scope of the convention altogether, i.e., "not governed" by it, will therefore usually have to be dealt with under the relevant rules of the applicable national law. However, it is not always a straightforward exercise to determine which matters are governed by a convention and which are not – a particular issue could be classified in more than one sense but that classification might determine whether the issue is governed by the CISG or not: for instance, a statement made during negotiations could be classified as misrepresentation or as an aspect of conformity, but only the latter would fall within the CISG.[90] Furthermore, whilst one might assume that matters of procedure generally fall outside the scope of a convention, it may not always be obvious where a particular question involves a question of procedure or substance (such as whether an expert report can be required as part of a claim that goods are not in conformity with the contract under the CISG).[91]

Furthermore, once it has been determined that a particular question concerns an internal gap, it becomes necessary to identify the general principles on which the convention in question is based. Unfortunately, there is rarely any indication in the text of the convention itself as to the general principles which it seeks to reflect, and so a national court faces the difficult task of working out what those general principles might be.[92] Some will be more obvious than others: party autonomy is undoubtedly a general principle underpinning all International Commercial Law conventions. The CISG also seems to be based on the *pacta sunt servanda* and security of transactions principle, evidenced by its remedial regime.[93] Perhaps more controversially, good faith is also regarded as a general principle underpinning many conventions, and it is possible to treat some provisions in a convention as specific instances of a wider good faith notion. The UNCITRAL Digest on the CISG mentions a large number of candidates for general principles on which the CISG is based, some of which are well supported by specific provisions of the CISG, but others seem more tenuous.[94] For each convention, however, this exercise needs to be attempted afresh – there is no guarantee that a general principle on which one convention was based also became a general principle on which another was based.[95] Even the general principle of party autonomy

---

90 See J.M. Lookofsky, "Loose ends and contorts in international sales: problems in the harmonization of private law rules" (1991) 39 *American Journal of Comparative Law* 403, pp.407–410.

91 A.J. McMahon, "Differentiating between internal and external gaps in the UN Convention on Contracts for the International Sale of Goods" (2006) 44 *Columbia Journal of Transnational Law* 992.

92 For examples, see J. Lookofsky, "Walking the Art.7(2) tightrope between CISG and domestic law" (2005–06) 25 *Journal of Law and Commerce* 87, pp.91–103.

93 See Chapter 4, sections 5 and 7.

94 UNCITRAL, *Digest of Case Law on the United Nations Convention on Contracts for the International Sale of Goods* (2016), pp.43–46.

95 For an attempt to distil the general principles from a number of conventions, see F. Ferrari. "General principles and international uniform commercial law conventions" (1999) 1 *European Journal of Law Reform* 217.

might not always be among the general principles on which a convention is based. Ultimately, if it is not possible to determine a relevant general principle to resolve the question before the court, the relevant rules of the applicable national law[96] should be used. It has been suggested that the UNIDROIT Principles of International Commercial Contracts might also fulfil a gap-filling role; this issue will be dealt with when we examine the UNIDROIT Principles later.[97]

5.1.3 Interpretation, gap-filling and avoiding the application of national law

It should be apparent now that the interpretation of provisions in a convention, as well as the approach to gaps on matters within the scope of a convention, should be resolved autonomously if at all possible. Indeed, in interpreting a convention, national courts or arbitrators should avoid any recourse to national law altogether. However, experience shows that this does not always happen: courts have at times interpreted provisions from a convention with reference to a national law using the same or similar concepts; also, gaps have sometimes been tackled by falling back on the applicable national law without first considering whether there is some general principle underpinning the convention which could be used as basis for filling the gap which has been identified. With regard to the interpretation of conventions, the so-called "homeward trend" is a rather too frequent occurrence still: courts interpreting a convention provision on the basis of the way the corresponding provision of national law has been interpreted.[98] A variation on this is the "outward trend", where a court interprets a convention provision on the basis of a national law other than its own which, in the court's view, is the inspiration for or basis of the convention provision.[99] Either approach conflicts with the fundamental obligation stipulated in the interpretation provision that regard should be had to the international character of a convention, i.e., that it should be interpreted autonomously.

The intention behind Art. 7 CISG and the corresponding provisions is that a convention is interpreted autonomously and free from the influences of national law, but this is almost impossible to do in practice. Whilst instances of "homeward" and "outward" trend should be reduced, this will not ensure that national courts are able to disconnect entirely their methodologies of interpretation; moreover, both internal and external gaps and the way these are dealt with by national courts, and the inherent ambiguity of many terms in conventions will mean that there will always be differences in the way conventions are interpreted by national courts.[100]

---

96 Determined on the basis of the rules of private international law of the forum.
97 See Chapter 10 at 3.1.1.
98 E.g., J.O. Honnold, "The sales convention in action: uniform international words: uniform applications?" (1988) 8 *Journal of Law and Commerce* 207; T Keily, "Good faith and the Vienna Convention on Contracts for the International Sale of Goods (CISG)" (1999) 3 *Vindobona Journal of International Commercial Law and Arbitration* 15.
99 F. Ferrari, "Autonomous interpretation versus homeward trend versus outward trend in CISG case law" (2017) 22 *Uniform Law Review* 244.
100 P.S. Berman, "The inevitable legal pluralism within universal harmonization regimes: the case of the CISG" (2016) 21 *Uniform Law Review* 23.

5.2 Model Laws

Unlike conventions, model laws are not intended to operate as free-standing legally binding texts. Rather, as their name suggests, they are offered as a template for national legislatures to enable them to reform, or to fill a gap in, their domestic laws. If numerous countries adopt national legislation which closely follows a model law, then practically speaking, a comparable level of harmonisation to that pursued by conventions could be achieved. In this regard, there is a parallel between conventions and model laws: both require a decision by national legislatures to make the international text part of their domestic law. As we saw above, in the case of conventions, this requires formal ratification; in the case of a model law, it requires the drafting and adoption of national legislation. However, unlike a convention, there is no minimum number of adoptions by countries required before national legislation based on a model law can take effect.

However, a model law may not result in the same degree of harmonisation among the countries adopting legislation based on it as would be achieved by a convention. Whilst a model law will usually take the form of legislation, individual countries are not faced with the take-it-or-leave-it choice they have in respect of conventions. In particular, a model law need not be transposed verbatim, and there is scope for adjusting the terminology in the national legislation based on the model law to suit the particular domestic context. Indeed, because a model law is not intended to be adopted "as is", the drafting process may not be as heavily concerned with anticipating resistance based on potential clashes between the international text and domestic law.

A further advantage of a model law is that it can be revised more easily than a convention, should this become necessary. Of course, any changes or additions made to a model law would have no effect in those countries which have adopted legislation based on it unless and until they decided to amend the national legislation to reflect the changes made to the model law.

5.3 Standard terms and international trade terms

Both conventions and Model Laws seek to achieve a degree of harmonisation of the laws in multiple jurisdictions in a particular area. However, as we saw earlier, the contract between the parties to an international commercial transaction is often just as important as, or more important than, the legal regime of whichever jurisdiction provides the law governing that contract. Inevitably, many commercial contracts involve limited negotiations, with the parties relying on pre-drafted standard terms. Broadly speaking, there are two categories of standard terms: the first is those drafted by an individual business for use in its contracts with other parties; the second is a set of standard terms drawn up by an industry body for general use across that industry. Some of the latter have become so well established that they are regarded as the *de facto* standard for certain types of transactions and are generally referred to as trade terms.

In essence, such standard terms are drawn up for use in international transactions by an industry-specific organisation such as the ICC or the GAFTA. These organisations have drawn up a range of standard terms to facilitate international contracting, which are generally based on established trade practices or usages. They are reviewed from time to time and amended in light of changes in the way transactions are arranged or carried out in order to reflect current practice. Such revisions are less difficult than revisions to conventions or Model Laws, because there is no requirement for any individual country to endorse the use of international trade terms. Indeed, the whole process of adoption is more straightforward. However, their significance depends on the extent to which the parties to an international contract in respect of which international trade terms are available actually incorporate them. The extent to which they align with commercial practice may be important, although some international trade terms have become so well established that they may be treated as the *de facto* legal rules for such transactions.[101]

International trade terms will only apply to a specific contract if the parties to that contract have expressly chosen to incorporate them. Such incorporation is often done through a term in the standard terms used by one, or both, of the contracting parties. In effect, therefore, these international trade terms become part of the contract between the parties and are, in one sense, part of all the terms according to which the contract is to be performed. However, matters are not quite as straightforward: international trade terms are primarily designed to reflect commercial practice and as such, are not always drafted on the basis of a particular legal system. This can create an obvious problem, because every international contract will be governed by a particular domestic law. As a consequence, there may be a clash between the requirements of the applicable domestic law and the intended operation of the international trade terms. Such a clash may be due to the specific requirements of the applicable law with regard to its requirements for enforceable contractual obligations, or the application of whatever vitiating factors are recognised in the applicable law. In respect of both, the Uniform Customs and Practices for Documentary Credits (UCP) illustrate both the problem and potential solutions: some of the undertakings enshrined in the UCP might not be treated as enforceable obligations if national law were applied strictly, although courts have generally refrained from undermining the UCP on this basis. Things have been more varied with regard to the use of doctrines permitting external factors to influence the operation of the UCP system: the impact of fraud, in particular, has given rise to conflicting case-law regarding the extent to which fraud could be a justification for not complying with a bank's obligations laid down in the UCP.[102]

There may also be particular mandatory rules of the applicable law which conflict with the international trade terms. A related question arises with regard to the extent to which the applicable law can be relied upon to deal with matters not expressly dealt with in the international trade terms.

---

101 The key example are the Uniform Customs and Practices for Documentary Credits, discussed in Chapter 9.
102 See further, Chapter 9 at section 5.

5.4 Guidelines

At a more general level, international organisations may issue guidelines on a particular topic which is of relevance to international commercial transactions. Such guidelines are not intended to provide model rules for adoption by national legislatures. Rather, they set out specific issues or factors which should be considered by national legislatures if they intend to adopt legislation on that topic. They therefore mainly serve as a source on which national legislators minded to adopt legislation on a given topic could draw.[103]

5.5 Statements of principles

A final tool for promoting greater alignment between national legal systems with regard to international commercial transactions may be achieved through so-called statements of principles. In the sphere of International Commercial Law, the UNIDROIT Principles of International Commercial Contracts[104] are the most significant.

Broadly speaking, such principles are best understood as a non-binding restatement of principles applicable to the area of law they cover. The UNIDROIT Principles, for example, provide a detailed statement of principles of contract law as it applies to international commercial contracts. In this regard, the use of the word "principles" may be misleading, because such principles generally take on the appearance of legal rules. They are usually drafted by a group of scholars who are experts in the particular field, and are based on comparative study of a range of international and national legal sources.

Statements of principles are becoming an increasingly popular way of developing new rules for emerging areas of commercial law. The growth of new business models utilising digital technology has resulted in several initiatives towards the adoption of principles. Thus, the European Law Institute has adopted *Model Rules on Online Platforms*,[105] which are akin to a statement of principles. Furthermore, the American and European Law Institutes collaborated on *Principles for a Data Economy*.

Principles are not intended as legally binding documents, nor are they Model Laws for adoption by national legislatures. They may simply be a general guide to commercial parties in drafting their contracts, or courts/arbitrators to assist with the adjudication of commercial disputes. It is also possible that national legislators may use such statements of principles as a source to guide the drafting of national legislation.

6. Conclusions

This chapter has unpacked many of the considerations which shape the process of making International Commercial Law. This process has driven a rich academic debate

---

103 See, e.g., UNCITRAL's *Legislative Guide on Insolvency Law* (2004).
104 See Chapter 10.
105 Available via https://www.europeanlawinstitute.eu/projects-publications/completed-projects-old/online-platforms/ [accessed December 2020].

about the merits of harmonisation of commercial law generally and the merits of different approaches utilised in this process. It has also explored the main instruments for making International Commercial Law in general terms. In the chapters which follow, we will examine a range of different topics in International Commercial Law for which concrete action has been taken at the international level. Many of these concern conventions, but we will also take a look at the Uniform Customs and Practices for Documentary Credits as one example of international trade terms, and the UNIDROIT Principles of International Commercial Contracts. Many of the general points made in this chapter will be revisited in the context of these specific areas and instruments.

What should have emerged from the discussion in this chapter is that International Commercial Law can fulfil multiple purposes. Whilst harmonisation, both as a technique and as an objective, have characterised much of the evolution of International Commercial Law, it is increasingly the case that International Commercial Law is deployed to address quite specific obstacles to international commercial transactions, or as a benchmark for the adoption of modern commercial law regimes on a wide range of issues. Indeed, the ideal of harmonisation as an objective for International Commercial Law as a whole may increasingly yield to sector-specific initiatives, driven by the interests of individual industries.[106] Moreover, it is clear that harmonisation will have a limited impact on the plurality of legal sources which shape the context for international commercial transactions,[107] which implies that harmonising efforts, whether through conventions or soft law, will reshape but not eliminate the pluralist structure of the legal regime for international commercial transactions.

---

106 See J. Karton, "Sectoral fragmentation in transnational contract law" (2018) 21 *University of Pennsylvania Journal of Business Law* 142.
107 Cf. G.-P. Callies and I. Buchmann, "Global commercial law between unity, pluralism, and competition: the case of the CISG" (2016) 21 *Uniform Law Review* 1.

4

INTERNATIONAL SALES

1. Introduction

In this chapter, we turn to the quintessential commercial contract: the contract of sale. It is also a topic which is a key element of International Commercial Law, thanks to the adoption of the UN Convention on Contracts for the International Sale of Goods 1980 (CISG). The CISG, which is the focus of this chapter, is among the most successful International Commercial Law conventions on the basis of the number of ratifications. At the time of writing, 94 countries had ratified the CISG, Portugal being the most recent.[1] However, it took almost eight years from its adoption before the required minimum number of 10 ratifications[2] was obtained, with the CISG entering into force on 1 January 1988.[3] To this date, neither the United Kingdom nor Ireland have ratified the CISG.

The CISG addresses only some aspects regarding contracts for the international sale of goods, in particular the formation of contracts, the respective rights and obligations of seller and buyer, and the remedies available to the other party if one party has breached one or more of its obligations.[4] It is, however, not a comprehensive convention. Some aspects of the law relating to the sale of goods are expressly outside the scope of the CISG at all, such as questions of validity or, more importantly rules regarding the transfer of ownership from seller to buyer.[5] The CISG also does not cover any liability on the part of the seller if the goods supplied cause death or personal

---

1   In September 2020; effective from 1 October 2021.
2   Art. 99(1) CISG.
3   The first 10 countries to ratify the CISG were Argentina, China, Egypt, France, Hungary, Italy, Lesotho, Syria, USA and Zambia.
4   Art. 4 CISG.
5   Art. 4(a) and (b) CISG.

DOI: 10.4324/9781315692807-4

injury to any person.[6] In respect of all these exclusions, it will be necessary to rely on the law applicable to the contract instead.

Furthermore, the CISG generally provides default rules, i.e., its provisions are not mandatory and can be disapplied by the parties either in their entirety or through terms in their contract which make express provisions for matters which are also covered by CISG (e.g., the time or place of delivery).

One characteristic feature of the CISG is its attempt to find a workable balance between the different legal families which were dominant at the time of its negotiation. There are a number of instances where a careful balance was found between more civil law-inspired provisions and those reflecting the common law. In addition, the approaches of the then socialist legal systems had to be taken into account. It is therefore not surprising that the CISG can be criticised for the way its provisions reflect compromises between approaches characteristic of one particular legal family, and there is a degree of vagueness or even ambiguity in some of its provisions.

In order to keep this chapter to a reasonable length, it is limited in its purpose to provide a general overview of the CISG. The literature on the CISG is vast, and there are several detailed article-by-article commentaries available,[7] as well as countless scholarly articles.

2. Scope of application

2.1 Contract of sale

Surprisingly, despite the fact that the CISG applies to contracts for the sale of goods, there is no comprehensive definition of that type of contract in the CISG itself.[8] One can infer that a central aspect of a sale is that the seller transfers ownership in the goods to the buyer from the obligations imposed on the seller.[9] On that basis, the CISG would not apply to other common supply transactions, such as a leasing contract or a hire-purchase contract, which involve the transfer of possession but not necessarily the transfer of ownership.

Furthermore, the CISG treats as a contract of sale a contract under which goods have yet to be manufactured, except where a substantial part of the materials is supplied by the buyer.[10] A distinction therefore has to be drawn between instances where goods are made to order or based on specifications drawn up by the seller, and instances where the

6 Art. 5 CISG.
7 The leading commentary is I. Schwenzer (ed.), *Schlechtriem & Schwenzer – Commentary on the UN Convention on the International Sale of Goods (CISG)*, 4th ed. (Oxford University Press, 2016).
8 There is no definition of goods, which raises the inevitable question of whether software/digital content could be treated as "goods" for the purposes of the CISG. For arguments in favour, see F. Diedrich, "Maintaining uniformity in international uniform law via autonomous interpretation: software contracts and the CISG" (1996) 8 *Pace International Law Review* 303; or E. Muñoz, "Software technology in CISG contracts" (2019) 24 *Uniform Law Review* 302.
9 Cf. Art. 30 CISG.
10 Art. 3(1) CISG.

"seller" assembles goods the materials for which have, to a large extent, been provided by the buyer. In the latter case, it would seem that the seller's role is primarily that of a provider of services rather than a seller of goods, and therefore the CISG does not apply. In a similar vein, if a contract primarily involves the provision of labour or other services, and the supply of goods is only ancillary to this, then the CISG does not apply at all.[11] In this sense, the CISG reflects a rather traditional view of the notion of a contract for the sale of goods. However, it will not always be easy to determine in practice whether the service element of a contract is dominant, or "preponderant"[12] so as to remove the contract from the scope of the CISG.

2.2 Internationality

The CISG only applies to contracts for the international sale of goods. There are several criteria which could be used to determine what makes a sale "international". For example, the fact that goods will cross a border could be a determining factor. An alternative criterion could be the location of the parties: if they are located in different jurisdictions, then the contract is international. A third approach might be to combine both requirements.

In the CISG, the chosen criterion is to determine internationality on the basis of where the parties to the contract of sale have their respective places of business.[13] If their places of business are in different States, then the contract is an international one.[14] The only thing which matters is where the parties' respective places of business are; their nationality is not relevant.[15] If a party has multiple places of business, then the relevant place of business will be that which has the "closest relationship to the contract and its performance",[16] taking into account what was known or contemplated by the parties before the contract was concluded.

It is clear that it does not matter whether the goods cross borders or not. However, it seems that the question of whether the parties have their places of business in different States is not assessed entirely objectively. Rather, the fact that parties have their places of business in different States has to be apparent from the contract itself, or from the dealings between, or information disclosed by, the parties before or at the time of conclusion of contract.[17] Presumably, the intention is that neither party should discover that they have inadvertently concluded a contract to which the CISG applies if they were not aware that the contract fulfils the requirement of internationality in the CISG.

As well as being an international sale of goods on this basis, there also has to be a factor which connects the contract with the CISG. There are two possible routes: the first is that

---

11 Art. 3(2) CISG.
12 The word used in Art. 3(2) CISG.
13 If a party has no place of business, the relevant criterion would be that party's habitual residence: Art. 10(2) CISG.
14 Art. 1(1) CISG.
15 Art. 1(3) CISG.
16 Art. 10(1) CISG.
17 Art. 1(2) CISG.

both the parties to the contract have their places of business in (different) Contracting States.[18] Where this is not the case, Art. 1(1)(b) provides as an alternative connecting factor that the law of a Contracting State is the law applicable to the contract under the rules of private international law. This means that parties from States which are not Contracting States could still make their contract subject to the CISG if the applicable law is that of a Contracting State. As we saw in Chapter 2, this may be either the result of a choice made by the parties, or it may be determined by the rules of private international law which determine the applicable law in the absence of party choice. However, it is not entirely clear what the effect of the choice of the law of a Contracting State by the parties would be for the application of the CISG. On the one hand, the choice of the law of a Contracting State would mean a choice of the legal regime which governs contracts for the international sale of goods in that country, and this would include the CISG. On the other hand, the choice of a particular national law could be seen as a choice of the national rules only, to the exclusion of the CISG. This second criterion is subject to Article 95, which permits a Contracting State to declare that it does not wish to be bound by Art. 1(1)(b). Such a reservation could mean that if the applicable law is that of a Contracting State which has made the reservation, then the national law of that State will apply. Alternatively, it could be understood in the sense that the courts of a Contracting State which has made a reservation under Art. 95 will not apply the CISG on the basis of Art. 1(1)(b).[19]

2.3 Excluded contracts

A number of sales contracts are excluded from the scope of the CISG.[20] The broadest exclusion is of contracts where the goods are "bought for personal, family or household use".[21] In essence, therefore, the CISG does not apply to international sales of goods to consumers. However, this is not an absolute exclusion, because it will only apply if the seller did not know, nor should have known, at any point before the contract was concluded that the goods were bought for such use. It is therefore possible that there may be instances when a contract falls within the scope of the CISG even though the buyer is acquiring the goods for non-professional purposes. The factor which determines the application of this exclusion is the knowledge the seller has, or should have had, about the use for which the goods are bought.[22]

---

18   Art. 1(1)(a) CISG.
19   See also UNCITRAL, *Digest of Case Law on the United Nations Convention on Contracts for the International Sale of Goods* (2016), p.426.
20   Art. 2 CISG.
21   Art. 2(a) CISG.
22   This may be contrasted with the way EU Law defines the scope of application of its consumer law measures. For example, Directive (EU) 2019/771 on certain aspects concerning contracts for the sale of goods (2019) OJ L 136/28 applies to contracts between a "seller" and a "consumer". As long as the buyer is within the definition of "consumer" ("any natural person who, in relation to contracts covered by this Directive, is acting for purposes which are outside that person's trade, business, craft or profession" (Art. 2(2)), the Directive applies. Knowledge on the part of the seller is not relevant for this purpose.

Other types of sale are also excluded. They are sales by auction; on execution or by other legal authority; of stocks, shares, investment securities, negotiable instruments or money; of shops, vessels, hovercraft or aircraft; and of electricity.[23]

2.4 Party autonomy

A key feature of the CISG, like most other conventions in the field of International Commercial Law, is that the parties are able to exclude the application of the CISG altogether, or, alternatively, derogate from some of its provisions or vary their effect.[24]

If the parties decide to exclude the CISG altogether, then their contract will be governed entirely by the rules of the applicable law, which would then not include the CISG for this purpose. Such an exclusion would most easily be achieved by a clearly worded term in the contract to that effect. It would also be the consequence of choosing the law of a non-Contracting State (such as English Law) as the law applicable to the contract.[25]

However, the parties may not wish to exclude the CISG altogether, but may wish to depart only from some of its provisions. Some provisions (e.g., those on delivery) already defer to the express provisions in the contract and will only apply if the contract does not address the matter in question. However, there may be other provisions in the CISG which the parties might wish to vary. For example, the parties might agree that the right to "substitute delivery" (replacement) under Art. 46(2) in the case of a non-conformity should be available even if the non-conformity falls short of constituting a fundamental breach.[26]

This provision is an important feature of the CISG. In one sense, it is the classic embodiment of party autonomy in that it allows the parties to an international sales contract to determine which default rules will apply to their contract. On the other hand, it can also undermine the harmonising effect if parties routinely exclude the CISG and continue to apply national law. However, that might be a conscious decision, perhaps out of a feeling that the CISG is no more preferable than any national law.[27]

2.5 Interpretation of statements by or conduct of one party

In Chapter 3, issues regarding the interpretation of conventions by national courts or arbitrators were discussed. There, we saw how Art. 7 CISG stipulates a number of criteria which need to be adhered to when interpreting the CISG, and how any gaps

---

23 Art. 2(b)–(f) CISG.
24 Art. 6 CISG.
25 Merely choosing the courts of a non-Contracting State as the forum for litigation would not guarantee the non-application of the CISG itself, because the private international law rules of the forum might still determine that the law applicable to the contract is, in fact, the law of a Contracting State.
26 All of this is discussed below at 5.1.
27 Coyle summarises a number of surveys on the application of the CISG which suggest that the CISG has been routinely excluded: J.F. Coyle, "Rethinking the commercial law treaty" (2011) 45 *Georgia Law Review* 343, pp.371–383.

in the CISG should be deal with. Whilst Art. 7 is concerned with the interpretation of the text of the CISG itself, Art. 8 also provides guidance on how the interpretation of statements made by the parties to the contract should be approached. This will be relevant whenever one party has to communicate something, whether by words or conduct, to the other party. Article 8 is effectively a two-pronged approach. The first is that the statements or conduct of a party is to be interpreted according to that party's intent, provided the other party knew of, or could not have been unaware of, what was intended.[28] However, a party's intent may not always be known, and so the second requires that, where the other party was not aware of the party's intent, the statement or conduct of that party should be interpreted according to the under-standing a reasonable person of the same kind as the other party would have had in the same circumstance.[29] So in the first instance, the enquiry is into what the other party actually knew, or should have known, about the intent of the party making a state-ment or acting in a particular way. Where the other party had no such knowledge, an objective test is applied to determine what a reasonable person would think the party had intended. In either case, all the relevant circumstances, including negotiations, established practices between parties, usages and any subsequent conduct of the parties, can be taken into consideration.[30]

2.6 Formal requirements

One important hallmark of the CISG is the absence of any formal requirements with regard to the way a contract is formed or recorded. In particular, Art. 11 CISG makes it clear that there is no requirement that a contract of sale has to be in writing, nor are there any other specific requirements as to form. However, this is subject to the pos-sibility of a Contracting State to require that a contract of sale be in writing,[31] and Contracting States can make a declaration under Art. 96 CISG to disapply Art. 11 where at least one party has its place of business in that Contracting State.[32]

Where the CISG refers to writing, this should be understood as including the use of "telegram and telex".[33] At the time of drafting the CISG, both were com-monly used technological means of instantaneous communication, but these have largely fallen into abeyance following the wide-spread introduction of e-mails and the internet in the 1990s. Although not immediately apparent from the wording of the CISG itself, one would expect that its provisions would apply where digital means of communication are used.[34]

---

28 Art. 8(1) CISG.
29 Art. 8(2) CISG.
30 Art. 8(3) CISG.
31 Art. 12 CISG.
32 This rule has mandatory status, i.e., the parties cannot rely on Art. 6 CISG to dispense with any requirements as to writing where Art. 12 applies.
33 Art. 13 CISG.
34 See, generally, Chapter 12.

3. Formation of contracts (Part II CISG)

The CISG contains a set of provisions which deal with the formation of contracts for the international sale of goods. It is based on the established idea that a contract is based on an agreement resulting from offer and acceptance, and so a contract is concluded once the acceptance of an offer becomes effective.[35] Whilst the idea of offer and acceptance is well established, it can seem somewhat artificial to apply this framework in the context of commercial negotiations, and identifying the precise point at which an offer was made and subsequently accepted may not always be easy.[36]

An offer is a proposal which is sufficiently definite and indicates the intention of the person making the proposal (the offeror) to be bound.[37] For such a proposal to be sufficiently definite, it has to indicate the goods covered by the proposal and either state the price and quantity of the goods expressly or implicitly, or set out a mechanism for determining the price and quantity of the goods.[38] In addition, this proposal must be addressed to (a) specific person(s); otherwise, the proposal is to be regarded as an invitation to others to make an offer.[39] An offer takes effect, and therefore becomes capable of being accepted, once it reaches the person or persons to whom it is addressed (the offeree).[40]

The meaning of "reach" is important for the application of this and other stages in the process of concluding a contract. In this context, something "reaches" a party either when it is made orally to that party, or if it is delivered in any other way to that party personally or to that party's place of business or mailing address.[41]

For instances when the offeror changes its mind, the CISG distinguishes between the possibility of *withdrawing* an offer and *revoking* it. It is possible to withdraw an offer if this is done before the offer has become effective, i.e., the withdrawal must reach the offeree before or at the same time as the offer.[42] However, once the offer has become effective, it can no longer be withdrawn. Nevertheless, the offer can be revoked, provided that the revocation of the offer reaches the offeree before the offeree has dispatched its acceptance.[43] However, revocation is not possible if the offer is stated to be open for a fixed period of time, if the offer is expressed to be irrevocable, or if the offeree could reasonably assume that the offer was irrevocable *and* the offeree has relied on this fact accordingly.[44]

---

35 Art. 23 CISG.
36 See, e.g., Lord Sumption in *Four Seasons Holdings Incorporated v Brownlie* [2017] UKSC 80 at para. 16, commenting, from an English Law perspective, on the artificial nature of rules "adopted for reasons of pragmatic convenience" (*Ibid.*).
37 Art. 14(1) CISG.
38 *Ibid.*
39 Art. 14(2) CISG. However, if the person making the proposal clearly indicates that it is intended as an offer addressed to anyone, then it will be treated as such.
40 Art. 15(1) CISG.
41 Art. 24 CISG. In the absence of either, something reaches a party if it is sent to that person's habitual residence.
42 Art. 15(2) CISG.
43 Art. 16(1) CISG.
44 Art. 16(2) CISG.

Finally, an offer is *terminated* if the offeree has rejected it and the rejection reaches the offeror.[45]

It is worth pointing out that the notion of an irrevocable offer is unfamiliar to English contract law, which generally permits the revocation of an offer at any time.[46] However, in the context of international transactions, it seems appropriate to recognise the concept of an irrevocable offer, particularly if this possibility is recognised elsewhere. In this sense, the recognition of irrevocable offers in the CISG is one of the many compromises that were made in its drafting.

In order to conclude a contract, an offer must be accepted. This requires the offeree to assent to the offer by words or conduct, but not through silence or inactivity.[47] An active step by the offeree is therefore required. Furthermore, the acceptance will only be effective, and a contract will only be concluded, once the acceptance reaches the offeror.[48] Until it does so, there is no contract between the parties. Should the offeree change its mind, it can withdraw its acceptance as long as the withdrawal reaches the offeror before, or at the same time as, the acceptance.[49]

The requirement that acceptance must reach the offeror could be cumbersome in some instances. For example, the offeree is a seller of goods responding to an order, and the offeree dispatches the goods to the buyer. There would be no binding contract until the goods reach the offeror unless the offeree separately notifies the offeror of the dispatch and thereby accepts the offer. However, if the offer makes it clear that no separate notification is required, or if there is an established practice between the parties that no notification is required, or even a usage to that effect, then simply performing the required act (dispatching the goods; making payment) would suffice to constitute acceptance.[50]

An acceptance may not be effective, and not result in the conclusion of a contract, if the acceptance reaches the offeror after the time for acceptance has expired.[51] Thus, if the offeror fixes a period of time for acceptance[52] or sets an end-date to its offer, and an acceptance arrives only after this date, it will not be effective and no contract will be concluded. Where no date for acceptance is fixed, acceptance has to reach the offeror within a reasonable period of time.[53] However, the offeror has the option of treating a late acceptance as effective by informing the offeror (including by dispatching a notice)

---

45 Art. 17 CISG.
46 *Routledge v Grant* [1828] 4 Bing 653. If an offer is to be kept open for a fixed period of time, a separate agreement to that effect, supported by consideration, must be reached.
47 Art. 18(1) CISG.
48 Art. 18(2) CISG.
49 Art. 22 CISG.
50 Art. 18(3) CISG.
51 In the case of an offer made orally, it has to be accepted immediately, unless it is clear from the circumstances in which the offer was made that it can be accepted at a later point: Art. 18(2), final sentence.
52 Art. 20 CISG spells out when such a period of time begins to run and how official holidays and non-business days affect the expiry of that period.
53 Art. 18(2) CISG. In order to determine what a reasonable period of time is, the circumstances of the transaction and the method of communication used by the offeror are relevant.

without delay about this.[54] Moreover, if an acceptance sent by means of a letter or by other writing was late, but would not have been late in the normal course of transmission, then the acceptance will still be effective unless the offeror tells the offeree that it considers the offer as having lapsed.[55]

It is, of course, not always the case that there is a simple pattern of an offer being made and that offer being accepted. In many commercial contracts, there will be an element of negotiation, and so an initial offer might not be met by an immediate acceptance, but by a counter-offer. Under the CISG, a purported acceptance which contains any additions or limitations to the offer, or any other modification, is treated as a counter-offer, as well as a rejection of the offer.[56] Read in combination with Art. 17 CISG, this means that a counter-offer extinguishes the original offer, which would then preclude a return to the previous offer if the counter-offer is rejected.[57] However, this seemingly strict rule is eased insofar as any additional terms, or different terms, included in a purported acceptance do not materially alter the terms of the offer. For these purposes a material alteration would encompass additional or different terms relating to the price, payment, the quality and quantity of goods, the place and time of delivery, the extent of one party's liability to the other, and provisions regarding the settlement of disputes.[58] Variations to any of these terms from those in the offer would be material and therefore constitute a counter-offer.

Other modifications, i.e., any which are not material, that are made in a purported acceptance are not treated as giving rise to a counter-offer, but as an acceptance of the offer with modifications. As a result, a contract is concluded on the terms of the offer as modified by the acceptance.[59] However, if the offeror objects to such non-material alternations "without undue delay", either orally or by notice to the offeree, then there will be no acceptance and no contract.

3.1. Modification and termination of contract

We have already seen that the conclusion of a contract under the CISG only requires an agreement established through offer and acceptances, and the intention to be legally bound. Nothing further is needed. The same approach applies in respect of modification of the contract, or its termination (other than for breach). Thus, modification or termination only requires that both parties are in agreement,[60] and nothing further. However, this leaves open the question of what should happen where the modification was brought about in a way that could be described as extortion or economic duress: it might be that this could be resolved on the basis of the obscure reference to

---

54 Art. 21(1) CISG.
55 Art. 21(2) CISG.
56 Art. 19(1) CISG.
57 This is akin to English Law: see *Hyde v Wrench* [1840] 3 Beav 334.
58 Art. 19(3) CISG.
59 Art. 19(2) CISG.
60 Art. 29(1) CISG.

good faith in Article 7(1),[61] and that allowing a variation in such circumstances to stand would not be in accordance with good faith in international trade, but it is also possible to argue that the question of duress, linked as it is to questions of validity, might be a matter for national law.[62]

However, if a written contract contains a term according to which an agreement to modify or terminate the contract has to be in writing, then such a term overrides the possibility to modify or terminate the contract by a simple agreement. This, in turn, is subject to the possibility of a waiver, i.e., a party will be precluded from insisting on compliance with such a term if their conduct so indicates, and the other party has relied on such conduct.[63]

4. Seller's obligations

The CISG deals with the respective obligations of seller and buyer in a contract for the international sale of goods, and provides a number of rights (or remedies) in respect of a failure by one party to perform its obligations. In this section, we concentrate on the obligations of the seller, before turning to the buyer's remedies for breach by the seller of its obligations.

The basic obligations of the seller are set out in Article 30 and comprise three aspects: (i) the obligation to deliver the goods; (ii) the obligation to hand over any documents relating to the goods (which is common in international commercial transactions); and (iii) to transfer the property in the goods. All of these obligations must be performed in accordance with both the relevant provisions in the CISG and any requirements stipulated in the contract itself.

4.1 Delivery

With regard to the seller's duty to deliver the goods, there are generally two aspects which need to be determined: (i) where to deliver the goods; and (ii) when to deliver the goods. Both aspects may be expressly agreed in the contract itself, in which case the contract will govern the seller's obligations regarding the place and time of delivery. Many international sales contracts involving the carriage of goods will rely on the ICC's INOCTERMS®,[64] which are a set of international trade

---

61 See Chapter 3 at 5.1.1.
62 J.M. Lookofsky, "Loose ends and contorts in international sales: problems in the harmonization of private law rules" (1991) 39 *American Journal of Comparative Law* 403, p.413 (suggesting the latter).
63 Art. 29(2) CISG. An English common lawyer might be tempted to equate this with the idea of an estoppel, but whilst there are obvious parallels between Art. 29(2) CISG and the doctrine of waiver/promissory estoppel, the imperative of Art. 7(1) CISG to interpret every provision autonomously must be remembered. Note that the UK Supreme Court side-stepped an opportunity to consider the effect of estoppel on so-called non-oral modification clauses in *Rock Advertising Ltd v MWB Business Exchange Centres Ltd* [2018] UKSC 24.
64 The most recent version is the INCOTERMS® 2020.

terms which include provisions on the seller's obligations with regard to delivery. These obligations vary, depending on whether carriage of the goods is involved and the extent to which this has to be arranged or provided by the seller.

However, for cases when the contract is silent, the CISG provides a number of rules to determine both where the seller has to fulfil its obligation to deliver, and when.

4.1.1 Place of delivery

Article 31 CISG sets out the seller's obligations regarding the place for delivery. The general rule is that the seller has to put the goods at the buyer's disposal at the place where the seller had its place of business at the time the contract was concluded.[65] In essence, the seller's obligation to deliver would be fulfilled by having them available for collection at its business premises. The particular reference to the place of business at the time of concluding the contract might produce odd results if the seller has subsequently abandoned that place of business and changed location – it would seem strange if the effect of Art. 31(3) CISG were to require the seller to return to their abandoned site. However, the solution to this conundrum lies in the ability of the parties to modify the contract by agreement, and so a notice from the seller to the buyer that the place of business has changed which is subsequently confirmed by the buyer (in practice, this would probably be achieved by an exchange of e-mail messages) would suffice to displace the default rule in Art. 31(3).

There are two variations to this basic provision. The first is where goods (whether specific, unidentified to be drawn from a specific stock, or to be manufactured/produced) were at, or to be made at, a particular place known to the parties at the time of concluding the contract. In this situation, the seller fulfils its obligation to delivery by putting the goods at the buyer's disposal at that place.[66]

Finally, if it is envisaged under the contract of sale that the goods are to be transported by a carrier, then the seller fulfils its obligations by handing over the goods to the first carrier for transmission to the buyer.[67] When handing over the goods to the carrier, they will often be clearly identified to the contract, e.g., by markings on the goods, shipping documents, etc.; however, where this is not the case, the buyer has to be given notice of the consignment specifying the goods.[68]

Article 32 further spells out the obligations on the seller with regard to arranging the carriage of goods and insurance. If the contract of sale incorporates the INCOTERMS®, then the relevant provisions of those will apply instead of Art. 32. In other cases, a seller who has to make arrangements for the carriage of goods has to make such contract(s) of carriage to the place agreed in the contract, using means of transportation appropriate in the circumstances, and on the basis of terms usual for such transportation.[69] The seller may also be required under the contract

65 Art. 31(c) CISG.
66 Art. 31(2) CISG.
67 Art. 31(1) CISG.
68 Art. 32(1) CISG.
69 Art. 32(2) CISG.

to insure the goods whilst they are in transit to the buyer, but if the seller is not required to do so, it must, if requested by the buyer, give the latter all the available information necessary to effect insurance.[70]

4.1.2 Time of delivery

The time of delivery may be fixed in the contract, in which case this is the date when the seller must deliver.[71] If the contract specifies a time period within which delivery is made, then the default position is that seller can deliver at any time during this period. However, if the contract, or the circumstances surrounding the contract, indicates that the buyer has to choose a date, then the seller would be obliged to deliver on that date.[72] If the contract is silent on the time for delivery, the fall-back position in Art. 33 (3) CISG is that delivery has to be made within a reasonable time after the contract was concluded. Invariably, this leaves open considerable room for arguments as to what sort of time-scale would be reasonable in any given context. One relevant consideration will be the nature of the goods (e.g., if they are perishable or not). Another relevant factor might be relevant trade usages regarding the time for delivery.[73]

4.2 Obligation to hand over documents

The second key obligation of the seller is to hand over any documents relating to the goods, where required under the contract of sale. These documents must be handed over at the time, place, and in the form required under the contract.[74] This may mean handing the documents to the buyer, but it might also mean handing the documents to another person specified in the contract, such as a bank to which documents are to be presented in accordance with a documentary credit.

There may be instances where the documents do not fully comply with the contractual requirements. As a result, the seller would be in breach of its contractual obligations. However, if the documents were handed over before the due date and time, the seller is given the right to correct any non-compliance in the documents, provided that this would not cause unreasonable inconvenience or unreasonable expense to the buyer.[75] However, the buyer would have a right to damages under the CISG in any case, and this is not affected by the seller's ability to correct the documents.

4.3 Transfer property in the goods

The third obligation of the seller in Art. 30 CISG is to transfer the property in the goods. However, there are no provisions in the CISG which deal with the transfer

---

70 Art. 32(3) CISG.
71 Art. 33(a) CISG.
72 Art. 33(b) CISG.
73 See Chapter 1 at 6.1.
74 Art. 34 CISG, first sentence.
75 Art. 34 CISG, second sentence.

of property from seller to buyer. Consequently, the transfer of property will be governed by the relevant rules of the law applicable to the contract of sale.

4.4 Goods to be in conformity with the contract

4.4.1 The conformity requirement

In addition to the obligations regarding delivery of the goods, the handing over of documents and the transfer of property, the seller is also under the obligation to ensure that the goods delivered to the buyer are in conformity with the contract. In essence, this means that the goods must be of the quantity, quality and description specified in the contract, and be contained or packaged as required by the contract.[76] It is important to note that conformity is primarily determined on the basis of the contract, which places the onus on the parties to ensure that they have reached a clear agreement regarding the quality of the goods and how they should the packaged.

In addition to whatever is provided in the contract, there are a number of default requirements which determine whether the goods are in conformity with the contract. These will apply unless the parties agree otherwise. Whereas any contractual agreement as to conformity will be based on the subjective requirements of the parties, the provisions of Art. 35(2) CISG, which set out the default requirements, apply objectively. According to Art. 35(2), goods are not in conformity with the contract unless they

a   Are fit for the purposes for which goods of the same description would ordinarily be used.
b   Are fit for any particular purpose made known, expressly or impliedly, to the seller at the time of concluding the contract, unless the buyer did not rely on the seller's skill and judgement, or it was unreasonable for the buyer so to rely.
c   Possess the qualities held out by the seller to the buyer as a sample or model.
d   Are contained or packaged in a manner usual for such goods, or adequate to preserve and protect the goods.

It will be immediately obvious that the default criteria for conformity are set at a relatively low level. The main requirement is that the goods are fit for the purposes for which they would ordinarily be used, as well as for any particular purpose made known to the seller. This suggests that, as long as the goods can be used for these purposes, they meet the conformity requirement in Art. 35(2) CISG. If the buyer has any particular expectations regarding the quality, durability or performance of the goods, then these need to be negotiated and included in the contract of sale as contractual requirements as to conformity.

As noted, the criteria in Art. 35(2) only apply insofar as they are not displaced by the contract. Moreover, the seller will also not be liable for a failure of the goods to

76 Art. 35(1) CISG.

comply with the requirements of Art. 35(2) if the buyer knew, or could not have been unaware, of the lack of conformity at the time the contract was concluded.[77]

4.4.2 Time at which conformity is assessed: transfer of risk

It is important to be clear about the time at which compliance with the seller's obligation to supply goods in conformity with the contract is determined. This could be determined either with reference to the point at which the seller transfers possession of the goods to the buyer, or at the moment when the risk of loss or damage is transferred to the buyer. In the CISG, the latter has been chosen. Thus, a seller is liable for any lack of conformity which exists when the risk passes to the buyer.[78] The fact that the lack of conformity must "exist" at that point does not mean that it must also have become apparent. The seller's liability extends to any lack of conformity which only manifested at a later point, as long as it can be shown to have existed at the point when risk passed to the buyer.

The CISG contains several provisions which deal with the transfer of risk. The general rule is that risk passes from the seller to the buyer when the buyer takes over the goods.[79] If, after the risk has passed, the goods are lost or damaged, the buyer will still be liable to pay for them, except where the loss or damage was caused by the seller.[80] However, if the goods had not been identified in the contract (e.g., because they were referred to by a generic description), they are not deemed to be at the buyer's disposal until they have been clearly identified to the contract.[81] Moreover, even if risk has passed, the buyer retains its remedies against the seller in respect of a fundamental breach of contract committed by the seller.[82]

If the buyer is required to collect the goods from a particular place other than the seller's place of business, risk will pass once delivery has become due and the buyer is aware that the goods have been put at its disposal.[83]

Risk will also pass to the buyer if the buyer has delayed taking delivery of the goods (or failed to take delivery altogether) as required under the contract; in this instance, the relevant point in time is when the goods were placed at the buyer's disposal.[84]

There are specific provisions in respect of contracts where the goods are to be transported to the buyer by carrier, and where the goods are already in transit when they are sold.

In respect of the first situation, where the contract of sale involves the carriage of goods, it is first necessary that the goods have been clearly identified to the contract.[85] Provided

77 Art. 35(3) CISG.
78 Art. 36 CISG.
79 Art. 69(1) CISG.
80 Art. 66 CISG.
81 Art. 69(3) CISG.
82 Art. 70 CISG.
83 Art. 69(2) CISG.
84 Art. 69(1) CISG.
85 Art. 67 (2) CISG.

that this has been done, the risk passes to the buyer once the goods have been handed over to the first carrier for transmission to the buyer, as specified in the contract.[86] This does not apply, however, if the contract requires the seller to hand the goods over at a particular place.[87] Should the seller be required to hand the goods over to the carrier at a particular place (such as a freight terminal in a nominated port), then the risk passes to the buyer once the seller has handed over the goods accordingly.[88] In any case, the fact that the seller has the authority to keep the documents which are necessary to control the disposition of the goods does not affect the passing of risk in these instances.

The second situation arises where the goods are already in transit when the contract of sale is made. This is common where goods are transported by ship over long distances and therefore in transit for a period of time. If the goods are already in transit, then risk passes when the contract of sale is made.[89] This does not apply, however, if the seller knew that the goods had been lost or damaged by that time and failed to disclose this to the buyer.

4.4.3 Freedom from third-party claims

As well as ensuring that the goods are in conformity with the contract under Art. 35 CISG, the seller is also required to make sure that the goods are free from any right or claim of a third party, except where the buyer has agreed to buy the goods subject to that right or claim.[90]

In addition, Art. 42 CISG deals with the seller's obligation to deliver goods free from claims of a third party which are specifically based on industrial or other intellectual property. For the seller to be liable under this Article, the seller must have known about (or could not have been unaware of) that claim, provided that such a claim arises either under the law of the State where goods will be resold or otherwise used if this was contemplated by parties; or, in any other case, under the law of the State where the buyer has its place of business.[91] However, this will not be the case if the buyer knew, or could not have been unaware, of the right or claim, or where this right or claim arises because the seller complied with technical drawings, designs, formulae or other specifications provided by the buyer.[92]

Where either situation under Art. 41 or Art. 42 arises, the buyer must notify the seller within a reasonable period of time of becoming aware of this, or when the buyer ought to have become aware of this, and specify what the right or claim of the third party is.[93] However, if the seller knew of the third party's right or claim,

---

86 Art. 67(1) CISG.
87 *Ibid.*
88 *Ibid.*
89 Art. 68 CISG. However, in some instances, the risk may be assumed by the buyer from time the goods were handed over to the carrier who issued the relevant documents.
90 Art. 41 CISG.
91 Art. 42(1)(a) and (b) CISG.
92 Art. 42(2)(a) and (b) CISG.
93 Art. 43(1) CISG.

the seller cannot rely on a failure by the buyer to notify it within a reasonable period of time as a ground for rejecting liability.[94]

4.5 Seller's right of cure

One interesting feature of the CISG is the possibility for the seller to put right ("cure") a delivery of goods which is not in accordance with the contract.[95] In order for this to arise, the seller must have delivered the goods *before* the date for delivery.[96] If there were parts missing from that delivery, or a smaller quantity than contractually agreed was delivered, then the seller can remedy this, provided this happens before the due date for delivery. Furthermore, if the goods delivered were not in conformity with the contract, the seller can provide a replacement of any such goods, but again only until the due date for delivery. This possibility to cure is subject to the proviso that doing so would not cause unreasonable inconvenience or expense to the buyer. In any case, the buyer retains the right to claim damages for any losses suffered as a result.

5. Remedies of the buyer

In the previous section, we examined the obligations of a seller under the CISG. In this section, the buyer's remedies for a breach of contract by the seller will be considered. It will become clear that the primary purpose of the CISG's remedial scheme is to ensure the performance of the contract, rather than allowing the buyer to terminate the contract too easily.

The buyer's remedies are based on two sets of provisions.[97] There are a number of specific remedies set out in Articles 46–52 CISG. In addition, there is a general section on claims for damages in Arts. 74–77 CISG. If the buyer opts for one of the specific remedies, it will still be able to claim damages for any further losses.[98]

We will first focus on the specific remedies of the buyer. Before doing so, it is necessary to consider one preliminary issue: the concept of "fundamental breach" under the CISG.

5.1 Fundamental breach

A pre-condition to the availability of some of the buyer's remedies (and also the seller's remedies, discussed in section 7 below) is that the breach of contract by the seller must amount to a *fundamental breach*. The test for determining whether a

---

94 Art. 43(2) CISG.
95 Art. 37 CISG.
96 Note that the seller may also effect cure *after* the due date, but subject to the buyer's right of avoidance: see Art. 48.
97 See Art. 45(1) CISG.
98 Art. 45(2) CISG. Once a buyer has sought a remedy for breach of contract, a court or arbitral tribunal is precluded from granting the seller a grace period: Art. 45(3).

breach of contract amounts to a fundamental breach is in Art. 25 CISG, which provides as follows:

> A breach of contract committed by one of the parties is fundamental if it results in such detriment to the other party as substantially to deprive him of what he is entitled to expect under the contract, unless the party in breach did not foresee and a reasonable person of the same kind in the same circumstances would not have foreseen such a result.

From a cursory reading, it is apparent that the threshold for determining whether a breach is fundamental is a high one. In order to apply this test to a breach in the context of a particular contract, it will be necessary to consider a number of issues. First, it must be considered what the party not in breach was entitled to expect under the contract. In other words, it needs to be established what the innocent party should have obtained, had the contract been performed in full by the other party. Secondly, it needs to be determined what the party not in breach actually obtained (if anything). This then needs to be compared to what was expected in order to address the third issue, which is whether what was actually received by the party not in breach did *substantially* deprive that party of what it expected under the contract.

However, matters do not stop there. If it is established that the breach resulted in the other party being substantially deprived of what was expected under the contract, it then becomes necessary to consider whether the party in breach would have foreseen that the breach would result in substantially depriving the other party of what was expected. The first question is whether it can be shown that the party in breach foresaw such a consequence as a result of its breach of contract. If so, foreseeability is established and the breach will be regarded as fundamental. However, if the party in breach did not foresee such a consequence (or if it cannot be shown on the facts that it did), the next question is whether a reasonable person in the position of the party in breach and in the same circumstances would have foreseen such consequences as resulting from the breach of contract. If this question is answered positively, then, again, the result was foreseeable and therefore the breach is treated as a fundamental breach.

In practice, the innocent party will establish that the other party's breach of contract had the effect of substantially depriving it from what was expected under the contract. The party in breach would then try to establish that it did not foresee this result, nor would a reasonable person in the same situation have done so, and that the breach should consequently not be treated as a fundamental breach.

5.2 Buyer's remedies under Arts. 46–52

In general terms, the buyer can require the seller to perform its obligations, unless the buyer has already opted for a remedy that would be inconsistent with this.[99] For example, if the seller has not delivered, or only delivered some of, the

---

99 Art. 46(1) CISG.

goods,[100] the buyer can require the seller to deliver all, or the missing portion of, the goods. If the contract has made any other stipulations which the seller is required to perform but has failed to do, then again, the buyer can require the seller to make good on this.

For a common lawyer, this remedy looks akin to the remedy of "specific performance". However, this remedy is not awarded as a matter of routine but only in exceptional cases.[101] The implications could be that a common law court might be obliged to make an order for specific performance in respect of contracts to which the CISG applies, when it would not do so if the contract was governed solely by the respective national law (not including the CISG). In order to forestall possible concerns from common law countries about this, Art. 28 CISG provides that a court is not required to make an award for specific performance if that court would not make such an order in the case of comparable contracts of sale outside the CISG's scope. In other words, a national court would not be obliged to make an order for specific performance in the context of the CISG where it would not do so under national law. The intention behind Art. 28 was undoubtedly to acknowledge the concerns of common law jurisdictions that specific performance would have to be awarded much more regularly, which, in turn, could result in specific performance also becoming more readily available in the context of contracts governed purely by national law.

5.2.1 Remedies for a lack of conformity

In addition to the general remedy of requiring the buyer to perform, there are a number of specific remedies for instances when the seller's breach of contract is due to a lack of conformity of the goods with the contract. If the contract involves the delivery of multiple goods, and only some are affected by a lack of conformity, then the remedies can be exercised in respect of those goods which do not conform with the contract.[102]

5.2.1.1 Buyer's duties to examine and notify

The availability of these remedies is subject to the buyer's duties to examine the goods and to notify the seller of a lack of conformity. First, the buyer must have examined the goods speedily, usually after they have been delivered. Thus, Article 38 CISG requires the buyer to examine the goods "within as short a period as is practicable under the circumstances". The duration of the period within which the buyer has to carry out this examination is therefore flexible and will vary according to the circumstances of the particular transaction, and may depend on factors such as nature and complexity of the goods and any particular understanding between seller and buyer as to when examination might be practicable. However, the over-

---

100 Art. 51(1) CISG.
101 *Co-operative Insurance Soc Ltd v Argyll Stores (Holdings) Ltd* [1998] A.C. 1.
102 Art. 51(1) CISG.

arching requirement is one of speedy action on the buyer's part. Of course, the buyer cannot examine the goods whilst they are in transit, and so it is acknowledged in the CISG that examination may not take place until after they have arrived at their destination.[103] Similarly, if they are redirected whilst in transit, or if the buyer immediately forwards the goods (e.g., to a sub-buyer, or to a different business location of the buyer) without having had a reasonable opportunity to examine the goods first, then the buyer's examination can be deferred until the goods have arrived at their destination; however, the seller must have known, or at least ought to have known, that this would happen.[104]

Secondly, if the buyer discovers a lack of conformity, this must be notified to the seller within a reasonable time after discovering this.[105] Thus, if a lack of conformity is apparent on examination of the goods, then the buyer must notify the seller within a reasonable time after the examination. If the lack of conformity only becomes apparent at a later point – and therefore could not have been discovered by reasonable examination – the buyer must notify the seller within a reasonable period of time afterwards. The obligation to notify also arises if the buyer ought to have discovered it; this might matter, e.g., if the examination was not as thorough as might have been reasonable and the defect would have been spotted by a more careful examination. If the buyer fails to notify the seller, it loses the entitlement to a remedy for the lack of conformity.[106]

Furthermore, Article 39(2) provides for a limited period of time during which a buyer could raise a lack of conformity; this period ends two years after the goods were "actually handed over to the buyer". Thus, if a lack of conformity materialises 25 months after the goods were delivered, then the buyer cannot bring a claim against the seller in respect of this, even if the buyer immediately notifies the seller. By way of exception, if the seller has given a contractual guarantee for a longer period of time than two years, then this longer period would determine the time-scale during which the buyer can hold the seller responsible for a lack of conformity.

There is therefore a not insignificant burden on a buyer to examine the goods promptly and to notify any lack of conformity swiftly. The effect of these provisions is to strike a balance between making available remedies for a buyer in case the seller has delivered non-conforming goods, but at the same time to provide a degree of finality by not permitting the buyer to wait for an unreasonable period of time before raising a lack of conformity with the seller.

As a further element of this balancing act, if the buyer has failed to notify the buyer within the reasonable period of time required by Art. 39(1) CISG, but has a reasonable excuse for its failure to do so, then the buyer would still be entitled to rely on the remedy of price reduction and to claim damages.[107] Moreover, if the seller was aware, or could not have been unaware, of the lack of conformity of the goods and did not

103 Art. 38(2) CISG.
104 Art. 38(3) CISG.
105 Art. 39(1) CISG.
106 *Ibid.*, opening words.
107 Art. 44 CISG.

disclose this, then the seller cannot evade liability even if the buyer had failed to examine the goods swiftly and/or failed to notify the seller within a reasonable period of time.[108] This would preclude a seller from deliberately not disclosing a known lack of conformity and then seeking to rely on the buyer's duties of examination and notification to prevent the buyer from seeking a remedy for this lack of conformity. As such, this could be seen as one instance of a substantive provision of the CISG reflecting a broader underlying principle of good faith.[109]

5.2.1.2 Repair or substitution

The primary remedy a buyer can seek in the case of most instances of a lack of conformity is to have the goods repaired.[110] The availability of this remedy is subject to the requirement that it must not be unreasonable for the seller to repair the goods, determined on the basis of the relevant circumstances.

The seller may also be required to provide replacement goods (deliver substitute goods), but only where the lack of conformity is so serious that it would constitute a fundamental breach of contract (see above). The threshold for this remedy is therefore a high one; this might be justified by the fact that in the context of many international sales contracts, the goods will have had to be carried over a considerable distance, and the cost of sending replacement goods might be unduly high.

In either case, the buyer must ask the seller to repair the goods or provide a replacement when it gives notice to the seller in accordance with Art. 39 CISG, or at the latest within a reasonable time after giving such notice.[111]

5.2.1.3 Price reduction

A further remedy in respect of non-conforming goods is the buyer's right to reduce the price, irrespective of whether the buyer has already paid or not. The calculation of the proportion by the price is reduced reduction is based on the value of the goods as actually delivered compared to the value the goods would have had, had they been in conformity with the contract.[112]

> Example: The seller has delivered goods with a lack of conformity which are worth £800 as delivered. Had the goods been in conformity, they would have been worth £1000. The proportion by which the price will be reduced is £800:£1000, or 0.8.
>
> The actual amount by which the price will be reduced is then determined on the basis of the contract price. Thus, if the contract price for the goods was £900, the reduced price would be £900 x 0.8 = £720, so the price would be

---

108 Art. 40 CISG.
109 See Chapter 3 at 5.1.2.
110 Art. 46(3) CISG.
111 Art. 46(2)/(3) CISG, final sentence.
112 Art. 50 CISG.

reduced by £180. If the contract price was £1000, the reduced price would be £800, and the reduction would be £200. Finally, if the contract price was £1100, the price payable after reduction would be £880, with the amount by which the price was reduced amounting to £220.

These examples illustrate that the proportionate approach to price reduction will produce the same outcome as a straightforward calculation of the difference in value if the contract price reflects the actual value of goods in conformity with the contract. It works to the advantage of a buyer who has secured a better price in that the price reduction will reflect the good bargain, but a buyer who has paid more than the goods are worth to begin with will still pay more than their true value after the price has been reduced.

The right to reduce the price will be lost if the seller was able to exercise its right to cure,[113] or if the buyer has refused to let the seller attempt to cure the breach of contract.[114]

5.2.2 Extension of period of performance

Where the seller has not performed its obligations, the buyer can set an additional period of time, of reasonable length, within which the seller must perform its obligations.[115] In effect, this would give the seller a second chance to perform all of its obligations. A buyer who sets such an additional period would not lose the right to claim damages for any losses which may have been suffered as a result of the seller's delay to perform its obligations by the initial due date.[116] However, during this period, the buyer is precluded from exercising any other remedy, unless the seller tells the buyer that it will not perform its obligations within the extended period.[117]

5.2.3 Declaring contract avoided (termination)

As the buyer's remedies under the CISG primarily seek to ensure the seller's performance of its contractual obligations, the right to bring the contract to an end is only available in some circumstances. First, the buyer can declare the contract avoided (the phrase used in the CISG) if the seller's breach of contract amounts to a fundamental breach.[118] Secondly, the buyer can also avoid the contract if, having set an additional period for performance in accordance with Art. 47 CISG, the seller has failed to perform within that period or has notified the buyer that it will not perform.[119] This would be so even where the initial breach of the seller in not performing all of its obligations by the due date was not so serious as to constitute a

113 Either before the due date for performance under Art. 37 CISG, or under Art. 48 (see below).
114 Art. 50 CISG, final sentence.
115 Art. 47(1) CISG.
116 Art. 47(2) CISG, final sentence.
117 Art. 47(2) CISG.
118 Art. 49(1)(a) CISG.
119 Art. 49(1)(b) CISG.

fundamental breach. Where the contract involves the supply of multiple goods, but only some are affected by a lack of conformity, the buyer can avoid the contract in respect of those goods if the conditions for avoidance are otherwise met. However, the buyer would only be entitled to avoid the contract as a whole where the fact that some of the goods delivered are not in conformity with the contract constitutes a fundamental breach in respect of the whole contract.[120]

5.2.3.1 Consequences of avoidance

The consequences of avoidance are dealt with in Arts. 81–84 CISG and apply to avoidance by either seller or buyer, but they are considered here for convenience.

The main effect of exercising the right of avoidance is that both parties are released from their obligations under the contract, with the exception of any provisions in the contract dealing with dispute resolution or any terms which make express provision for the consequences of either party avoiding the contract.[121]

Following avoidance, a party which has already rendered some or all of its performance under the contract can claim restitution of whatever they have provided to the other party from that party.[122] If the seller has to provide restitution, this will usually mean that the seller has to refund the price paid by the buyer. In addition, the seller is required to pay interest on the price from the date on which the price was paid.[123] In the buyer's case, as well as returning the goods (or part of them), the buyer has to account to the seller for all the benefits it may have derived from the goods.[124] This also applies if the buyer is unable to make restitution as required by returning the goods substantially in the condition which they were received, but has still declared contract avoided or required substitute goods.[125]

5.2.3.2 Loss of the right to avoid

The buyer will not be able to exercise the right to avoid the contract in a number of instances.[126] A distinction is made between a breach of contract involving late delivery, and other breaches of contract. In the former instance, where the seller has delivered the goods late, the buyer will lose the right to avoid the contract (assuming this right is available to the buyer) unless it exercises it within a reasonable period of time from becoming aware that delivery has been made.[127] In other

---

120 Art. 51(2) CISG.
121 Art. 81(1) CISG.
122 Art. 89(2) CISG. If both parties are required to provide restitution, they must do so concurrently, i.e., one party cannot wait for the other party to have made restitution before it makes restitution.
123 Art. 84(1) CISG.
124 Art. 84(2)(a) CISG.
125 Art. 84(2)(b) CISG. See below for instances when the inability to make restitution may preclude the buyer from avoiding the contract and exceptions thereto.
126 See Art. 49(2) CISG.
127 Art. 49(2)(a) CISG.

cases, the right to avoid will be lost unless exercised within a reasonable period of time after the buyer knew, or ought to have known, about the breach of contract.[128] If the buyer has set an additional period for the seller to perform in accordance with Art. 47, then the right to avoid will be lost unless exercised within a reasonable period of time after the additional period for performance has expired, or after the seller has told the buyer that it will not perform.[129]

A further instance when the right to avoid will be lost is when the buyer cannot make restitution of the goods "substantially in the condition in which he received them".[130] This is because the buyer is required to return anything it has received to the seller following the exercise of the right of avoidance.[131] However, the loss of the right to avoid on this basis does not deprive the buyer of any other remedies, whether contractual or available under the CISG, in respect of the seller's breach of contract.[132] Furthermore, there are a number of exceptions to the loss of the right to avoid for inability to make restitution, which recognise that the buyer's inability to make full restitution of the goods in the required condition may not be the buyer's fault. Thus, if the buyer's inability to return the goods in the required condition was not due to an act or omission on the buyer's part, the right to avoid the contract is preserved.[133] Moreover, if some or all of the goods have perished or deteriorated as a result of the examination the buyer is required to undertake in accordance with Art. 38 CISG (see above), then this will also not result in the loss of the right of avoidance.[134] The third instance where the right to avoid is not lost is when the goods were resold by the buyer in the normal course of its business, or consumed or transformed in the normal use by the buyer, before the lack of conformity was, or ought to have been, discovered.[135]

5.2.4 Seller's right of cure

We saw earlier that the seller can cure an initial failure to perform its obligations where the time for delivery has not yet passed. Article 48 CISG provides for a further opportunity for the seller to cure a breach even after the time for delivery has passed. The seller will be permitted to do so if this can be done without an unreasonable delay, and without causing the buyer unreasonable inconvenience, or uncertainty in respect of the reimbursement by the seller of any expenses advanced by the buyer.[136] If able to cure a breach in these circumstances, the seller would have to do so at its own expense.

128 Art. 49(2)(b)(i) CISG.
129 Art. 49(2)(b)(ii) CISG.
130 Art. 82(1) CISG.
131 Art. 81(2) CISG.
132 Art. 83 CISG.
133 Art. 82(2)(a) CISG.
134 Art. 82(2)(b) CISG.
135 Art. 82(2)(c) CISG.
136 Art. 48(1) CISG.

The seller can make a request to the buyer to ask whether the buyer would accept whatever performance is required to cure the breach; if the buyer does not respond to this request within a reasonable period of time, the seller can proceed with curing the breach within the period the seller stated in its request.[137] During this period, the buyer is precluded from exercising any remedy which would undermine the seller's ability to provide the performance needed to cure the breach.[138] Should the seller simply send a notice stating that the seller can perform within a specified period of time, then this is presumed to include also a request to the buyer to indicate whether the buyer would accept the seller's performance.[139]

5.2.5 Remedies for incorrect delivery

A final set of provisions deals with a failure by the seller to deliver the goods as required under the contract or the CISG. Whilst late delivery or non-delivery will constitute a breach of contract, delivering early may not be such. If the seller tenders delivery before the due date, then the buyer has the option of accepting the delivery then, or the seller can refuse to take delivery at that point.[140]

A shortfall in delivery will constitute a breach of the contract, and the buyer's remedies as discussed above apply in respect of the shortfall accordingly.[141] Should the buyer deliver goods in excess of the contract quantity, the buyer has the choice between rejecting the excess or retaining the excess quantity. In the latter case, the buyer would be required to pay the corresponding price for the goods based on the contract price.

5.3 Duty to preserve goods

In circumstances when the buyer has already received the goods but exercises a remedy under the CISG which involve the rejection of the goods (e.g., substitute goods or avoidance), then the buyer comes under a duty to take reasonable steps to preserve the goods. The buyer will be entitled to retain the goods until the seller has reimbursed it for any expenses incurred as a result.[142] Moreover, where the goods were dispatched by the seller and placed at the buyer's disposal at their destination, but the buyer rejects the goods, then the buyer is required to take possession of the goods on behalf of the seller. However, the buyer will only be required to do so if this can be done without having to pay the price of the goods and without causing unreasonable inconvenience or unreasonable expense. It will

---

137 Art. 48(2) CISG.
138 *Ibid.*
139 Art. 48(3) CISG. The request or notice, as the case may be, will only be effective once received by the buyer: Art. 48(4) CISG.
140 Art. 52(1) CISG.
141 Art. 51(1) CISG.
142 Art. 86(1) CISG.

also not be required if the seller or a person authorised by the seller is present at the good's destination at the time.[143]

5.3.1 Preserving the goods

Although the CISG does not fully expand on what would be required in order to comply with the obligation to preserve the goods, it contains a number of ancillary provisions which set out the rights and obligations of the party charged by the CISG with preserving the goods.[144]

First of all, the party responsible for preserving the goods may place them in a warehouse of a third person. The other party will have to pay the reasonable expenses incurred for doing so.[145]

Secondly, the party who has preserved the goods may sell them if the other party unreasonably delays taking possession of goods or taking them back or paying for their preservation. Before reselling, reasonable notice of the intention to sell the goods must be given to the other party.[146]

In the case of goods which are liable to deteriorate rapidly, or where the preservation of the goods would cause unreasonable expense, the party charged with their preservation must take reasonable steps to resell them. If possible, notice of the intention to sell must be given to the other party.[147]

Finally, the party who has resold the goods in one of these situations can retain a sum which covers that party's reasonable expenses for preserving and selling the goods, but any surplus exceeding such a sum has to be accounted for to the other party.[148]

6. Buyer's obligations

This section sets out the duties of the buyer under the CISG. They are simple to state: the buyer must pay the price and take delivery of the goods, as required under the relevant provisions of the CISG and any terms of the contract of sale.[149]

6.1 Payment of the price

The CISG contains several provisions that deal with the buyer's obligation to pay the price. Some seek to provide default rules to provide clarity and remove any doubts as to what the obligation to pay the price entails. Thus, Art. 54 CISG states that the duty to pay includes an obligation to ensure that the buyer takes all the

---

143 Art. 86(2) CISG.
144 The seller can be under an obligation to preserve the goods in certain circumstances: see 7.4, below.
145 Art. 87 CISG.
146 Art. 88(1) CISG.
147 Art. 88(2) CISG.
148 Art. 88(3) CISG.
149 Art. 53 CISG.

necessary steps and formalities, both under relevant laws and regulations and the contract, to make payment. In addition, Art. 56 CISG makes it clear that if the price to be paid depends on the weight of the goods, then the price is to be determined on the basis of the net weight of the goods; this is for the avoidance of doubt and if the contract specifies otherwise, then whatever the contract requires applies instead.

We saw earlier that, for the formation of a contract of sale under the CISG, an offer, i.e., a sufficiently definite proposal, needs to be made, and that a proposal is sufficiently definite if, *int. al.*, it expressly or implicitly fixes the price or makes provision for doing so.[150] However, if a contract has been validly concluded but the price has not been fixed, nor is there provision for doing so, then Article 55 provides a fall-back rule to determine the price. Unless there is any indication to the contrary, the price would be that generally charged at the time of concluding the contract for such goods sold under comparable circumstances in the relevant trade sector.[151]

6.1.1 Place where payment to be made

The contract of sale will usually specify how the buyer should make payment, and consequently also the location of where this has to be done. In most international sales contracts, this will usually be arranged via an electronic funds transfer or by means of a documentary credit.

However, the CISG provides default rules in case the contract does not specify where payment has to be made. In such a case, there are two alternatives provided for in the CISG. The general default rule is that payment has to be made at the seller's place of business.[152] If payment must be made in return for the seller or someone else handing over the goods or relevant documents to the buyer, then the place for payment is where such handing-over takes place.[153] Moreover, if the seller changes its place of business after the conclusion of the contract, then the seller is to bear increase in the expenses which are incidental to the payment resulting from this change of location.[154]

6.1.2 Time for payment

As with the method and place of payment, the contract of sale will also usually specify the time for making payment, and the general rule is that the buyer must pay the price on the date fixed in, or determinable on the basis of, the contract, without the seller having to request payment or comply with any formalities

---

150 Art. 14(1) CISG.
151 This provision seems to be in conflict with Art. 14(1) regarding the requirements for a definite proposal: E.A. Farnsworth, "Unification and harmonization of private law" (1996) 27 *Canadian Business Law Review* 48, p.61.
152 Art. 57(1)(a) CISG.
153 Art. 57(1)(b) CISG.
154 Art. 57(2) CISG.

first.[155] The same rule applies where the time for payment is determined on the basis of the CISG.

As a general rule in the absence of a contractual requirement as to the time for payment, payment has to be made when seller places the goods, or the relevant documents, at the buyer's disposal as required by the contract and/or the CISG.[156]

The seller can make payment a pre-condition for handing over the goods or the relevant documents.[157] Moreover, if the contract involves the carriage of the goods, the seller can effectively dispatch the goods subject to a requirement that the goods or documents controlling their disposition will not handed over to the buyer unless the buyer makes payment in return.[158]

Finally, there is no obligation on the buyer to pay the price until it has had an opportunity to examine the goods. However, this rule will not apply if the delivery or payment procedures agreed between the parties would not allow for the buyer to have such an opportunity before making payment.[159]

6.2 To take delivery

The buyer's obligation to take delivery is comparatively straightforward and comprises two aspects. First, the buyer has to do whatever could reasonably be expected of it to enable the seller to make delivery.[160] Secondly, the buyer has to take over the goods.[161]

7. Remedies of the seller

The CISG provides a number of remedies for the seller for breaches of contract by the buyer. As with the buyer's remedies in respect of breaches of contract by the seller, the seller's remedies primarily seek to ensure the performance of the buyer's obligations under the contract and the CISG. There are several specific, performance-focused remedies available to the seller, alongside the possibility of claiming damages.[162] Claiming one of the specific remedies will not preclude the seller from claiming damages, as well.[163]

7.1 Seller may require buyer to perform

The general remedy available to the seller is to require the buyer to pay for the goods, take delivery of the goods, or to perform any other obligation, unless the

---

155 Art. 59.
156 Art. 58(1) CISG.
157 *Ibid.*
158 Art. 58(2) CISG.
159 Art. 58(3) CISG.
160 Art. 60(a) CISG.
161 Art. 60(b) CISG.
162 Art. 61(1) CISG.
163 Art. 61(2) CISG.

seller has also sought to exercise a remedy that would be inconsistent with requiring performance (such as avoiding the contract).[164]

7.2 Seller may fix additional period for performance

As we saw earlier, the contract (or the default rules of the CISG) will usually determine the time when and how the buyer has to pay the price, and to take delivery. Where the buyer has failed to do so, the seller may wish to give the buyer a further opportunity to perform its obligations. The seller is therefore able to set a further period, of a reasonable length, within which the buyer must perform its obligations.[165] During this additional period of time for performance, the seller cannot exercise any other remedy so as to give the buyer a chance to perform its obligations. However, if the buyer gives notice to the seller that it will not perform during this additional period either, then the seller may opt for one of the other remedies instead.[166] In any case, the seller's right to claim damages remains unaffected.

7.3 Seller may declare contract avoided

In some instances, the seller will be able to bring the contract to an end by declaring it avoided. There are only two instances when this will be possible: the first is where the buyer's breach of contract or of any of its obligations under the CISG is so serious as to constitute a fundamental breach.[167] The second instance arises only if the seller has given the buyer an additional period of time within which to pay the price or take delivery of the goods in accordance with Art. 63 CISG, but the buyer has either failed to do so by the new due date, or has told the seller that it will not do so.[168] The consequences of the seller's decision to exercise the right of avoidance have already been discussed earlier in the context of the buyer's right of avoidance.[169]

However, there are limitations on the seller's right of avoidance, which apply if the buyer has paid the price for the goods, and so the breach of contract concerns other matters than payment of the price. In this situation, the seller will lose the right to avoid the contract, except in the following circumstances: first, the buyer has performed its obligations late, and the seller had not yet become aware of the buyer's performance when the right to avoid the contract was exercised.[170] Secondly, for other breaches, the right is lost once a reasonable period of time has passed from the point at which the seller knew, or ought to have known, about

164 Art. 62 CISG.
165 Art. 63(1) CISG.
166 Art. 63(2) CISG.
167 Art. 64(1)(a) CISG.
168 Art. 64(1)(b) CISG.
169 See 5.2.3, above.
170 Art. 64(2)(i) CISG.

the breach. It will similarly be lost after a reasonable time after the additional period for performance fixed by the seller has expired, or after the buyer has stated its refusal to perform within this additional period.[171]

7.4 Seller's obligation to preserve goods

In certain circumstances, the buyer's failure to perform its obligations can trigger a duty on the seller to preserve the goods.[172] This will arise where the buyer has delayed taking delivery of the goods, or where the buyer was required to pay the price on delivery but has failed to do so. Whilst the seller is still in possession of the goods, or still able to control their disposition, it is required to take whatever steps would be reasonable in the circumstances to preserve the goods.[173] This is likely to be of particular importance where the goods are at risk of deterioration or perishing. The seller is entitled to retain the goods until the seller has been reimbursed for its reasonable expenses by the buyer. If the buyer fails to correct its non-performance and the seller avoids the contract, the seller will be able to recover its losses by way of damages.

8. Damages and interest

In addition to the specific remedies for the buyer and seller, as discussed in sections 5 and 7 above, both parties are also able to claim damages. The basis on which damages can be awarded are the same for both parties.

8.1 Damages: general rules

The basic measure of damages to which a party may be entitled is the sum which is equal to the loss which that party has suffered as a consequence of the breach of contract by the other party.[174] There has to be a causal link between the breach of contract and the losses claimed for. Such losses expressly include a loss of profits.[175] However, in order to limit the kinds of losses for which a party can recover, there is a requirement of foreseeability, and not every loss that could conceivably be described as a consequence of the breach will be recoverable. Article 74 CISG provides that damages may not exceed those losses which the party in breach foresaw, or ought to have foreseen, at the time when the contract of sale was concluded. Relevant factors for determining what the party in breach did foresee or should have foreseen are determined with reference to the facts and matters this party knew or ought to have known would arise as possible consequence of breach.

171 Art. 64(2)(ii) CISG.
172 See 5.3.1 for the rights and obligations on the party charged with preserving the goods.
173 Art. 85 CISG.
174 Art. 74 CISG.
175 *Ibid.*

In addition to limiting recoverable losses to those which were foreseeable, the innocent party is placed under a duty to mitigate its losses. Article 77 CISG requires the innocent party to take such measures as are reasonable in the circumstances to mitigate its loss. A failure to take such steps would allow the party in breach to claim that the overall damages it is liable for should be reduced by a sum based on the losses which would not have been suffered, had the innocent party taken reasonable steps to mitigate its losses.

8.2 Damages after avoidance and substitute transaction

As seen above, both buyer and seller are entitled to avoid the contract in certain circumstances. As a result of exercising that right, the innocent party's expectations under the contract will not have been met: a buyer will not have received the goods expected, and a seller will be left with unsold goods. In either instance, the innocent party may have to enter into a substitute transaction, not least in order to fulfil its duty to mitigate its losses. Thus, an innocent buyer will endeavour to source replacement goods, and an innocent seller will try to resell those goods to another buyer. However, a buyer sourcing replacement goods might have to pay a higher price; similarly, a seller reselling the goods to another buyer might only obtain a lower price. Article 75 CISG therefore provides that in either situation, the damages awarded to the innocent party should include the difference between contract price and price paid, or obtained, for the goods in the substitute transaction. Additional losses would be recoverable in accordance with Art. 74 CISG. However, if there is no substitute transaction, then damages should be calculated by taking the difference between the contract price and the current price for the goods at it was at the time of avoidance, as well as additional losses.[176] The current price is defined as the price prevailing at the place where the goods should have been delivered.[177] In the absence of a current price at that place, the current price at a reasonably comparable place should be used instead.

8.3 Interest

In addition to damages, the CISG also provides for the imposition of interest in respect of any late payments, whether of the price or any other charges (cost of inspection; customs charges) which are due. Article 78 states that, if a party fails to pay the price or any other sum which is in arrears, the other party is entitled to interest on the overdue sum. This is separate, and therefore without prejudice, to any damages claim which the other party might have.

---

176 Art. 76(1) CISG. If the contract was avoided after the party claiming damages had taken over the goods (which will usually be the buyer), the relevant date for establishing the current price is date of taking over goods.
177 Art. 76(2) CISG.

9. Other common provisions

9.1 Anticipatory breach

The availability of the remedies discussed above is generally triggered by a breach of contract by one of the parties, i.e., the breach must have occurred before any of the remedies can be exercised. However, there are instances when it becomes clear to one party that the other party will not perform some or all of its obligations under the contract. At that point, there is no actual breach of contract yet, but one party "anticipates" a breach by the other party. It would be a waste of time and resources for one party to continue its performance if there was a serious doubt about the likelihood that the other party will perform its obligations; however, if that party also suspended its performance, then it might be at risk of breaching the contract of sale itself. The CISG contains several provisions in order to deal with a situation when an anticipatory breach is likely and the other party wishes to suspend its performance.

Article 71(1) spells out when a party may suspend its performance because of concerns about performance by the other party. Thus, a party may suspend its performance if it becomes clear (after the contract has been concluded) that the other party will not perform a substantial part of its obligations. The other party's inability may be (i) due to a serious deficiency in that party's ability to perform its obligations; (ii) due to a serious deficiency in its creditworthiness; or (iii) based on that party's conduct in preparing its performance or the performance rendered up to that point. The party suspending its performance in these circumstances must give notice of its decision to the other party immediately. If the other party then is able to give an adequate assurance that it will perform, the party intending to suspend its obligations must continue with its performance.[178]

In a situation where the seller seeks to suspend its performance for an anticipatory breach by the buyer, but has already dispatched the goods, then the seller can prevent the goods from being handed over to the buyer, even if the buyer already has the document entitling it to take possession of the goods.

Whereas Art. 71 deals with an anticipatory breach suggesting that one party will not perform a substantial part of its obligations, Art. 72 addresses the type of anticipatory breach which would amount to a fundamental breach of the contract if it materialises. As the remedy for a fundamental breach is for the innocent party to declare the contract avoided, this route is also available in the case of an anticipatory breach, i.e., where it is clear before the date of performance that one party will commit a fundamental breach. Time permitting, the party seeking to avoid the contract in these circumstances must give reasonable notice to the other party, so as to give that party the opportunity to provide adequate assurance that it will be able to perform its obligations.[179] However, if the other party has made it clear that it

---

178 Art. 71(3) CISG.
179 Art. 72(2) CISG.

will not perform, then this anticipatory breach justifies immediate avoidance of the contract.[180]

9.2 Instalment deliveries

In many international commercial contracts, the goods which are the subject of the contract will not all be delivered at once, but instead delivered over time. This will particularly be the case where the contract envisages a regular supply of a raw material to be used by the buyer in the manufacture of a finished product. The CISG contains a set of rules which deal with a failure of one party to perform its obligations in respect of a particular instalment. Where this constitutes a fundamental breach in respect of that instalment, the other party is entitled to avoid the contract in respect of that instalment,[181] i.e., there is a right to partial avoidance. An example where this might occur is where a seller has failed to deliver an instalment by the due date, and the buyer subsequently set an additional period within which the seller should have delivered. At that point, the seller's failure would be a fundamental breach in respect of that instalment, and so the buyer can exercise this right to partial avoidance.

Furthermore, if a party's failure to perform in respect of one instalment suggests to the other party that a fundamental breach will occur in respect of the future instalments, the other party, acting within reasonable time, can declare the contract avoided with prospective effect.[182] The important point here is that this is not the same as avoidance of the contract as a whole, assuming that the parties' respective obligations with regard to earlier instalments were performed.

Finally, if a buyer has declared the contract avoided in respect of one delivery, and if deliveries under the contract are interdependent and the other deliveries can consequently no longer be used for their intended purpose, then the buyer can declare the contract avoided in respect of both previous and future deliveries.[183]

9.3 Exemption from liability to perform

The CISG deals with two instances when a party who would otherwise be liable for a failure to perform its obligation is exempt from that liability. The first is where the failure to perform is due to a matter beyond the party's control; the second is where the failure of one party to perform was brought about by the other party.

9.3.1 Impediment beyond party's control

The first situation concerns a party which has failed to perform its obligations, but where this was due to an "impediment beyond his control" which that party could

---

180 Art. 72(3) CISG.
181 Art. 73(1) CISG.
182 Art. 73(2) CISG.
183 Art. 73(3) CISG.

not reasonably have been expected to have taken into account at the time of contracting, or have avoided or overcome it or its consequences.[184] Provided that this can be proven as the reason for the failure to perform, then that party will not be liable for such failure. This exemption from liability only applies for the duration of the impediment.[185] Moreover, notice must be given to the other party that there is an impediment and how this has affected the ability to perform the contract.[186] Such notice must be received by the other party within a reasonable time once the party who is unable to perform realised, or should have realised, that an impediment has arisen. Failure to do so will allow the other party to claim damages for any losses resulting from the fact that notice was not received.

Finally, where a party cannot perform its obligations because of a failure by a third party it has engaged to perform, then that party will only be exempt from liability if it is exempt for inability to perform due to this impediment, and the third party would also be exempt on the same basis.

9.3.2 Party's failure to perform caused by other party

A second exemption for liability of one party for not performing some or all of its obligations is provided in Article 80 CISG. It applies if the failure of one party to perform was caused by an act or omission of the other party, then the other party cannot use this failure to perform as a basis for seeking a remedy under the CISG.

10. Conclusions

The CISG is one of the most ratified International Commercial Law conventions. It has given rise to a great deal of case-law, and an even greater amount of scholarly writings, and both continue to grow in volume. From that perspective alone, the CISG is undoubtedly a remarkable achievement. However, anyone familiar with the law on the sale of goods will look at the substance of the CISG and will not see much that is innovative. It is true that the CISG adopts an approach which straddles the line between different approaches in national sale of goods regimes, e.g., by prioritising the performance of the contract over termination in case of breach. However, its broad scope also suggests that there was not much concern over the identification of specific obstacles to international sales transactions. Instead, the harmonisation of international sales law seems to be its over-arching objective. And in a way, it has succeeded, because more and more countries have ratified the CISG, and its role as the dominant legal regime for international sales transactions seems assured. Yet, one can see why Stephan concluded that "the Convention inflicts no great injury, but it seems a somewhat hollow accomplishment".[187] Whilst that might be striking too negative a

---

184 Art. 79(1) CISG.
185 Art. 79(3) CISG.
186 Art. 79(4) CISG.
187 P.B. Stephan, "The futility of unification and harmonization in international commercial law" (1999) 39 *Virginia Journal of International Law* 743, p.779.

tone, there is some truth in the suggestion that the CISG was neither revolutionary nor innovative, but at the same time offers something which appeals to a wide number of countries and commercial actors alike. It therefore seems right to say that the CISG has served the "primary key purpose to serve as an acceptable set of default rules for international transactions [and] to increase certainty and predictability for commercial parties".[188]

---

188 U.G. Schroeter, "Has the UN Sales Convention achieved its key purpose(s)?" in D. Saidov, *Research Handbook on International and Comparative Sale of Goods Law* (Elgar, 2019).

5

AGENCY

1. Introduction

Commerce has always relied on intermediaries to assist with growing the customer base of a business. This is common in a domestic setting, but in international commerce, there is a much greater need for such intermediaries. Any business which seeks to expand into new markets will have to develop an appropriate strategy for attracting customers from those markets. One way of doing so is simply to rely on advertising, and perhaps an online presence, in the hope that this might result in orders from new markets. However, such a passive strategy may not yield many new orders, so a more strategic way of growing a customer base would be required. One such strategy involves the use of intermediaries in the target jurisdiction. The advantage of doing so is that such intermediaries will have knowledge about local market conditions, customs, and the conduct of commercial negotiations in the target country. Enabling such intermediaries to proactively seek new customers, negotiate and possibly conclude contracts, could be an effective way of creating new business. A local intermediary might be more trusted than a salesperson from another country, and might therefore be able to secure orders better than a representative of that business from its home jurisdiction.

In law, these types of intermediaries are usually referred to as "agents". An agent is someone who has been authorised by someone else, the agent's "principal", to do certain things on behalf of that principal. Such an authorisation may be very broad and allow an agent to negotiate and conclude contracts with a third party without restriction, although often, some limit on that authorisation is stipulated by the principal. In some instances, the law will recognise that the agent has the power to act on behalf of their principal without having been authorised. The effect of agency is that the agent will take all the steps which are necessary to conclude a contract, but the final contract will then bind the principal and the third party only, with the agent usually having no further involvement.

DOI: 10.4324/9781315692807-5

The role of agents in international commerce seems obvious, and it is not surprising that there is an international convention which seeks to provide a uniform regime on agency law in international commerce. This is the UNIDROIT Geneva Convention on Agency in the International Sale of Goods, which was adopted in 1983.[1] However, the Convention has never entered into force, as only 5 of the 10 ratifications required for the Convention to come into effect have occurred. In this chapter, we will examine the substance of the Agency Convention and identify why it might have failed to gain sufficient acceptance to enter into force.

2. What is agency?

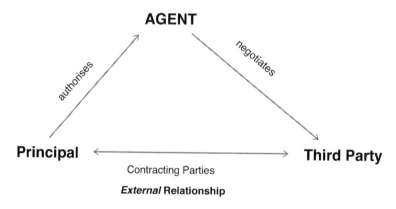

FIGURE 5.1. Elements of agency

As we have seen, businesses need many people to act on their behalf to find customers and to negotiate and conclude contracts. Businesses which have been incorporated are legal constructs and cannot act for themselves, so need individuals to act on their behalf. These individuals are known as "agents" in law.[2] The person on whose behalf an agent acts is known as the "principal". The essence of agency is that an agent has certain powers to bring about legal relationships between its principal and a third party. For our purposes, this will be the negotiation and conclusion of a contract. The agent's power to bind its principal is based on the authorisation which the principal has given to the agent. Such authorisation may be based on a formal contract, but could also be based on the appointment of the agent to a particular role, perhaps indicated by a job

---

1   For a useful account of its history, see M. Bonnell, "The 1983 Geneva Convention on Agency in the International Sale of Goods" (1984) 32 *American Journal of Comparative Law* 717.

2   For a concise overview of the English law on agency, see, e.g., H. Bennett, *Principles of the Law of Agency* (Hart, 2013). Most standard textbooks on English commercial law contain chapters on agency.

title, which brings with it a usual set of powers to act on behalf of and bind the principal.

The authority which a principal confers on an agent can be express or implied. It is express when the principal has set out in detail what the agent is empowered to do. Authority will be implied when the principal has given the agent a task, or a range of tasks, which necessitates that the agent is empowered to do certain things. This kind of authority is sometimes referred to as "usual" authority, i.e., the authority that usually comes with the particular task the agent has been engaged to carry out. Moreover, where an agent has been given express powers to act, there may still be certain matters which have not been set out in detail, but which are essential, and such matters are "incidental" to the authority which has been given. For example, if an agent has been appointed to sell espresso machines, then the agent may have to demonstrate how the machine works, and perhaps allow a prospective customer to test the machine, and the agent may have to purchase a quantity of coffee in order to do this. It would be strange if a principal were to deny that this agent was authorised to do this, and the agent's authority would be recognised as incidental to the main task it has to undertake. These different instances of an agent's authority are commonly known as *actual* authority.

As we will see later, an agent may also at times act without having been authorised by the principal, and the agent's actions would not be covered by the authority usual for its role, or incidental to what the principal has authorised the agent to do. In that case, there would not normally be any legal relationship between principal and third party, although the agent may be liable towards the third party for any financial losses the third party has suffered. However, in some instances, despite the absence of actual authority conferred by the principal, the law will recognise that from the third party's perspective, the agent's actions appeared to be within that agent's authority, and that the third party should therefore be able to hold the principal to the contract seemingly concluded by the agent on the principal's behalf. This is known as *apparent* or *ostensible* authority. Where the law recognises that the agent had apparent authority, the third party will therefore be able to hold the principal to the contract. However, in domestic law, the principal will have recourse against the agent for exceeding its authority. If, however, the law does not recognise apparent authority for the contract concluded with the third party, the agent will be liable to the third party for any loss it has suffered.

Moreover, if the agent has acted without any authority, the principal may nevertheless authorise the agent retrospectively. This is known as *ratification* of the contract by the principal. The legal effect is that the principal and third party will be bound by the contract negotiated by the agent in the same way as if the agent had been authorised from the outset.

So far, we have assumed that the third party knows that it is dealing with an agent, and so is fully aware that the agent is acting on behalf of a different person. However, there may be instances when the existence of the agency relationship is not disclosed to the third party, and the third party dealing with the agent will assume that this is, in fact, the person with whom it will enter into a contract. This might not make much difference as long as the transaction in question is performed as both parties expect; however, once there is a problem, the principal may wish to intervene, or the third party which has discovered the true state of affairs may wish to take action against the principal. The question of how to deal with an "undisclosed principal" is often mentioned as a typical instance where common law and civil law take divergent views, with the former accepting the possibility that a principal may be undisclosed and yet the contract negotiated by the agent will bind principal and third party, whereas the civil law will not recognise the principal as being party to the transaction at all.[3] However, it is important to appreciate that this is not a simple juxtaposition; in particular, there are differences as between individual civil law jurisdictions.[4]

In this chapter, we will see how the Agency Convention deals with some of these issues. However, it is important to note here that the Convention focuses on the effects of an agent's action on the *external* relationship, i.e., the relationship between principal and third party, and how the agent brings this about.[5] One significant omission from the Agency Convention is the *internal* relationship between principal and agent, in particular what should happen if the agent acts without authority and causes loss to the principal (e.g., because the third party can enforce the contract on the basis of apparent authority), or the way an agent is remunerated for its efforts in finding customers for the principal.

3. UNIDROIT Convention on Agency in the International Sale of Goods 1983

3.1 Scope

3.1.1 Agency in contracts for the international sale of goods

The Agency Convention only applies to agency relationships for contracts for the sale of goods,[6] and covers the conclusion of the contract itself, as well as the steps leading up to its conclusion and its subsequent performance.[7] However, this does not seem to include agents where there is no authority to conclude contracts on the principal's behalf – it is only concerned with the conclusion of contracts by the agent with third parties on behalf of the principal. Moreover, the Convention applies whether or not

---

3 M. Bonnell, "The 1983 Geneva Convention on Agency in the International Sale of Goods" (1984) 32 *American Journal of Comparative Law* 717, pp.718–720.
4 K. Grönfors, "Unification of agency as a legislative challenge" (1998) *Uniform Law Review* 467, p.473. This article also provides a useful account of the differences between the common law and the civil law, including some of the nuances within the civil law jurisdictions.
5 Cf. Art. 1(3).
6 Art. 1(1).
7 Art. 1(2).

the agent is acting in its own name, or in the name of the principal.[8] This means that the Convention's scope is not limited to instances where the agency relationship is disclosed, but can also cover those circumstances where the agent is acting in its own name, but, in reality, on behalf of an undisclosed principal. However, as we will see, the role of undisclosed agency under the Convention is more limited than it would be in those common law jurisdictions which recognised undisclosed agency.

As with all other International Commercial Law conventions, it only applies to agency relationships with an international dimension. Article 2 determines stipulates when the internationality requirement is met. As there are three parties in an agency set-up, this is more complex than, e.g., under the Convention for the International Sale of Goods (CISG).[9] First, the principal and third party must have their places of business[10] in different States. This mirrors the requirement in Art. 1(1)(a) CISG, although for the purposes of the Agency Convention, these States need not be Contracting States. Secondly, the agent must have its place of business in a Contracting State. This means that the connecting factor for engaging the Convention is solely based on the agent's place of business. In practice, the agent's place of business could be in the same State as that of either principal or third party, although this would not be essential. The Agency Convention therefore could apply where neither principal nor third party have their place of business in a Contracting State. A familiar alternative to the second element of the internationality criterion is that the rules of private international law would lead to the application of the law of a Contracting State.[11] If principal and agent have chosen an applicable law to govern the contract between them which is the law of a Contracting State, then the Convention would apply. In the absence of a choice, the relevant rules of private international law would determine this.[12]

There is an additional requirement for instances where the third party did not know, nor ought to have known, that the agent was acting as an agent at the time of entering into the contract. As well as satisfying one of the two combinations set out above, it will also be required that both agent and third party have their places of business in different Contracting States.[13]

---

8   Art. 1(4).
9   See Chapter 4.
10 In the case of parties with multiple places of business, the one with the closest connection to the contract of sale will be the relevant one: Art. 8(a). In the absence of a place of business, a party's habitual residence is used instead: Art. 8(b).
11 Note Art. 28, which permits a declaration by a Contracting State not to be bound by this provision.
12 Note that the Hague Convention on the Law applicable to Agency 1978 would, in the absence of choice by the parties, point to the law of the country where the agent has its business establishment or habitual residence (Art. 6(1)), except where the agent will primarily act in the country where the principal's business establishment/habitual residence is located (Art. 6(2)). However, this Convention only applies in four countries (Argentina, France, Netherlands and Portugal).
13 Art. 2(2).

3.1.2 Exclusions

Several instances which might fall within the Convention's broad conception of agency are excluded by Articles 3 and 4. Thus, the Convention does not apply to the agency of a dealer on a financial market, nor to that of an auctioneer.[14] Moreover, agency situations arising by operation of law from family, matrimonial or succession law are excluded.[15] Other exclusions concern agency arising from a statutory or judicial authorisation of a person to act on behalf of a person who does not have any capacity to act, and agency which arises as result of a decision by a judicial or quasi-judicial authority.[16] Furthermore, a person acting for a company, association or partnership or similar (irrespective of whether this has separate legal personality) is not treated as an agent insofar as that person is acting under any authority conferred by law or the constitutive documents of the company or partnership.[17] Such a person would still be regarded as an agent if the authority in issue was simply conferred, e.g., under a contract of employment, though. Finally, a trustee is deemed to be neither an agent of the trust, its creator or its beneficiaries.[18]

3.1.3 Party autonomy

The provisions of the Convention are not mandatory law, and the autonomy of the parties to exclude, limit or vary the application of the Convention to a specific situation is preserved by Art. 5. Any agreement not to apply the Convention as it is has to be made by the principal and the third party, although the agent can do so if acting under the express or implied instructions of its principal. However, Article 5 cannot be relied on if a Contracting State requires that the authorisation of an agent, the ratification of an unauthorised act, or the termination of the agent's authority, has to be made in writing and the Contracting State in question has made a declaration to apply this to those provisions of the Convention which would otherwise not require writing to be used.[19]

3.1.4 Interpretation

Article 6 of the Agency Convention replicates the interpretation provision from Art. 7 CISG. Thus, regard must be had to the Convention's international character (autonomous interpretation), the need to promote uniformity in its application, and the observance of good faith in international trade. Moreover, any gaps

---

14 Art. 3(1)(a) and (b).
15 Art. 3(1)(c).
16 Art. 3(1)(d) and (e).
17 Art. 4(a).
18 Art. 4(b).
19 See Arts. 11 and 27. The relevant provisions are Art. 10, Art. 15 or Chapter IV of the Convention.

("matters governed by this Convention which are not expressly settled in it") need to be addressed on the basis of the general principles on which the Convention is based, or, insofar as there are no such principles, on the basis of the applicable law. The corresponding provision was discussed in detail in Chapter 3, and the observations made there are also relevant for present purposes.

3.1.5 Usages

Article 7 deals with usages and established practices. Usages are relevant as between principal or agent, and the third party. They are bound by any usages to which they have agreed. Moreover, unless there is an agreement to the contrary, they will also be bound by any usages of which they know (or ought to have known), and which are both widely known and regularly observed by parties to agency relationships in the particular trade concerned. Moreover, principal or agent, and third party, will be bound by any practices which they have established between themselves. This provision also mirrors the corresponding provision in the CISG, as discussed in Chapter 1.

3.2 Establishment and scope of agent's authority

Chapter II of the Agency Convention deals with the establishment and scope of an agent's authority. There are no formal requirements in order to authorise an agent to act on behalf of a principal; in particular, this need not be done in writing.[20] If there is a dispute about the authority of an agent, any means of proof is permissible. This reflects the general attitude in International Commercial Law conventions that there are few, if any, formal requirements.

An agent can be authorised expressly or impliedly. Express authorisation might, for example, be done through a contract between principal and agent, but an informal arrangement would suffice. A basic e-mail which clearly reflects the willingness of the principal to engage the agent and which sets out what the agent is authorised to do might suffice, for example. Often, an agent will be appointed to a particular role, and this will bring with it the kind of authority that a person in that role would usually have. In that case, there is no need to spell out the extent of the agent's authority expressly, and the authority which ordinarily comes with the role in question will be implied. However, this does not preclude the principal from adding express limitations on an agent's authority, e.g., by setting a maximum value for each contract concluded by the agent.

In addition, the Convention also deems an agent to have been authorised to carry out "all acts necessary in the circumstances to achieve the purposes for which authorisation was given". This provision avoids any doubt about whether acts of an agent which were not expressly mentioned, but are incidental in order to ensure the agent is able to carry out its duties effectively, are covered by this authorisation. A principal

---

20 Art. 10. This is subject to Art. 11 and Art. 27 declarations.

should not be able to refuse to be bound by such incidental acts of the agent, nor claim that the agent has acted in breach of the agency agreement.

3.3 Legal effects of acts carried out by agent

Chapter III of the Convention focuses on the legal effects of the acts carried out by the agent. In addition to dealing with acts which fall within the agent's authority as determined by Chapter II, it also covers circumstances where the existence of a principal has not been disclosed, and acts which fall outside the agent's authority.

3.3.1 Acts within agent's authority

The first situation is the most straightforward one: where the agent acts within the scope of its authority, and the third party with whom the agent was dealing knew, or ought to have known, that the agent was acting in that capacity, then the legal effect is that the agent's acts result in a contract between principal and third party.[21] Where the authority is conferred under a contract, the terms of that contract will set out the extent of the agent's authority. This would be subject to Art. 9(2) on an agent's incidental authority.

However, if the circumstances suggest that the agent undertakes to be the party to the contract (e.g., in the case of a commission contract), then the contract will be between agent and third party, notwithstanding the fact that the agent might also have been authorised by the principal to act as agent.

3.3.2 Acts by an undisclosed agent

We noted earlier that there may be instances when the existence of a principal is undisclosed, and the third party will therefore assume that it is dealing with the agent as a principal. Broadly speaking, the common law would permit a principal to intervene in some circumstances and effectively replace the agent as the seeming contract party, although this will only be possible where the agent acted within the scope of its actual authority (which is logical, as apparent authority is considered from the third party's perspective, and until the principal is disclosed, the third party will not know that the agent is in fact an agent). In contrast, civil law jurisdictions broadly require that the agent has to be acting on behalf of, *and in the name of*, the principal, which means that the idea of an undisclosed principal is not accepted at all. In a situation where the agent does not disclose that it is acting for a principal, the contract will simply be one with agent and third party as the contracting parties. *Prima facie*, the approaches taken by the common law and civil law respectively seem irreconcilable. Nevertheless, both disclosed and undisclosed agency are within the scope of the Convention.[22]

---

21 Art. 12.
22 Art. 1(4).

Furthermore, in the substantive rules of the Convention, an attempt was made to find a compromise which would, on the one hand, take into account the position in the civil law that a contract negotiated by an agent who has not disclosed that it is acting on behalf of a principal is one which binds only agent and third party, and on the other, the circumstances when enabling a principal to be disclosed might be necessary when there has been a failure to carry out the transaction as agreed. The compromise adopted in the Agency Convention seeks to reflect this in Article 13.

The starting point is that if there is a situation where the third party had no knowledge of the existence of an agency relationship, or where the circumstances indicate that the agent intends to bind itself only, then the effect is that only agent and third party are legally bound. In essence, this is the way in which the civil law treats instances of an undisclosed agency relationship. The matter could have been left there, but, in order to acknowledge the different treatment of undisclosed agency at common law, two instances were included in the Agency Convention when an undisclosed principal can be disclosed, and then sue, or be sued by, the third party directly. However, it is important to bear in mind that the Convention provides that the contract is only between agent and third party. This does not change as a result of the provisions in Art. 13: although the principal gains a limited right of intervention (as well as being the target of action by the third party), this does not have the effect of making the principal a party to the contract with the third party.

So, what is the effect of Art. 13? If the contract is one for the supply of goods to the third party, the principal will supply those goods to the agent, or possibly directly to the third party, and the third party will then pay the agent. As between principal and agent, the agent will be required to pay the principal for those goods. Alternatively, if the contract is one for the purchase of goods, the principal will provide the necessary funds to the agent, who will pay the third party and will receive the goods from the third party in return. Conversely, the agent will need the co-operation of the principal in order to fulfil its obligations towards the third party. Thus, where the agent is selling the principal's goods, the agent needs the principal to deliver the correct goods either to the agent or directly to the third party. Where the agent is buying goods for the principal, the agent needs the principal to provide it with the necessary funds to pay the third party.

As long as all of this happens in such a way that the transaction is completed as all parties expect, then it does not matter, at least from a practical perspective, that the agency was not disclosed. However, if either principal or third party fail to do what is required for the performance of the transaction, then the agent will be in a difficult position. Take the example of a contract for the supply of the principal's goods to the third party, and assume that the third party, having taken delivery of the goods, now refuses to pay. Having handed over the goods, the principal expects the agent to forward the payment, but the agent is unable to do so. As the agent is the only person in a contractual relationship with the third party, the agent would now have to sue the third party for payment of the price, or, if the principal sues the agent for payment of the price, the agent's claim against the third party might become part of the proceedings.

In order to short-circuit this, the Agency Convention contains a mechanism which would enable the principal to take action directly against the third party. The trigger point for this is that the agent is unable to fulfil its obligations towards the principal. First, the agent would be obliged to tell the principal who the third party is.[23] Secondly, the principal can then take action against the third party in the same way as the agent could have done – the "principal can exercise against the third party the rights acquired for him by the agent".[24] However, before the principal can do this, it must give notice to both the agent and the third party of its intention to act against the third party directly. Once notice has been given, the third party cannot escape a claim by the principal by then performing its contractual obligations under the contract with the agent.[25]

There are then two further important qualifications to this right: first, if the third party could raise a defence when sued by the agent, then that defence could similarly be raised against the principal. One instance might be where the third party could rely on the right of set-off against the agent, e.g., where the third party might be entitled to a reduction in the price to be paid to the agent. Secondly, the principal cannot act against the third party where the circumstances show that the third party would not have contracted with the principal, had the third party known of the principal's identity.[26] Quite what might be required here is not clear, though. It may be that third party and agent had an unhappy experience in the past, which might justify the agent's refusal. The difficulty is that the Convention does not indicate whether the agent must have reasonable grounds for any such refusal which existed at the time the contract in issue was concluded.

In the converse situation where the principal has not done what it should do to allow the agent to perform the contract with the third party, the agent has to communicate the principal's name to the third party.[27] The third party can then sue the principal directly to enforce the rights it has under the contract with the agent, but, once again, only after having given notice.[28] However, again, this is subject to any defences which the agent would have against the third party, if sued by the third party. In addition, any defences which the principal might be able to raise against the agent could also be raised against the third party.

This is an attempt to find a way of reconciling the conflicting approaches to undisclosed agency between the common law and civil law. Crucially, it does not change the fact that the contract is only binding on agent and third party. The disclosure of the undisclosed principal only permits action in respect of the

---

23 Art. 13(5).
24 Art. 13(2)(b).
25 Art. 13(3).
26 Art. 13(6).
27 Art. 13(4).
28 Art. 13(3).

particular non-performance which has occurred, but does not have the effect of making the principal a party to the contract; otherwise, the third party and principal would be directly bound towards one another in respect of other elements of the contract, such as future deliveries.

3.3.3 Unauthorised acts

So far, we have considered those instances where the agent acts within the authority conferred on it by the principal. We now need to turn to how the Agency Convention deals with acts by an agent, purportedly done on behalf of the principal, but without authority. The basic position is as simple as it is unsurprising: Article 14(1) states that where an agent acts beyond the scope of its authority, or without any authority, the agent's acts do not bind the principal and third party to one another. This is a fundamental aspect of agency law: only those acts which have been authorised can bind a principal, because the agent is given the power to create or alter legal relationships affecting the principal, without the principal reviewing or consenting to this on each occasion.

However, the third party may not always know whether an agent is acting within or beyond its authority. For example, an agent may have been appointed to sell the principal's goods in a new country, but the maximum order value the agent can agree with any one customer is £50,000. A third party wishing to place an order with a higher value is unlikely to know of this limitation, and the agent may agree to the order if it seems particularly lucrative. However, the agent has now acted beyond its authority, and principal and third party would not normally be bound. From a commercial perspective, the advantage of the bright-line rule in Art. 14(1) is also a disadvantage, as it might catch out a third party which is unaware of the limits on an agent's authority, and might reasonably expect that the scope of the agent's authority is wider, e.g., because this would be usual for agents of this type.

So in order to balance the need to protect the principal against unauthorised acts by its agent with the need to promote commercial activity, Art. 14(2) provides some protection for the third party. It provides that, where the principal's conduct leads the third party to believe that the agent has authority for the act in question, and this belief is held reasonably and in good faith, then the principal cannot claim that the agent's act was unauthorised. What this means is that the third party can seek to enforce a contract against the principal, and the principal cannot resist that claim on the basis that the agent exceeded its authority. This is a derogation from the basic principle that an agent's acts must have been authorised which is common to jurisdictions around the world, and is variously known as "apparent" authority or "ostensible" authority. A crucial aspect of this provision is that the principal has, through its actions, created the impression that the agent has the required authority to conclude the contract in question. The provision would not assist a third party where the agent has claimed to have been authorised by the principal.

3.3.4 Ratification of unauthorised acts

In addition to the derogation in Art. 14(2), there is a further mechanism through which unauthorised acts can be turned into an obligation binding as between principal and agent. This is the process of "ratification", which is essentially a means for a principal to confer retrospective authorisation for the act in question, even though this exceeded the agent's authority. Ratification is possible irrespective of whether the third party was aware of the lack of authority.

Any act by an agent which exceeded the agent's authority, or which was concluded without any authority, can be ratified by the principal. The legal effect of ratification is to treat the agent's act as if it had been authorised at the time it occurred.[29] A ratification becomes effective once notice of it reaches the third party, or the ratification comes to the third party's attention in other ways.[30] The latter instances might be simply the principal delivering the goods to the third party. Once a ratification has become effective, both principal and third party are bound, and the ratification cannot be revoked.[31] There is no particular requirement as to how a principal should ratify an unauthorised act. It could be an express statement to that effect, or be inferred from the principal's conduct (e.g., by the principal starting to perform the contract in question, such as paying for goods ordered by the agent on its behalf).[32] The Convention specifies that ratification is effective even if the act itself could not have been carried out at the time of ratification,[33] e.g., because the principal at the time lacked the relevant capacity.[34]

However, the principal's right to ratify an unauthorised act is not unlimited, and there is some protection given to the third party. The Agency Convention distinguishes between instances where the third party did not know, nor ought to have known, about the agent's lack of authority, and those where it did know. The reason for allowing a third party to resist ratification of authorised acts by the principal is that this retains a degree of balance between principal and third party. A principal might delay a decision to ratify to monitor the market price of the goods in question, and only ratify where the contract would be advantageous to it. A third party should not be exposed to such market speculation by the principal and be kept in limbo indefinitely.

In the former instance, the right of the principal to ratify is restricted in two ways: first, the third party can effectively resist being bound if a notice of refusal to be bound is given to the principal before ratification occurs. This might happen, e.g., where the third party discovers that the agent did not have the relevant authority before the principal ratifies, and the third party seeks to escape the contract. The

---

29 Art. 15(1).
30 Art. 15(5).
31 *Ibid.*
32 Art. 15(8).
33 Art. 15(6).
34 Note the particular provision regarding acts entered into on behalf of a company or other legal entity before it was incorporated in Art. 15(7): such "pre-incorporation contracts" can only be ratified if the law where the legal entity is incorporated so permits. In the UK, the Companies Act 2006, s.51, would preclude such a possibility.

second situation is where the principal ratifies only after a reasonable time has passed, and the third party promptly gives notice of its refusal to accept ratification to the principal. Invariably, determining what would be a reasonable time will be context specific, and might depend on the nature of the goods, the reasons why the third party wanted to buy (or sell) goods, etc.

In the converse situation, where the third party knew or ought to have known about the agent's lack of authority, the third party may either stipulate a reasonable period of time within which the principal has to ratify, or, reach agreement with the principal as to the time by which the principal has to ratify. Once that time has expired, the third party can refuse to become bound by any attempt by the principal to ratify the act.

3.4 Agent's liability towards third party

We have seen above that there are two instances where an unauthorised act by an agent may still result in binding obligations between principal and third party: either the third party can rely on the appearance of authority to hold the principal to the contract, or the principal ratifies the act subsequently and thereby creates a binding obligation between it and the third party. In these two instances, the third party will be able to enforce whatever contract it assumed it had entered into with the principal, notwithstanding the agent's lack of authority.

However, it will not always be possible for the third party to rely on the agent's apparent authority, nor will a principal decide to ratify an unauthorised act. In such circumstances, the third party may incur losses for which it needs to be compensated, e.g., because the third party required the goods for a particular purpose and now has to source replacement goods in the market at a higher price.fig

The obligation to compensate the third party falls on the agent, although it only arises where the third party did not know, nor ought to have known, about the agent's lack of authority.[35] In those circumstances, the agent will be liable to pay the third party "such compensation as will place the third party in same position as he would have been in if the agent had acted with authority and within the scope of his authority".[36] It seems that the effect of this provision is to hold the agent liable for damages in the same way the principal would have been liable for damages for not performing the contract. This is because, had the agent acted within its authority, there would have been a contract between principal and third party. In the absence of such authority, and in light of the refusal by the principal to ratify, there is no such contract, but had there been a contract, either the third party would have received the principal's performance of that contract, or would have been able to sue the principal for breach of that contract. For example, if the contract had been for the sale of goods to the third party, then damages would have been awarded for the principal's failure to deliver the goods, usually based on the difference between the contract price and the

---

35 Art. 16(2).
36 Art. 16(1).

cost of obtaining replacement goods in the market.[37] The effect of Art. 16 is that the agent will now be liable for these losses, notwithstanding the absence of any contract.

There are difficulties with this provision, because it imposes liability on the agent without adding any duties on the third party to mitigate its losses. Moreover, in contrast with Art. 13, which recognises the existence of possible defences which an agent might have against the third party, there is no indication that the agent's liability to pay compensation would be restricted by any defences which the agent might have against the third party, nor, indeed, any defences the principal might have had against the third party. These omissions might be less significant than might be thought: the agent's liability is effectively analogous to the principal's liability, had there been a binding contract, and any claim for damages by the third party against the principal would have been subject to a duty of mitigation under law applicable to that contract. For the same reason, any defences the principal might have had against the third party's claim should be available to the agent, because these would have affected the third party's ability to seek compensation from the principal. This leaves the possibility for the agent to raise any defences it might have against any claims brought by the third party, and for this, the national law governing any proceedings would determine if those defences could be raised.

3.5 Termination of authority

The final substantive chapter is Chapter IV, dealing with the termination of an agent's authority. Such termination may be through natural expiry, e.g., because the authority had been time-limited by the principal, or it might be when the principal decides to terminate the authority for a variety of reasons.

Article 17 sets out the instances when the authority of an agent is terminated. The first of this is where the termination is agreed between principal and agent. This agreement might be part of a contract under which the agent was appointed, e.g., where this was a fixed-term appointment. Alternatively, where the initial authorisation had been on a continuing basis, both parties may agree to bring this arrangement to an end.

The second instance is relevant in circumstances where the agent's authority was granted in respect of one particular transaction, or a specific number of transactions, and these transactions have been completed.[38]

Finally, the principal may simply revoke the agent's authority, or the agent might renounce the grant of authority.[39] In either case, this terminates the agent's authority. The decision by either principal or agent in this situation might be contrary to any agreement they may have concluded about the duration of the agent's authority, and may therefore constitute a breach of that agreement. However, Art. 17(c) makes it clear that the agent's authority is terminated irrespective of whether this would be in

---

37 See Art. 75 CISG.
38 Art. 17(b).
39 Art. 17(c).

accordance with the agreement. This might mean that this provision would override the ability of either party to seek specific enforcement of the contract, although this is not clear from the wording of the Article.

One further instance which results in termination of the agent's authority is where this is the effect of the law applicable to the relationship between the principal and the agent.[40]

It is clear that termination will bring to an end the agent's authorisation, but what does this mean for any third party the agent had been dealing with? The third party may not know about the agent's termination, and if the agent continues to act despite the termination of its authority, the third party may assume that the agent's actions continue to result in a contract between the third party and the principal. This is not dissimilar to the situation dealt with in Art. 14(2) on an agent's apparent authority. Article 19 effectively treats the situation of an agent whose authority has been terminated in a similar way to a situation where the agent acted without authority in the first place but where the principal's conduct has led the third party to believe that the agent had authority, although it expresses this in a much more straightforward fashion. Thus, unless the third party did know, or ought to have known, about the termination of the agent's authority, the fact that the authority has been terminated does not "affect" the third party. This, presumably, means that the third party can proceed as if the agent was still acting with authority and continue to hold the principal bound by any of the agent's actions which fall within the scope of the (terminated) authority, except that there would be no need to prove the criteria of Art. 14(2) or rely on the principal's ratification.

3.6 Final provisions

Articles 21–35 in Chapter 5 deal with a range of non-substantive issues, such as the process of ratification, as well as any permissible declarations to modify the scope of the Convention in relation to the Contracting State making that declaration. We have already noted the option under Art. 27 for a Contracting State to declare that it requires certain actions to be made or evidenced in writing. Article 26(1) deals with the instance where two Contracting States have the same or very similar rules on the matters governed by the Agency Convention. It permits those States to declare that the Convention will not apply to instances where principal and third party (or agent and third party for the purposes of Art. 2(2)) have their places of business in those particular Contracting States. Similarly, Art. 26(2) permits such a declaration where a Contracting State has the same or similar rules as non-Contracting States.

An interesting provision is Article 30, which is effectively a "soft harmonisation" provision. This permits a Contracting State to extend the rules from the Convention to instances which fall outside its scope, such as contracts other than those for the sale of goods, or cases where there is no connection with a Contracting State as required under Art. 2(1).

---

40 Art. 18.

Finally, we may note Art. 33(1), which states that the Convention comes into force a year after 10 States have ratified it. That threshold has not been reached, and only five States ever ratified the Agency Convention: France, Italy, the Netherlands, Mexico and South Africa. As a result, the Convention has never entered into force.

4. Evaluation

The Agency Convention is widely regarded as being unsuccessful, because it has failed to achieve the minimum number of ratifications required. This fact alone may be surprising, because agency is a fundamental aspect of commercial law, and most students of commercial law have to grapple with the principles of domestic agency law as part of their studies.

This lack of enthusiasm cannot be explained purely on the basis that agency is insufficiently relevant to international commerce. Instead, possible reasons for this might be the scope of the Convention, i.e., the matters it addressed, or its substantive provisions. In terms of scope, the Convention is limited to contracts for the international sale of goods. On the one hand, this might have made sense at the time, with this Convention following hot on the heels of the CISG. On the other hand, this is quite a narrow scope and might exclude many other international commercial contracts negotiated by agents. Furthermore, the Convention does not address all aspects of the agency relationship. Crucially, it does not deal with the internal relationship between principal and agent.[41] However, if the main reason for engaging an agent is to negotiate contracts in the jurisdiction where the agent is active, and the principal is located in another jurisdiction, then it might be that this aspect of agency is more likely to raise problems for international commerce than questions of authority.

As far as its substance is concerned, a key objective seems to have been to find a compromise between the different approaches taken to the situation where a principal is undisclosed. One view might be that the solution adopted in Art. 13 might be seen as striking the balance in the right place between generally requiring that the principal is disclosed, but permitting that the principal can sue, or be sued by, the third party in those situations where there has been a failure to perform the contract as agreed. It certainly has the appeal of showing how divergent approaches could be reconciled, but one has to question whether this is more of an intellectual achievement than a solution to a problem which poses an obstacle to international commercial activity. In any case, it may be that, on reflection, this compromise was acceptable from neither perspective. Grönfors concluded his discussion with the observation that the solution adopted in Article 13

---

41 As Bonnell explains, earlier drafts had included provisions on the internal relationship between principal and agent, but a first diplomatic conference for the adoption of the Convention in 1979 failed because no agreement on this issue could be reached. See M. Bonnell, "The 1983 Geneva Convention on Agency in the International Sale of Goods" (1984) 32 *American Journal of Comparative Law* 717, p.724.

seems feasible from a technical standpoint. However, it has the drawback of leaving both the common lawyer and the civil lawyer "in distress": the former cannot recognise his usual machinery for transforming a contract situation into an agency situation, while the latter searches in vain for his usual starting point, viz. the distinction between direct and indirect agency.[42]

In other words, this is a compromise which does not satisfy anyone. It is worth noting that Art. 2.2.4 of the UNIDROIT Principles[43] follows the substance of Art. 13(1) in that an undisclosed principal is not a party to the contract with the third party, but only the agent is; there is no equivalent to the derogation which Art. 13(2) contains.

Without wishing to overstate the point, one could conclude that the Agency Convention shows why harmonisation should not be seen as an end in itself, but rather as an instrument to tackle specific obstacles to international commercial activity. Not every difference between legal systems needs to be overcome by harmonisation, no matter how strange such differences may seem. Had the Convention addressed more of those issues likely to be of practical concern to international commerce instead of reconciling legal differences for the sake of it, the Convention might have stood a better chance of success.[44]

---

42 K. Grönfors, "Unification of agency as a legislative challenge" (1998) *Uniform Law Review* 467, p.474.
43 See Chapter 10.
44 See also M. Bonnell, "The 1983 Geneva Convention on Agency in the International Sale of Goods" (1984) 32 *American Journal of Comparative Law* 717, pp.747–749, for an early discussion of the Convention's shortcomings from a practical perspective, notwithstanding his more favourable view of the compromise in Art. 13 (see p.746).

6

FINANCIAL LEASING

1. Introduction

We have already come across the most common type of commercial contract, the contract for the sale of goods.[1] The purpose of a contract of sale is to transfer two types of interest in goods, ownership and possession of the goods, to the buyer. These two interests can be separated, and so it is possible to transfer possession (and the corresponding right to possession) independently from ownership. For instance, a seller of goods may be willing to transfer possession of the goods to a buyer, but retain ownership in those goods until the buyer has paid for them. Such "retention of title" clauses are common in commercial contracts and can perform the function of a security interest, without necessarily having to be treated as such under a particular domestic law.[2] The reason for including such a term is to manage a risk that commonly arises with commercial transactions where payment for goods is not required on delivery, but instead to be made over time and possibly in instalments. There will be a period of time during which the buyer will have possession of the goods before paying the seller. Should the buyer fail to make payment as required, or become insolvent, a retention of title clause will allow a seller to retake possession of those goods it has supplied which have not yet been consumed or resold.

The possibility to separate ownership and possession has also made it possible to have transactions for the supply of goods other than an outright sale. One of these is a contract under which possession is transferred for a fixed period, without envisaging

---

1   See Chapter 4.
2   In fact, there are variations between jurisdictions as to whether a retention of title clause is a purely contractual arrangement (as is the case in English Law: see *Clough Mill v Martin* [1984] 3 All ER 982), whereas elsewhere, it will be a security interest which has to comply with the formal requirements of the relevant secured transactions rules, such as registration, to be effective.

DOI: 10.4324/9781315692807-6

the transfer of ownership. Such contracts are known as contracts of hire, or leasing contracts. These contracts, and their treatment in International Commercial Law, are the focus of this chapter.

2. Leasing

When we speak of "leasing", we need to deal with two separate categories of leasing. First, there are "operating leases". Here, the person acquiring the goods (the lessee) needs goods for a limited period of time, often for a specific purpose. The owner of those goods (the lessor) will agree to supply the goods in question to the lessee for an agreed period of time, in return for which the lessee will make a payment (whether as a lump-sum or through regular instalments, depending on the duration of the leasing period). The payments will generally reflect the value to the lessee of being able to use the goods and the profit margin for the lessor. At the end of the leasing period, the lessee will return the goods to the lessor, who can then lease the same goods again to another lessor. An operating lease is a standard hire agreement and is commonly used where short-term use of goods is all that is needed. Examples include car hire, hiring construction machinery for a period of time, or scaffolding for construction projects.

The second category is a rather different type of arrangement. This is the finance lease. Rather than the simple two-party arrangement of an operating lease, a finance lease involves three parties: the seller/supplier of the goods in question, a finance company and the person seeking to acquire the goods. Finance leases may be used where the person seeking to acquire the goods does not necessarily wish to become the outright owner of the goods but still wishes to have long-term use of the goods, usually for most of their product life-span. Instead of acquiring those

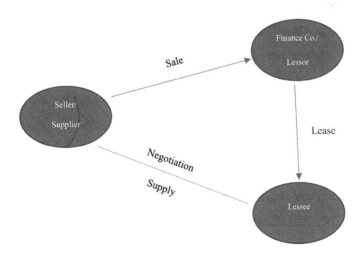

FIGURE 6.1. Structure of a financial leasing transaction

goods directly from the seller/supplier, the goods are sold to a finance company which then enters into a leasing agreement with the lessee.

The basic mechanism of a leasing arrangement is as follows: first, the supplier of the goods and the prospective lessee agree on the goods to be supplied. Then, a finance company – the lessor – agrees to buy the goods from the supplier. The lessor will then enter into a separate contract with the lessee for the supply of the goods in return for regular payments. The lessee may or may not decide to acquire outright ownership at the end of the agreed leasing period.[3] The advantage for the supplier is that it will be paid immediately by the lessor. For the supplier, this is an advantage because it eliminates the risk of non-payment in the case of a contract of sale under which payment is deferred. The lessee is able to acquire goods for which it could not pay in full upfront and to utilise them in its business activities, which in turn will generate the funds needed to pay the lessor. The lessor, as the owner of the goods, has some protection against the lessee's failure to pay in that it can assert its rights as owner and reclaim possession if the buyer defaults. The charges to be paid by the lessee will be designed to allow the lessor to recover the cost of the goods over the duration of the leasing agreement, together with a profit element for the lessor.

In addition to the distinct practical differences between an operating lease and a finance lease, there are also a number of distinctive legal features with regard to a finance lease. It will already be apparent that such an arrangement involves three parties, rather than two. Furthermore, there are at least two separate contracts involved: the contract for the sale of the relevant goods from supplier to lessor, and the leasing contract between lessor and lessee. There will not always be a direct contractual relationship between supplier and lessee. This is significant, because under a contract of sale, the buyer of the goods will have recourse against the seller if the goods are not in conformity with the contract, e.g., when they are faulty.[4] In the case of a finance lease, the immediate contractual supplier to the lessee will be the lessor, but the lessor will usually be a finance company and have no specific expertise in respect of the goods. Moreover, the selection of the goods will have been discussed between lessee and supplier. A lessor will therefore usually seek to limit, or exclude altogether, any liability towards the lessee in respect of the goods. A supplier and lessee could enter into a separate contract in respect of the quality and fitness for the purpose of the goods to be supplied under the finance lease, but this will not always be the case.[5]

We can see, therefore, that the role of the lessor is mostly to provide finance for the acquisition of the goods by the lessee. This arrangement is not dissimilar from a loan

---

3   As we will see, the Leasing Convention applies to a finance lease irrespective of whether the lessee could become the owner at the end of the leasing period. English Law, for instance, makes a strict distinction between contracts of hire and contracts of hire-purchase (which are contracts of hire which include a contractual option to acquire ownership of the goods at the end of the hire period).
4   Cf. Art. 35 CISG (see Chapter 4).
5   There may be instances when a separate, collateral, contract might arise between supplier and lessee which might provide the lessee with a remedy against the supplier if the goods are faulty.

provided to a borrower in return for which the lender takes a security interest (a charge) over an asset belonging to the borrower. Should the borrower fail to repay the loan, the lender can exercise the security interest to take over the asset, realises its value and clear the loan (with any surplus returned to the borrower). In a sense, a finance lease performs a similar function: in both situations, the finance company provides money, with its interest "secured" over an asset: in the case of a finance lease, this security is the fact that the lessor is the legal owner of the goods and the lessee only takes possession; in the case of a charge, the security is a legal interest in goods which are owned by the borrower. In both situations, the lessor/lender can take possession of the asset in case the lessee/borrower defaults on its repayment obligation. In this sense, both leases and charges perform the same practical function. However, the fact that the lessor under a finance lease is the owner of the goods means that, in some legal systems, this arrangement is not characterised as a security arrangement but a contractual one, whereas a charge-style arrangement is generally always treated as a form of security to which specific and rather strict rules apply.[6]

Finally, we should note a variant of the financial leasing arrangement explained above: the "sale-and-leaseback" arrangement. In one sense, this is very similar to a financial leasing arrangement in that the lessor will be a finance company acquiring the goods in question for immediate lease to the lessee. The difference is that the supplier of the goods is their future lessee. The goods which become subject to a sale-and-leaseback are owned by the future lessee, who sells them to the lessor and takes an immediate lease over those goods back to it. An owner of goods might use such an arrangement as a useful means of raising funds to improve the owner's overall cashflow by unlocking the value of the goods while still being able to continue to use the goods.

Our focus will primarily be on financial leasing. This is the focus of the UNIDROIT Convention on International Financial Leasing, adopted 1988, to which we now turn.

3. UNIDROIT Convention on International Financial Leasing 1988

In order to facilitate financial leasing transactions with an international dimension, UNIDROIT promoted a Convention on International Financial Leasing (the "Leasing Convention"), which was agreed in Ottawa in 1988 alongside the Factoring Convention, discussed in Chapter 7. The Leasing Convention deals with the respective rights and obligations of all three parties usually involved in a financial leasing transaction, the supplier, lessor and lessee. It does not deal with other leasing transactions, such as the operating lease, because of the particular nature of a financial leasing transaction; attempts to include these in the draft Convention were rebuffed.[7]

---

6   See, e.g., C. Walsh, "'Functional formalism' in the treatment of leases under secured transactions law: comparative lessons from the Canadian experience" in S. Bazinas and O. Akseli, *International and Comparative Secured Transactions Law* (Hart, 2017).

7   R. Goode, "Reflections on the harmonisation of commercial law" (1991) *Uniform Law Review* 54, p.62.

The Convention entered into force in 1995, and there are 10 Contracting States at the time of writing.[8] Although this is a rather small overall number, the Convention only required three ratifications to enter into force,[9] so it fared better than, e.g., the Agency Convention.[10]

3.1 Scope of application

We begin by examining the scope of application of the Leasing Convention. The relevant contract type to which the Convention applies is a financial leasing transaction, which also satisfies the Convention's criteria as to internationality.

3.1.1 Financial leasing transactions

The Leasing Convention applies to financial leasing transactions (except where the lessee acquires the equipment primarily for personal, family or household purposes,[11] i.e., as consumer) under which a lessor enters into a supply agreement with the supplier of goods, on terms specified by the lessee and approved insofar as they relate to its interests, to acquire equipment, and then enters into a leasing agreement with the lessee under which the lessee gets the right to use the equipment in return for regular rental payments.[12] In addition, the financial leasing transaction must have the following characteristics: first, the lessee chooses the equipment and supplier without relying primarily on the lessor's skill or judgement; secondly, the lessor acquires the equipment for the purposes of leasing them with the knowledge of the supplier; and third, the rental payments are designed to cover the whole or substantial part of the cost of the equipment.[13] We can see immediately that this definition reflects the commercial realities of most finance leases: the real negotiations about the goods to be supplied are conducted between supplier and lessee without the lessor's involvement, with the lessor's role essentially the provision of upfront finance to pay the supplier and then to become the supplier in law of the goods to the lessee (in practical terms, the supplier will usually supply the goods directly to the lessee).

The Leasing Convention operates with an extended notion of "lease": at the end of the leasing period, the lessee may have the option to buy the equipment outright or to conclude a further lease,[14] or to return the equipment to the lessor.

Further, should the equipment which is subject to the lease become a fixture or incorporated in land (as determined by the law of the State where the land is

8   Belarus, France, Hungary, Italy, Latvia, Nigeria, Panama, Russia, Ukraine and Uzbekistan.
9   Art. 16(1).
10 See Chapter 5.
11 Art. 1(4).
12 Art. 1(1). The Convention also applies to sub-leases involving the same equipment, whereby the first lessor enters into a sub-leasing agreement; the lessor is treated as "supplier" for the purposes of the Convention.
13 Art. 1(2).
14 Art. 1(3).

situated[15]), the provisions of the Convention continue to apply,[16] although the rights as between the lessor and the person with a proprietary interest in the land are determined on the basis of the law of the State where the land is situated.[17]

However, it seems that the Leasing Convention does not apply in respect of sale-and-leaseback arrangements, i.e., to instances where the supplier and the lessee are the same person. This is suggested by the wording of Art. 1(1)(a), referring to "one party (the lessor)", "another party (the lessee)" and "a third party (the supplier)". The assumption is that the types of financial leasing transactions within the scope of the Leasing Convention involve three separate parties. This would exclude the two-party sale-and-leaseback arrangement.

3.1.2 Internationality and connecting factors

The Leasing Convention, as other International Commercial Law conventions, needs a criterion to determine when a transaction is international so as to engage the provisions of the Convention. The requirement of internationality in the Leasing Convention is that lessor and lessee must have their places of business[18] in different States.[19]

The connecting factor with the Convention is established if (i) lessor, lessee and supplier all have their respective places of business in a Contracting State,[20] or (ii) both the supply agreement and the leasing agreement are governed by the law of a Contracting State.[21] In the second instance, it would therefore be possible to engage the Leasing Convention by choosing the law of a State which has ratified the Convention, even where one or more of the parties involved has their place of business in a non-Contracting State.

3.1.3 Party autonomy and interpretation

Reflecting the general principle of party autonomy in International Commercial Law, the Convention can be excluded from applying to a finance lease to which it would otherwise apply, but only if all the parties to both the supply agreement and the leasing agreement agree to do so.[22] This could be done through an appropriately worded standard term excluding the application of the Convention. Alternatively, the parties to each agreement can agree to derogate from or vary the effect of individual provisions of the Convention without excluding it in its entirety.[23]

---

15   Art. 4(2).
16   Art. 4(1).
17   Art. 4(2).
18   In the case of multiple places of business, the relevant place of business would be that with the closest connection with the relevant agreement and its performance (Art. 3(2)).
19   Art. 3(1) opening sentence.
20   Art. 3(1)(a).
21   Art. 3(1)(b).
22   Art. 5(1).
23   Art. 5(2).

The rules on interpretation and gap-filling[24] are analogous to those in Art. 7 CISG,[25] with the addition of the obligation to take the Convention's object and purpose, as set out in the Preamble, into account when interpreting the Convention.[26] With regard to the general principles on which the Leasing Convention is based, relevant to gap-filling under Art. 6(2), Ferrari has suggested that party autonomy, protection of the lessee's interests, preservation of the contract (allowing termination only in limited circumstances) and reciprocity of performance (allowing a party to withhold its performance when the other party has not performed when obliged to), the protection of the lessor's interests in case of the lessee's insolvency, and the need to mitigate losses, would all qualify as relevant general principles.[27] All of these find expression in specific provisions of the Convention, so it would seem reasonable to treat them as relevant general principles.

3.2 Rights and duties of the parties

The substance of the Leasing Convention is concerned with the respective rights and obligations of the lessor, lessee and supplier towards one another. When compared with the way a finance lease would be treated under domestic law, the Convention contains a number of novel provisions which are directed at the particular legal issues created by the triangular arrangement of a finance lease, and which depart, to some extent, from what would be the situation under the various contractual relationships.

3.2.1 Lessor

A number of issues regarding the position of the lessor are addressed in the Convention.

3.2.1.1 Rights of lessor as owner

The first aspect is the protection of the lessor's rights and interests as owner of the equipment subject to the leasing agreement, and therefore the lessor's financial interest. In particular, the lessor's rights as owner are protected in the case of the lessee's insolvency, and can be asserted against the lessee's trustee-in-bankruptcy[28] and other creditors.[29] This is subject to any requirement of the applicable law

---

24 Art. 6.
25 See discussion in Chapter 3 at 5.1.1.
26 Art. 6(1).
27 F. Ferrari, "General principles and international uniform law conventions: a study of the 1980 Vienna Sales Convention and the 1988 Conventions on International Factoring and Leasing and the UNIDROIT Principles" (1999) 1 *European Journal of Law Reform* 217, pp.237–238.
28 An umbrella term which encompasses "a liquidator, administrator, or other person appointed to administer the lessee's estate for the benefit of the general body of creditors" (Art. 7(1)(b)).
29 Art. 7(1)(a).

(usually the law where the equipment is situated[30]) which renders the effectiveness of the lessor's rights subject to a public notice requirement,[31] such as registration in a register of security interests.[32] This proviso is significant: some jurisdictions will equate a finance lease with a security arrangement and require registration of a lease in respect of such equipment. The lessor's right as owner under the Convention is therefore subject to registration under the relevant national law, and failure to do so would mean that the lessor's rights would not be enforceable as against the lessee's trustee-in-bankruptcy and creditors. The Leasing Convention does not point to a single State that determines where registration is required; in particular, in respect of equipment which normally moves between States, the relevant State is the one where the lessee has its principal place of business,[33] whereas for other equipment, it is the State where the equipment is situated (which could be different from the State of the lessee's principal place of business).[34] There is therefore a risk that the lessor might fail to realise that a registration requirement exists, or the financial leasing transaction might be entered on the register in the "wrong" State.

3.2.1.2 Lessor's liability in respect of equipment

The second aspect concerns the lessor's liability for the equipment itself. As explained earlier, the lessor is the contractual supplier of the goods to the lessor, but in a commercial sense, the lessor's role is essentially limited to providing finance for the acquisition of the goods by the lessee. Usually, the lessor will neither have expertise in respect of the goods, nor will it have been involved in the process of selecting the goods. Reflecting this, the general position under the Leasing Convention is that the lessor is not liable to the lessee in respect of the equipment.[35] This approach, which largely isolates the lessor from any claims by the lessee, accords with the nature of a financial leasing transaction.[36] However, there are a number of qualifications to this position. The first is where the leasing agreement itself provides otherwise. This acknowledges the possibility that lessor and lessee might agree that some liability for the equipment should be assumed by the lessor directly.

Secondly, the lessor will be liable in respect of the equipment if the lessee has suffered a loss because of its reliance on the lessor's skill or judgement and because the lessor intervened in the selection of the supplier or the specifications of the equipment.[37]

---

30 Art. 7(3)(d). Note the special requirements relating to ships, aircraft and other mobile equipment (including aircraft engines) moving between jurisdictions in Art. 7(3)(a)–(c).
31 Art. 7(2).
32 Note that the priority of a creditor arising from consensual or non-consensual liens or security interests arising other than by attachment or execution if preserved, as are rights of arrest, disposition or detention in relation to ships or aircraft: Art. 7(5).
33 Art. 7(3)(c).
34 Art. 7(3)(d).
35 Art. 8(1)(a).
36 R. Goode, "Reflections on the harmonisation of commercial law" (1991) *Uniform Law Review* 54, p.62.
37 Art. 8(1)(a).

In contrast, there is no liability on the lessor, in its capacity as lessor, to third parties for death, personal injury or property damage caused by the equipment.[38] Instead, such liability may fall on the lessee if the cause of liability to third parties was due to the lessee's actions, where they result in liability under the applicable national law, or on the manufacturer of the equipment where provided for under national law on product liability.

In any event, and in contrast to the limited imposition of liability on the lessor set out above, the lessor may be liable under other rules of law, e.g., where the applicable law imposes particular obligations on an owner of equipment.[39] The legal position of the lessor as owner is therefore distinct from the lessor's liability as lessor under the leasing agreement.

3.2.1.3 Lessor's warranty of quiet possession

Moreover, the lessor is deemed to warrant that the lessee will be able to enjoy "quiet possession" of the equipment, i.e., that no other person will seek to interfere with the lessee's ability to use the equipment on the basis that they have, or claim to have, a superior title or right.[40] The exception to this is where such a title, right or claim is due to an act or omission of the lessee. The provision has mandatory effect insofar as the superior title, right or claim is due to an intentional or grossly negligent act or omission by the lessor.[41] Additionally, there may be a broader warranty of quiet possession under the applicable law.[42]

The explanation for this is that the purpose of the leasing agreement is to enable the lessee to take full possession of the equipment which is the subject of the leasing agreement, and to use this freely for its commercial activities. With the exception of any rights the lessor might have in respect of the leased equipment under the leasing agreement, the lessee's ability to use the equipment should not be interfered with by any other party.

3.2.1.4 Lessor's rights in case of payment default by lessee

The main advantage of a financial leasing transaction is that the lessor remains the legal owner of the equipment in question, and, as a final resort, can assert those rights in case the lessee fails to comply with the leasing agreement. Usually, such a failure will be a payment default, i.e., a failure to keep up the instalment payments under the leasing agreement.

A payment default by the lessee entitles the lessor to recover any accrued rental payments which remain unpaid, together with interest.[43] The important point here is

38 Art. 8(1)(b).
39 Art. 8(1)(c).
40 Art. 8(2).
41 Art. 8(3).
42 Art. 8(4).
43 Art. 13(1).

that a right to interest on missed payments is granted under the Convention. Furthermore, damages for any related losses can also be recovered,[44] subject to a duty to take reasonable steps to mitigate losses.[45] If there is only one, or a small number of missed payments, then recovery of those payments should suffice as a remedy and the leasing agreement can remain in place. One might expect both parties to seek an informal solution to a payment default by the lessee, rather than invoking formal legal steps. However, if the lessee is in serious financial difficulties, missed payments may soon build up.

The Leasing Convention therefore contains a further provision for instances when the default by the lessee has become "substantial". There is no further indication in the Leasing Convention as to the criteria that should be applied in determining whether a default is substantial. Relevant factors might consider the proportion of the default in comparison to the total number of payments under the leasing agreement; how far into its term the leasing agreement is, or any customary understanding of what is regarded as a substantial default.

Where the default is substantial, the lessor should first give the lessee notice that the lessee has a reasonable opportunity of remedying its default, if it can be remedied.[46] Where it cannot be remedied, or once the reasonable opportunity has passed, the lessor may, if provided for in the leasing agreement, require the accelerated payment of future rentals, i.e., require the lessee to pay the balance of rental payments before they fall due.[47]

Alternatively, the lessor can terminate the leasing agreement, recover possession of the equipment and recover damages to put the lessor in the position it would have been in, had the lessee performed its obligations in accordance with the agreement (subject to the lessor's duty to mitigate).[48] The lessor cannot require accelerated payment as well as terminate the contract, although the value of future rentals can be taken into account in calculating damages.[49]

The calculation of the damages due to the lessor, if it terminates the leasing agreement, might be provided for in the leasing agreement and will apply to determine the damages due to the lessor,[50] except where this would be "substantially in excess" of the quantum of damages that could be recovered by applying the general damages rule in Art. 13(2)(b).[51] Thus, a liquidated damages clause in the leasing agreement would be effective, even where the sum to be paid under the clause is higher than the damages recoverable under the Convention. A clause

---

44   *Ibid.*
45   Art. 13(6).
46   Art. 13(5).
47   Art. 13(2).
48   Art. 13(2)(a) and (b).
49   Art. 13(4). This limitation is mandatory and cannot be derogated from by the parties agreeing otherwise.
50   Art. 13(3)(a).
51   Art. 13(3)(b). This provision has mandatory effect, i.e., the limitation of s.13(2)(b) as to the measure of damages cannot be derogated from in favour of a contractual term which is more generous to the lessor.

such as this has the advantage of providing greater certainty to both parties at the outset as to what the lessee's liability might be in the case of termination. However, where the sum stipulated in the clause were to be so much higher than the damages recoverable under the Convention so as to be regarded as "substantially in excess", then the clause will not be enforceable. As a consequence, only damages as permitted under the Convention would be recoverable. A challenge for the parties is that it might be difficult to say in advance whether the sum stipulated in a liquidated damages clause would be regarded as being "substantially in excess" of the damages recoverable under the Convention. Establishing the quantum of damages in advance of a breach will always be an imprecise exercise, so there is some leeway built in. Again, it will turn on whether a higher sum is *substantially* in excess of regular damages, and on the criteria which can be deployed in determining when this threshold has been crossed.

3.2.2 Lessee

3.2.2.1 Duty to maintain equipment

For the duration of the leasing agreement, the lessee will be in possession of the equipment. Consequently, the lessee is obliged to take proper care of it, use it reasonably and maintain it in the condition in which it was delivered (subject to fair wear and tear, and whatever modifications to the equipment may have been agreed by the parties).[52] On the expiry of the leasing agreement, the lessee has to return the equipment to the lessor in the appropriate condition, unless the lessee agrees to buy the equipment at that point, or both parties agree a further term of lease.[53]

3.2.2.2 Relationship between lessee and supplier of the equipment

The supplier of the equipment will owe duties as a seller to the lessor under the supply contract (which will normally be a contract of sale). As the lessee is not a party to that contract, the supplier would not normally owe any duties, nor be directly liable, to the lessee.[54] However, under the Convention, the supplier's duties under the supply agreement are extended to the lessee, so the lessee is treated as if it were a party to the supply agreement and the equipment had been supplied directly to the lessee.[55] This has the effect of reducing the impact of rules of the applicable law regarding the exclusion of a third party from the benefit of a contract (privity). It is also quite a radical solution to the problem which privity of contract would otherwise create in this context. Unless the lessee has the right to enforce the supplier's obligations under the supply contract under the rules of the applicable law, then the lessee could only fall back on its contract with the

---

52 Art. 9(1).
53 Art. 9(2).
54 There may, of course, be collateral agreements between supplier and lessee, and other duties owed by the supplier to the lessee based on rules outside the supply agreement may apply.
55 Art. 10(1).

lessor. However, as we saw above, the lessor's liability in respect of the equipment is limited under the Leasing Convention. The solution adopted in the Leasing Convention reflects the commercial reality of a financial leasing transaction, where the role of the contractual supplier of the equipment (i.e., the lessor) is limited to the provision of finance to enable the supply of the goods to the lessee. All the negotiations regarding the equipment itself will have been between lessee and supplier, and so it seems much more sensible, from a commercial perspective, to allow the lessee to be able to rely on the contractual duties owed by the supplier to the lessor.

However, the extent to which the supplier owes any duties to the lessor under the supply agreement will depend on the precise terms of that agreement. In particular, the supply agreement may provide for a more limited liability of the supplier in respect of the goods. Furthermore, unless expressly provided for in the supply agreement, any specific agreements reached in respect of the goods between supplier and lessee may not invariably be part of the supply agreement. The Leasing Convention assumes that the lessee will have agreed to the terms of the supply agreement "so far as they concern [the lessee's] interests",[56] but this does not mean that those terms will mirror the terms that would be part of a direct contract of sale between supplier and lessee. The respective commercial bargaining strength of all three parties might have a bearing on how much real scope there is for the lessee to approve the terms of the supply agreement. The Leasing Convention offers some protection to a lessee who has approved the terms of the supply agreement by providing that any rights of the lessee under the Convention in respect of the supply agreement will not be affected by a variation of the supply agreement where the lessee had previously approved the term in question, unless the lessee gives its consent to the variation.[57] This ensures that the supplier and lessor cannot vary the terms of the supply agreement after gaining the lessee's approval and thereby reduce the lessee's rights under the Convention against the supplier.

In any case, the supplier's liability is qualified by a limitation to the effect that there cannot be liability on the part of the supplier to both lessor and lessee in respect of the same damage. Moreover, the lessee is not entitled to set aside ("terminate or rescind") the supply agreement without the lessor's consent.[58]

3.2.2.3 Rights against lessor

In addition to the rights against the supplier,[59] the lessee also has some rights against the lessor. Thus, if the equipment is not in conformity with the supply agreement, or if the equipment is delivered late, then the lessee is treated as if it had agreed to buy the equipment from the lessor on the same terms as those of the actual supply agreement. In effect, the Leasing Convention creates a legal fiction to the effect that there is a supply agreement between lessor and lessee, even though

---

56   Art. 1(1)(a).
57   Art. 11.
58   Art. 10(2).
59   The rights set out in this paragraph do not affect the lessee's rights against the supplier discussed in the previous section (Art. 12(6)).

no such agreement actually exists. The effect of this legal faction is that the lessee gains the right to reject the equipment as against the lessor, or to terminate the leasing agreement,[60] where there is a non-conformity under the terms of the supply agreement. However, the lessor has the right to remedy the failure to provide equipment which is in conformity with the contract.[61] In the latter case, the lessee can withhold any rental payments until the lessor has remedied its failure, or until the lessee has lost the right to reject the equipment.[62] If the lessee terminates the leasing agreement, any rentals already paid can be recovered, subject to a "reasonable sum" to reflect any benefit which the lessee did get from the equipment until the point of termination.[63]

Once more, the solution adopted in the Leasing Convention is interesting. For the purposes of dealing with a non-conformity of the equipment under the terms of the supply agreement, it effectively creates a right of action for the lessee against the lessor on the basis of a fictitious sales contract between lessor and lessee, subject to the conditions and restrictions which would arise if there were such a contract in place. Of course, it is open to the parties to exclude or vary the operation of this provision under the terms of their contract.[64] The real importance of this provision is that it provides a backdrop against which the parties might negotiate different contractual arrangements, should they wish to do so. Furthermore, there is nothing to stop the parties from excluding the Convention in its entirety and thereby avoid the application of these rules altogether.[65]

3.2.3 Transfer of rights

Both lessor and lessee may be able to transfer their rights to third parties, but only under certain conditions. The lessor can transfer or deal with its rights in the equipment or under the leasing agreement, but this will neither affect its *duties* under the agreement, nor the nature of the leasing agreement or the legal rules applicable to it under the Convention.[66]

In a similar way, the lessee can transfer its right to use the equipment, or other rights under the leasing agreement, but only with the consent of the lessor, and subject to any third-party rights.[67]

---

60 Art. 12(1)(a).
61 Art. 12(1)(b). Either right is subject to the same conditions and limitations that would arise if there had been a direct contract of sale between lessor and lessee on the same terms as the actual supply agreement (Art. 12(2)).
62 Art. 12(3).
63 Art. 12(4). No other claims against the lessor for non-delivery, late delivery or delivery of non-conforming equipment are permitted except where these are the result of an act or omission by the lessor (Art. 12(5)).
64 Art. 5(2).
65 Art. 5(1).
66 Art. 14(1).
67 Art. 14(2).

3.3 UNIDROIT Model Law on Leasing 2008

The Leasing Convention has only secured 10 ratifications, but the Convention has been influential beyond the countries which have ratified it by serving as a model for the modernisation of national legislation on leasing contracts. In view of this, UNIDROIT decided to develop a Model Law which took the provisions of the Leasing Convention as its starting point, but the Model Law has a wider scope, including a broader notion of the assets which can be leased, and the applicability of some provisions to leases which are not "leasing agreements".

The Model Law operates with a simplified definition of financial lease (Art. 2), requiring only that the lessee specifies the asset to be leased, and that the supplier is aware that the asset will be leased when supplying to the lessor. The Model Law follows the Leasing Convention in granting the lessee the benefit of the supplier's duties under the supply agreement (Art. 7(1)), but contains a new provision that the lessee can request the lessor to assign rights under the supply agreement to the lessee. However, if the lessor does not do so, the lessor is deemed to have assumed the same duties towards the lessee as those of the supplier under the supply agreement (Art. 7(2)). Other provisions derived from the Leasing Convention have been amplified or clarified.

Furthermore, the Model Law contains provisions on matters which were not addressed in the Leasing Convention. This includes Article 11 on the transfer of risk of loss to the lessee (in the case of a financial lease, but not under other types of lease), Article 12 on the consequences of damage to the asset before delivery to the lessee, and Article 13 on deemed acceptance of the asset which precludes the lessee's right to reject once a reasonable period of time for inspection has passed.

As we saw in Chapter 3, the advantage of a Model Law compared to a convention is that the need to find a solution that is agreeable to a sufficient number of States is less pressing. A convention can, subject to any permissible declarations, only be ratified as it is, whereas there is scope for a State seeking to introduce national legislation based on a Model Law to make any changes to the wording it regards as necessary – although if too many changes are made, this could undermine the harmonising effect which a Model Law seeks to provide. The Model Law also goes beyond the substantive scope of the Convention itself to offer a more comprehensive template and deal with a wider range of issues which were either not considered for the Convention, or on which an agreement could not be reached at the time. Individual States seeking to introduce legislation based on the Model Law can decline to follow any provisions which they do not wish to introduce domestically.

3.4 Conclusions

The Leasing Convention contains a number of interesting and innovative solutions to reflect the commercial realities of a financial leasing transaction. In particular, it recognises the fact that the contractual pattern of a financial leasing transaction, under which the user of the equipment (lessee) may not have directly enforceable rights against the actual supplier of the equipment, is out of step with the commercial nature of this arrangement. It offers a solution which enables the lessee to rely on the supplier's duties directly despite the absence of a contractual nexus. This illustrates how International Commercial Law fulfils a specific problem-solving role which is not confined to doctrinal limitations which would otherwise exist; instead, it puts forward a commercially focused solution to the particular features of a financial leasing transaction. Whether this is palatable to the parties involved in financial leasing transactions is a different question, of course: even without the Convention, there are mechanisms by which a comparable outcome could be achieved on the basis of exceptions to the doctrine of privity, where these exist, or the possibility of a separate collateral contract between supplier and lessee. However, the provisions of the Leasing Convention might encourage the parties to make appropriate arrangements – the Convention's provisions only apply insofar as they have not been disapplied by the parties. And where they do not, the Leasing Convention might offer a more balanced commercial solution than would otherwise be the case under the applicable domestic law.

7

RECEIVABLES FINANCING

1. Introduction

Whenever a business supplies goods, services or digital content to a customer, it does so to receive payment in return. Depending on the nature of the contract, such payment may be immediate, or deferred. Deferred payment might merely defer the payment of the full sum due until a set date, often based on a period of time after delivery (e.g., "payment within 30 days of delivery"). Alternatively, it may be an arrangement to pay in instalments over a period of months or years. Another common situation is that of a finance company (lender) which has advanced funds to its customers, who will repay this over time, usually with interest. This type of income which a business or lender expects to receive from its customers is known as "receivables", or "book debts". In legal terms, a "receivable" is a right under a contract – whether a contract of sale, or a loan agreement – to receive payment for whatever has been provided by the other party. As these are contractual rights, they are capable of being transferred to a third party which is not involved in the original contract, through a legal process known as "assignment".

This transferability can be important to a business, because it is possible to sell the right to receive payment to another person. The person who buys the right to receive payment, i.e., the receivables, will pay for this, albeit that a sum that will be paid is going to be lower than the total value of the receivables. Once a receivable has been sold, the seller's debtor will pay the buyer of the receivables who will become the new creditor.

The advantage of such an arrangement is that it can be a useful way for a business to increase liquidity. It avoids the need to wait for a customer to make payment, as well as the risk of late payment or default by a customer. The drawback is that the sum actually received will be less than the value of the receivables, but this will be outweighed by the benefit of having a fixed payment for the receivables from the buyer.

DOI: 10.4324/9781315692807-7

The legal process to "sell" receivables is to *assign* the right to receive payment to the buyer of the receivables, usually a bank or some other finance company. Whilst it is possible to have discrete, or one-off, arrangements, for individual contracts, it is more often the case that there will be a continuing arrangement between the supplier of goods or services and a finance company for the assignment of the supplier's receivables, usually on a discounted basis. Within these arrangements, it is important to distinguish between assignments on a "recourse" and "non-recourse" basis. In essence, a non-recourse assignment of a receivable means that, once the receivable has been sold, there would be no claim by the finance company against the seller, if there was subsequently a default to make payment by the debtor.

As an alternative to selling receivables outright, it may be possible to securitise them, i.e., to use them as an asset over which a security interest is granted in favour of a lender, in return for a loan or other type of financing facility.

The ICC identifies four distinctive techniques for receivables financing:[1]

i   *Receivables discounting*: covers a wide range of transactions where receivables (individual or multiple) are sold to a finance company at a discount compared to their actual value, whether with or without recourse. This may be done with or without notifying the debtor of such an arrangement. Collection of payment is made either by the finance company (where notice has been given to the debtor) or the supplier as agent for the finance company.

ii *Forfaiting*: a specialist type of receivables financing arising out of payment instruments (such as bills of exchange, or documentary credits) rather than a supply contract and are usually sold without recourse.

iii *Factoring*: involves the sale by a supplier of goods or services of receivables, i.e., outstanding invoices, to a finance company known as a "factor". Payment by the factor to the supplier is usually advanced. The factor usually takes over the responsibility for collecting the debt. It is normally disclosed to the buyer who is required to pay the outstanding amounts to the factor directly. It is available both with and without recourse.

iv *Payables finance*: a receivables discounting method used in the context of supply chains where there are multiple sellers in the buyer's supply chain. The buyer enters into a payables finance arrangement with a finance company, which then offers early payment to the various sellers in the buyer's supply chain at a discount. Those that decline are paid in full by the finance company when payment is due.

Distinguishing between these four broad techniques is useful to understand the complexity of receivables financing, although it should be noted that there is some

---

1   International Chamber of Commerce, *Standard Definitions for Techniques of Supply Chain Finance* (2016), pp.27–48, providing a detailed explanation of all four techniques. Available at https://iccwbo.org/content/uploads/sites/3/2017/01/ICC-Standard-Definitions-for-Techniques-of-Supply-Chain-Finance-Global-SCF-Forum-2016.pdf [accessed December 2020]. The explanations below draw on these definitions.

overlap between these categories, and changing practices might change the label attached to any particular arrangement.[2]

The practical benefit of receivables has not always been matched by a willingness for the law to recognise the effectiveness of such arrangements. In particular, there have, historically, been concerns about the practice of transferring rights under contracts in order to raise money, or to use such rights as security. The common law has now generally recognised the possibility of receivables financing, but from the civil law perspective, there are still a number of concerns regarding some of the business practices associated with receivables financing. First, whilst the common law recognises the possibility of assigning future receivables, i.e., receivables under contracts which have not yet been concluded at the time the receivables financing arrangement is agreed, the civil law is more reluctant to permit this. Related to this is the second concern, which is the need for specificity in the civil law, i.e., each contract needs to be specified clearly in an instrument of assignment. Third, there has to be notification of the assignment to the debtor before it can take effect, or there has to be registration of the assignment. The common law has been willing to accommodate the assignment of future receivables without the need for each contract to be identified, and, through equity, has recognised the effectiveness of assignments without notice (albeit not of the full legal interest in the receivable[3]).[4]

These concerns could affect the extent to which a useful financing arrangement can be operated in practice. This area is a useful illustration of the potential clashes between commercial practice and commercial law. Two attempts have been made to try and facilitate receivables financing at the international level. The first was the UNIDROIT Convention on International Factoring, agreed in 1988. The second is the UN Convention on the Assignment of Receivables in International Trade, adopted in 2001. Both are covered in this chapter.

2. UNIDROIT Convention on International Factoring 1988

UNIDROIT's initial attempt to create an international regime for receivables financing focused on one particular method for this: factoring. This is an established, and increasingly international, business model for dealing in receivables.[5] A supplier of the goods or

---

2   For instance, Alexander, writing in 1989, noted that factoring was confined to non-recourse assignments, whereas "accounts receivable financing" covered "with recourse" assignments: M.R. Alexander, "Towards unification and predictability: the international factoring convention" (1989) 27 *Columbia Journal of Transnational Law* 353, p.358.

3   In English Law, a statutory assignment under s.136 of the Law of Property Act 1925 would be required.

4   See generally, E. Peel, *Treitel – The Law of Contract*, 15th ed. (Sweet & Maxwell, 2020), Chapter 15.

5   For a (now dated) account of factoring in international commercial transactions, see W. C. Philbrick, "The use of factoring in international commercial transactions and the need for legal uniformity as applied to factoring transactions between the United States and Japan" (1996) 99 *Commercial Law Journal* 141.

services, known as the client, will assign the debts due from customers (the debtors) to a factor. If the supply contract is an international contract, then the factor may, in turn, assign the collection of the debt to a factor located in the debtor's country. Once assigned, the factor will assume the risk that the debtor might default, if the factoring provides for an assignment without recourse. Where a factor has only been willing to agree to an assignment with recourse, the client could be required to "repurchase" any remaining debts where the debtor has defaulted on its obligations to make payment; effectively, this means that the factor will require the client to pay the outstanding amount to the factor. Under a factoring agreement, the factor will usually collect the debts due from the debtor. A particular variation is an "invoice discounting" arrangement, under which a factor selects specific invoices from all the supplier's outstanding receivables and only includes those in the factoring arrangement.[6] Usually, the client will continue to collect the receivables on behalf of the factor, and the debtor is not given notice of the assignment of the debt to the factor. The client acts as the factor's agent in collecting the debts, although the customer/debtor would not be aware of this arrangement. The advantage of this approach is the element of confidentiality of the factoring arrangement.

Factoring takes on an international dimension where supplier and debtor are located in different countries. A factor will usually be from either of the two countries. If the factor is located in the supplier's country, then it may either engage directly in the collection of the debts due from the customer/debtor, or it may transfer (re-assign) the right to receive payment to a factor in the debtor's country. In the former situation, the factor is involved in "direct export factoring". The latter arrangement means that the factor is acting as an export factor. The factor located in the customer's/debtor's country is an "import factor". Despite the costs involved, factoring is generally regarded as cheaper than other financing methods where a third party is interjected between a supplier and a customer, such as the documentary credit system discussed in Chapter 9.

The main objective pursued in the UNIDROIT Convention on International Factoring 1988 (the "Factoring Convention") is to remove some of the legal obstacles to international factoring resulting from the different national rules on the assignment of receivables.[7] In particular, it seeks to ensure that an agreement for the assignment of future receivables, i.e., receivables arising under contracts yet to be concluded, would be effective. There would therefore be no need for a new act of assignment once a particular receivable comes into existence, nor would it be necessary to identify that debt or the identity of the debtor.[8]

6   ICC, *Standard Definitions for Techniques of Supply Chain Finance* (2016), p.44.
7   For a general discussion of the Convention, see M.R. Alexander, "Towards unification and predictability: the International Factoring Convention" (1989) 27 *Columbia Journal of Transnational Law* 353.
8   Cf. Art. 5.

2.1 Scope

2.1.1 Factoring

The Factoring Convention applies to the assignment of receivables in the context of a factoring contract. The main features of factoring were summarised above. A factoring contract is one which is concluded between the supplier of goods (which "includes" services[9]) and the factor, under which the supplier will assign to the factor receivables from the contracts for the sale of goods between the supplier and its (business) customers.[10] Moreover, the factor has to perform at least two functions out of (i) providing finance to the supplier (such as loans or advance payments); (ii) keeping the accounts relating to the receivables; (iii) collecting the receivables; and (iv) protecting the supplier against payment defaults by the customers (debtors). These criteria reflect the particular features of factoring.

Finally, notice of the assignment of the receivables has to be given to the debtors. The effect of this criterion is that a factoring arrangement under which the debtor is not given notice of the assignment, is excluded from the scope of the Convention. It is possible that no-notice assignments were excluded from the Convention because of the additional complexities this would raise from the perspective of national law.

2.1.2 Internationality and connecting factor

The Convention will only apply to an *international* factoring arrangement.[11] The crucial contract for determining internationality is the one between supplier and customer/debtor, whose places of business must be in different States.[12] The internationality of the arrangement is therefore determined on the basis of the internationality of the *receivables*, rather than of the assignment. The factor could therefore have its place of business in the same State as the supplier. Furthermore, the connecting factor for engaging the Convention is that all three parties (supplier, customer and factor) have their respective places of business in a Contracting State. Alternatively, the Convention applies when both the supply contract and the factoring contract are governed by the law of a Contracting State.

2.1.3 Party autonomy and exclusion of the Convention

Where the Convention would apply based on the criteria outlined above, there is a possibility for it to be excluded.[13] One important point in this regard is that the

---

9   Cf. Art. 1(3) – references to goods and sale of goods includes services and the supply of services.
10 Art. 1(2). This does not apply to receivables arising from consumer transactions (customers buying goods "primarily for their personal, family or household use").
11 For a fuller discussion, see F. Ferrari, "The international sphere of application of the 1988 Ottawa Convention on International Factoring" (1999) 8 *International Business Law Journal* 895.
12 Art. 2(1).
13 Art. 3.

Factoring Convention can only be excluded in its entirety. This is a difference from many other conventions, which permit for the selective exclusion of individual provisions or their modification by the parties. The decision to exclude the Factoring Convention may be taken either by the parties to the factoring contract, or by the parties to the supply contract insofar as the exclusion relates to receivables arising only after the point in time at which the factor has received written notice of the decision to exclude the operation of the Convention. This invariably opens the question as to when such written notice might be deemed to have been received, and how this would be satisfied when using electronic means of communication.[14]

2.1.4 Interpretation and gap-filling

A more familiar provision is Article 4 on the interpretation of the Convention and gap-filling, which follows the template set by Art. 7 CISG,[15] with the addition of the obligation to take the Convention's object and purpose, as set out in the Preamble, into account when interpreting the Convention. With regard to gap-filling, the task of identifying the "general principles on which [the Convention] is based"[16] is more challenging than, e.g., under the CISG because the latter covers a much broader range of issues.[17] Ferrari suggested that relevant general principles might be: (i) encouragement of assignments, (ii) good faith, and (iii) debtor not to be put in a disadvantageous position.[18] However, he is "doubtful"[19] as to whether party autonomy would qualify as a general principle under the Factoring Convention, both because the ability to exclude the Convention is restricted to an either-or-choice, and, as we will see below, because of the specific provision regarding clauses which prohibit assignments. If party autonomy were to be regarded as a general principle on which the Factoring Convention is based, it would certainly not be a dominant principle and would not be well suited to guide the process of gap-filling.

2.2 The contract of assignment

2.2.1 The assignment

Receivables are transferred from supplier to the factor through effecting a valid contract of assignment. The Convention includes a number of provisions to clarify which elements of an assignment are regarded as effective under a factoring

---

14 See Chapter 12 for a discussion of these issues.
15 See discussion in Chapter 3 at 5.1.1.
16 Art. 4(2).
17 F. Ferrari, "General principles and international uniform law conventions: a study of the 1980 Vienna Sales Convention and the 1988 Conventions on International Factoring and Leasing and the UNIDROIT Principles" (1999) 1 *European Journal of Law Reform* 217, p.234.
18 *Ibid.*, pp.235–236.
19 *Ibid.*, p.235.

contract within its scope. The core of the factoring contract is the assignment of the supplier's receivables due from its customers under contracts for the sale of goods (which includes the supply of services).

In addition, the contract may also provide that any other of the supplier's rights under a supplier–customer contract may be assigned, in particular the benefit of a reservation of title clause, or a clause creating a security interest over any goods supplied to a customer.[20] For such additional rights, the contract may state whether a separate act of transfer of such additional acts is required.[21] The reason why such rights might be the subject of assignment is because they seek to provide a mechanism by which the supplier can take steps to recover the goods from the debtor where the debtor has failed to pay what is due under the terms of the contract. However, the Convention does not regulate priority issues, nor the impact on the validity of a retention-of-title clause, which could be problematic because of differences in the recognition of such clauses at national law.[22]

Furthermore, there is no need to specify each existing or future receivable individually in the factoring contract. The Factoring Convention only requires that all existing and future receivables which are intended to be covered by the factoring agreement can be "identified to the contract", either at the point when the factoring contract is concluded (in the case of existing receivables), or when the receivables come into existence.[23] It is likely that a broad phrase in general terms would satisfy this requirement: for instance, "an assignment of all current or future debts due to the supplier" would suffice for the purposes of a general factoring agreement. It is also important to note that, in the case of future receivables, there is no need to execute a new act of transfer in order to assign them if the factoring contract is already intended to cover future receivables.[24] Here, we have an example of how the Convention seeks to remove one of the obstacles to factoring under those national laws which do not allow for the assignment of future receivables without a fresh act of transfer.

2.2.2 Treatment of non-assignment clauses in the supply contract

An even bolder, and crucial, provision is Article 6, which deals with so-called "non-assignment" clauses. Such clauses are not uncommon, and are often included in standard form contracts.[25] The essence of such a clause is to prohibit the possibility of assigning any rights under the contract, particularly the right to receive

20 Art. 7.
21 *Ibid.*
22 M. Torsello, "The relationship between the parties to the factoring contract according to the 1988 UNIDROIT Convention on International Factoring" (2000) 1 *International Business Law Journal* 43, pp.52–53.
23 Art. 5(1)(a).
24 Art. 5(1)(b).
25 Some useful information is provided by H. Beale, L. Gullifer and S. Paterson, "A case for interfering with freedom of contract? An empirically-informed study of bans on assignment" (2016) *Journal of Business Law* 203.

payment, to another party. A customer/debtor may insist on such a clause, because it might only wish to have a payment obligation towards its supplier. This may be because of the nature of their business relationship, or because the customer/debtor might wish to preserve any rights of set-off or similar defences it might have against the supplier.[26] Furthermore, there is the practical risk that the customer/debtor may somehow miss the notice of assignment and might therefore continue to make payment to the supplier when it should be making payments to the factor. A non-assignment clause is designed to eliminate that risk.

However, a non-assignment clause, especially if it is part of the supply contract on the basis of a standard form contract rather than after individual negotiation, acts as an obvious major block to the use of receivables financing. The Convention takes a simple approach to resolving this issue by providing that an assignment of a receivable will be effective, "notwithstanding any agreement between the supplier and the debtor prohibiting"[27] this. As a consequence, a non-assignment clause loses much of its force by permitting exactly what the clause seeks to preclude. Article 6 (1) of the Convention therefore overrides the intentions of the contracting parties as expressed in the terms of their contract. This seems to collide with the strong emphasis placed on freedom of contract and party autonomy in International Commercial Law: the effect of Art. 6(1) is to undermine the autonomy of the parties and the exercise of their contractual freedom by rendering a non-assignment clause largely ineffective. It is generally rare to intervene in contracts between commercial parties, except where there are strong overriding reasons to do so. Factoring is generally important for some suppliers to get rapid access to finance as an alternative to taking out a loan and offering its physical assets as security; for some businesses, factoring (and related forms of receivables financing) might be the only way of improving their financial situation. In order to preserve the possibility of accessing factoring, overriding the effect of a non-assignment clause is a reasonable solution, despite the fact that it is in conflict with party autonomy.[28] The fact that this might be unpalatable for some States is recognised in the possibility that a Contracting State may make a declaration under Article 18 which would disapply Art. 6(1) where the debtor has its place of business in that Contracting State.[29]

However, the effect of Art. 6(1) is not to invalidate the non-assignment clause in its entirety. An assignment attempted in breach of a non-assignment clause is

---

26 This concern is addressed in Art. 9, discussed further below.
27 Art. 6(1).
28 For this reason, the UK (which is not a Contracting State to the Factoring Convention) introduced legislation which has the same effect in the context of a limited range of contracts, where the supplier qualifies as a small or medium-sized enterprise: see *Business Contract Terms (Assignment of Receivables) Regulations 2018 S.I. 2018/1254.*
29 Art. 6(2). The effect of this is that Art. 6 no longer applies, but this does not mean that the non-assignment clause will be effective; instead, the relevant provisions of the domestic law governing the supply contract will be applied instead to determine the effectiveness of the clause: M.R. Alexander, "Towards unification and predictability: the International Factoring Convention" (1989) 27 *Columbia Journal of Transnational Law* 353, p.370.

effective where the Factoring Convention applies. This does not provide any relief for the supplier if the customer brings a claim against the supplier in respect of the breach of that clause, and the remedies which the customer could exercise under the applicable law remain available. Nor does it affect the supplier's duty of good faith, if this is imposed by the applicable law.[30] So whilst an assignment of receivables under a contract which includes a non-assignment clause is effective, the customer/debtor may nevertheless have a claim arising from the supplier's breach of contract, although in the absence of a quantifiable loss, this may not lead to an award of substantive damages. In some instances, the breach of a non-assignment clause may justify termination of the supply contract by the customer/debtor (for example, if the contract is governed by English Law and the term is classified as a condition), which, if exercised, could affect the assignment. This issue has not been addressed in this Convention.[31]

2.3 Notice requirement

The obligation of the customer/debtor to make payment to the supplier will change to an obligation owed to the factor only if a notice in writing of the assignment has been given by the supplier, or by the factor if so authorised by the supplier.[32] For these purposes, "notice in writing" encompasses means of electronic communication as long as it is possible to reproduce that communication in tangible form.[33] Although the Convention pre-dates the widespread use of electronic communications, the definition seems broad enough to encompass e-mail and other forms of electronic communication. There is no requirement for such a notice to be signed, although the person who gives notice (or in whose name it is given) must be identified in the notice.[34] Notice is effective once given, i.e., once it is received by the intended recipient[35] (in this case, the customer/debtor).

The notice has to reasonably identify the receivables which are subject to the assignment, as well as the factor to whom the customer/debtor should now make payment. Moreover, the notice must relate to a supply contract which was made at the latest by the time notice is given to the customer/debtor. So a notice of assignment can be given immediately if the contract of supply between supplier and customer is subject to a factoring agreement which includes future receivables. However, the notice would not be effective if it related to a supply contract which is only concluded after the notice has been given. In practical terms, this would

---

30 Art. 6(3).
31 But see Art. 9(2) of the UNCITRAL Receivables Convention, discussed below, which states that a breach of the non-assignment clause would not in itself suffice to allow termination of the supply contract.
32 Art. 8(1)(a). This duty does not arise if the debtor has knowledge of another person's superior right to payment.
33 Art. 4(b).
34 Art. 4(a).
35 Art. 4(c).

require fresh notice to be given for receivables assigned to a factor which arise under a supply contract concluded after the previous notice had been given. This suggests that a general notice given to the customer/debtor to cover all future contracts between it and the supplier would not be effective notice for the purpose of the Convention.

Provided the customer/debtor pays the factor, having received the required notice, then this discharges the debtor's liability to make payment under the supply contract.[36]

2.4 Defences of the customer/debtor

Under a contract for the sale or supply of goods or services, the supplier will have a number of obligations, e.g., with regard to the quality of what it has provided to the customer/debtor. Should the supplier's performance fall short of what was required by the contract, the customer/debtor will have a number of remedies open to it, including the possibility to set off its claim for compensation against the supplier's right to receive full payment. As seen, one of the reasons why a customer might want a non-assignment clause in a contract is to protect this possibility. Article 9 preserves the defences a customer/debtor would have under the supply contract against the supplier after the assignment of the receivables to a factor. Thus, the general rules is that if the factor brings claim against the customer/debtor for failure to pay as required under the supply contract, the customer/debtor can invoke all the defences which would have been open to it against a claim made by the supplier.[37] More specifically, this includes any rights of set-off available to the customer/debtor at the time notice of the assignment was given, where these rights relate to claims against the supplier which were already in existence when notice was given.

However, the customer/debtor will not be able to recover payments made to the factor if the supplier has not performed its obligations, or if the performance was late or defective, in circumstances where the customer/debtor has a right to claim those payments from the supplier.[38] There are exceptions to this, which allow a customer/debtor to claim back payments from the factor. This is the case where (i) the factor has not yet made payment to the supplier in respect of the receivable under the supply contract in issue; or (ii), the payment was made when the factor knew that the supplier had not properly performed its obligations to which the payments made by the customer/debtor relate.[39]

In short, therefore, the Factoring Convention protects the debtor's position in that any defences it has against the supplier are not undermined as a result of the assignment, whilst requiring the debtor to enforce its rights under the supply contract against the supplier.

36 Art. 8(2).
37 Art. 9(1).
38 Art. 10(1).
39 Art. 10(2).

2.5 Subsequent assignments

A final issue addressed in the Convention is a situation where a factor, having been assigned a receivable, subsequently assigns this to another person (who may, in turn, further assign this to other subsequent assignees). The Convention applies to such subsequent assignments as if these were the first assignment by the supplier to a factor.[40] However, if the factoring contract prohibits a subsequent assignment, the Convention does not apply to this, and the consequences of a subsequent assignment in breach of that prohibition would have to be dealt with under the applicable law.[41] The override of a non-assignment clause under the Factoring Convention therefore only applies to such clauses in the supply contract.

2.6 Status of the Convention

More than three decades after its adoption, the Convention has only secured nine ratifications.[42] It has come into force as between the Contracting States, as only three ratifications were required for the Convention to enter into force.[43] In light of the commercial importance of factoring, this seems disappointing. It may be that limiting the scope of the Factoring Convention to notice-based factoring, and thereby exclude no-notice factoring from its scope, made the Convention less attractive. Consequently, few States decided to ratify, and in the absence of strong pressure from the factoring industry, there would have been little incentive for States to consider ratification.

Another reason for the limited support for the Factoring Convention could be due to the limited use of factoring of international receivables, with factoring of greater significance in a domestic setting. With this in mind, UNIDROIT has started work on a Model Law on Factoring, and the Working Group tasked with preparing the Model Law started its work in 2020.[44]

3. UN Convention on Assignment of Receivables 2001

As we have seen, the UNIDROIT Convention on International Factoring has quite a narrow scope, and, in particular, does not apply to no-notice assignments of receivables. The more recent UN Convention on the Assignment of Receivables 2001 (the "Receivables Convention")[45] has a much broader scope in that it is not limited to notice-based factoring of receivables; however, it has not (yet) managed

---

40 Art. 11.
41 Art. 12.
42 Belgium, France, Germany, Hungary, Italy, Latvia, Nigeria, Russia and Ukraine.
43 Art. 14(1).
44 See UNIDROIT, *Factoring Model Law*, at https://www.unidroit.org/work-in-progress/factoring-model-law [accessed December 2020].
45 For a general overview, see S. Bazinas, "Multi-jurisdictional receivables financing: UNCITRAL's impact on securitization and cross-border perfection" (2002) 12 *Duke Journal of Comparative & International Law* 365.

to attract a sufficient number of ratifications to enter into force. One reason might be the fact that its provisions, in some respect or another, depart from established domestic rules on assignment,[46] which might have prompted a degree of reluctance to ratify.

3.1 Scope of the Receivables Convention

The Receivables Convention applies to a broad range of assignments of receivables (the "assignor's contractual right to payment of a monetary sum from a third party"[47]). For the purposes of the Convention, an assignment is a "transfer by agreement" from the assignor to the assignee "of all or part of an undivided interest in the assignor's [receivable]".[48] This includes the use of receivables as security for the assignor's indebtedness or other obligations owed to the assignee. The Convention only refers to assignor and assignee, because it applies to both the assignment of receivables under the original contract and subsequent assignments by an assignee to another assignee. The "original contract" is the contract between the creditor/assignor and the debtor.[49] It is not limited to contracts for the supply of goods or services, but extends to any contractual right to receive payment (such as loan receivables, royalties from licensing contracts, damages claims for breach of contract, etc.). It does not, however, extend to rights to receive payments of different origin, such as damages claims in tort.

The Convention is intended to apply to a wide range of receivables, going beyond the trade receivables to which the Factoring Convention applies. The Receivables Convention also covers loan receivables, consumer receivables, receivables arising from transactions with a public body, as well as asset-based financing and the various forms of factoring and forfaiting, whether with or without notice to the debtor. It also covers the securitisation of receivables and project financing (which involves the assignment of receivables arising from future incomes from the project).[50]

However, despite this broad scope, a range of assignments are excluded from the scope of the Receivables Convention, listed in Article 4. For example, whilst assignments of receivables arising from consumer transactions are covered by the Convention,[51] assignments of receivables *to* a consumer are not.[52] Transactions on a regulated exchange are also excluded[53] because they are already subject to detailed rules. Other exclusions are receivables arising from financial transactions

---

46 The possible concerns, both from a civil law and common law angle, are succinctly noted in B.A. Markell, "UNICTRAL's Receivables Convention: the first step, but not the last" (2002) 12 *Duke Journal of Comparative & International Law* 401.
47 Art. 2(a) RC.
48 *Ibid.*
49 Art. 5(a) RC.
50 See *United Nations Convention on the Assignment of Receivables in International Trade – Text and Explanatory Notes*, para. [10], p.30.
51 Although note that any rules of consumer law which apply to the original contract with the debtor are not affected by the Convention: Art. 4(4).
52 Art. 4(1)(a).
53 Art. 4(2)(a).

governed by netting agreements,[54] foreign exchange transactions, inter-bank payments, transfers of intermediated securities, bank deposits or letters of credit.[55] For present purposes, it is not necessary to explore the precise scope of these exceptions further, other than to note that despite these specific exclusions, the Receivables Convention covers a much broader range of receivables financing than the narrow Factoring Convention.

3.2 Internationality and connecting factors

The Convention applies to two types of international transactions:[56] (i) the assignment of international receivables, where assignor[57] and debtor under the original contract are located in different States at the time of conclusion of that contract;[58] (ii) international assignments of receivables, where the assignor and assignee[59] are located in different States at the time the contract of assignment was concluded.[60] There are therefore two different ways of establishing internationality: either with reference to the underlying supply contract, or to the assignment of the receivables.

The Convention also applies to subsequent assignments of a receivable, provided that an earlier assignment in the same sequence of assignments was covered by the Convention. Thus, it can apply to a non-international (i.e., domestic) subsequent assignment, if the receivables had previously been subject to an assignment of international receivables or been subject to an international assignment.[61] It can also apply to a subsequent assignment which is either an international assignment of receivables or an assignment of international receivables, despite the fact that previous assignments of the same receivable were not within the scope of the Convention.[62]

The connecting factor with the Convention is the assignor's location in a Contracting State.[63] A second connecting factor in relation to the rights and obligations of the debtor is either that at the time of concluding the original contract, the debtor was located in a Contracting State, or the original contract was governed by the law of a Contracting State.[64] If the debtor is not so connected with the Convention, then the Convention does not affect the rights and obligations of the debtor.[65]

---

54 Defined in Art. 5(l).
55 Art. 4(2)(b)–(g).
56 Art. 1(1)(a) for the general scope; Art. 3 for the definition of the two types of international transaction.
57 The term used in the Receivables Convention for "supplier" and "client".
58 Art. 3.
59 The assignee could be a factor or other type of commercial entity engaging in receivables financing.
60 Art. 3.
61 Art. 1(1)(b).
62 Art. 1(2).
63 Art. 1(1)(a).
64 Art. 1(3).
65 *Ibid.*

It is useful to note at this point that the Receivables Convention operates with a narrower definition of where a party is located. Whilst it follows the general position in International Commercial Law that a party is located in the State where it has its place of business, a party is located in the State where the party has its central administration if the assignor or assignee has places of business in more than one State. This is a departure from the criterion used in other contexts, including for the determination of the debtor's location under the Convention, but a rule with greater certainty was regarded as beneficial.[66] In relation to the debtor with multiple places of business, the place of business which has the closest relationship to the original contract is determinative.[67]

3.3 Party autonomy and interpretation

In common with other international law conventions, it is permissible to derogate from the provisions of the Convention, or to agree to vary its provisions, relating to the rights and obligations of assignor, assignee and debtor.[68]

Article 7 of the Receivables Convention deals with interpretation. As well as the criteria familiar from Article 7 CISG, there is also the additional criterion that regard must be had to the object and purpose of the Convention as set forth in the Preamble. Relevant points from the Preamble would include the desire to establish certainty and transparency and to promote modern laws on the law relating to the assignment of receivables; the desire to protect existing practices as well as facilitating the development of new practices; and to ensure the adequate protection of the interests of the debtors whose obligation to pay is being assigned.

In addition to these standard guiding criteria for the interpretation of the Convention, Article 5 provides definitions of several key terms used throughout the Convention. In comparison to other conventions, this may seem unusual, but the technical nature of the subject-matter of the Convention requires clarity on how key terms are intended to be understood for the purposes of the Convention.

3.4 Assignment

3.4.1 Effectiveness of assignment

The Receivables Convention, in a similar way to the Factoring Convention, seeks to remove any obstacles to the effectiveness of the assignment of receivables. Thus, Article 8(1) stipulates that an assignment is not ineffective between assignor and assignee merely because the assignment covers more than one receivable, future

---

66 S. Bazinas, "Multi-jurisdictional receivables financing: UNCITRAL's impact on securitization and cross-border perfection" (2002) 12 *Duke Journal of Comparative & International Law* 365, p.367.

67 This is set out in Art. 5(h). In the absence of a place of business, a party's habitual residence is used instead.

68 Art. 6. This is subject to Art. 19, noted below.

receivables or parts of undivided interests in receivables. For the same reasons, an assignment cannot be ineffective against the debtor or a competing claimant, nor can the right of an assignee be denied priority. However, this is on condition that the receivables must either have been identified individually as covered by the assignment;[69] or described in another manner which allows them to be identified as being covered by the assignment at the time of the assignment (or the time of conclusion of the original contract in the case of future receivables).[70] With regard to future receivables, it will usually not be possible to identify them individually in advance because the assignor may not yet know which contracts it might enter into in the future, so these would have to be described in more general terms. Furthermore, the Convention facilitates the automatic assignment of future receivables in that no further act of transfer is required to assign the receivable once it has come into existence, unless the parties agree otherwise.[71]

3.4.2 Effect of non-assignment clauses

We saw earlier that a non-assignment clause could be a significant obstacle to receivables financing. Article 9(1) brushes aside the effect of any contractual agreement not to assign a receivable, whether between the assignor and the debtor in relation to the original contract, or as between a subsequent assignor and a subsequent assignee. In this regard, it prioritises the wider economic benefits of enabling receivables financing over the exercise of party autonomy and freedom of contract.[72] This means that any limitation of an assignor's right to assign its receivables would be ineffective. Indeed, Article 9(1) refers to an agreement "limiting in any way" the right to assign receivables. This suggest that the override does not only apply to non-assignment clauses *strictu sensu*, but also other clauses (such as confidentiality clauses) in the contract between assignor and debtor which would limit or render impossible the assignment of the receivables under that contract. The extent to which Art. 9(1) stretches beyond immediate non-assignment clauses would, invariably, be a matter of interpretation, although in view of the general objective of the Convention, one would expect courts to take a broad view of what might constitute a limitation on the assignor's ability to assign the receivable.

However, the liability of an assignor for breach of a non-assignment agreement is not affected, except that the other party to the non-assignment agreement cannot terminate (avoid) the contract.[73] Moreover, a person who is not a party to

---

69   Art. 8(1)(a).
70   Art. 8(1)(b).
71   Art. 8(2).
72   Cf. S. Bazinas, "Multi-jurisdictional receivables financing: UNCITRAL's impact on securitization and cross-border perfection" (2002) 12 *Duke Journal of Comparative & International Law* 365, p.373.
73   Art. 9(2). The contract here is the original contract if the non-assignment agreement is as between assignor and debtor, or the assignment contract if the non-assignment agreement is as between assignor and assignee.

the non-assignment agreement (i.e., the person to whom the receivables are to be assigned) will not incur any liability merely because it knew of the existence of the non-assignment agreement.

Article 9 does not apply to all the assignments to which the Convention applies. Article 9(3) limits the scope of Article 9 to receivables arising from an original contract which is for the supply or lease of goods, supply of services (other than financial services), a construction contract, or a contract for the sale or lease of real property;[74] a contract for the sale, lease or licence of industrial or intellectual property or proprietary information;[75] the payment obligation of a credit card transaction;[76] or receivables following the net settlement of a multi-party netting agreement.[77] This is still an extensive range of contracts, and in respect of these, the effect of a non-assignment clause is overridden as far as the assignment itself is concerned. For assignments arising from other types of contract, the national law governing the receivable[78] determines whether an assignment in breach of a non-assignment clause is effective or not. If it is effective under the national law, the remaining provisions of the Convention will apply.[79]

In order to secure payment of a receivable, the receivable may be subject to a personal or property right (such as a retention of title clause, or rights under a security interest). This is treated as an accessory right to the receivable and is transferred with the receivable to the assignee without the need for a separate act of transfer. However, if the law governing the right requires a new act of transfer, then such an act will have to be executed, i.e., the assignor is required to take the steps to transfer the right (and any proceeds) to the assignee.[80] Moreover, if there are form requirements or registration requirements in respect of these security rights, they need to be complied with.[81]

3.5 Rights and obligations as between assignor and assignee

The Receivables Convention deals with a number of aspects regarding the relationship between an assignor and assignee. Article 11 reflects the general position in International Commercial Law that the mutual obligations between assignor and assignee arise from their agreement (contract), as well as any usage or practices they have established between themselves. Furthermore, in the case of an international assignment, any usage which is widely known to and regularly observed by parties to the type of assignment, or to assignments of particular categories of receivables,

---

74 Art. 9(3)(a).
75 Art. 9(3)(b).
76 Art. 9(3)(c).
77 Art. 9(3)(d).
78 Art. 29.
79 S. Bazinas, "UNCITRAL's contribution to the unification of receivables financing law: the United Nations Convention on the Assignment of Receivables in International Trade" (2002) 7 *Uniform Law Review* 49, p.51.
80 Art. 10(1). A non-assignment clause is treated in the same way as under Art. 9 (Art. 10 (2)), and Art. 10 only applies to the receivables to which Art. 9 applies (Art. 10(4)).
81 Art. 10(6).

is implicitly applicable to their agreement. However, assignor and assignee may agree not to apply such usages, nor their established practices. In essence, this provision reflects those found in other conventions which seek to confirm the relevance of established usages.[82]

In addition, the Convention implies a number of representations into the assignment contract, although the parties can agree to exclude these (in line with party autonomy). These default representations are that the assignor has the right to assign the receivable, that it has not previously assigned the receivable to another assignee, and that the debtor does not, nor will have, any rights of set-off.[83] On the other hand, the assignor does not represent that the debtor will be able to pay the sums that are being assigned.[84] This is also subject to the parties agreeing otherwise. No specific remedies for a breach of any of these representations are envisaged under the Convention itself, so this would be a matter for the national law applicable to the assignment agreement.

The parties may agree who should notify the debtor of the assignment,[85] but in the absence of such agreement, either party, or both, may send a notification to the debtor. A payment instruction may be sent at the same time as giving notice, but if this is not done at that time, then only the assignee is able to send a payment instruction after notice of the assignment has been given.[86]

Finally, there are several default rules regarding the assignee's right to receive payment (also subject to agreement to the contrary).[87] These rules apply irrespective of whether notice of the assignment has been sent to the debtor, so will be of relevance to all types of assignment. In essence, these provisions confirm that the assignee is entitled to the proceeds of any payment made and goods returned in respect of any receivable assigned to it. Any such payment made to the assignee can be retained by the assignee. However, if such payment is made to the assignor, or to another person over whom the assignee has priority, then the assignee is entitled to be paid the proceeds and to obtain any goods returned to the assignor or such other person. However, the assignee may only retain proceeds and/or goods up to the value of its right in the receivable.[88]

3.6 The position of the debtor

The basic position to protect the debtor is that its rights and obligations are unaffected by an assignment, unless any of the provisions in the Convention adjust

---

82 See discussion in Chapter 1 at 6.1.1.
83 Art. 12(1).
84 Art. 12(2).
85 A notice sent in breach of such agreement would not affect its validity, but the party in breach would still be liable to pay damages for any losses resulting from such a breach (Art. 13(2)).
86 Art. 13(1).
87 Art. 14(1).
88 Art. 14(2).

these.[89] The standard of debtor protection under the Convention is therefore a high one and a general principle underpinning the Convention.[90] An obvious effect of an assignment will be that the mechanics for payment which were agreed originally will probably change – at the very least, the account into which payment has to be made may differ. Any adjustments to the payment instructions are limited to what is essential for an assignment of receivables. Thus, an instruction to the debtor regarding payment may only change the person, address or account to which payment must be made, but it may not change the currency of payment, nor the State where payment is to be made, stated in the original contract.[91] Importantly, the debtor's defences and rights of set-off which would have been available in respect of the original contract are preserved when a claim for payment is made by an assignee[92] (although not in relation to remedies arising from a breach of a non-assignment clause in the original contract[93]). Also, the debtor can raise, against the assignee, any other rights of set-off it may have, if that was available at the time notification of the assignment was notified to the debtor.[94] Notification therefore effectively freezes the set-offs the debtor could raise against the assignee to those available at the time of notification.[95] This is subject to the possibility that debtor and assignor may agree in writing that the debtor will not raise any defences or rights of set-off against the assignee, except those relating to fraud by the assignee or the debtor's incapacity.[96]

As we have already seen, notification to the debtor of the assignment or a payment instruction is common in receivables financing. Notification of either is deemed to be effective once received by the debtor, but it has to be in a language in which the debtor can reasonably be expected to understand the content of the notification, such as the language of the original contract.[97] Unlike the Factoring Convention, under the Receivables Convention, any notification can extend to receivables which only arise after notification.[98]

Here, it is appropriate to note what is required to give notification of an assignment. Such a notification has to be in writing, and reasonably identify the assigned receivables and the assignee.[99] Presumably, the requirement that the receivable must be *reasonably* identifiable relates to the fact that a notification can

---

89   Art. 15(1).
90   S. Bazinas, "UNCITRAL's contribution to the unification of receivables financing law: the United Nations Convention on the Assignment of Receivables in International Trade" (2002) 7 *Uniform Law Review* 49, p.57.
91   Art. 15(2).
92   Art. 18(1).
93   Art. 18(3).
94   Art. 18(2).
95   S. Bazinas, "Multi-jurisdictional receivables financing: UNCITRAL's impact on securitization and cross-border perfection" (2002) 12 *Duke Journal of Comparative & International Law* 365, p.375 and p.379.
96   Art. 19.
97   Art. 16(1). If a debtor is notified only of a subsequent assignment, then this is deemed to constitute notification of all prior assignments (Art. 16(3)).
98   Art. 16(2).
99   Art. 5(d).

extend to future receivables, which cannot be identified precisely. The notion of "writing" is given an extended definition to reflect the technologically neutral definition first used in the Model Law on Electronic Commerce, i.e., "any form of information that is accessible so as to be usable for subsequent reference".[100] Moreover, if a signature is required on the written notice, then this is satisfied if the writing "identifies the person and indicates that person's approval to the information contained in the writing".[101] In drafting the Convention, the rise of electronic communication and the replacement of physical documents with electronic equivalents was taken into account, although whether a given electronic document satisfies these requirements is not always easy to establish.[102]

Notification is important, because until the debtor has been notified of the assignment, it can be discharged from its obligations under the original contract by paying as agreed in that contract.[103] However, once notification has been received, the debtor must pay the assignee, or follow whatever payment instructions are subsequently given,[104] although if the notification has come from the assignee, the debtor can ask for "adequate proof" (such as communications from the assignor confirming the assignment[105]) that there was an assignment by the assignor who was the debtor's contracting party.[106] There is no obligation on the debtor to request such proof. Should a debtor receive notification that was sent fraudulently, i.e., without any assignment having taken place, then this would fall outside the Convention and would have to be considered under the applicable national law. The Convention is also silent as to what should happen when payments are due whilst the debtor is still awaiting the "adequate proof",[107] and the appropriate solution in such a context may fall to national law, although the principle of debtor protection entails that the debtor cannot be required to pay the assignee whilst adequate proof has yet to be provided.

The Convention deals with various instances of multiple payment instructions (i.e., different and potentially conflicting instructions as to when, how and whom to pay) and notifications, and sets down several rules for dealing with such instances. In the case of a single assignment of the same receivable, i.e., with no subsequent assignment, in respect of which the debtor is given multiple payment instructions, the payment obligation is discharged by paying in accordance with the instructions that were received last before payment.[108] The same applies where notification of multiple subsequent assignments is received – paying in accordance with the notification of the last subsequent assignment would discharge the debtor's payment

---

100 Art. 5(c).
101 *Ibid.*, final sentence.
102 This issue is discussed more fully in Chapter 12.
103 Art. 17(1).
104 Art. 17(2).
105 Art. 17(7), final sentence.
106 Art. 17(7). The right to request proof extends to any intermediate assignments.
107 S. Bazinas, "UNCITRAL's contribution to the unification of receivables financing law: the United Nations Convention on the Assignment of Receivables in International Trade" (2002) 7 *Uniform Law Review* 49, p.59.
108 Art. 17(3).

obligation.[109] On the other hand, if there are multiple notifications of an assignment of the same receivable by the same assignor, the debtor should pay in accordance with the first instruction.[110] Finally, in the case of a partial assignment, or an assignment of an undivided interest in receivables, the debtor must either pay in accordance with the notification, or pay as if no notification had been received (i.e., pay the original assignor, or an earlier assignee who had received an outright assignment).[111]

3.7 Relevance of the original contract

Whilst an assignment changes the payment obligation of the debtor, it does not generally affect the remainder of the original contract. Thus, the assignor's failure to perform its obligations under the original contract does not result in any liability for such a breach of contract on the part of the assignee.[112]

Furthermore, assignor and debtor may agree to vary the original contract, although this could affect the assignee's position. To resolve any potential conflict in this regard, the Convention provides that any modification made to the original contract before notification of the assignment will bind the assignee.[113] Modifications made after notification will not affect the assignee's position unless the assignee has consented to the modification.[114] Moreover, if there was a basis for the modification in the original contract, or if a reasonable assignee would have agreed to the modification, then a modification will be affected in respect of unearned receivables.[115]

3.8 Third parties and competing rights

Conflicts may arise between an assignee and other creditors of the assignor, or an insolvency administrator if the assignor becomes insolvent. This could result in competing claims over the same receivable, and the question will be as to who is entitled to receive payment first. This is known as a question of priorities. However, unlike the Cape Town Convention,[116] there are no substantive priority rules in the Receivables Convention. Instead, there are conflict-of-law rules which essentially refer these issues to the law of the State where the assignor is located (applying the Convention's provision determining location in Art. 5(h)).[117] These

---

109 Art. 17(5).
110 Art. 17(4).
111 Art. 17(6).
112 Art. 21.
113 Art. 20(1). However, the assignor may incur liability to the assignee if the assignment agreement contains a clause by which the assignor undertakes not to modify the original contract (Art. 20(3)).
114 Art. 20(2)(a).
115 Art. 20(2)(b).
116 Discussed in Chapter 8 at 4.1.5.
117 Art. 22. See M. Deschamps, "The priority rules in the United Nations Receivables Convention" (2002) 12 *Duke Journal of Comparative and International Law* 389.

are to take precedence over mandatory rules of the Forum State or any other State, except for the public policy rules of the Forum State.[118] This is not uncontroversial, because there are divergent views as to which conflicts rule would be appropriate for determining priority issues.[119] In contrast, if insolvency proceedings have started in a different State from that of the assignor's location, any rights having priority over those of an assignee in the Forum State can be given priority in those proceedings,[120] even though the Convention would ordinarily refer priority matters to the assignor's State of location.

An assignee with priority as to the receivable can keep any proceeds it has received which fall within the priority it has been accorded. More importantly, if such proceeds were paid to the assignor under instructions from the assignee to hold these for the assignee's benefit, and the proceeds were kept separately and are reasonably identifiable, then the assignee has a priority claim to those proceeds which are in the assignor's hands.[121] The latter situation will be important in the case of non-notice assignments, as well as other arrangements where the assignor continues to be paid by the debtor. The recognition that the assignee's interest in the receivable translates into an interest in the proceeds on realisation is an important aspect of the Convention and should reduce the impact of divergent national rules on tracing the assignee's interest into the proceeds. Such national rules are not altogether redundant, however; Art. 24 does not address the difficulties which might result from mixing the proceeds with the assignor's general funds. This may not be problematic, practically speaking, as long as the assignor is solvent, but could cause difficulties when the assignor is insolvent.

An unusual feature of the Convention is its Annex, which contains a number of model priority provisions which a Contracting State could adopt if they do not have a clear priority system, or if they wish to modernise it. There are three models based on different yardsticks – notice filing (registration), notification of the debtor or timing of the assignment. The Convention therefore not only seeks to provide binding rules, but also contains a mini "Model Law" in respect of priority rules which individual States can decide to use as the basis for reforming domestic law. This may have been intended to compensate for the fact that it was not possible to agree on a priority rule within the Convention itself, but it does nothing to promote harmonisation and essentially allows countries to retain their current priority rules.[122]

118 Art. 23(1) and (2).
119 C. Walsh, "Receivables financing and conflict of laws: the UNCITRAL Draft Convention on the Assignment of Receivables in International Trade" (2001) 106 *Dickinson Law Review* 159, p.167.
120 Art. 23(3).
121 Art. 24.
122 C. Walsh, "Receivables financing and conflict of laws: the UNCITRAL Draft Convention on the Assignment of Receivables in International Trade" (2001) 106 *Dickinson Law Review* 159, p.170.

3.9 Autonomous conflict-of-laws rules

One other feature of the Receivables Convention is that it provides separate, autonomous conflict-of-laws rules for application by Contracting States in respect of the assignment of international receivables and the international assignment of receivables to which the Convention would not apply otherwise.[123] This might be the case where there is no connecting factor of such assignments with the Convention, but a court of a Contracting State is seized with an issue involving the assignment. In such a situation, Part V of the Receivables Convention provides the relevant conflict-of-laws rules which determine the governing law to be applied in dealing with a number of aspects.

Thus, the validity of contract of assignment is determined either with reference to the law applicable to that contract, or the law of the State in which the parties are located.[124] If the parties are located in different States, then the law of either State, or the applicable law if different, can determine the issue of validity.[125] The law applicable to the assignment itself is either the law chosen by the parties, or, failing that, the law of the State which has the closest connection with the assignment.[126] The rights and obligations are between debtor and assignee are determined based on the law applicable to the original contract.[127] Finally, the priority rights of an assignee are determined on the basis of the law where the assignor is located.[128] By way of derogation from these provisions, the court of the Forum State can apply any relevant mandatory rules,[129] as well as refuse the application of a provision of another law which is contrary to the public policy of the Forum State.[130]

3.10 Status

As mentioned earlier, the Receivables Convention is not in force. At the time of writing, only two countries had ratified the Convention. In fact, for many years after its adoption, the only State which had ratified the Convention was Liberia, but in 2019, the United States of America also ratified the Convention. There have been no other ratifications since, and there are only two other signatories, Luxembourg and Madagascar, neither of which have ratified the Convention. It will not enter into force until five States have ratified the Convention. Ordinarily, the fact that after almost two decades, an insufficient number of countries have ratified a convention would suggest that it is unlikely ever to enter into force, but the fact that the USA decided to ratify

---

123 See generally, J. Krupski, "Cross-border receivables financing at the crossroads of legal traditions, capital markets, uniform law and modernity" (2007) 12 *Uniform Law Review* 57.
124 Art. 27(1).
125 Art. 27(2).
126 Art. 28.
127 Art. 29.
128 Art. 30, mirroring Art. 22 of the Convention.
129 Art. 31.
130 Art. 32.

the Receivables Convention in 2019 might encourage more States to ratify the Convention in the near future.

4. Conclusions

All forms of receivables financing are of considerable commercial significance in that they enable a supplier of goods, services or other products to access finance faster and at lower risk than would be the case if the supplier had to await payment from its customers. Although the amount of money provided by a factor or other assignee will be lower than the value of the receivable itself, the fact that the supplier can minimise, or at least reduce, the risk of non-payment by its customers and that money is available faster than it would otherwise be make receivables financing a useful means for a business to manage its cash-flow.

Both the Factoring Convention and the Receivables Convention seek to facilitate the use of receivables financing in an international context. The narrow scope of the Factoring Convention may explain its limited take-up, although it is surprising that the broader Receivables Convention has not yet secured the required number of ratifications to come into force. Whether the ratification by the United States in 2019 will encourage more States to ratify remains to be seen; in any case, events in 2020 will probably have delayed any immediate plans to do so where they existed.

Both Conventions seek to address a number of aspects where differences in national law could create obstacles to international receivables financing. Most noteworthy is the fact that both take the sting out of non-assignment clauses in the contract giving rise to the receivables so as to enable receivables financing, contractual prohibitions notwithstanding. Indeed, the Receivables Convention seems to be broader in respect of this override, focusing not only on contractual prohibitions on assignments, but any clause which somehow limits the ability of the assignor to effect an assignment. This is significant because it would be a much more extensive interference with party autonomy and freedom of contract, but one which is justified by the desire to facilitate receivables financing.

Both Conventions also take a direct approach with regard to national variations as to which receivables are capable of being assigned, by including future receivables and permitting general identification of the receivables covered by an assignment, rather than a high degree of specificity which would make assignment of future receivables a much more cumbersome process.

Both Conventions are examples of the facilitative focus of commercial law generally, and also show how International Commercial Law serves not only to reduce obstacles to international commercial transactions, but also to provide novel solutions for domestic law reform.

8

SECURED INTERESTS IN MOBILE EQUIPMENT

1. Introduction

In this chapter, we turn to an area of International Commercial Law of considerable importance: the protection of security interests in high-value assets which are mobile and used across multiple jurisdictions on a regular basis. By their very nature, such assets are expensive and the acquirer of such an asset will rarely be able to pay for this outright at the time of acquisition, i.e., these assets are not transferred under simple contracts of sale. Instead, the acquirer will either agree credit terms with the supplier or obtain finance from a lender. In either instance, the supplier or lender will seek to ensure that there is protection of their financial interests in place in case the acquirer becomes unable to pay as agreed. Although there will be a contractual right to payment which can be enforced against the acquirer, this will only be of any use whilst the acquirer has sufficient funds to pay. Once the acquirer has become insolvent, a contractual claim will be worthless. Therefore, it is common practice for a supplier or a lender to take a security interest over the asset itself, which will give it some security in case the acquirer defaults. The advantage of this is that the security interest gives the supplier or lender a proprietary interest in the asset, which can be asserted against a liquidator as well as other creditors who do not have a secured interest over the same asset.

There are three common arrangements for a supplier of high-value assets, or a lender advancing money for the acquisition of such an asset, to establish a proprietary interest over an asset which has been supplied to the acquirer. The first is a reservation, or retention, of title clause in favour of a seller of goods. The purpose of a contract of sale is to transfer ownership in goods from seller to buyer, but legal systems generally recognise the possibility to stipulate conditions which need to be met before ownership is transferred. Where a seller supplies goods on credit terms, with the purchase price to be paid by the buyer at a later date and/or in instalments, the seller will retain ownership over those goods until full payment has been made. As a consequence, if

DOI: 10.4324/9781315692807-8

the buyer becomes insolvent before the goods have been paid for, the seller is generally able to take back possession of the goods. In some jurisdictions, such as England, a retention of title clause takes effect as a term of the contract, and is generally effective as long as it seeks to attach only to the goods as supplied, as well as goods supplied to the same buyer under other contracts. In other jurisdictions, such as the United States, Canada and New Zealand, a retention of title clause is regarded as a type of security interest, and its effectiveness depends on compliance with the relevant legal regime for the creation of security interests over goods.

The second arrangement arises where the buyer of goods obtains finance (a loan) from a lender to finance the acquisition of an asset. The lender will seek a security interest over assets belonging to the borrower, which might include the asset to be acquired. This security interest will be created as soon as ownership in the asset has been transferred from the seller of the asset to the buyer. The buyer will create a charge, or mortgage, over the asset in favour of the lender, and this gives the lender a proprietary interest over the asset which can be exercised in case of the buyer's insolvency. Should this happen, the lender will take over the asset and sell it, using the proceeds to settle the outstanding amount of the loan it had advanced to the buyer. Any excess usually has to be returned to the liquidator for distribution to other creditors. The important point here is that the charge or mortgage is a security interest which has to comply with the formal requirements of the legal regime on such interests and usually requires registration in a register of security interests.

The third common means of supplying goods where these cannot be paid for in full is to rely on a leasing arrangement. In contrast to a contract of sale, the purpose of a leasing arrangement is to transfer long-term possession of the asset to the acquirer (known as a lessee in this instance), but ownership will remain with the lessor. The lessee will have use of the goods during the period of the leasing arrangement and will make regular payments to the lessor. Should the lessee fail to make the agreed payments or become insolvent, the lessor, who is still the legal owner of the goods, will terminate the leasing agreement and retake possession of the asset in question.

2. The international dimension

The arrangements described above are very common and familiar to most legal systems. Within a particular jurisdiction, there will be a legal regime which deals with the effectiveness and enforceability of each of these arrangements. As long as all the parties and the asset itself are located in one jurisdiction, these types of arrangements should work effectively.

However, the legal regimes applicable to these arrangements are not consistent throughout the world. For example, a retention of title clause may be effective and enforceable in one jurisdiction purely on the basis of the contract of sale in which it has been included, whereas in another jurisdiction, it would be regarded as a security interest and might be ineffective unless the relevant formalities (such as registration of the security interest on a public register) have been complied with. When it comes to enforcing a particular arrangement, it may be difficult at times to persuade a court in one jurisdiction to recognise a security interest created under the laws of another jurisdiction. However, this could be problematic where the asset in question is mobile and has crossed the border into a jurisdiction other than that where the security interest was created. Any uncertainty over the enforceability of a security interest will mean that a lender will have to factor the risk of non-enforceability of a security interest into the overall cost of the agreement, which could make it more difficult to obtain finance. Similarly, a seller of goods may not be willing to supply goods on retention of title terms at all, or only at a significantly higher cost to the buyer. The upshot is that a prospective acquirer of such an asset may find it much more difficult and costly to finance that acquisition.

At the root of these difficulties is the fact that, in private international law, the general principle for determining the existence and enforceability of rights over property is the *lex loci rei sitae*, or simply *lex situs*, principle. According to this, it is the law of the jurisdiction where the property in question is located. This works fine for fixed assets or real estate, but it is clearly unsuitable for assets which are mobile and cross jurisdictional boundaries frequently. Whether or not a particular security interest is enforceable would depend on the particular jurisdiction a mobile asset is in when the holder of that interest seeks to enforce it. Take as an example a seller who has retained ownership of an asset under a basic retention of title clause in the contract of sale governed by English Law. The clause is effective without further formalities under English Law.[1] However, when the seller seeks to enforce the clause due to the buyer's non-payment, the asset is located in the US, where retention of title clause is treated as security interests and therefore needs to be registered there in order to be recognised. As a result, the clause has effectively become worthless as the seller cannot enforce it.

It is therefore unsurprising that this problem has been a particular issue for high-value assets which by their very nature are mobile and move between different jurisdictions frequently, such as aircraft, trains, ships or lorries. It therefore seems to be an obvious candidate for action at the international level. However, it was only in 2001 that a solution for security interests in certain times of mobile equipment was eventually adopted, the Convention on International Interests in Mobile Equipment, better known as the Cape Town Convention after the city where the diplomatic conference leading to its adoption was held.

The Cape Town Convention is interesting for several reasons. First, it provides a solution for the problem of enforcing security interests over certain movable assets in a cross-jurisdictional setting. Secondly, the drafting of the Convention gave rise to an innovative use of a main Convention and protocols to the Convention, known as the "two-instrument" or "Cape Town" approach. Thirdly, the drafting

---

1   *Aluminium Industrie Vaasen B.V. v Romalpa Aluminium Ltd.* [1976] 1 WLR 676; *Clough Mill Ltd. v Geoffrey Martin* [1985] 1 WLR 111; *Armour v Thyssen Edelstahlwerke AG* [1990] 3 All ER 481.

of the Convention and its protocols is noteworthy because of the close co-opera-tion between legal specialists and representatives from the industry sectors to which the Convention would apply in the first instance: aircraft, railway rolling stock and space equipment.[2] We will take a closer look at these issues in this chapter, although a discussion of the various protocols is beyond its scope.

In seeking to address the enforceability of security interests, it had to be accepted that it was possible to deal with property interests in the context of an international convention. We have already seen, for example, that there are no provisions in the CISG which regulate the transfer of ownership from seller to buyer under a con-tract of sale.[3] In seeking to find a solution for the recognition and enforceability of security interests, the Convention would touch upon a central aspect of personal property law. This provided a significant challenge, not only because it might prove difficult to find a workable solution to this issue, but also because any solu-tion would need to gain support from a large number of States if it was to have a significant impact.

3. The road to the Convention

The Cape Town Convention was carefully prepared.[4] Following an initial sug-gestion that this was a topic which might merit an international initiative, UNI-DROIT decided to undertake a scoping study to consider feasibility of uniform rules for security interests in mobile equipment. This resulted in a project which would consider the possibility of creating an international interest in such equip-ment. As this project progress, it was eventually limited to security interests in air-craft, railway rolling stock, space equipment and possibly ships, although ships were subsequently excluded from the project. A further question was how the different types of arrangement discussed earlier (charges, retention of title, leasing) should be treated under a potential international instrument.

The Convention began to take shape, and as it developed, specialist lawyers and industry representatives worked together to identify how the concerns on the business side could be reflected in the Convention.[5] In particular, the International Civil Aviation Organization (ICAO) was a key player in this process.[6] It became apparent that, whilst there were themes common to the three sectors involved in the prepara-tion of the Convention, each sector also had distinct concerns. These were fleshed out in different working groups. As work on the aircraft aspects developed more rapidly

2   Cf. Art. 2(3).
3   See Chapter 4 at 4.3.
4   See further R. Goode, "The Cape Town Convention on International Interests in Mobile Equipment: a driving force for international asset-based financing" (2002) 7 *Uniform Law Review* 3.
5   Cf. S. Gopalan, "Harmonization of commercial law: lessons from the Cape Town Convention on International Interests in Mobile Equipment" (2003) 9 *Law and Business Review of the Americas* 255, esp. pp.268–270.
6   The ICAO is a specialist agency of the United Nations, with 185 Member States.

than those on space assets and railway rolling stock, a novel approach was adopted: rather than seeking to have one convention which brought together all three categories of equipment in one convention, it was decided that there should be a base convention which would lay down common aspects, such as the recognition of the international interest, the International Registry, priorities between different interests in the same asset, and assignment. Additional matters specific to a particular category of equipment would be covered in a separate protocol to the Convention, with a separate protocol being developed for each category of asset. Although not uncontroversial, this approach won the day, and it was possible to complete the Convention and the protocol dealing with aircraft at a diplomatic conference in Cape Town on 16 November 2001.

3.1 The two-instrument approach

As already noted, one of the features of the Cape Town Convention is its combination of the main, or base, Convention with the use of protocols. The immediate practical benefit of this approach was the timely adoption of the Convention and at least of the Aircraft Protocol. However, there were further reasons for adopting this approach. The subject-matter of the Convention is very technical, and despite the common objective of creating an international interest over these assets, there are different ways of doing this. The use of protocols made it possible to deal with the detailed technical requirement of each category of equipment separately. For each category of equipment, the Convention and the relevant protocol are to be read as a single text.[7] If there are inconsistencies between the Convention and a protocol, the protocol is to prevail,[8] not least because it contains detailed provisions and definitions relevant to the category of equipment it covers, but also because it modifies the provisions of the Convention itself to reflect particular industry practices.

Inevitably, there was considerable debate about this approach, and not all delegations were supportive. They preferred a consolidated text for each type of equipment, so effectively entirely separate conventions. As a compromise, the UNIDROIT and ICAO secretariats have produced a consolidated text of the Cape Town Convention and the Aircraft Protocol, but this is non-binding.[9]

Although this process helped to accelerate the drafting and adoption of the Convention, it also added an additional challenge: the drafting of the Convention had to ensure that it provided a clear overall structure whilst retaining sufficient flexibility to allow for modifications by each protocol.

The Convention itself is confined to aircraft, railway rolling stock and space assets,[10] but Article 51 provides for the possibility of extending the scope of application to other categories of high-value mobile equipment, as long as each item

---

7   Art. 6(1).
8   Art. 6(2).
9   Accessible via https://www.icao.int/secretariat/legal/DCME2011/Pages/doc.aspx [accessed December 2020].
10 Art. 2(3).

within such a category is uniquely identifiable. In 2005, UNIDROIT decided to commence work on a further protocol, focusing on Mining, Agricultural and Construction equipment ("MAC Protocol"), and this was eventually adopted in 2019.[11] In the future, other protocols might be added,[12] although experience to date indicates that negotiations are likely to be lengthy, and there is no guarantee that the final product will receive a sufficient number of ratifications.

It is noteworthy that the Cape Town Convention relies on protocols in a novel manner. Sundahl noted that protocols have traditionally been used in one of four ways: (i) protocols of signature (adding provisions not suitable for the main convention); (ii) protocols of amendment to modify or delete provisions in a convention; (iii) optional protocols containing additional commitments; and (iv) protocols to a framework convention to flesh out detailed obligations in respect of broad commitments set out in the convention.[13] In short, protocols generally supplement a Convention. In contrast, the Cape Town Convention *relies* on its protocols to have any effect in the first place: on its own, the Convention does not work, and Contracting States also need to ratify at least one protocol. For the Cape Town Convention, the protocols are therefore an integral feature and not an optional addition to the Convention. The advantage of this approach is to start with provisions which are broadly suitable for different types of equipment, and to use each equipment-specific protocol to supplement and, where necessary, modify the provisions of the main Convention. This approach allows the development of a basic system which can then be adjusted for specific types of equipment as necessary, and may ultimately result in a broadening of the Convention's reach beyond the initially envisaged types of equipment. However, it does bring with it the risk of fragmentation if protocols adjust too many of the common provisions from the Convention, and the varying speed at which protocols might be developed could make the process of achieving the key objectives of the Convention a lengthy one.[14] Nevertheless, the novel approach for utilising conventions via the two-instrument method could become a template for the adoption of conventions in other areas, whether in the field of International Commercial Law, or elsewhere.

---

11 See T. Rodríguez de las Heras Ballell, "Complexities arising from the expansion of the Cape Town Convention to other sectors: the MAC Protocol's challenges and innovative solutions" (2018) 23 *Uniform Law Review* 214.

12 E.g., on renewable energy equipment: O. Böger, "A possible protocol to the Cape Town Convention on renewable energy equipment" (2018) 23 *Uniform Law Review* 242; or ships and maritime equipment: O. Böger, "The case for a new protocol to the Cape Town Convention covering security over ships" (2016) 5 *Cape Town Convention Journal* 73, although see B. Köhler, "Heading towards Cape Town? Some remarks on the preparation of a future protocol to the Cape Town Convention with respect to ships and maritime equipment" (2017) 22 *Uniform Law Review* 507.

13 M.J. Sundahl, "The 'Cape Town approach': a new method of making international law" (2006) 44 *Columbia Journal of Transnational Law* 339, pp.355–358.

14 Sundahl discusses 10 advantages (pp.360–364) and seven disadvantages (pp.364–369) of this approach.

3.2 Ratification of the Convention and its protocols

The Convention and its Aircraft Protocol rapidly gained the minimum number of ratifications, and it entered into force on 1 March 2006, which, by International Commercial Law standards, is extremely swift. By December 2020, there were a total of 82 Contracting States, including the EU.[15] There are also now three protocols in place. The one regarding aircrafts was adopted at the same time as the Cape Town Convention. Since then, 79 States have ratified the protocol. It is the only one which has entered into force thus far. The Railway Protocol was adopted in Luxembourg on 23 February 2007, but as of December 2020 had only been ratified by three States, whereas four are required before the Protocol will come into effect.[16] There are six further signatories, and only one additional ratification is required for it to enter into force, so there is a reasonable prospect that this might happen in due course. Finally, the protocol dealing with space assets was adopted in Berlin on 9 March 2012, more than a decade after the Cape Town Convention itself was adopted. It requires 10 ratifications before it can take effect, but so far, only four States have signed it and none has ratified it.

The UK was among the original signatories, but only ratified the Convention as a whole in July 2015, and it came into effect in the UK from 1 November 2015, together with the Aircraft Protocol.[17] In February 2016, the UK also signed the Railway Protocol, but has not yet ratified this.[18]

The fact that the Aircraft Protocol was not only ready for adoption alongside the Convention, but also its ratification by a large number of States, confirms that there was a real and urgent need for an international instrument that would ensure the recognition of security interests over aircraft. Indeed, its positive impact on the aircraft financing market was noted not long after its entry into force.[19] The significant time-lag between the adoption of this and the two other protocols (and the recent addition of the MAC Protocol) indicates that the work on the aircraft aspect of the Cape Town system was significantly more advanced than those for the other two categories of equipment, and the decision to pursue the two-instrument approach has been vindicated. Had this approach not been adopted, then final agreement on a convention

---

15   Note that the EU's ratification only relates to some aspects within its competence, and that each EU Member State also has to ratify the Convention separately in order to become a full Contracting State.

16   Art. XXIII of the Luxembourg Protocol.

17   The International Interests in Aircraft Equipment (Cape Town Convention) Regulations 2015, S.I. 2015/912.

18   France signed in March 2017. The Channel Tunnel train service might be a factor that will encourage both France and the UK to ratify the Railway Protocol.

19   G. Mauri, "The Cape Town Convention on Interests in Mobile Equipment as applied to aircraft: are lenders better off under the Geneva Convention?" (2005) 13 *European Review of Private Law* 641; L. Weber, "Public and private features of the Cape Town Convention" (2015) 4 *Cape Town Convention Journal* 53; S. Gopalan, "A demandeur-centric approach to regime design in transnational commercial law" (2008) *Georgetown Journal of International Law* 327, p.352.

covering all three categories of equipment would have taken a lot longer, and possible put the entire project in jeopardy.

4. The Cape Town Convention

The Cape Town Convention is a good example of how conventions in the field of International Commercial Law can be used successfully to provide an international-level solution to a problem which could not have been tackled by one jurisdiction acting on its own. The Preamble emphasises the desire for the Convention to be practical by reflecting the principles underpinning asset-based financing and leasing and to support party autonomy. Party autonomy is reflected in various substantive provisions, as well as the right of the parties to agree in writing[20] which court will have jurisdiction over any claims brought under the Convention, irrespective of whether the chosen court has any connection with the parties or their transaction.[21]

Moreover, because of the nature of these financing arrangements, the Convention aims for a high degree of predictability, reflected in particular in the large number of definitions both in the Convention itself and in the protocols. The Convention alone provides 40 definitions of various terms and phrases used throughout the Convention in Article 1. Another feature of the Convention is that its drafters were mindful of the impact it might have on national laws, practices and procedures regarding secured trans-actions. This resulted in a list of declarations which could be made by a Contracting State regarding the application of certain provisions. All of these features are discussed below.

Substantively, the Cape Town Convention found a novel solution for dealing with the problem of ensuring the recognition and enforceability of security inter-ests across jurisdictions. One possible approach was to provide for the mutual recognition of security interests by the Contracting States, but whilst this might have provided greater assurance of enforceability, it still would have had the drawback of not providing sufficient information to lenders or suppliers about the existence of security interests. So, a lender being asked to advance money in return for a security interest over a particular asset might have had to take numerous steps to discover the existence of any prior security interests over the same asset.

So instead, the Convention introduces a new type of security interest, the *inter-national interest*. This is combined with the creation of an International Registry, where any international interests can be registered. This allows anyone to search one single register to discover the existence of an international interest over a par-ticular asset. Many of the substantive provisions of the Conventions deal with the creation of the international interest, its perfection through registration in the International Registry, the priorities as between competing interests, the rights of the holder of a particular security interest, and the effects of an assignment of the

---

20 The meaning of "writing" for the purposes of the Convention is discussed below.
21 Art. 42. However, this does not apply to insolvency proceedings: Art. 45. For a dis-cussion, see K.F. Kreuzer, "Jurisdiction and the choice of law under the Cape Town Convention and the protocols thereto" (2013) 2 *Cape Town Law Journal* 149.

"associated rights", i.e., the rights to payment or other performance of a supplier, lessor or lender secured by the asset in question.[22]

4.1 An overview of the key provisions of the Cape Town Convention

The Convention is an interesting and somewhat complex combination of public features (such as the public register and its complex system of declarations) and private features (default, self-help remedies).[23] In this part, the main features of the Convention will be discussed so as to provide a general explanation of the Cape Town system. For present purposes, the detailed interaction between the Convention and the various protocols is not necessary.[24]

4.1.1 Sphere of application

The Cape Town Convention will apply if the debtor[25] is situated in a Contracting State at the time the agreement which gives rise to the international interest is concluded.[26] For this purpose, a debtor is "situated in a Contracting State" if a Contracting State is where (i) the debtor is incorporated; (ii) the debtor has its registered office or statutory seat; (iii) it has its central administration; or (iv) it has its place of business.[27] This ensures that any connection of the debtor with a Contracting State suffices to engage the Convention. It does not matter that the debtor might be incorporated in one Contracting State and have its central administration in another, as long as the debtor can be connected to at least one Contracting State. This is the only connecting factor to bring the Convention into play – the creditor[28] does not have to be situated in a Contracting State for the Convention to apply.[29] It is possible for a Protocol to add additional criteria for the Convention to apply. The Aircraft Protocol, for example, adds that the asset is a

---

22   Art. 1(c).

23   See further, L. Weber, "Public and private features of the Cape Town Convention" (2015) 4 *Cape Town Convention Journal* 53.

24   For an authoritative discussion, see R. Goode's commentaries: *Official Commentary on the Cape Town Convention and the Protocol Thereto on Matters Specific to Aircraft Equipment*, 4th ed. (UNIDROIT, 2019); *Official Commentary on the Cape Town Convention and the Protocol Thereto on Space Assets* (UNIDROIT, 2014); and *Official Commentary on the Cape Town Convention and the Luxembourg Protocol on Matters Specific to Railway Rolling Stock*, 2nd ed. (UNIDROIT, 2014).

25   Defined as "a chargor under a security agreement, a conditional buyer under a title reservation agreement, a lessee under a leasing agreement or a person whose interest in an object is burdened by a registrable non-consensual right or interest" (Art. 1(j)).

26   Art. 3(1).

27   Art. 4(1). Where the debtor has multiple places of business, the principal place of business is determinative. In the absence of a place of business, the debtor's habitual residence is used as the relevant criterion instead (Art. 4(2)).

28   Defined as "a chargee under a security agreement, a conditional seller under a title reservation agreement or a lessor under a leasing agreement" (Art. 1(i)).

29   Art. 3(2).

helicopter or an airframe which has been registered in an aircraft register of a Contracting State.[30]

4.1.2 Interpretation and applicable law

Article 5(1) deals with the interpretation of the Convention. Unlike many other International Commercial Law conventions, this provision does not simply replicate Art. 7(1) CISG. Instead, it provides that the criteria to guide the Convention's interpretation are (i) the purpose as set out in the Preamble to the Convention, (ii) its international character, (iii) the need to promote uniformity in its application, and, crucially, (iv) the need to promote predictability in its application. It will be immediately apparent that there is no mention of "good faith" in this instance, which contrasts with all the other International Commercial Law conventions examined in this book. Instead, the need for predictability is stressed. The difficulties with the "good faith" reference in the interpretative articles in other conventions are well known,[31] and so it was felt that retaining this in the Cape Town Convention would create a potential risk of uncertainty in the way the Convention might be interpreted by a court.

With regard to matters "governed by" the Convention but "not expressly settled in it", i.e., gaps in the Convention, Art. 5(2) requires such matters to be resolved in line with the general principles on which the Convention is based (some of which are set out in the Preamble). This is comparable to the corresponding provision in other Conventions. Where there are no principles, the matter should be resolved in line with the applicable law, which, in this instance, are the rules of the national law which apply "by virtue of the rules of private international law of the forum State".[32]

4.1.3 International interest

Perhaps the biggest novelty for International Commercial Law in the Cape Town Convention is its creation of an "international interest". A number of requirements have to be met before an international interest over a particular asset is created. The first is that there has to be one of these three types of arrangement:[33]

a   A charge over an asset granted by a chargor;[34]
b   A title reservation/conditional sale agreement, under which a seller retains title/ownership of the asset in question;
c   A leasing agreement, under which the owner (lessor) leases the goods to a lessee.

---

30 Art. IV(1) Aircraft Protocol.
31 See Chapter 3 at 5.1.1.
32 Art. 5(3).
33 Art. 2(2).
34 In this situation, the chargor is already the owner of the asset in question, but uses this as security for finance.

As noted earlier, the classification of these arrangements varies between jurisdictions, and so it is for the law applicable to the arrangement to determine which of the three types of arrangements exists.[35] The Convention itself does not contain any provisions dealing with the classification of the underlying agreement – it takes the existence of one of these three types of agreement as the starting point for the creation of the international interest.

These arrangements must relate to an asset which is *uniquely identifiable* and be an asset belonging to one of three categories: (i) airframes, aircraft engines and helicopters; (ii) railway rolling stock; and (iii) space assets.[36] The asset must also have been "designated in the Protocol", which means that a protocol in relation to the category in question must exist and be in force. A challenge which arose for drafting the MAC Protocol was that it covers a much wider range of equipment, and so the drafters came up with a novel way of determining the types of mining, agricultural and construction equipment which would come within the scope of the Protocol. Rather than listing every item which might be covered, the MAC Protocol instead refers, in three separate annexes, to the codes used by the World Customs Organization in its six-digit Harmonized System in respect of a range of mining, agricultural and construction equipment. Equipment will therefore fall under the Cape Town system if it is of a type covered by one of these codes *and* is uniquely identifiable, e.g., through the manufacturer's serial number.[37]

Article 7 of the Convention then introduces a number of formalities which are required before an international interest can be recognised under the Convention. First, the agreement which creates or provides for the interest[38] must be in writing.[39] It is not necessary that the agreement is contained in a physical document, however. An extended notion of writing applies under the Convention, covering a record of information which is "tangible or other form and is capable of being reproduced in tangible form", and this includes information "communicated by teletransmission".[40] The definition also requires that this record "indicates by reasonable means a person's approval of the record".[41] Although not expressed in those terms, this seems to require that the document has been signed, or has had a seal affixed to it, as this would be a common means of indicating consent.

Secondly, the agreement must relate to an asset (object) which the person creating the interest has the power to dispose.[42] So, for example, a conditional seller must be the owner of the asset and be able to sell it to the buyer. Similarly, a

---

35 Art. 2(4).
36 Art. 2(3). Note the final sentence of Art. 2(2), which seeks to prevent the classification of an arrangement under more than one heading.
37 Art. XVII, MAC Protocol.
38 I.e., "a security agreement, a title reservation agreement or a leasing agreement" (Art. 1 (a)).
39 Art. 7(a).
40 Art. 1(nn).
41 *Ibid.*
42 Art. 7(b).

chargor must be able to create a charge over an asset. The third requirement is that the asset can be identified in accordance with the criteria for identification laid down in the relevant protocol.[43] Finally, if the agreement in question is a security agreement, it is possible to determine the obligations which have been secured on the asset from the agreement, although it is not necessary to state a sum or specify a maximum sum which has been so secured.[44]

Once all these requirements have been satisfied, an "international interest" has been created. One final point is important to note: the international interest covers not only the particular asset, but also the *proceeds* of that asset.[45] However, for the purposes of this Convention, the term "proceeds" has a distinct meaning. Article 1 (w) defines it as "money or non-money proceeds of an object arising from the total or partial loss or physical destruction of the object or its total or partial confiscation, condemnation or requisition". Consequently, "proceeds" here does not relate to the proceeds that might have been obtained from reselling the asset, but instead covers things such as insurance payment or compensation payments.

However, these requirements merely deal with the *creation* of the international interests. A second essential step for the international interest to fulfil its intended purpose is the *registration* of that interest in the database maintained by the International Registry. Once this has been done, the international interest has been perfected.

4.1.4 International Registry

The Convention establishes the International Registry, where international interests created in accordance with Arts. 2 and 7 can be registered.[46] In fact, the Registry is intended to permit the registration of more than just an international interest. In addition, it is possible to register a prospective international interest,[47] registrable non-consensual rights and interests,[48] assignments[49] and prospective assignments[50] of international interests, as well as acquisitions of an international interest through legal

---

43 Art. 7(c).
44 Art. 7(d).
45 Art. 2(5).
46 The only registry currently in operation is the one for aircraft equipment. See www. internationalregistry.aero [accessed December 2020].
47 Defined as "an interest that is intended to be created or provided for in an object as an international interest in the future, upon the occurrence of a stated event (which may include the debtor's acquisition of an interest in the object), whether or not the occurrence of the event is certain" (Art. 1(y)).
48 This phrase refers to a right or interest intended to secure the performance of an obligation, and which arises under the law of a Contracting State, where that State has made a declaration under Art. 39 (cf. Art. 1(s)).
49 Defined as "a contract which, whether by way of security or otherwise, confers on the assignee associated rights with or without a transfer of the related international interest" (Art. 1(b)).
50 Defined as "an assignment that is intended to be made in the future, upon the occurrence of a stated event, whether or not the occurrence of the event is certain" (Art. 1 (x)).

or contractual subrogation, notices of national interests[51] and any subordinations of any of these interests.[52]

The Registry is to be established under the auspices of a Supervisory Authority[53] and to be operated by a Registrar, as detailed in the relevant Protocol. The activities by the Registrar are to be monitored by the Supervisory Authority.[54] The Registrar may be liable to pay compensation if an error or omission by the Registrar or a malfunction of the registration system results in loss to a person.[55] However, there will be no liability where the event was of an "inevitable and irresistible nature", which could not have been prevented.[56] Furthermore, the Registrar's liability does not extend to inaccurate information provided to the Registrar, or any matters beyond the Registrar's responsibility which arose before the registration information had been submitted to the register.[57]

In essence, the Registry works on a "notice-filing" approach, which requires the provision of basic information about the transaction giving rise to the interest, and the interest itself. The Registry itself is intended to be electronic.[58] The requirements for registration are specified in the relevant protocol and any regulations which the Supervisory Authority has determined in accordance with the protocol, notably the criteria by which an asset is identifiable.[59] Some requirements are also stipulated in the Convention itself. In particular, a registration will only be valid if this is done in accordance with the requirements of Article 20.[60] This specifies that, in order to register an international interest (as well as prospective international interest, or a (prospective) assignment of an international interest), both parties have to consent to its registration. Either party may register the interest, and the other party's consent to that registration has to be made in writing.[61] The extended meaning of "writing" was noted earlier. Similarly, where an international interest is to be subordinated to another international interest, this subordination can be registered either by the party whose interest is to be subordinated, or by another person with the written consent of that party.[62] For other types of registrable interest (those arising from subrogation, registrable non-consensual rights or interest, or notice of a national interest) may only be registered by the person in whose favour that interest operates, i.e., the subrogee or holder.

---

51 Defined as "an interest held by a creditor in an object and created by an internal transaction covered by a declaration under Article 50(1)" (Art. 1(r)).
52 Art. 16(1).
53 The supervisory authority is to enjoy international legal personality (Art. 27(1)).
54 The detailed obligations of the Supervisory Authority are laid down in Art. 17(2).
55 Art. 28(1).
56 *Ibid.*
57 Art. 28(2).
58 On the possible reason for its swift success, see J.K. Winn, "The Cape Town Convention's International Registry: decoding the secrets of success in global electronic commerce" (2012) 1 *Cape Town Convention Journal* 25.
59 Art. 18(1).
60 Art. 19(1).
61 Art. 20(1).
62 Art. 20(2).

The registration is complete once all the required information has been entered on the International Registry's database and the entry has become searchable.[63] An entry is searchable once it has been allocated a file number, all the registration information has been stored in durable form, and the entry can be accessed via the Registry.[64] Registrations have to be entered in chronological order of receipt, and the entry has to record the date and time when it was received by the International Registry.[65]

As the Convention permits the registration of a prospective international interest, questions arise as to what should happen once a prospective interest becomes an actual interest. If the information provided at the time of registering the prospective interest is sufficient to fulfil the requirements for registering an international interest, then no further registration of the international interest is required.[66] Moreover, the time of the creation of the international interest will be the time when the prospective interest was registered, as long as that registration was still current.[67]

Once an international interest has been registered, it will remain effective until it is either discharged, or when any period of registration specified when registering the interest has expired.[68]

4.1.4.1 Searching the Register

The Register must be searchable.[69] The requirements for making a search and for the issuing of search certificates are determined in the relevant protocol and any regulations adopted by the Supervisory Authority.[70] Generally, any person[71] is permitted to search the Register for any interests or prospective interests which have been recorded on the Register in respect of a particular asset.[72] Such searches are to be conducted by electronic means. The Registrar has to issue an electronic search certificate which states all the registered information in relation to the asset, including the date and time of registration,[73] as well as that the creditor named in the registration information has acquired, or intends to acquire, an international interest (but not whether the registration relates to an international or prospective international interest).[74]

Where no information relating to the particular asset has been recorded on the Register, then a certificate to that effect has to be issued.[75]

63 Art. 19(2).
64 Art. 19(3).
65 Art. 18(4).
66 Art. 18(3).
67 Art. 19(4). The same applies to a prospective assignment.
68 Art. 21.
69 Art. 19(6).
70 Art. 18(2).
71 Art. 26 states that no person can be precluded from accessing the registration and search facilities of the Register, unless that person has failed to comply with the procedures laid down in the Convention.
72 Art. 22(1).
73 Art. 22(2)(a).
74 Art. 22(3).
75 Art. 22(2)(b).

4.1.4.2 Discharge of a registration

Registration of an international interest will only be required as long as the international interest itself continues to exist. Thus, if a buyer has completed all its payments under a conditional sale agreement, the debt is paid and ownership of the asset is transferred to the buyer. Similarly, once a borrower has paid back a loan, the lender's security interest over the buyer's asset(s) ceases. Where this happens, the international interest needs to be removed from the Register.

There are a number of instances when a registration can or must be discharged. An existing registration may be discharged either by the party in whose favour the interest was created, or with that party's written consent.[76] Furthermore, if the obligations or conditions for which the interest had been created have been fulfilled, and once the debtor has demanded in writing that the interest be discharged, the holder of the interest is required to request that the registration is discharged without undue delay.[77]

In the cases of prospective interests or prospective assignments where no value has been transferred nor a commitment to give value been entered, the intending debtor or assignor can demand in writing that the prospective creditor/assignee discharge that registration.[78] A similar obligation exists where the obligations secured by a national interest have been fulfilled and the debtor has made a written demand for the discharge of the registration of that interest.[79]

Finally, if a registration should not have been made at all, or where it is incorrect, the person in whose favour the registration was made is responsible for asking for the registration to be either discharged or corrected, again at the written demand of the debtor.[80]

4.1.5 International interest: priorities and effects of insolvency

So far, we have seen how an international interest is created, and what needs to be done to ensure that the correct information about the interest is recorded on the Register. One of the reasons for registering the interest is the transparency element – the Register is searchable by anyone, and so anyone can discover whether a particular asset is subject to an existing international interest, or whether one is about to be created. This will be important for conditional sellers and lessors of mobile assets because registration will ensure that anybody who might consider advancing finance on the security of that asset is made aware of the existing international interest. Similarly, a lender can verify whether an asset is already subject to an existing international interest before agreeing the terms for providing finance secured on that asset. Registration has two further important consequences, though: the first is that registration is important

---

76   Art. 20(3).
77   Art. 25(1).
78   Art. 25(2).
79   Art. 25(3).
80   Art. 25(4).

for determining the priorities of multiple interests over the same asset, i.e., which interest should prevail over other interest when it comes to either retaking possession of the asset or taking over the asset in order to realise its economic value. Generally speaking, the timing of registration determines the order of priorities as between different interests.[81] Secondly, registration ensures that the international interest is effective against a liquidator (or similar), and the holder of the interest can exercise whichever remedies are available where there has been a default by the acquirer under the agreement which gave rise to the interest.

4.1.5.1 Priorities

A crucial effect of registering an interest is that it gains priority over any unregistered interests which might also have been created over the same asset.[82] Moreover, if there is more than one *registered* interest, the timing of registration determines the order of priority as between those registered interests, reflecting the "first in time prevails" principle. The importance of registration is underlined by the fact that whoever registers their interest first will have the highest priority, even if that interest was acquired or registered with knowledge of the existence of other as yet unregistered interests.[83] This can have the effect that a person in whose favour an international interest was created *after* an earlier agreement which also gave rise to an international interest can jump to the top of the order of priorities if that person registers the interest before anyone else registers their interest.

If the asset is sold, then the buyer of the asset will be subject to any interest which had been registered before the buyer acquired its interest in the asset as owner, i.e., ownership in the asset is transferred to the buyer subject to any existing and registered interests.[84] If the asset is transferred under a title reservation agreement or lease, then the person acquiring the asset takes subject to any interests which were registered prior to the interest which the conditional seller or lessor will have over the asset.[85] However, in either situation, the asset will be transferred free from any interest which existed but had not been registered at the time of sale or transfer of the asset, even where the acquirer had actual knowledge of the existence of an existing unregistered interest.[86] Here, the Convention uses a bright-line rule to determine priority: all that matters is registration of the international interest, and any actual knowledge about the existence of other, unregistered interests is generally irrelevant.

Although these rules are broadly clear, the Convention emphasises the importance of party autonomy in its Preamble. It is therefore possible for the holders of

---

81 Cf. Art. 29(1). The priority given to an interest in the asset extends to the proceeds from that asset (Art. 29(6)), the meaning of proceeds being the one in Art. 1(w), mentioned earlier.

82 Art. 29(1).

83 Art. 29(2).

84 Art. 29(3)(a).

85 Art. 29(4)(b).

86 Art. 29(3)(b) and (4)(b), respectively.

competing interests to agree on a different order of priorities from the one stipulated under Art. 29(1).[87] This could have the effect of "subordinating" an interest with higher priority under Art. 29(1) to one of lower priority. As we saw earlier, an agreement to subordinate an interest can be registered by or with the consent of the person whose interest has been subordinated,[88] and so once an agreement to change the order of priority has been reached, this can be registered. Indeed, such registration is important in case there is a subsequent assignment of a subordinated interest, because an assignee would not be bound by a subordination agreement which had not been registered.[89]

Finally, Art. 29(7) deals with "items installed on an object". For example, it may be that specialist equipment, e.g., to conduct search and rescue missions, is installed on an aircraft. That equipment may have been supplied subject to a lease or title reservation agreement. If the installation of this on an aircraft does not have the effect of extinguishing the rights of the conditional seller or lessor under the applicable law, then those rights will also not be affected by the registration of an international interest over the airframe. This means that, should the holder of the international interests exercise the default remedies in relation to the airframe, the holder of the interest in the equipment can continue to assert its rights over the equipment.[90]

4.1.5.2 Insolvency

A further beneficial effect of registration becomes relevant, should the debtor become insolvent and insolvency proceedings commence. In that case, a registered international interest is effective, which means that the holder of the interest takes priority over anyone else in the insolvency proceedings, and can exercise the default remedies.[91] Moreover, if under the applicable law, the interest is effective without having been registered in accordance with the requirements of the Convention, then the interest will still be effective.[92]

However, insolvency proceedings can often be complex and may involve close scrutiny of the conduct of the debtor's business in the period leading up to the insolvency. In particular, the directors of a company approaching insolvency may take steps to dispose assets so they are beyond the reach of the company's creditors and the insolvency administrator. Where this happens, it may be possible under national insolvency law to have such transactions set aside on the basis that it is an unlawful

---

87 Art. 29(5).
88 Art. 20(2).
89 Art. 29(5).
90 Art. 29(7)(a). Article 29(7)(b) is a corresponding provision for instances where the rights over the item are created after installation of the item on an object. In the example in the text above, this might be where the equipment was owned by the acquirer of the aircraft and then used as security to raise finance.
91 Art. 30(1).
92 Art. 30(2).

preference,[93] or that it was a transaction which amounted to a fraud on the company's creditors.[94] The priority rules under the Cape Town Convention are not intended to affect the possibility of taking action under such national laws.[95] Furthermore, once insolvency proceedings have commenced, all the assets belonging to, or in the possession of, the debtor will be controlled by the insolvency administrator, and national law may impose procedural requirements which need to be complied with for a holder of a registered interest to exercise their default remedies. These procedural requirements are also not affected by the priority given to a registered international interest in insolvency proceedings.[96]

4.1.6 Default remedies

The Convention specifies what the remedies of a creditor will be in case the debtor is in default. The parties can agree, in writing, the events which they regard as putting the debtor in default under their agreement,[97] reflecting the importance given by the Convention to party autonomy. Where there is no specific agreement as to the events which are deemed to constitute a default, the Convention provides that a default is a default which "substantially deprives the creditor of what it is entitled to expect under the agreement".[98] This seems to be setting a high threshold for establishing that a default has occurred – "substantial deprivation" would suggest that the creditor would not receive most of the expected performance under the agreement. However, there is a degree of inherent vagueness in this threshold standard, which leaves room for argument as to whether the effect of a default was such as to cross that threshold.[99] It falls somewhere between a "minor" deprivation and a total deprivation, but quite where the threshold falls on this spectrum is a matter of debate in the context of each particular agreement. A creditor keen on a high level of predictability might therefore prefer to seek an agreement with the debtor to apply a clearer standard, or at least to specify that events which are less detrimental than the fall-back notion of "default" are sufficient to constitute a default. For example, the creditor and debtor could agree that a number of late or missed payments might be sufficient to constitute a default, particularly where there is no track-record of previous dealings which would give the creditor sufficient confidence as to the reliability of the debtor.

Once a default has happened, the remedies available to a creditor will depend on the nature of the agreement between it and the debtor. If the arrangement is a title reservation agreement or a lease, the creditor will simply take possession of the asset

93 See, e.g., s.239 of the Insolvency Act 1986 (UK).
94 See, e.g., s.213 of the Insolvency Act 1986 (UK).
95 Art. 30(3)(a).
96 Art. 30(3)(b).
97 Art. 11(1).
98 Art. 11(2).
99 See further, S. Saidova, *Security Interests under the Cape Town Convention on International Interests in Mobile Equipment* (Hart, 2018), pp.180–185.

and terminate the agreement.[100] Under the Convention, this is treated as a "self-help" remedy, i.e., it is not envisaged that it would be necessary to seek a court order before this remedy could be exercised.[101] However, it is possible for a Contracting State to make a declaration to the effect that leave of a court is required before exercising this remedy.[102] Even where a leave of the court is not required under the applicable law, the creditor may seek a court order which authorises repossession or directs the handing-over of the asset which is the subject of the agreement.[103]

There are more detailed rules in respect of rights granted to the chargee because a chargee will not usually be the owner of the asset. Chargor (debtor) and chargee (creditor) should have agreed the remedies which the chargee may exercise in the event of the default. The remedies which may be available are (i) to take possession or control of any object over which the chargee has a charge; (ii) sell or lease a charged asset; or (iii) collect or receive any income/profits which stem from the use or management of the asset.[104] These are also regarded as self-help remedies, but once again subject to any declarations made by a Contracting State to require leave of a court before exercising the remedy.[105] Furthermore, a chargee could seek a court order to authorise its exercise of a remedy in any event.[106] Other remedies agreed by the parties or provided by the applicable law can also be exercised, but only to the extent that they are not inconsistent with the provisions on default remedies which the Convention regards as mandatory.[107]

Article 8(3) stipulates that the chargee must exercise any remedy in a "commercially reasonable manner", which seems to require no more than that the remedy is exercised in accordance with the agreement which created the chargee's interest in the asset, i.e., the security agreement. However, party autonomy in this regard seems to be limited by the proviso in Art. 8(3) that any term in a security agreement regarding the remedies which can be exercised by a chargee is not "manifestly unreasonable". Quite how this is to be determined is not further specified in the Convention and seems to introduce a surprising element of uncertainty. It seems clear that "commercial reasonableness" will be context specific, i.e., it will depend on the particular circumstances of the contract. Saidova has suggested that there are two general factors in addition to this: first, the creditor is required not only to act in its own interest but to have regard to the interests of the debtor; and secondly, as the Convention is

---

100 Art. 10(1).
101 The exact procedure under which any remedy can be exercised is the procedure laid down in the law of the place where the remedy is to be exercised: Art. 14.
102 Art. 54(2).
103 Art. 10(2).
104 Art. 8(1).
105 Art. 54(1).
106 Art. 8(2).
107 Art. 15 stipulates that the provisions of Art. 8(3)–(6) (notice before sale or lease, and application of sums received), Art. 9(3) and (4) (requirements for court order to vest ownership in chargee and effects of redemption of security), Art. 13(2) (protection of interested persons when ordering interim relief) and Art. 14 (applicable procedural requirements for exercising a remedy) are mandatory.

concerned with economic efficiency, the creditor should act in a manner which minimises economic waste.[108] In contrast, Veneziano[109] argues for a more restrictive interpretation of commercial reasonableness, arguing for an autonomous interpretation which gives priority to the contract between the parties and the possibility to spell out what might be commercially reasonable within that context. If the contract does not do so, then relevant considerations should be industry standards and customary practices with regard to financing in the particular sector.[110]

A chargee can only recover what is necessary to settle the outstanding debt. A chargee is therefore likely to sell or lease the asset after taking possession of it. The proceeds which are received by the chargee by virtue of any sale or lease are first used to settle the outstanding amount which has been secured by the charge,[111] as well as any reasonable costs which were incurred when exercising the remedy.[112] Insofar as the chargee obtains sums which exceed the secured amount and costs, any surplus is first distributed, in the order of priority, among the holders of other registered interests or those of which the chargee has been given notice.[113] Any remaining sums have to be passed to the chargor/debtor.

However, before the chargee can sell or leave the asset in question, reasonable prior notice of its intention to do so must be given to "interested persons",[114] i.e., the debtor and "any person who, for the purpose of assuring performance of any of the obligations in favour of the creditor, gives or issues a suretyship or demand guarantee or a standby letter of credit or any other form of credit insurance"; as well as any other person having rights over the object who have given notice to the chargee of their rights within a reasonable period of time before the asset is sold or leased.[115]

As well as exercising any of the remedies set out above, the chargee may agree with the debtor and other interested persons that ownership in the asset (or whatever interest the debtor has in the asset) is to vest in the chargee, either in or towards satisfaction of the obligations secured by the interest.[116] Alternatively, the chargee may ask for a court order to that effect,[117] which will be useful if no agreement can be reached. In the latter case, a court order can only be made if the value of the asset is commensurate with the amount secured taking account of any payment which the chargee has to make to any of the interested persons.[118]

The interest of a chargee is limited to securing the chargor's obligations under the security agreement. Consequently, once the chargor fulfils these obligations, the security

---

108 S. Saidova, *Security Interests under the Cape Town Convention on International Interests in Mobile Equipment* (Hart, 2018), pp.185–188.

109 A. Veneziano, "The contours of 'commercial reasonableness' under the Cape Town Convention" (2018) 7 *Cape Town Convention Journal* 83.

110 *Ibid.*, p.91.

111 Art. 8(5).

112 Art. 8(6).

113 *Ibid.*

114 Defined in Art. 1(m).

115 Art. 8(4).

116 Art. 9(1).

117 Art. 9(2).

118 Art. 9(3).

interest is discharged. In most cases, this will simply be full payment of the sums due to the chargee which have been secured by the security interest. Therefore, if the chargor pays the secured amount in full before the charged asset is sold, or before a court makes an order transferring ownership in the asset to the chargee, then the security interest is discharged.[119] However, where the chargee has already exercised the remedy of granting a lease, or where this has been ordered by a court, then the discharge will be subject to that lease.[120]

It is also possible that another interested person might pay the chargee the amount which has been secured. In that case, the effect of the payment by an interested person is that this person is "subrogated to the rights of the chargee", i.e., the person will assume the rights of the chargee as against the debtor. This effectively means that this person will become the new chargee under the security agreement, and is able to register that interest.[121]

Finally, where the chargee exercises the right to sell the asset on default by the debtor and ownership is transferred to the buyer, or where the ownership is transferred to the chargee as set out above, the transfer is free from any other interest over which the chargee's interest has priority.[122] In effect, any lower-ranking interests become ineffective in these circumstances.

4.1.7 Interim relief

A creditor who can provide evidence which shows that the debtor is in default may ask a court to make an order for interim relief whilst its claim is resolved and to the extent that the debtor has agreed to this. The courts which have jurisdiction to make such orders are either the court chosen by the parties, or the courts of the Contracting State on which the asset is situated.[123]

Such interim orders may provide for (a) the preservation of the asset; (b) transfer of possession, control or custody of the asset to the creditor; (c) immobilisation of the asset; or (d) lease or management of the object and income from this.[124] Any court order may make this subject to terms to protect interested persons, in case the creditor, when implementing the order, fails to perform its obligations towards the debtor under the Convention/protocol; or in case the creditor does not succeed in establishing its claim when it is finally determined. Moreover, a court may require that any interested person is given notice of the creditor's request for a court order for interim relief before making any order.[125] The final determination

---

119 Art. 9(4).
120 *Ibid.*
121 Cf. Art. 20(4).
122 Art. 9(5).
123 Art. 43(1).
124 Art. 13(1). In the case of (d), the court with jurisdiction is either one chosen by the parties, or the courts of the Contracting State where the debtor is located.
125 Art. 13(3).

of the creditor's claim may be dealt with by a court in another Contracting State, or through arbitration.[126]

4.1.8 Assignments

As we have seen, the purpose of a security interest is to ensure that the supplier of goods, or a lender, is protected in case the acquirer fails to make the agreed payments. In the language of the Convention, a security interest secures "associated rights", i.e., the right to payment or other performance by the debtor,[127] on the asset. However, as we have already seen, it is common for a creditor to assign, or factor, the right to receive payment ("receivables"), in order to receive funds more quickly than under the agreement with the debtor. If the creditor's right to receive payment is secured through an international interest, the question arises what should happen to the interest when there is an assignment of the right to receive payment. This is dealt with in Chapter IX of the Convention.[128] This sets out the formalities for an assignment, the effect on the international interest, as well as the debtor's duty towards the assignee (i.e., the person to whom the associated rights have been assigned).

For the purposes of the Convention, an assignment confers on the assignee the associated rights. This could be an outright assignment, or an assignment by way of security.[129] Not every assignment will have the effect of transferring the international interest, and the agreement between assignor and assignee may provide that the international interest should not be transferred.[130] Where this is the case, the Convention does not apply to that assignment.[131]

However, the basic position under the Convention is that an assignment of the associated rights which complies with the formalities laid down in Article 32 has the effect of transferring both the international interest *and* the interests and priorities of the assignor under the Convention to the assignee.[132] These formalities are that the assignment has to be made in writing and that it enables the identification of the associated rights under the contract from which they arise.[133] Additionally, if the assignment is by way of security, the obligations which have been secured by the assignment need to be determined in accordance with the provisions of the relevant protocol.[134] An assignment which only seeks to assign the international

---

126 Art. 43(3).
127 Art. 1(c).
128 The Convention is to prevail over the UN Convention on the Assignment of Receivables 2001 insofar as the assignment is one of receivables which are associated rights relating to international interests in the categories of assets to which the Cape Town Convention applies: Art. 45*bis*.
129 Art. 1(b). For instances where the assignment is by way of security, Art. 34 provides that the rights of a chargor under Arts. 8, 9 and 11–14 apply *mutatis mutandis*.
130 Art. 31(1), first seven words.
131 Art. 32(3).
132 Art. 31(1).
133 Art. 32(1)(a) and (b).
134 Art. 32(1)(c).

interest without assigning at least some of the associated rights is not valid,[135] which is logical as the international interest seeks to ensure the performance of those rights.

As assignment of the associated rights may be partial, i.e., the assignor may retain some of the associated rights and assign others. Where the assignment is partial, the assignor and assignee need to agree what their respective rights regarding the international interest are. However, this must not affect the debtor's position without its consent.[136]

If a valid assignment has been made, the debtor will be bound by the assignment and required to pay or perform the assigned obligations to the assignee, provided that notice in writing of the assignment has been given to the debtor, and that notice identifies the associated rights which have been assigned.[137] However, the debtor may have defences or rights of set-off as against the assignee under the applicable law and could rely on these,[138] unless the debtor has agreed in writing to waive these defences and rights of set-off.[139]

A difficult situation arises when there are competing assignments in relation to the associated rights. If at least one of these assignments also involves the assignment of the international interest, and this assignment has been registered, then the provisions of Article 29 dealing with priorities of interests are applied to determine the priorities as between the competing assignments.[140] However, the priority of an assignee of associated rights and the international interest requires that the contract under which these associated rights arise (i.e., the contract between the debtor and the creditor) must state they are secured by the asset, and only to the extent that these rights consists of the right to payment or performance of other obligations relating to the acquisition of the asset.[141] Where this is not the case, the applicable law determines the priority of competing assignments.

4.2 Use of declarations

It will be apparent from the discussion of the Convention's provisions that these are detailed and have an impact on national laws dealing with the enforcement of security interests. Many States might be reluctant to ratify the Convention because of the possible effect on established national procedures. This risk is addressed in the Convention by providing Contracting States with a range of permissible declarations, which allow them to adjust the scope of the Convention, or to maintain certain

---

135 Art. 32(2).
136 Art. 31(2).
137 Art. 33(1).
138 Art. 31(3).
139 Art. 31(4). This does not extend to defences in case the assignee has acted fraudulently.
140 Art. 35(1). Similarly, Art. 30 is applied *mutatis mutandis* in case of the debtor's insolvency.
141 Art. 36. The specific rights relating to the acquisition of the asset are set out in Art. 36 (2)(a)–(e).

national procedural requirements which are not required under the Convention. In view of the large number of Contracting States and the possible combinations of declarations that might be made, the Registrar is obliged to maintain a list of all the declarations which have been made by the Contracting States,[142] and this list can be searched on the Register.

A distinction is made between "opt-in" and "opt-out" declarations.[143] The former are made under Articles 39 and 40. Under Article 39, a Contracting State can make a declaration to the effect that certain non-consensual rights or interests are to have priority over an international interest, without the non-consensual right/interest having to be registered. Article 40 allows a Contracting State to specify those non-consensual rights/interests which are to be registrable in the International Registry, and will only have priority once registered.

In contrast, there are permitted opt-out declarations under Articles 54 and 55. The declarations under Art. 54 were already noted earlier. The first declaration under this Article is that a charge is not allowed to grant a lease of the charged asset whilst that asset is situated within, or controlled from, the Contracting State which has made the declaration. A second declaration may be made to require that any remedy to be available to a creditor may only be exercised with the leave of a court. The effect of this declaration is to opt-out from the "self-help" approach preferred under the Convention. Article 55 allows a Contracting State to declare that it will not apply the provisions for interim relief under Article 13 and/or the provisions in Article 43 on the courts which have jurisdiction for making an order under Article 13.

The possibility for a Contracting State to make multiple declarations could have the effect of undermining the uniformity and certainty pursued by the Convention. That said, the types of declarations relate primarily to procedural issues and do not affect the substantive scope of the Convention.

5. Conclusions

The Cape Town Convention is a novel way of creating International Commercial Law, which is suggest that conventions still have a role to play in the context of International Commercial Law. In a general sense, the Convention is a paradigm example of how conventions should be used in the context of International Commercial Law: a clear problem had been identified (concerns over the enforceability of security interests over mobile equipment and the resulting negative impact on raising finance) which required a tailored solution at the international level (provided through the international interest and the International Registry). The solution to the problem was developed in close co-operation with affected business sectors and therefore aligns

142 Art. 23.
143 There are additional declarations permitted under Arts. 52, 53, 57, 58 and 60 as well as the mandatory requirement for a regional development organisation to declare the matters in respect of which it has the competence to become a party to the Convention under Art. 48(2). The European Union is the only regional development organisation which has become a party to the Convention thus far.

as much as possible with the needs of commercial parties. At least in respect of aircraft, the Cape Town Convention entered into force rapidly and has been widely ratified. It has also had an immediate practical impact: the registration system is being used extensively, and there is evidence that cost of loans has been reduced. In focusing on facilitating the particular types of commercial transactions within the Convention's scope, it not only demonstrates the continuing role of conventions in the field of International Commercial Law, but also shows how conventions can bring about concrete economic benefits.[144]

One obvious *caveat* to regarding the Cape Town Convention as a success story has to be made, though: designed to apply to a number of different types of high-value mobile equipment, it has yet to secure sufficient support from individual States for the Cape Town system to extend to equipment other than aircraft. One can remain hopeful that this will happen in the not too distant future in respect of at least one of the other protocols.

The Cape Town Convention is significant well beyond its scope of application. The combination of the base convention with its equipment-specific protocols might lend itself to application in other areas of International Commercial Law, and beyond. For instance, some of the novel legal questions of the digital economy[145] might point to the need for international solutions, e.g., for the various kinds of digital platforms which are increasingly the focus of national and regional lawmakers. In this context, the two-instrument approach pioneered in the Cape Town Convention might be a template for future action.

It is also important to stress that the Cape Town Convention focuses on a sub-category (high-value, uniquely identifiable mobile assets) of a much broader element of commercial law: the treatment of secured transactions generally. A key development since the Cape Town Convention is the UNCITRAL Model Law on Secured Transactions, adopted in 2017. This is a comprehensive Model Law which offers a template for national legislators for developing a modern secured transaction law.[146] Furthermore, Mooney has suggested that the success of the Cape Town's International Registry might have laid the foundations for a general international secured transactions registry.[147]

---

144 J. Wool, "Treaty design, implementation and compliance benchmarking economic benefit – a framework as applied to the Cape Town Convention" (2012) 17 *Uniform Law Review* 633.
145 See Chapter 12.
146 A full discussion of this Model Law is beyond the scope of this book.
147 C.W. Mooney, "The Cape Town Convention's improbable-but-possible progeny part one: an international secured transactions registry of general application" (2014) 55 *Virginia Journal of International Law* 163.

9

DOCUMENTARY CREDITS

1. Introduction: payment in international commercial contracts

A common concern in many international contracts, particularly where the parties do not have an established business relationship, or when the goods which form the subject-matter of the contract are particularly high-value, is that both parties will be concerned that their performance will not be fully reciprocated by the other party's contractual counter-performance. Thus, a seller may be concerned that the buyer will not pay for goods after they have been despatched, particular if the seller has had no previous dealings with the particular buyer and therefore has no experience as to the buyer's reliability, or solvency. Conversely, a buyer may be reluctant to pay until the goods have been delivered and checked for their conformity with the contract. It would not be realistic for either party to insist on the other party performing its obligations before performing itself.

In order to resolve this impasse, international commerce has developed a system in which banks perform the role of a neutral and reliable intermediary to provide greater reassurance to both parties that the contract will be performed as expected. This is the documentary credit system. In essence, a documentary credit, or letter of credit, is an undertaking given by a bank to a seller of goods to pay the price due for the goods once the seller has fulfilled specified conditions. The seller has to provide the bank with the shipping documents and other documents as stipulated by the buyer. If all the documents are in order, the bank will pay the seller for the goods and hold the documents until the bank has been reimbursed by the buyer. The advantage for the seller is that the bank will pay once the seller has provided the required documents, and therefore the seller is less dependent on the buyer. At the same time, the buyer will be reassured that the seller has performed its obligations before payment is released (although there are residual risks whilst the goods are in transit to the buyer, of course).

DOI: 10.4324/9781315692807-9

2. What are documentary credits?

The system of documentary credit is based on the fact that in international commercial contracts, a seller of goods will not only have to ensure that the goods themselves are delivered, but will also be required to transfer a range of documents to the buyer. As goods are most commonly shipped using a third-party carrier, the *bill of lading* issued by the carrier will be the most significant document. A bill of lading is a commercial document which is issued by a carrier once goods have been received for transmission to the buyer. Crucially, a bill of lading is a document of title to the goods and the person named in the bill of lading is *prima facie* regarded as the owner of the corresponding goods. A bill of lading may be negotiable, which means that the bill of lading can be transferred to different persons, and whoever is the holder of the bill of lading will be recognised as the *prima facie* owner of the goods. This feature of a bill of lading is important for the documentary credit system, because a bank which has paid a seller for the goods will receive various documents including the bill of lading in return.

A documentary credit will be the agreed or stipulated method of payment in the contract of sale between seller and buyer. The buyer fulfils its obligation to pay for the goods by opening a documentary credit which identifies the seller as the beneficiary of the credit. The bank undertakes to pay the price of the goods to the seller once the seller has presented the shipping and other documents specified by the buyer when opening the documentary credit, provided that the information contained in those documents matches the information stipulated by the buyer. As such, the documentary credit system seeks to assure the buyer that funds will only be released to the seller when the specified documents are presented and in order, whilst assuring the seller that payment will be released once the required documents have been presented to the bank. The bank's role as intermediary is therefore crucial in providing those assurances to both seller and buyer.

However, banks will be concerned about the amount of risk they will be exposed to. A bank will be exposed once it has paid the seller in return for the required documents, as the buyer may not reimburse the bank for its expenditure, particularly if the buyer is concerned that the documents received by the bank are not what the buyer was expecting. Therefore, a bank will require clarity from the buyer as to the documents the seller must present and the information those documents must contain. A bank cannot investigate whether the documents presented by the seller are genuine, but can only verify the documents for their compliance with the requirements stated by the buyer. A bank which has paid a seller against documents which, on their face, conform, must therefore be able to claim reimbursement from the seller. We will see how the documentary credit system under the Uniform Customs and Practices for Documentary Credits (UCP) deals with this and other aspects.

Before we take a closer look, it is useful to distinguish documentary credits from two other ways of dealing with payment uncertainties in international commerce. The first is a *demand guarantee*. This is essentially an undertaking given by a bank in favour of a recipient of goods or services. It acts as a fall-back for instances when the supplier of the goods or services fails to perform its obligations. This means that it essentially serves as safeguard against the supplier's default, and in that sense has a different purpose than the documentary credit system. The second is the so-called *stand-by letter of credit*, which combines the features of a demand guarantee and a documentary credit. Payment will be made by the bank which has issued the stand-by letter of credit on presentation of the stipulated documents. However, its role is also to be utilised in cases of default, rather than as an integral part of the performance of the transaction.

3. The legal framework for documentary credits

Unlike other areas of International Commercial Law discussed in this book, the rules governing documentary credits are largely based on banking customs and practice. More significantly, they are not enshrined in a convention or model law, but rather in the Uniform Customs and Practices for Documentary Credits, known as the UCP600.[1] The current version of the UCP took effect from 2007, and is the seventh version of the UCP. The first version was published in 1933 and there have been reviews roughly every decade or so.[2] The body responsible for revising the UCP is the International Chamber of Commerce (ICC). The UCP are note-worthy because of their origins in usages developed between banks, rather than having been imposed by legislation. They govern almost all documentary credits, and are usually engaged by the parties to a documentary credit through incor-poration, although they can also be implied on the basis of an established course of dealings or even on the basis of international trade usage. Although documentary credits are used in order to ensure that payment is made under a contract for the sale of goods, they are an abstract form of undertaking operating independently from the underlying contract of sale. This is significant because of the specific role banks have with regard to the processing of payment for the goods, without being interested in the performance of other aspects of the contract of sale.

3.1 A brief outline of the process

3.1.1. Opening the credit

The starting point is the contract for the sale of goods between seller and buyer, under which the buyer will be required to open a documentary credit in order to ensure that the seller is paid. The buyer will approach a bank and open a doc-umentary credit. One of the things the buyer will have to do is to stipulate the conditions which must be met by the seller before payment can be made and the

---

1   For a concise discussion, see J. Ulph, "The UCP 600: documentary credits in the 21st century" (2007) *Journal of Business Law* 355.
2   Revisions were issued in 1951, 1962, 1974, 1983 and 1993.

documents which must be submitted in respect of each condition. Any conditions in respect of which no document to confirm compliance is specified will be disregarded when considering whether the seller has fulfilled all the stipulated conditions.[3]

The bank at which the buyer (in this context known as the *applicant*) opens the documentary credit is known as the *issuing bank*, because this is the bank which issues the documentary credit. The issuing bank will usually be located in the buyer's jurisdiction. Having received instructions to open the documentary credit, the issuing bank either advises the seller (the *beneficiary*) directly that a documentary credit has been opened, or the issuing bank makes arrangements with another bank, usually located in the seller's jurisdiction, to advise of the opening of the credit. This bank is referred to as the *advising bank*. The advising bank might not only agree to communicate the opening of the documentary credit to the seller/beneficiary, but also undertake to pay the seller/beneficiary on a correct presentation of the stipulated documents. In the latter case, the advising bank takes on the role of a *confirming bank*. The advantage to the seller/beneficiary is that the bank where the documents are to be presented and which has undertaken to make payment is located in the same jurisdiction as the seller/beneficiary. The documentary credit may indicate where it is available, i.e., in addition to the issuing bank, as well as the confirming bank, there might be another *nominated bank* at which the documentary credit is available.

3.1.2 Payment choreography

Before requesting payment from the bank, the seller has to obtain the relevant documents and despatch the goods. As noted earlier, one of the key documents will be a bill of lading to confirm that the right goods have been received by the carrier in good condition. The terms of the documentary credit will specify other documents which the seller has to provide, e.g., insurance documents to cover the goods in transit, quality certifications, certification of compliance with relevant technical standards, etc. Once the seller has all the required documents, they are submitted to either the issuing or confirming bank. The bank will then compare the documents provided by the seller with the requirements of the documentary credit. If the documents are as required, the seller's presentation of the document is a *complying presentation*. The bank will pay the seller for the goods in accordance with the terms of the documentary credit.

The confirming bank then transfers the documents to the issuing bank, and is reimbursed by the issuing bank. At that point, the issuing bank holds all the relevant documents, including the bill of lading in respect of the goods. If the buyer has not already put the issuing bank into funds to cover the cost of the documentary credit, the buyer will do so on notification from the issuing bank. Once the issuing bank has been paid, it will release the documents to the buyer. Once the goods have arrived at their destination, the buyer will take possession of the goods, and the process is complete.

3   See Art. 14(h) UCP600.

This short description summarises how things should ideally happen, but this will not always be the case in practice. In particular, it is not uncommon that there will be discrepancies between the documents presented by the seller/beneficiary and the requirements in respect of those documents stated in the documentary credit. It will be seen below how this is dealt with under the UCP600. Moreover, it can also happen that the goods as delivered fail to be in conformity with the contract. However, in such a situation, the buyer's only recourse will be against the seller, and not against any of the banks involved in the documentary credit – provided that the documents were in order. This is because of the so-called "autonomy of the credit", which means that the banks are only concerned with the documents presented by the seller and the requirements stated in the documentary credit, but not in the performance by the seller of the underlying contract of sale. This is made clear by Art. 4 UCP600, which confirms that the documentary credit is a separate transaction from the contract of sale, and "banks are in no way concerned with or bound by such contract".[4] Significantly, an undertaking by a bank to fulfil an obligation under the documentary credit is not affected by any claim or defence which the applicant might have against the beneficiary.[5] Additionally, Art. 5 UCP600 stresses that "banks deal with documents and not with goods, services or performance to which the documents may relate". This reflects the fact that the only concern of the banks is to examine the documents submitted by the seller/beneficiary for their compliance with the requirements of the documentary credit.

4. Documentary credits – key principles

Whilst this chapter is not intended to provide a detailed account of the documentary credit system, it is useful to highlight its key features to show how a solution to a commercial problem was developed, and continues to develop, through commercial and banking practice rather than legislative intervention.

4.1 Irrevocability of documentary credit

A documentary credit becomes irrevocable from the time it is issued, i.e., it cannot be revoked by the bank once it has been issued.[6] Prior to the UPC600, it was possible to have both revocable and irrevocable credits, but in light of changes in banking practice, only irrevocable credits are now envisaged under the UCP600.

4.2 Undertakings by issuing and confirming banks

It was already explained above that the seller/beneficiary may be able to claim payment, on presentation of the required documents, from the issuing bank, the confirming bank

---

4   Art. 4(a) UCP600.
5   *Ibid.*
6   Art. 7(b) UCP600 (issuing bank); Art. 8(b) UCP600 (confirming bank).

(if one is involved) or another nominated bank. However, only the issuing bank and the confirming bank are subject to specific undertakings, as set out in Articles 7 and 8 UCP600. Fundamentally, the issuing bank must "honour"[7] if the required documents are presented to the issuing bank and the presentation is a complying presentation.[8] "Honour" is defined in Art. 2 UCP600 as one of three actions: (i) payment at sight, i.e., on presentation of the documents, if the documentary credit is available by sight payment; (ii) if the credit is available by deferred payment, to undertake to pay at maturity, i.e., the due date; or (iii) if the credit is available by acceptance, to accept a bill of exchange drawn by the beneficiary and pay at maturity. If the presentation is made to the nominated bank, and the nominated bank does not honour as required, the issuing bank has to step in instead and honour in accordance with the terms of the credit.[9] However, if the nominated bank has honoured, then the issuing bank undertakes to reimburse the nominated bank once the documents have been forwarded to it.[10]

A confirming bank undertakes to honour if a complying presentation is made[11] on the same basis as the issuing bank.[12] Additionally, if the credit is available by negotiation with the confirming bank, the confirming bank undertakes to negotiate without recourse.[13] "Negotiation" means purchasing drafts and/or documents by advancing, or agreeing to advance, funds to the beneficiary. Furthermore, the confirming bank also undertakes to reimburse another nominated bank which has honoured or negotiated a complying presentation.[14]

4.3 Complying presentation and examination of documents

The seller/beneficiary must present all the documents required in accordance with the terms of the documentary credit itself, as well as with the provisions of the UCP600 dealing with particular documents,[15] and international standard banking practice. When a presentation is made, the bank must examine the documents presented to determine whether this constitutes a complying presentation. This examination must be undertaken purely on the basis of the documents,[16] and must be in accordance with international standard banking

---

7   Art. 15(1) UCP600.
8   A presentation which complies with the terms of the credit, the relevant provisions of the UCP600 and international standard banking practice: Art. 2 UCP600.
9   Cf. Art. 7(a)(ii)–(v) UCP600.
10 Art. 7(c) UCP600.
11 Art. 15(2) UCP600.
12 Art. 8(a)(i) UCP600.
13 Art. 8(a)(ii) UCP600.
14 Art. 8(c) UCP600.
15 Arts. 17–28 UCP600 deal with the requirements that must be met by particular documents, such as the commercial invoice (Art. 18), the bill of lading (Art. 20) or the insurance document (Art. 28).
16 Art. 14(a) UCP600.

practice.[17] Banks are required to act swiftly and have a maximum of five banking days to establish compliance.[18]

If the documents presented comply with the requirements stated in the documentary credit, the issuing bank must honour the credit in line with its undertakings as per Art. 7 UCP600.[19] A confirming bank, in turn, is required to either honour or negotiate, and also forward all the documents to the issuing bank.[20] Finally, a nominated bank which honours or negotiates has to forward the documents to either the confirming or the issuing bank.[21] Note, however, that a nominated bank neither undertakes to honour or negotiate under the UCP600, nor is it obliged to honour or negotiate (unless the nominated bank is also the confirming bank).

4.3.1 Strict compliance and tolerances

In principle, the documents presented by the seller/beneficiary must comply strictly with the requirements of the documentary credit.[22] However, the UCP600 contain several provisions to mitigate this strictness to ensure that the documentary credit system can operate in a commercial sensible manner. For example, Art. 14(d) UCP600 provides that the data in a document, read in its context and in light of international standard banking practice, does not have to be identical with data in another document or the documentary credit, as long as it is not in conflict with such documents. Similarly, documents other than the commercial invoice can give a general description of the goods, services or performance, again provided that this is not in conflict with the credit.[23] If the seller/beneficiary presents any documents which are not required under the terms of the documentary credit, then they will be disregarded and returned to the beneficiary.[24] Furthermore, Art. 30 UCP600 deals with tolerances in respect of the credit amount, quantity and unit prices. Thus, if the credit states that the amount, quantity or unit price must be "about" or "approximately" a stated figure, then there is a tolerance margin of 10% either way.[25] Furthermore, there is a tolerance of 5% either way in respect of the quantity of goods in any case, except when the quantity stated refers to a set number of packaging units or individual items.[26]

17   See ICC, *International Standard Banking Practice for the Examination of Documents under UCP600* (ISBP 745) (Paris, 2013).
18   Art. 14(b) UCP600.
19   Art. 15(a) UCP600.
20   Art. 15(b) UCP600.
21   Art. 15(c) UCP600.
22   For English authorities on this, see, e.g., *Equitable Trust Co of New York v Dawson Partners Ltd.* [1927] 27 Ll. L. Rep. 49; *JH Rayner & Co Ltd v Hambro Bank Ltd* [1943] KB 37.
23   Art. 14(e) UCP600. For an instance where a discrepancy between the credit and the commercial invoice was held not to give rise to a non-complying presentation because the description of the goods in the commercial invoice was within the generic description of the credit, see *Glencore International AG v Bank of China* [1996] 1 Lloyd's Rep 135.
24   Art. 14(g) UCP600.
25   Art. 30(a) UCP600.
26   Art. 30(b) UCP600.

4.3.2 Non-complying presentation

If a bank[27] determines that the presentation made by the beneficiary does not constitute a complying presentation, then the bank may refuse to honour or negotiate.[28] Alternatively, if the issuing bank has determined that the presentation is a non-complying one, it has the discretion to contact the applicant/buyer and ask if the applicant would waive the discrepancy.[29]

If a bank has refused to honour or negotiate, notice must be given, by telecommunications or another expeditious method,[30] to the presenter stating that the bank has refused to honour or negotiate the credit.[31] The notice also has to specify each discrepancy in respect of which bank refuses to honour/negotiate.[32] The bank may retain the documents pending further instructions (or waiver, in the case of the issuing bank), or the bank returns documents to the presenter.[33] However, the bank has to act within the five-banking-day limit;[34] otherwise, it will be precluded from claiming that the presentation was not a complying one.[35]

5. Challenges for domestic courts

As mentioned earlier, the UCP have no independent force of law and take effect through incorporation into the contract between the buyer/applicant and the issuing bank. The UCP therefore take their legal effect as contract terms, and, in principle, would be subject to the doctrinal requirements of the national law which governs the documentary credit. This could give rise to a conflict between the system as it is designed to function under the UCP600 and specific doctrinal requirements of the applicable law. For instance, English Law requires that any contractual obligation must be supported by consideration, and the arguable absence of consideration moving from the seller/beneficiary to one of the banks involved could cause difficulties. A seller/beneficiary does not provide consideration to either the issuing or confirming bank for the bank's undertaking to pay the seller on presentation of the relevant documents, unless the act of presentation constitutes the requisite consideration. Whatever the analysis might be, however, the system for documentary credits under the UCP600 has never been challenged on such a ground; moreover, the English courts have been sensitive to the fact that "an elaborate commercial system has been built up ... and ... it would be wrong to interfere with that established practice",[36] which is a strong indication that any attempt to undermine the

---

27 Nominated, confirming or issuing bank.
28 Art. 16(a) UCP600.
29 Art. 16(b) UCP600.
30 Art. 16(d) UCP600.
31 Art. 16(c)(i) UCP600.
32 Art. 16(c)(ii) UCP600.
33 Art. 16(c)(iii) UCP600.
34 Art. 16(d) UCP600.
35 Art. 16(f) UCP600.
36 *Per* Jenkins LJ in *Hamzeh Malas & Sons v British Imex Industries Ltd.* [1958] 2 QB 127 at p.129.

operation of the UCP600 system would be given short shrift by the courts. Indeed, Thomas LJ has observed that the "courts must interpret [the UCP] in accordance with [their] underlying aims and purposes reflecting international practice and the expectations of international bankers and international traders so that [the UCP] underpins the operation of letters of credit in international trade. A literalistic and nationalistic approach must be avoided."[37] And more recently, the Supreme Court firmly closed off any argument that obligations under the UCP600 might somehow not be enforceable for lack of consideration in a case where such an argument was attempted.[38] Lord Clark agreed with Moore-Bick LJ's observation in the Court of Appeal that "he would be loath to hold, particularly in a commercial context, that a promise which both parties intended should be relied on was unenforceable for want of consideration. So would I."[39] Lord Mance (who dissented on other issues) said in respect of a consideration-based argument that "There is not, and could not consistently with important and well-established principles governing letters of credit be, any suggestion that these arrangements were not supported by consideration",[40] and further "It is … now accepted, realistically, that whatever contractual arrangements are contained in the letters of credit are binding, and that no problem relating to absence of consideration arises."[41]

However, this does not mean that principles of contract law have no room within the documentary credit system. On the one hand, the matters covered by the UCP600 will be dealt with on the basis of its rules, and there is no room for domestic law to undermine the direct application of any of the UCP600 provisions. However, there may at times be issues raised before a court which are not directly addressed by the UCP600 itself. Perhaps the most difficult issue is what to do when the documents presented by the seller/beneficiary are somehow affected by fraud, i.e., where they have been deliberately completed so as to give the impression that all the requirements of the documentary credit have been complied with when this is in fact not the case. This was the issue in the controversial House of Lords ruling in *United City Merchants (Investments) Ltd v Royal Bank of Canada (The American Accord)*.[42] A fraudulently issued bill of lading showed the wrong shipping date of manufacturing equipment. When it was presented to the confirming bank by the seller/beneficiary, who was unaware of the fraud, the bank refused to pay because it *was* aware that the goods had not been shipped on the date stated. The House of Lords had to consider whether in these circumstances, the bank could refuse to pay notwithstanding the fact that presentation made by the seller was, on the face of it, complying. It held that because the seller had not been fraudulent himself and was unaware that the date was incorrect, the bank was obliged to honour its commitment to pay on presentation of the documents. Lord

37 *Fortis Bank SA/NV v Indian Overseas Bank* [2011] EWCA Civ 58, para. [29]. Emphasis added.
38 *Taurus Petroleum Ltd v State Oil Marketing Company of the Ministry of Oil, Republic of Iraq* [2017] UKSC 64.
39 At [25].
40 At [95].
41 At [100].
42 [1983] 1 AC 168.

Diplock said that documentary credits are autonomous and the parties only deal with each other on the basis of the documents. Consequently, if the documents presented by the seller/beneficiary are, on their face, in compliance with the documentary credit, then the bank is obliged to pay. He rejected the argument that the bank's obligation to pay would not arise if the documents contained a material inaccuracy despite appearing to be in order. Lord Diplock held that accepting this argument "would, in my view, undermine the whole system of financing international trade by means of documentary credits".[43] He thought that any other conclusion would be "strange from the commercial point of view".[44] The only instance when a court should permit a bank to refuse to pay is where the seller/beneficiary themselves fraudulently present documents which they are inaccurate or wrong.[45]

The decision by the House of Lords in *United City Merchants* is squarely based on what the UCP provide and in light of the needs of commerce.[46] Yet, the reasoning has been heavily criticised on the basis that it misunderstood the relevant provisions of the UCP and for the assumptions that were made with regard to the obligations undertaken by a bank under a documentary credit. Goode has pointed out that the bank is not under an *obligation* to pay, but is *entitled* to do so if it has concluded after reasonable examination of the documents that they are in order.[47] Therefore, this is a rule which protects a bank which has paid out, but not a positive obligation to pay out once a presentation which, on its face, is complying has been made. However, the wording of the relevant UCP provisions is expressed in terms of an obligation on the bank that it "must honour"[48] if the seller/beneficiary correctly presents all the documents required under the documentary credit. In earlier rulings, the courts have certainly treated this as an obligation binding on the banks.[49]

In the more recent case of *Montrod Ltd v Grundkötter Fleischvertriebs GmbH*,[50] the Court of Appeal stressed that a "fraud exception" should be limited to "fraud or knowledge of fraud on the part of the beneficiary",[51] and should not be extended, e.g., to instances where the documents presented are flawed without the presenting party acting in bad faith or with knowledge of this. Potter LJ stressed that fact that any exception to the UCP system should be narrowly construed, not least because a broader exception would require banks to look beyond the documents which is precisely what the UCP system does not require them to do. Moreover, a seller/beneficiary may be exposed to excessive risk as the seller/beneficiary themselves have to rely on documents handed to them by other parties.

43 [1983] 1 AC 168, p.184.
44 [1983] 1 AC 168, pp.184–185.
45 [1983] 1 AC 168, p.183.
46 D. Irvine, "The law: an engine for trade" (2001) 64 *Modern Law Review* 333, p.341.
47 See R. Goode, *Commercial Law*, 3rd ed. (Penguin, 2004), p.994.
48 Art. 7(a) UCP600 (issuing bank); Art. 8(a) UCP600 (confirming bank).
49 *Hamzeh Malas & Sons v British Imex Industries Ltd.* [1958] 2 QB 127 at p.129.
50 [2002] 1 WLR 1975.
51 *Ibid.*, p.1991.

In contrast, the Singapore Court of Appeal in *Beam Technology v Standard Chartered Bank*[52] took a different view from the House of Lords in *United City Merchants*. In this case, the required clean air waybill which was presented had purportedly been issued by a freight forwarding company, but that company did not exist; the confirming bank declined to pay. The Court agreed that, if a presentation complies on its face with the requirements of the documentary credit, the bank is authorised to honour, even if it subsequently transpires that one of the documents was a forgery. However, if the bank discovers, within what is now a five-day timescale[53] that one of the documents is a forgery, then the bank should be able to refuse to honour. Otherwise, the bank would deliberately ignore an obvious problem, and this, in the view of the Singapore Court of Appeal, cannot be the intention under the UCP. However, this does not mean that a bank is required to look beyond the documents, and if there is nothing to suggest that the documents are tainted, then the bank can honour if the beneficiary's presentation was a complying one. The reasoning of the Singaporean Court seemingly reflects the commercial realities of the situation in that a bank should not be obliged to pay when it has knowledge that something is wrong with the documents presented by the seller. The House of Lords took a more literal reading of the relevant provisions of the UCP, which may have the advantage of providing greater certainty, particularly to an innocent seller/beneficiary. The crucial point these cases illustrate is that different views as to the extent of any kind of exception to the UCP system which develops through national case-law can put the operation of the UCP system, the risk allocation between the parties, and therefore its commercial benefits, under strain.[54] A study by Johns and Blodgett has suggested that there are signs of other exceptions, particularly based on unconscionability and illegality, taking hold; something they regard as problematic:

> Unconscionability and illegality damage the independence principle, in particular, and commercial certainty, in general, by elevating fairness-based judgments about the risk-allocation choices of the parties to the underlying contract above the certainty-dependent environment that underpins international transactions.[55]

They are right to raise their concerns about these developments; commercial parties, particularly in international commercial contracts, are expected to consider the allocation of risk between them, and any grounds for intervening in that allocation should be limited. A similar position was expressed by Ren thus:

---

52   [2003] 1 SLR 597.
53   Art. 14(b) UCP600.
54   R.J. Johns and M.S. Blodgett, "Fairness at the expense of commercial certainty: the international emergence of unconscionability and illegality as exceptions to the independence principle of letters of credit and bank guarantees" (2011) 31 *Northern Illinois Law Review* 297, p.309.
55   *Ibid.*, p.333.

the public policy to maintain the commercial utility of letters of credit as a reliable payment mechanism in international transactions underlies the autonomy principle. Exceptions to the principle, such as the fraud exception, should be made where the policy underlying the exception is judged to be as important or more important that the competing policy to maintain credits' commercial utility.[56]

For this reason, Ren disagrees with the approach of the Singaporean Court of Appeal in *Beam Technology*, which seemed to recognise nullity of a document identified by a bank as a possible ground for refusing to honour. National courts therefore need to be mindful that they do not undermine the effectiveness of the UCP600, as well as other types of international trade terms, by recognising various exceptions.

6. Concluding observations: documentary credits and International Commercial Law

The brief flavour of the documentary credit system given in this chapter suffices to illustrate how it is possible to create a set of rules for an international commercial transaction which is firmly rooted in commercial practice, and which can be regularly revised as practices evolve. These rules are compiled by an organisation representing international commerce rather than a law-making body, and as such, they do not depend on ratification or implementation by national governments in order to be effective. Rather, the UCP are chosen by the parties to a documentary credit. Nevertheless, they have taken on a special role in International Commercial Law, because the UCP are more than just standard terms incorporated into a contract; rather, they are recognised as an established regime governing a particular commercial transaction. Whilst they do not have the force of law as such, their status is akin to that of binding law.

---

56 J. Ren, "A nullity exception in letter of credit law?" (2015) *Journal of Business Law* 1, p.16.

10

UNIDROIT PRINCIPLES OF INTERNATIONAL COMMERCIAL CONTRACTS

1. Introduction

Much of this book has focused on legal rules of varying kinds adopted at the international level to support international commercial activity by tackling selected legal issues pertaining to such activity. This shows that, whilst there has been a significant amount of activity in developing such international-level rules, the current picture at the international level is rather fragmented and piecemeal. It is therefore unsurprising that there are occasional calls for a much broader initiative towards the establishment of an International Commercial Code.[1] Indeed, some of the academic debate surrounding the *lex mercatoria* is shaped by the desire for a more comprehensive International Commercial Law. However, such an endeavour is unlikely to gain much traction because of the difficulties associated with drafting legal rules which would be acceptable to a large enough number of countries, and the inevitable difficulties in negotiating something like this in a timely manner.

International Commercial Law has instead evolved into a fairly complex, multi-level system which combines rules from different origins in creating the legal context for an international commercial transaction. However, this has not stopped initiatives which seek to encourage more coherent and comprehensive legal rules to facilitate international commercial transactions. Whilst it may not be possible to achieve this through top-down harmonisation through conventions and model

---

1   Such calls go back over 50 years. UNIDROIT suggested an ambitious codification as far back as 1970: see *Progressive Codification of the Law of International Trade: Note by the Secretariat of the International Institute for the Unification of Private Law (UNIDROIT)* in UNCITRAL, *Yearbook Vol. I: 1968–1970*, p.285; H.D. Gabriel, "UNIDROIT Principles as a source for global sales law" (2013) 58 *Villanova Law Review* 661; I. Schwenzer, "Global unification of contract law" (2016) 21 *Uniform Law Review* 60; for a more cautious view, see M.J. Bonnell, "Do we need a global commercial code?" (2000) 5 *Uniform Law Review* 469.

DOI: 10.4324/9781315692807-10

laws, there might be scope for progressive approximation of national laws. This would not mean that each jurisdiction would apply the same, or very similar rules (as is the objective of conventions or model laws), but rather that national laws would become substantively aligned so as to reduce the practical impact of having different commercial law regimes at national level.

The key initiative of this type for International Commercial Law are the UNI-DROIT Principles of International Commercial Contracts ("UPICC").[2] First launched in 1994, the UPICC have been revised and extended on three occasions (2004, 2010 and 2016). The UPICC have become a key document in International Commercial Law, and a vast amount of scholarly literature and reference works have been published. Despite the extensive academic output on the UPICC, it is important to stress at the outset that the UPICC are a non-binding statement, or rather restatement, of principles rather than a template for a convention or a Model Law. Nevertheless, their influence has been substantial. This chapter provides a general introduction and highlights key features of the UPICC, but it would require a separate book to provide a full discussion of all of the UPICC.

2. The UPICC as a restatement of principles

The UPICC are best characterised as a type of restatement. This is a well-established means of trying to distil common principles on particular topics based on a comparative survey of multiple jurisdictions. Often, as well as trying to identify what is common, a restatement might propose a "best solution" principle for matters on which there is a degree of discrepancy between the jurisdictions surveyed or where a particular principle would be better suited to the context for which the restatement is intended.

Restatements were first developed by the American Law Institute (ALI), which was founded in 1923. The impetus for the development of restatements was the fact that there was a perception that the main principles of the common law had become obscured by the volume of decided cases, and also that the same problem might lead to different results at State level. A restatement could therefore serve to identify the fundamental features of a given branch of the common law, such as the contract law or tort law. The *Handbook for ALI Reporters* offers the following definition of a "restatement":

> Restatements are primarily addressed to courts. They aim at clear formulations of common law and its statutory elements or variations and reflect the law as it presently stands or might appropriately be stated by a court.[3]

2   UNIDROIT, *UNIDROIT Principles of International Commercial Contracts 2016*. The full text of the UPICC contains explanatory comments and illustrations in respect of each principle. These are collectively referred to as "*UPICC Comments*" in this chapter.
3   American Law Institute, *Capturing the Voice of the American Law Institute: A Handbook for ALI Reporters and Those That Review Their Work*, revised edition (ALI, 2015), p.4, available at https://www.ali.org/media/filer_public/08/f2/08f2f7c7-29c7-4de1-8c02-d66f5b05a6bb/ali-style-manual.pdf [last accessed March 2021].

The primary concern of a restatement is therefore to provide a clear statement of the law in a particular area in its current state. They are addressed to those charged with the task of applying the existing law, i.e., the courts, rather than legislators. A restatement may appear in a form which is similar to a statute or a code, and those tasked with drafting a restatement should "aspire toward the precision of statutory language",[4] but it is not intended to be in a prescriptive form.

However, whilst the main objective is to provide a statement of the current law which has the benefit of greater clarity and precision, this does not mean that a restatement could not project how the law might develop in the future. As any common lawyer will only know too well, whilst the doctrine of precedent (*stare decisis*) governs the development of the common law, there are judgments which may be inconsistent with other cases or have been decided without full account of previous case-law. Moreover, on any given issue, it may be possible to identify trends between some jurisdictions adhering to established precedents whereas others may have shifted in their interpretation in light of new commercial, or other, developments. In short, the survey of the jurisdictions on which the restatement is based may reveal several different approaches to any particular issue. In drafting a restatement, there is the freedom to consider whether such a judgment might, in fact, chart a better way forward for the law. A restatement can, therefore, with appropriate justification, choose what is regarded as the better rule. Moreover, a restatement can be used to anticipate how the law might develop in the future and propose rules which would align with previously established principles.[5] This does not mean that those drafting a restatement will make up rules, but rather drawn on indications in the existing common law to suggest the best way for the law to develop:

> It will operate to produce agreement on the fundamental principles of the common law, give precision to use of legal terms, and make the law more uniform throughout the country. Such a restatement will also effect changes in the law, which it is proper for an organization of lawyers to promote and which make the law better adapted to the needs of life.[6]

The kinds of best rules which a restatement might suggest, therefore, are based on the greater scope for legal scholars to research different candidate rules and test their application against a range of factual situations.[7]

The ALI approach to restatements developed within the context of a country which comprises a large number of separate, State-level, jurisdictions which developed from a common base-line (the common law of England), which all follow the common law legal tradition,[8] and which all use the same language. At the international level, the starting point is rather different. There are, of course, many other

4   *Ibid.*, p.5.
5   *Ibid.*, p.5.
6   Cited *Ibid.*, p.6.
7   *Ibid.*, p.6.
8   With the exception of Louisiana, whose legal system has strong civil law influences, particularly in the private law field.

countries whose legal systems are rooted in the common law, but others follow the various branches of the civil law tradition as well as other legal traditions which are well established around the world.

Nevertheless, the restatement approach has been used elsewhere, most prominently in the *Principles of European Contract Law (PECL)*. The basic methodology is not that different from the ALI restatements. Starting with a range of topics on, say, contract law, experts from all the jurisdictions involved in the restatement survey "their" legal system and feed this into a comparative law exercise which seeks to identify whether there are commonalities among these jurisdictions on any particular issue, and also whether among the divergent approaches one particular approach might lend itself to be the preferred one for the restatement. The task is therefore fundamentally the same, in that both "common solutions" and "best solutions" are identified in this process.[9] This approach was used with success in drafting the *PECL*, and was subsequently broadened in the development of the *Principles, Definitions and Model Rules of European Private Law*, also known as the *Draft Common Frame of Reference (DCFR)*. A similar approach was also adopted in preparing the UPICC,[10] although as well as drawing on a range of national jurisdictions, the drafters of the UPICC also took account of the various international texts. In some instances, this resulted in UPICC provisions which closely mirrored the corresponding provisions in other International Commercial Law instruments; whereas in others (such as the UPICC provisions on agency), the UPICC departed significantly from the approach taken in instruments adopted previously.

3. The UNIDROIT Principles of International Commercial Contracts

As explained above, in one sense, the UPICC are a form of restatement with a specific focus, i.e., international commercial contracts. As such, the principles restated in the UPICC are designed to work in the context of such contracts, and not to all types of contract. In the same way as other restatements, the UPICC are fundamentally a scholarly product, albeit one compiled under the auspices of an international body which is also involved in the creation of international conventions and model laws. This means that the UPICC are not intended to be a legally binding instrument which can be adopted by individual countries through ratification or adoption of a Model Law. As the UPICC are not intended to have the status of legally binding rules, they cannot be selected as the law to govern a commercial contract under most private international law regimes,[11] because there is generally a requirement to select the legal rules of a specific jurisdiction.[12] However, it is possible to permit an arbitration panel

---

9   See, e.g., M.J. Bonnell, "The law governing international commercial contracts and the actual role of the UNIDROIT Principles" (2018) 23 *Uniform Law Review* 15 at p.22.

10   Cf. H.D. Gabriel, "The use of soft law in the creation of legal norms in international commercial law: how successful has it been?" (2019) 40 *Michigan Journal of International Law* 413.

11   See further, Chapter 2.

12   Under Art. 3 of the Hague *Principles on Choice of Law in International Commercial Contracts*, however, it is envisaged that "rules of law", such as the UPICC, could be chosen as a governing law. See the discussion in Chapter 2 at 2.x.

to use the UPICC as the substantive rules of law to be deployed in the context of international commercial arbitration, a widely used alternative form of dispute resolution.[13]

3.1 Purposes of the Principles

The UPICC are not intended to be legally binding, so the obvious question is what the purposes might be for which the UPICC were created. In considering this question, it is necessary to distinguish between the purposes for which the UPICC were intended, and the actual uses to which the UPICC have been put in practice. The former can be gleaned from the Preamble to the UPICC. For the latter, empirical research on the application of the UPICC is required. Although there is, as yet, not a great deal of such research available, research has been published which sheds some light on the actual use of the UPICC.[14]

3.1.1 Intended purposes

According to the UPICC's Preamble, the UPICC should be applied where the parties have agreed that their contract should be governed by them. This immediately runs into the problem identified above that most private international law rules do not permit the choice of a non-State law as the law governing a contract. In the comments to the Preamble, it is noted that the UPICC might be chosen as the governing law in combination with a national law, in which case the UPICC will apply unless there are rules of national law which are inconsistent with the UPICC and which cannot be contracted out of.[15] The national law which has been chosen would then also apply to any aspects not covered by the UPICC at all. The sole choice of the UPICC would only be possible if permitted by the relevant rules of private international law or in the context of international commercial arbitration.

Rather than applying where the parties have expressly chosen the UPICC, it is also stated in the Preamble that the UPICC could apply where the parties have not chosen the law applicable to their contract. This would mean that, instead of applying whichever national law would govern the contract under general private international rules,[16] the UPICC would be a default regime which would apply instead of any national law. Again, the main potential context in which this role would be possible is international commercial arbitration, rather than litigation.[17]

More controversially, it is envisaged in the Preamble that the UPICC could be applied where the parties have decided that their contract should be governed by general principles of law, the *lex mercatoria*, or similar. Again, such a choice would not be recognised in most private international law systems, but might be possible

---

13 This is explored further in Chapter 11.
14 See 3.1.2, below.
15 *UPICC Comments*, p.3.
16 See Chapter 2 at, section 3.
17 *UPICC Comments*, p.4.

in the context of international commercial arbitration. In the *UPICC Comments*, it is suggested that the UPICC could be used in such instances because this would help to overcome the inherent vagueness which would otherwise stem from the choice of the *lex mercatoria* or similar as the applicable law. However, this possible application of the UPICC might be criticised because it would seem to conflict with the widely accepted understanding of the *lex mercatoria* as a custom-based, evolving system which is unlikely to be amenable to capture in the form of a statement of principles or similar.[18] The UPICC are unlikely to qualify as a representation of international trade custom – for that, the UPICC would have to be widely known in the trade, but as Bridge observed, "despite the great success the PICC have already demonstrated in becoming known to arbitrators and scholars, they are a long way short of becoming known to those in any trade".[19]

The first three intended purposes are essentially concerned with party choice to apply the UPICC. The other intended purposes are addressed at courts, adjudicators and legislators. Thus, one purpose of the UPICC is to use them in the interpretation or supplementation of "international uniform law instruments", i.e., the various conventions in the field of International Commercial Law. We saw earlier[20] that one of the challenges of international conventions is both their interpretation, and the way gaps (whether internal or external) should be dealt with. As the UPICC are generally more comprehensive than any international convention, they could be used in both circumstances, and, indeed, have been used for this. The fact that the UPICC are designed to offer a restatement of principles particularly designed for international commercial contracts is a strong reason in favour of taking the UPICC into account, both when it comes to the interpretation of a particular provision of a convention and in finding appropriate gap-fillers.

However, there are also a number of counter-arguments to this application of the UPICC.[21] First, each international convention will have gone through a lengthy drafting period, a diplomatic conference and subsequent ratifications by individual countries. Unless the possibility of using the UPICC as an aid to interpretation and gap-filling was discussed favourably particularly in the preparatory stages, the use of a non-binding text which does not require endorsement by national governments might seem incompatible with the nature of a binding international convention.[22] This argument has some force in it, but as the UPICC have become more ubiquitous,

---

18 See Chapter 1 at 6.2.
19 M. Bridge, "The CISG and the UNIDROIT Principles of International Commercial Contracts" (2014) 19 *Uniform Law Review* 623 at p.629. Bridge is generally sceptical about the role the UPICC could play in supporting the CISG.
20 See Chapter 3 at 5.1.1.
21 Noted and not endorsed by R. Michaels, "The UNIDROIT Principles as a global background law" (2014) 19 *Uniform Law Review* 643, pp.665–666, nor by M.J. Bonnell, "The law governing international commercial contracts and the actual role of the UNIDROIT Principles" (2018) 23 *Uniform Law Review* 15, p.33.
22 Cf. M. Bridge, "The CISG and the UNIDROIT Principles of International Commercial Contracts" (2014) 19 *Uniform Law Review* 623 at p.625 ("These instruments are not to be supplemented by the PICC purely on the *ipse dixit* of the PICC").

and those involved in drafting more recent conventions are likely to be at least aware, and often familiar with the detail, of the UPICC, it lacks persuasion as the UPICC are now firmly part of the International Commercial Law landscape. Therefore, it is now just as arguable that the UPICC are part of the overall legal context within which more recent conventions were drafted and adopted. However, in respect of the many international conventions which pre-date the first version of the UPICC, this argument is less persuasive and the objection to using the UPICC is stronger.

However, this should not mean that the UPICC cannot have any role to play. In order to explain how the UPICC can still be relevant, it is first necessary to consider a further, rather technical but no less forceful, objection. This starts from the fact that the interpretative provisions generally found in international convention (mostly modelled on Art. 7 CISG)[23] provide a two-stage process for dealing with internal gaps: first, it should be attempted to deal with the gap on the basis of whichever underlying principles of the convention at issue can be identified; and secondly, if this is unsuccessful, to refer to the national law otherwise applicable to the contract. This would seem to leave no room for the UPICC, leading to the argument that the interpretative provisions do not permit recourse to anything but the two elements mentioned in the interpretative provisions. However, such a formalistic analysis, whilst technically correct, seems ill-suited to International Commercial Law. First, one needs to bear in mind the wider mandate to respect the international character of a convention and the need to promote uniformity in its application. Whilst these factors relate primarily to the interpretation of the text of a convention, this cannot mean that they have no relevance to the process of gap-filling, particularly with regard to internal gaps. Therefore, the mandate to pursue a high degree of consistency applies here, too. This suggest that recourse to the applicable national law should be a matter of last resort, and that the UPICC could be an appropriate intermediate step. However, even if the direct application of the UPICC in this context might be resisted, it may nevertheless be possible to apply them indirectly. This would be possible if there was an ambiguity, or even a gap, in the relevant provisions of national law, requiring the court or arbitrator to select the appropriate of several ways of interpreting the national law. Here, the UPICC can serve as a guide to the court/arbitrator in identifying the interpretation that would be most suitable for international commercial contracts. This indirect application of the UPICC would also be a response to concerns about drawing on the UPICC in respect of pre-UPICC conventions.

Overall, therefore, there is no convincing reason to disallow the application of the UPICC when interpreting or supplementing an international convention, although this does not mean that the UPICC should be readily applied for this purpose – the UPICC do not have the force of law in the way that international conventions do.

It is further suggested that the UPICC could be used to interpret or supplement domestic law. It has already been explained how a national court, faced with competing interpretations of national law, might opt for an interpretation which aligns most closely with the UPICC. This would ensure that the interpretation adopted is

---

23 See Chapter 3 at 5.1.1.

more likely to be suitable for international commercial contracts. However, national courts may not always wish to do so. This is because their task is to interpret national law, and the interpretation chosen would establish a precedent which would also apply to domestic, and possibly even non-commercial, situations. If an interpretation which most closely aligns with the UPICC would not be suitable for purely national contexts, or for contracts other than international commercial ones, then a national court may decline to draw on the UPICC to interpret, let alone supplement, national law. In international commercial arbitration, it may be easier for an arbitrator to adopt an interpretation of national law which aligns most closely with the UPICC, and may also be willing to use the UPICC to supplement national law, because an arbitrator is primarily concerned with resolving the particular dispute in hand, and less so with the implications for future cases.

Finally, the Preamble states that the UPICC might serve as model for national and international legislators when drafting legislation in the field of contract law. This is surprising, because the UPICC, as primarily a scholarly product, do not aspire to be a Model Law. However, this does not mean that the UPICC could not serve as a Model Law regardless of this, because the essence of a Model Law is merely to offer a template on which national legislators can draw when developing national legislation. In the same way, the UPICC could be a starting point for developing a new international convention or Model Law. It is important to appreciate that the notion of a model in this regard may be looser than when used in the context of a Model Law. In the present context, it is unlikely to mean that a legislator, whether national or international, would simply take one or several of the UPICC Principles and simply copy them into new legislation. Rather, the UPICC might better be understood akin to the toolbox function also once envisaged for the European Union's *DCFR*,[24] i.e., more as a source of inspiration or a starting point for the development of new legislation than a ready-made template.

3.1.2 Evidence of actual use

In order to gauge the real impact of the UPICC in international commercial contracting practice, it will be instructive to consider some of the available empirical work on their application. In an early review of statistics, Agrò[25] identified four dominant ways in which the UPICC had been used, based on 230 arbitral awards and judgments recorded in the UNILEX database[26] up to 31 August 2011 which mentioned the UPICC. Her findings suggested that 27% of decisions which mentioned UPICC, mostly arbitral awards, involved an application of the UPICC as the rules of law which governed the substance of the dispute. In 33% of decisions, the UPICC were used as a means of interpreting and supplementing the domestic law governing the contract,

---

24 See C. Twigg-Flesner, *The Europeanisation of Contract Law*, 2nd ed. (Routledge, 2013), ch.5.
25 E.F. Agrò, "The impact of the UNIDROIT Principles in international dispute resolution in figures" (2011) 16 *Uniform Law Review* 719.
26 This can be accessed at http://www.unilex.info/instrument/principles [last accessed March 2020].

and in 15% of decisions, the UPICC were referred to when interpreting and supplementing an international convention. Finally, in 25% of decisions, the UPICC were used to test the provisions of the law governing the contract against an international yardstick. The final finding is perhaps the most noteworthy, not least because it is not among the express purposes stated in the preamble.

An interesting analysis of the application of the UPICC, also based on case statistics in the UNILEX database, was provided by Michaels some years ago.[27] Although not very recent, the findings nevertheless provide interesting trends some two decades after the UPICC were first adopted. First, he discovered that the UPICC were rarely chosen by the parties, whether as the applicable rules of law or for the purposes of arbitration.[28] Secondly, the UPICC were referred to by both courts and arbitrators of their own motion, but usually in the context of a comparative discussion of several jurisdictions.[29] There was no strong difference between the respective proportions of judges and arbitrators referring to the UPICC, suggesting that they are applied with comparable frequency in all types of adjudication.[30] In some instances, this has involved treating the UPICC as trade usages/customs, despite their origins in legislation and international conventions rather than commercial usages.[31] Michaels also identified different ways in which the UPICC were applied by national courts: in several common law jurisdictions, UPICC provisions – such as Art. 1.7 on good faith and fair dealing or Art. 4.3 on factors relevant to contract interpretation – were considered but their solution rejected rather than followed.[32] By contrast, in many civil law jurisdictions, the UPICC are used to verify whether a preferred interpretation of domestic law accords with the global consensus reflected in the UPICC.[33] In all of these instances, the UPICC are not used as a coherent system; instead, particular provisions are referred to instead, often in connection with other laws.[34] Finally, rather than being a model for the development of international legislation, the UPICC have been taken into account more in the context of domestic law reform.[35] Taken collectively, these findings suggest that, far from being regularly chosen as an applicable law by the parties to a contract as a system, the UPICC are used on a much more selective basis when tackling specific issues.[36] Michaels therefore concluded that the UPICC seem to have assumed the status of a "global background law", i.e., not a set of rules of law being applied directly but rather as a benchmark

---

27 R. Michaels, "The UNIDROIT Principles as a global background law" (2014) 19 *Uniform Law Review* 643.
28 *Ibid.*, pp.646–647.
29 *Ibid.*, pp.647–648.
30 *Ibid.*, pp.649–651.
31 *Ibid.*, p.649.
32 *Ibid.*, p.651. Michaels regards this as a success in that the UPICC are being considered seriously, even if not followed.
33 *Ibid.*, p.652.
34 *Ibid.*, pp.654–655.
35 *Ibid.*, pp.656–657.
36 *Ibid.*, p.657.

or global consensus.[37] This conclusion suggests that the UPICC are applied rather differently from what is envisaged in the Preamble and the way the UPICC are discussed in the scholarly literature, but it would be much more in tune with the idea of the UPICC as a restatement.[38]

However, there are also more recent indications that courts might, on occasion at least, be willing to apply the UPICC directly. Bonnell,[39] who otherwise broadly echoes the findings made by Michaels, discusses two cases from Brazil in which preference was given to applying the UPICC and the CISG instead of the otherwise applicable law, where the parties had omitted to choose the governing law. However, Bonnell refers to these as "isolated" examples, and in most instances, national courts continue to refer to the UPICC, if at all, in a "subordinate role".[40]

A specific focus on the way the UPICC have influenced the development of national laws was adopted by Estrella Faria.[41] The UPICC were considered extensively, although not incorporated wholesale, in reforms in Russia, China, Estonia and Lithuania, with the latter drawing most extensively on the UPICC.[42] The UPICC were also used as background material for Germany's 2001 reform of its law of obligations in the civil code. More extensive use of the UPICC was made in preparing the new Mercantile Code for Spain, as well as in preparing Argentina's and Japan's respective new civil codes. He also finds many parallels with the UPICC in the revised French Contract Law. These findings would appear to align with Michaels' argument that the UPICC's dominant use is that of a background law which is drawn on for various purposes, but the provisions of which are not often applied or copied directly.

3.2 Scope of the Principles: international commercial contracts

As their name suggests, the UPICC are intended to apply to international commercial contracts. This invites a closer look at how the UPICC define "international" and "commercial". In previous chapters, it was seen that each International Commercial Law convention specifies what makes a transaction "international" for the purposes of this convention. It will be recalled that the usual criterion is that the respective places of business of the parties to a transaction are located in different States. In the UPICC, however, there is no set criterion for determining whether a contract is international. The Comment to the Preamble notes that there are multiple ways of determining whether a contract is international, and that any of these would suffice for the purposes

37 Ibid., p.658.
38 Ibid., p.688.
39 M.J. Bonnell, "The law governing international commercial contracts and the actual role of the UNIDROIT Principles" (2018) 23 Uniform Law Review 15, p.28.
40 Ibid., p.29.
41 J.A. Estrella Faria, "The influence of the UNIDROIT Principles of International Commercial Contracts on national laws" (2016) 21 Uniform Law Review 271.
42 Latvia, on the other hand, seems to have ignored the UPICC: Ibid., pp.249–250.

of the UPICC.[43] For the purposes of the UPICC, the internationality criterion is only deployed to exclude purely domestic contracts from the scope of the UPICC, although, as the Comment makes clear, parties to a domestic contract could opt into the UPICC subject to any mandatory rules of the national law.[44]

Similarly, there is no specific definition of "commercial"; rather, it is mainly there to exclude consumer transactions from the scope of the UPICC. This is because consumer transactions are already heavily regulated at national and/or regional level and subject to many mandatory rules.[45]

3.3 Format

The UPICC provide *principles* of international commercial contracts, rather than model rules or similar. In this context, principle has a particular meaning which differs from the way the term is more generally understood in the context of law. Generally speaking, the term "principle" might refer to a value or broader norm underpinning specific rules of law in a given area. For instance, it is often said that *pacta sunt servanda* is a general principle of contract law (and, indeed, other areas of law) which stresses the fact that parties to an agreement must adhere to their agreement and perform whatever acts they have agreed to perform. Such a general principle is difficult to apply in specific circumstances, and so legal rules are needed which give effect to this principle in a particular context, e.g., with regard to the remedies an innocent party can exercise when the other party has breached their contract.

In the context of the UPICC, the notion of principles is somewhat different and does not refer to the principles which might be underlying specific legal rules, but rather denotes the non-binding nature of the UPICC. A closer look at the individual UPICC articles soon reveals that these state quite specific rules, albeit not at the level of detail one would expect to see in a full code. For example, the provisions on contract formation[46] closely mirror the corresponding provisions of the CISG[47] and are written very much like a legal rule.

Each provision, or article, is presented in the same way. It starts with a "black-letter" *rule*, which is essentially a rule of law akin to a provision in a statute or international convention (such as "An offer becomes effective when it reaches the offeree"[48]). Each rule is then supplemented by an explanatory *comment*, which explains what the intended meaning of the provision is. Sometimes, it might also explain the origin of the rule.[49] However, there is no reference to any of the national laws which might have inspired the development of particular rules, so it is

---

43 *UPICC Comments*, p.1.
44 *UPICC Comments*, p.2.
45 *Ibid.*
46 See *Chapter 2*, section 1.
47 See Chapter 4 , section 3.
48 Art. 2.1.3, para. (1) UPICC.
49 For example, the comment to Art. 2.1.3, para. (1) UPICC states that is it "taken literally from Article 15 CISG" (*UPICC Comments*, p.38).

not always clear what the origins of a particular rule might have been.[50] Many comments also include a number of *illustrations*, which are short factual scenarios which explain how the *rule* might be applied in a specific context. The comments and the illustrations are a very useful way of working out what each particular rule was intended to mean and should thereby facilitate their application. For each article, the black-letter rule, the comment and any illustrations should be treated as being integral features of the UPICC.

3.4 Key underlying principles

Whilst it is not possible to cover every aspect of the UPICC in this chapter, it will be useful to highlight a few key features. The UPICC's first substantive provision reflects their broad approach to *freedom of contract*, appropriate to commercial transactions, by confirming that the parties are free to decide whether to enter into a contract, and that they can determine its content, i.e., the terms of the contract.[51] The UPICC do provide for a good number of rules concerning most aspects of the different stages of a contract, but almost all of these can be modified or excluded by the parties through the terms of their contract. This accords with a generous view of *party autonomy*, which is the hallmark of most International Commercial Law instruments discussed earlier in this book. Generally, the parties to a contract have the autonomy to decide whether to apply the UPICC at all, and, if they choose to do so, whether to exclude or modify any of the individual provisions of UPICC in their application to the contract.[52] However, the UPICC contain a handful of provisions which are regarded as so important that they are classified as mandatory and therefore cannot be excluded or modified, such as the duty to act in accordance with good faith and fair dealing in international trade.[53]

A third key principle is usually referred to by the maxim *pacta sunt servanda*, i.e., once a contract has been validly concluded, it is binding and therefore must be performed, except to the extent that modification or termination is permitted under the terms of the contract or a provision in UPICC.[54] This presupposes that the conclusion of the contract was valid, so if there was a flaw in the process of contract formation which affects its validity, the parties may no longer be bound by the contract. It also means that if one party has not performed its obligations, the aggrieved party's primary remedy will be to require performance first rather than immediate termination of the contract.[55] Only exceptional circumstances might excuse non-performance.[56]

---

50 The enormity of such a task should not be underestimated. The full version of the European Draft Common Frame of Reference also contains comments and illustrations, but additionally, there are national notes for each article which explain how each rule relates to the national laws of the then EU Member States. It is therefore not surprising that the full version of the *DFCR* is distributed across six volumes and runs to some 6600 pages.
51 Art. 1.1 UPICC.
52 Art. 1.5 UPICC.
53 See Art. 1.7 UPICC, discussed below.
54 Art. 1.3 UPICC.
55 See *Chapter 7* of the UPICC.
56 Art. 7.1.7 UPICC.

3.5 Overview of contents

Although this chapter cannot offer a detailed account of the contents of the UPICC, it is nevertheless helpful to provide a brief overview of the various topics it covers. In 2016, six provisions[57] were amended so as to ensure that the UPICC took better account of the specific features of long-term contracts, mostly by amending the comments.[58]

Chapter 1 covers general provisions, including general principles such as, *int.al.*, freedom of contract,[59] *pacta sunt servanda*,[60] interpretation of the Principles[61] and the treatment of usages.[62]

Chapter 2 is sub-divided into two sections. The first contains rules on the formation of contracts and is heavily influenced by the corresponding provisions of the CISG. Section 2 deals with the role of agents and their authority. This section departs from the UNIDROIT Agency Convention[63] in several ways, and also includes additional provisions not found in that Convention.

Chapter 3 focuses on the validity of transaction and is divided into three sections: general provisions, grounds for avoidance and illegality. The grounds for avoidance covered in section 2 include mistake,[64] fraud,[65] threats by wrongful acts or omissions,[66] or where the agreement was tainted by gross disparity between the parties.[67] It also contains a set of rules on the right of avoidance and its exercise.

Chapter 4 provides the rules for the interpretation of a contract, which combines both subjective and objective elements. The basic rule is that a contract is interpreted according to a common intention of the parties,[68] where this can be established; otherwise, the contract is interpreted by applying a "reasonable person" test.[69]

Chapter 5 then deals with the content of a contract (section 1), third-party rights (section 2) and conditions for a contractual obligation to be activated (suspensive condition) or brought to an end (resolutive condition).[70] Section 1 on the content of a contract covers not only the express obligations as expressed through the terms of the contract, but also obligations which can be implied in certain circumstances.[71] It also

---

57   The Preamble, and Arts. 1.11 (definition of "long-term contract" added), 2.1.14 (terms left deliberately open), 5.1.7 (price determination), 5.1.8 (termination of contract of indefinite duration) and 7.3.7 (restitution in respect of long-term contracts following termination).
58   "Introduction to the 2016 edition", p.vii.
59   Art. 1.1 UPICC.
60   Art. 1.3 UPICC.
61   Art. 1.6 UPICC.
62   Art. 1.9 UPICC.
63   See Chapter 5.
64   Arts. 3.2.1–3.2.4 UPICC.
65   Art. 3.2.5 UPICC.
66   Art. 3.2.6 UPICC.
67   Art. 3.2.7 UPICC.
68   Art. 4.1, para. (1) UPICC.
69   Art. 4.1, para. (2) UPICC.
70   Chapter 5, section 3 UPICC.
71   Art. 5.1.2 UPICC.

impose a duty of co-operation,[72] and deals with duties to achieve a specific result or to act with best efforts.[73] It also contains provisions for determining the quality of performance and the price payable,[74] as well as provisions regarding the termination of contracts of an indefinite period,[75] and consensual release.[76] Section 2 on third-party rights deals with the possibility of a person who is not a party to the contract to enforce a right which the contract seeks to grant it. In essence, this is an exception to the general privity of contract rule.

Chapter 6 then turns to the performance of the contract. Section 1 contains a set of rules dealing with the performance of the parties' obligations in general, including the time of performance,[77] payment[78] and instances where there is a requirement for public permission for the contract.[79] Section 2 concerns hardship arising from events arising after the contract had been concluded and which would not reasonably have been foreseen.[80] The response to a hardship situation is first an attempt to renegotiate the contract, followed by assistance from a court which may order the termination or adaptation of the contract.[81]

Chapter 7 deals with the consequences of non-performance of its obligations by one of the parties. Section 1 deals with general provisions regarding non-performance, including the possibility of the non-performing party to cure its breach,[82] and for the aggrieved party to fix an additional period of time in which the non-performing party can provide its performance.[83] It also contains a provision on *force majeure* ("an impediment beyond its control"), excusing non-performance in certain circumstances.[84] Many of these provisions are inspired by the corresponding provisions in the CISG.[85] The right of the aggrieved party to require the non-performing party to perform its obligations is dealt with in section 2. These include requiring the non-performing party to perform,[86] or requiring the repair or replacement of a defective performance.[87] Section 3 then deals with the instances when[88] and how the aggrieved person can terminate the contract, including for instances of anticipatory non-performance.[89] Finally, section 4 deals with the

---

72   Art. 5.1.3 UPICC.
73   Arts. 5.1.4 and 5.1.5 UPICC.
74   Art. 5.1.6 and 5.1.7 UPICC.
75   Art. 5.1.8 UPICC.
76   Art. 5.1.9 UPICC.
77   Arts. 6.1.1 to 6.1.5 UPICC.
78   Arts. 6.1.7 to 6.1.12 UPICC.
79   Arts. 6.1.14 to 6.1.17 UPICC.
80   Art. 6.2.2 UPICC.
81   Art. 6.2.3 UPICC.
82   Art. 7.1.4 UPICC.
83   Art. 7.1.5 UPICC.
84   Art. 7.1.7 UPICC.
85   See Chapter 4.
86   Art. 7.2.1 UPICC (payment) and Art. 7.2.2 (performance of non-monetary obligations).
87   Art. 7.2.3 UPICC.
88   Art. 7.3.1 UPICC.
89   Art. 7.3.3 UPICC.

aggrieved party's right to claim damages to compensate it for any harm[90] suffered as a result of the non-performance, as well as the requirement to mitigate the harm the aggrieved party suffers,[91] payment of interest[92] and the effectiveness of agreed damages clauses.[93]

Chapter 8 is a short chapter of five articles dealing specifically with the right of set-off where two parties owe each other money or other performances of the same kind,[94] and the requirements for,[95] and consequences of,[96] exercising that right.

Chapter 9 focuses on assignment and transfer of obligations. Section 1 deals with the assignment of rights under a contract[97] and the various conditions attached to this. Whilst the assignment of contractual rights is a familiar practice, section 2 deals with the transfer of obligations which is not something every legal system recognises. This allows a person contractually obliged to make a payment or render some other performance to transfer that obligation to another person,[98] provided that the party to whom this obligation is owed agrees.[99] Section 3 then effectively combines both elements and provides for the assignment of entire contracts,[100] i.e., all the rights and obligations of a contracting party to another person.[101]

Chapter 10 then deals with an issue which straddles the boundary between substantive and procedural law: limitation periods. A limitation period sets the timescale within which a party must exercise its rights.[102] The UPICC's general limitation period is three years from when a party was, or should have been, aware of the ability to exercise a right, capped by a 10-year long-stop period.[103] This chapter contains various provisions regarding the limitation period and associated consequences.

Chapter 11 addresses a complex contracting situation involving more than two parties. Section 1 deals with the plurality of obligors, i.e., a situation where a number of parties owe the same obligation towards another party, and the rights of the obligee against the obligors and their associated liability. Conversely, section 2 covers a plurality of obligees, i.e., a situation in which there are several parties to whom an obligation is owed by another party.

---

90 Arts. 7.4.2 to 7.4.6 UPICC.
91 Art. 7.4.8 UPICC.
92 Arts. 7.4.9 and 7.4.10 UPICC.
93 Art. 7.4.13 UPICC.
94 Art. 8.1 UPICC.
95 Arts. 8.3 and 8.4 UPICC.
96 Art. 8.5 UPICC.
97 We have already examined the importance of assignment in the context of receivables financing. See Chapter 7.
98 Art. 9.2.1 UPICC.
99 Arts. 9.2.3 and 9.2.4 UPICC.
100 In English Law, it is not possible to assign a contract as a whole; however, a similar effect can be achieved through novation.
101 Art. 9.3.1 UPICC.
102 Art. 10.1 UPICC.
103 Art. 10.2 UPICC.

3.6 A closer look at some provisions

The previous section has provided a very concise summary of the many aspects covered by the UPICC. A number of features merit a closer look.

3.6.1 Good faith as substantive obligation

One of the most striking features is the inclusion of a duty imposed on each party to a contract to act in accordance with "good faith and fair dealing in international trade".[104] In fact, the notion of "good faith and fair dealing" has a number of functions in the context of the UPICC. As well as being a duty imposed on the party, it is also an underlying "fundamental idea".[105] In that sense, several of UPICC's articles directly or indirectly reflect this notion. The purpose of adding a free-standing general duty to act in good faith and fair dealing is to provide a catch-all duty which applies to those circumstances for which no specific provision exists elsewhere in the UPICC.

One common concern about the use of standards of behaviour such as "good faith and fair dealing" is their inherent vagueness. The conception of standards such as good faith varies even as between jurisdictions which have some kind of good faith requirement as an integral part of their legal system.[106] In the context of the UPICC, therefore, the criterion is expressed as "good faith and fair dealing *in international trade*". The reference to "international trade" is to make it clear that the UPICC notion is not interpreted with reference to any corresponding national standards but instead on the basis of "the special conditions of international trade"[107] in the context of each specific trade sector.[108] In the comment to Art. 1.7 UPICC, the specific example of acting in breach of this duty is a situation where a party exercises a legal right in a manner not envisaged in order to gain from this, or harm the other party (abuse of rights).[109] In addition, Art. 1.8 UPICC, which precludes a party from acting inconsistently with an understanding it has created in the other party and on which that party has reasonably relied, is a further application of the good faith and fair dealing duty.[110]

A final point regarding the duty to act in accordance with good faith and fair dealing in international trade is that it has been given a mandatory character, and the parties cannot modify or exclude it.[111] It may seem surprising, and even contradictory, to have a mandatory provision in an instrument that is not legally binding. Indeed, Art. 1.5 UPICC confirms the non-mandatory character of UPICC by permitting the parties to exclude the UPICC altogether or to vary the

---

104 Art. 1.7 UPICC.
105 *UPICC Comments*, p.18.
106 Cf. P.J. Powers, "Defining the undefinable: good faith and the UN Convention on Contracts for the International Sale of Goods" (1999) 18 *Journal of Law and Commerce* 333.
107 *UPICC Comments*, p.20.
108 This is because expectations between trade sectors are likely to vary.
109 *UPICC Comments*, p.19.
110 *Ibid.*, p.21.
111 Art. 1.7, para. (2) UPICC: "The parties may not exclude or limit this duty".

effect of any of the UPICC provisions (mirroring the approach to party autonomy taken in the many International Commercial Law conventions). The comment to Art. 1.5 UPICC explains that a small number of provisions are regarded as so important to the UPICC system that they should not be excludable – although as the comment also acknowledges, there is nothing to stop the parties from ignoring the designation of certain provisions as mandatory.[112]

The key point therefore is that good faith and fair dealing in international trade is fundamental both as an underpinning value of many UPICC provisions as well as a duty with which parties to an international commercial contract should be expected to comply. As the UPICC are generally only engaged through party choice, the duty to act in good faith and fair dealing in international trade is therefore in some ways merely an opt-in duty.

3.6.2. Interpretation of contracts

A second feature, of particular interest from a common law perspective, are the provisions dealing with the interpretation of contracts. The main criterion is that the interpretation of a contract should be done on the basis of the common intention of the parties.[113] To that extent, the interpretation is subjective, but only if it is possible to attribute clearly the same intention to all of the parties in respect of the contract provision at issue. Where this cannot be done, the criterion is the "meaning reasonable persons of the same kind as the parties"[114] would attribute to the provision at issue.

Article 4.3 UPICC requires that in determining the meaning to be given to the provision at issue, regard is to be had to all the circumstances. A number of factors are then listed as among the circumstances to be taken into account: (i) preliminary negotiations between the parties; (ii) practices which parties have established between themselves; (iii) conduct of the parties subsequent to conclusion of the contract; (iv) the nature and purpose of the contract; (v) the meaning commonly given to terms and expressions in trade concerned; and (vi) usages.

An (English) common lawyer will immediately see that (i) and (iii) are factors which have expressly been excluded[115] from the matrix of fact,[116] or context, against which a contract should be interpreted. With regard to pre-contractual negotiations, English courts have on several occasions made reference to Art. 4.3 UPICC,[117] but have declined to follow its lead. In *Chartbrook Ltd v Persimmon Homes Ltd*, Lord Hoffmann rejected the approach of Art. 4.3 UPICC (and a similar provision in Art. 5:102 of the

---

112 *UPICC Comments*, p.14.
113 Art. 4.1, para. (1) UPICC.
114 Art. 4.2, para. (2) UPICC.
115 For pre-contractual negotiations, see *Chartbrook Ltd v Persimmon Homes* [2009] UKHL 38; for post-contract formation conduct, see *Schuler AG v Wickman Machine Tool Sales Ltd* [1974] AC 235.
116 *Investors Compensation Scheme Ltd v West Bromwich Building Society* [1998] 1 WLR 896.
117 *Proforce Recruit Limited v The Rugby Group Limited* [2006] EWCA Civ 69; *Chartbrook Ltd v Persimmon Homes Ltd* [2008] EWCA Civ 183 (Court of Appeal); [2009] UKHL 38 (House of Lords).

Principles of European Contract Law) because both "reflect the French philosophy of contractual interpretation, which is altogether different from that of English Law".[118] That would not, of itself, be a sufficient reason to reject the approach in Art. 4.3 UPICC, but Lord Hoffmann continued by observing that "One cannot in my opinion simply transpose rules based on one philosophy of contractual interpretation to another, or assume that the practical effect of admitting such evidence under the English system of civil procedure will be the same as that under a Continental system."[119] Whether one agrees with this analysis or not may be a matter of debate, but this attitude is also indicative of an altogether different issue regarding the UPICC. Its provisions purport to provide "best solutions" for international commercial contracts. However, English Law is still a popular law of choice for many types of international commercial contracts, and its reluctance to take pre-contractual negotiations into account when interpreting a contract does not seem to deter commercial parties in large numbers. This suggests that there may be alternative candidates for "best solutions", and to some extent, the decision of which one to accept for something like the UPICC might not be obvious. However, the UPICC have adopted a solution which might work well for many international commercial contracts; indeed, at times, both pre-contractual negotiations and subsequent conduct might be useful factors to be taken into account to confirm an interpretation already preferred on different grounds.

3.6.3 Force majeure *and hardship*

One further element of the UPICC merits mention: the provisions dealing with circumstances where it is not possible to perform a contract as intended as a result of events beyond the control of the parties. Thus, Art. 7.1.7 UPICC on *force majeure* provides that a party's non-performance is excused if this was "due to an impediment beyond its control".[120] This is subject to the requirement that the non-performing party "could not reasonably be expected to have taken the impediment into account at time of the conclusion of the contract"[121] or have mitigated the impediment or its consequences. Although not phrased in these terms, this presumably entails that the impediment in question was neither foreseen nor reasonably foreseeable by the parties to the contract. Where the impediment is temporary rather than permanent, non-performance is only excused for a period which is reasonable in view of the effect the impediment has had on the performance of the contract.[122]

The party unable to perform due to the impediment must give notice of the impediment and its impact on the party's ability to perform to the other party, and do so within a reasonable time; failure to do so can result in liability for damages which result from the other party not receiving notice.[123]

---

118 [2009] UKHL 38 at para. [39].
119 *Ibid.*
120 Art. 7.1.7(1) UPICC.
121 *Ibid.*
122 Art. 7.1.7(2) UPICC.
123 Art. 7.1.7(3) UPICC.

The effect of Art. 7.1.7 UPICC is not to bring the contract to an end, nor to excuse both parties from further performance. Rather, it merely excuses non-performance which is due to the impediment so no liability for non-performance would arise. In practical terms, it might simply have the effect of extending the period for performance of the affected party's obligation. However, this does not affect the right of the other party to terminate the contract where the non-performance is fundamental.[124]

Furthermore, the UPICC deal with the situation where performance of the contract has not become impossible as such, but where continuing with performance would result in hardship for one or both of the parties. The mere fact that performance of a contract has become more onerous does not affect the parties' obligation to perform the contract.[125] However, where hardship arises, this position is modified. A situation involving hardship occurs "where the occurrence of events fundamentally alters the equilibrium of the contract", either because the cost of performing has increased or the value of the performance provided has reduced.[126] The event which is said to have caused hardship has to fulfil for criteria to engage Art. 6.2.2 UPICC: (i) it must have occurred or become known after the contract was concluded; (ii) it could not reasonably have been taken into account before the contract was concluded; (iii) it is beyond the control of the party suffering hardship; and (iv) it must be one in respect of which the party suffering hardship did not assume the risk. Once it has been established that a situation of hardship exists, the party which is now at a disadvantage is entitled to request renegotiation of the contract,[127] although this does not mean that that party's obligation to perform is suspended.[128] Should the renegotiations be unsuccessful, either party may involve a court, which may either terminate the contract on terms, or modify the contract in light of the circumstances to restore its equilibrium.[129]

Both provisions are novel in how they deal with the impact of unforeseen circumstances on the performance of a contract, and both reflect the underpinning principle of *pacta sunt servanda*. Neither provision leads to the contract coming to an end as a primary consequence.

These provisions attracted some attention as a result of the consequences of the 2020–21 period of the SARS-CoV-2 (COVID-19) pandemic. This pandemic significantly disrupted commercial activity around the world and tested the suitability of national laws on dealing with the impact of unforeseen events on contracts. The UNIDROIT Secretariat published a detailed note to explain how the UPICC provisions on *force majeure* and hardship would apply in the context of the pandemic to offer guidance on how the unprecedented impact of a global health crisis on commercial contracts could be dealt with.[130]

---

124 Art. 7.1.7(4) UPICC.
125 Art. 6.2.1 UPICC.
126 Art. 6.2.2 UPICC.
127 Art. 6.2.3(1) UPICC.
128 Art. 6.2.3(2) UPICC.
129 Art. 6.2.3(4) UPICC.
130 UNIDROIT Secretariat, *Note on the UNIDROIT Principles of International Commercial Contracts and the COVID-19 Health Crisis* (UNIDROIT, 2020).

4. Concluding observations

The UPICC have become an important feature of the International Commercial Law landscape, albeit perhaps in a way which differs from what was originally imagined. However, this does not weaken their significance; rather, the UPICC have gained a different but no less important status within International Commercial Law. They are a very useful starting point for comparative discussions of how different legal systems might address an issue relevant to international commercial contracts but not covered by a harmonising instrument of some kind, for example. However, contrary to what the drafters of the UPICC might have intended, it seems that they are rarely used in their entirety. In lamenting this, Bonnell claims that this is due to "the inherent conservatism, coupled with a good deal of provincialism, of the legal profession".[131] A different approach to legal education, which would include the UPICC as an integral part of the curriculum, could change this.[132]

---

131 M.J. Bonnell, "The law governing international commercial contracts and the actual role of the UNIDROIT Principles" (2018) 23 *Uniform Law Review* 15, pp.39–40.
132 *Ibid.*

11

DISPUTE RESOLUTION

International commercial arbitration

1. What is arbitration?

In this chapter, we will consider the typical means by which international commercial disputes are resolved. Instead of litigating a dispute before a court of law in a particular jurisdiction, the parties to an international commercial contract may prefer to have their dispute resolved through arbitration. It will be seen in this chapter that there are several advantages to arbitration compared to litigation, including its more flexible nature and the near-global enforceability of arbitration awards under the UNCITRAL Convention on the Recognition and Enforcement of Foreign Arbitral Awards 1958, often referred to in this context as the "New York Convention". Arbitration is a form of alternative dispute resolution in the sense that it is an alternative to litigating before a national court. Whilst the procedure of arbitration proceedings can to a large extent be determined by the parties, the final outcome of any arbitration proceedings will be a decision made by the arbitrator(s) which is binding on the parties in much the same way as a court judgment. The decision by the parties to an international commercial contract to take any disputes which might arise to arbitration rather than litigation is based on their contractual agreement. This can be achieved either by means of an arbitration clause included in the contract between the parties, or through a separate agreement to submit a dispute which has arisen to arbitration (a "submission agreement"). As we will see in this chapter, this agreement will determine matters such as the choice of arbitrators, the location of the arbitration proceedings, the procedural rules under which the proceedings will be conducted, and the substantive rules of law which the arbitrators will apply in resolving the dispute.

1.1 Why choose arbitration?

One might ask why parties to international commercial contracts might prefer arbitration to litigation. There are a number of reasons, some practical and some reflecting

DOI: 10.4324/9781315692807-11

the particular characteristics of arbitration. As we saw in Chapter 2, litigation has to be conducted before a national court, either chosen by the parties through a choice-of-forum clause in their contract or determined on the basis of whatever rules of private international law apply to their situation. This court will have set rules of procedure which will have to be followed. The national court hearing the dispute will consist of a judge or several judges who will be excellent lawyers, but may not know a great deal about the particular trade sector in which the parties operate, nor have the particular technical expertise which might be relevant in resolving the dispute. To overcome this, the parties, or rather their lawyers, would have to present a potentially substantial amount of background material to the court to ensure that all relevant non-legal factors are before the court to assist the judge(s) with their task. Arbitration, on the other hand, can be located wherever the parties might choose (although it will often be one of the leading global arbitration organisations), the parties can select arbitrators with relevant expertise, and the parties can determine how formal or informal the proceedings need to be. Moreover, a national court has to resolve the dispute on the basis of the law applicable to the contract between the parties, whereas in arbitration, the parties are able to ask the arbitrators to resolve the dispute on the basis of rules of law which may differ from the applicable law. Once a decision has been handed down by a court, it may become necessary to take steps to enforce the judgment in another jurisdiction, but unless there is an agreement for the recognition of judgments from a foreign court in place, this could be a complex and time-consuming process. Awards handed down in international commercial arbitration proceedings are recognised in almost every jurisdiction around the world.

However, as well as these practical advantages, arbitration proceedings are conducted in private. The privacy of arbitration proceedings is important because it avoids both unnecessary publicity and the wider economic impact this could have on the parties involved, and it also protects the details of the parties' commercial relationship and any proprietary knowledge from becoming public. Moreover, arbitration proceedings are subject to a duty of confidentiality, which means that nothing from the proceedings – whether evidence, witness statements or the final award – may be made public unless all parties consent to this. In *Ali Shipping Corporation v Shipyard Trogyr*,[1] the English Court of Appeal held that the duty of confidentiality of arbitration proceedings would prevent a party in arbitration proceedings from relying on evidence obtained during a previous arbitration between the same parties. The Court noted that the duty of confidentiality was an incident of the private nature of arbitration proceedings and recognised, in English Law, as an implied term arising as a "necessary incident of a definable category of contractual relationships",[2] i.e., it would be implied into an arbitration because of the fact that it is an arbitration agreement,[3] without further need to consider whether such a term would be required on the basis of the

1 *Ali Shipping Corporation v Shipyard Trogyr* [1999] 1 W.L.R. 314.
2 The formulation used by Lord Bridge in *Scally v Southern Health and Social Services Board* [1992] 1 A.C. 294 at p.307 to explain one of two instances when a term is implied into a contract.
3 Potter LJ in *Ali Shipping* at p.326.

business efficacy or officious bystander tests.[4] There would only be a limited number of exceptions to this principle: (i) disclosure of confidential material with the consent of the person who originally produced it; (ii) by order of a court (e.g., an order for disclosure where court proceedings result from the arbitration); and (iii) where this is reasonably necessary for the protection of the legitimate interests of an arbitrating party.[5]

1.2 The legal framework for international commercial arbitration

In this chapter, we will examine the legal framework which supports international commercial arbitration. There are two international texts which are of particular relevance. The first is the New York Convention on the Recognition and Enforcement of Foreign Arbitral Awards 1958, which has been ratified by 168 countries[6] around the world. Its primary purpose is to deal with the recognition and enforcement of both arbitration agreements and arbitration awards. Thus, it seeks to ensure, where parties have agreed to resolve their dispute by arbitration, that courts do not allow the parties (usually one of the parties) to take this dispute to court instead. More importantly, it provides for the recognition of an arbitration award in all of the Contracting States, which makes their enforcement considerably easier.

The second is the UNCITRAL Model Law on International Commercial Arbitration, which was first issued in 1985, and amended in 2006. This Model Law is intended to provide national legislatures with a template for modernising, or creating, a domestic legal regime which facilitates all stages of the process of international commercial arbitration. It is necessary to have national legislation on international commercial arbitration, because arbitration effectively diverts the parties' dispute from the court system, and so there needs to be a clear framework which governs the process of international commercial arbitration. In a sense, just as any international commercial contract ultimately has to be governed by a particular national law, so do arbitration proceedings. It will be explained later that each arbitration must be located somewhere, even if only notionally. This location is known as the "seat of arbitration", and the country, or jurisdiction, where the seat is located provides the legal regime governing the arbitration (often referred to as the *lex arbitri*). The *lex arbitri* deals, in particular, with the process by which a jurisdiction recognises the existence of an arbitration tribunal and the conduct of its proceedings, as well as relevant procedural aspects. The UNCITRAL Model Law therefore offers a model for each jurisdiction to ensure that its *lex arbitri* is suitable for international commercial arbitration, and to ensure a high level of convergence among different jurisdictions.[7]

4   These are the alternative formulations for determining whether to imply a term into a particular contractual relationship between identified parties: see *Marks and Spencer plc v BNP Paribas Securities Services Trust Company (Jersey) Ltd* [2015] UKSC 72.

5   Potter LJ in *Ali Shipping* at p.327. For an example of the final situation (treating it as disclosure in the interests of justice), see *John Foster Emmot v Michael Wilson & Partners Ltd* [2008] EWCA Civ 184.

6   Figure correct as at April 2021.

7   Legislation based on the Model Law has been adopted in 85 countries (a total of 118 jurisdictions): see https://uncitral.un.org/en/texts/arbitration/modellaw/commercial_arbitration/status [accessed May 2021].

The Model Law addresses a range of issues: the recognition of the arbitration agreement; the composition of the arbitral tribunal; the jurisdiction of the tribunal; the conduct of the arbitration proceedings; issuing of the arbitration award; possible recourse against the award; and recognition of the award. Many of its provisions are default rules which apply in respect of matters which the parties to the arbitration have not settled in their arbitration agreement.

In addition to these two UNCITRAL texts, there are other sets of international rules of relevance to the conduct of the arbitration proceedings. Whilst arbitration is, in principle, a flexible process and the parties have considerable leeway in determining the procedural aspects of their arbitration, in practice, many arbitration proceedings will be conducted by or under the auspices of the established arbitration centres. Each of these will have its own set of procedural rules which will be applied in arbitration proceedings conducted at these arbitration centres. In addition, both UNCITRAL and the International Chamber of Commerce (ICC) have published their own set of arbitration rules,[8] which can be adopted by the parties to arbitration proceedings to set out the procedure which will be followed in their proceedings. In addition, the International Bar Association has published *Rules of Ethics for International Arbitrators*[9] and *Guidelines on Conflicts of Interest in International Arbitration*,[10] both of which seek to ensure the proper conduct of arbitrators, especially with regard to impartiality and independence.

1.3 Private international law aspects

Although arbitration is separate from the court system of any particular jurisdiction, we have already seen that arbitration proceedings are governed by the law of the country/jurisdiction where the arbitration has its seat (*lex arbitri*). Therefore, in choosing the location for their arbitration, the parties may need to consider the requirements of the *lex arbitri*.

For a time, there was a debate as to whether control of international commercial arbitration under the *lex arbitri* was necessary at all. In particular, Paulsson[11] claimed that there was no need for the *lex arbitri* to play any role, and that any control regarding the validity or enforceability of arbitration proceedings and the resulting award should purely be a matter for the State where enforcement of the award is sought. This claim was justified on the basis that international commercial arbitration, by its very nature, should be disconnected from national controls and be governed solely by the

---

8   UNCITRAL, *UNCITRAL Arbitration Rules and Rules on Transparency in Treaty-Based Investor-State Arbitration* (New York, 2014); International Chamber of Commerce, *Arbitration Rules – Mediation Rules* (Paris, 2017), text available at https://iccwbo.org/dispute-resolution-services/arbitration/rules-of-arbitration/ [accessed February 2020].
9   International Bar Association, *Rules of Ethics for International Arbitrators* (London, 1987).
10 International Bar Association, *IBA Guidelines on Conflicts of Interest in International Arbitration* (London, 2014).
11 J. Paulsson, "Abitration unbound: award detached from the law of its country of origin" (1981) 30 *International and Comparative Law Quarterly* 358; Paulsson, "Delocalisation of international commercial arbitration: when and why it matters" (1983) 32 *International and Comparative Law Quarterly* 53.

provisions of the New York Convention. However, this idea of "delocalisation" of arbitral proceedings did not gain much traction and has failed to gain acceptance.

In addition to the *lex arbitri*, it will also be necessary to have regard to the law governing the contract between the parties itself, particularly where this contains an arbitration clause. The law governing the contract will also be relevant for resolving the dispute between the parties, unless the parties have asked the arbitrators to decide on the basis of different rules of law (see below). Where a separate arbitration agreement is concluded, this may be subject to a different governing law than the law applicable to the contract itself. Finally, as discussed below, the parties may choose whether the arbitrators should apply the law governing the contract or a different law/set of legal rules when resolving the dispute.

2. The international nature of international commercial arbitration

As with any other aspect of International Commercial Law, the scope of application of the rules on international commercial arbitration requires there to be an international dimension. Article 1 of the UNCITRAL Model Law provides the criteria for determining whether an arbitration is international. The criterion in Art. 1(3)(a) of the Model Law is familiar: it treats an arbitration as international if the parties to an arbitration agreement[12] have their respective places of business[13] in different States at the time the arbitration agreement is concluded. However, there are a number of alternative ways of treating an arbitration as international where the parties have their places of business in the same State. Thus, if either the place of arbitration, identified on the basis of the arbitration agreement, is located outside of the State where the parties have their places of business, or if the place where a substantial part of the obligations under the main contract is to be performed, or the place with which the subject-matter of the dispute is most closely connected, is located outside of that State, then the arbitration is also treated as international.[14] Finally, an arbitration will be international if the parties agree expressly that the subject-matter of the arbitration agreement relates to more than one country.[15]

3. The arbitration agreement

The decision to go to arbitration is essentially consensual in that the parties to a contract either agree in their contract or after a dispute has arisen that they will seek a resolution through arbitration rather than litigation. If there is an arbitration clause in the commercial contract between the parties, the principle of the separability, or

---

12 Which would also include an arbitration clause in the contract between the parties.
13 As is common in other International Commercial Law instruments, if a party has multiple places of business, the relevant place of business is that with the closest relationship to the arbitration agreement. Moreover, for a party without a place of business, its habitual residence is used instead (see Art. 1(4) of the UNCITRAL Model Law).
14 Art. 1(3)(b)(i) and (ii).
15 Art. 1(3)(c).

autonomy, of the arbitration clause is crucial. For example, Art. 16(1) of the UNCI-TRAL Model Law provides that "an arbitration clause which forms part of a contract shall be treated as an agreement independent of the other terms of the contract" and that, consequently, a decision regarding the effectiveness or validity of the commercial contract does not affect the validity of the arbitration agreement.

The arbitration agreement between the parties is therefore essential. Generally, the parties have the freedom to determine a whole range of issues in the arbitration agreement,[16] although often, parties will not set out the detail but rather defer to the rules of their chosen arbitration institution or specify the rules on the basis of which the arbitration should be conducted. If the parties decide not to do this, they will have to use the arbitration agreement to determine a range of issues.

The first is to decide on the individual arbitrators, and the number of arbitrators (usually, there will be a sole arbitrator or a panel of three, with one appointed by each party, and a neutral third one chosen by the two others). Secondly, the seat of the arbitration has to be chosen. This will determine the *lex arbitri*, i.e., the legal regime governing the arbitration. Third, the parties have to agree on the scope of the arbitration, i.e., they need to set out the issues which they wish to refer to arbitration. The arbitrator(s) can only consider those issues which have been referred for arbitration and they are not permitted to consider other issues which are only raised at a later point; otherwise, the award is can be challenged[17] and/or refused recognition.[18] Fourth, the arbitration agreement needs to set out the procedural rules which the arbitrators must follow. Finally, the arbitration agreement should state which substantive rules the arbitrators should use in resolving the dispute, particularly if the parties intend for this to be done on the basis of legal rules which differ from the law applicable to their commercial contract.

3.1 Validity

In order to be valid and therefore enforceable, there are a number of formal conditions which an arbitration agreement must satisfy. The criteria for validity can be determined on the basis of Art. II of the New York Convention, which sets out the criteria for recognising arbitration agreements. The first requirement is that it has to be in writing.[19] The New York Convention pre-dates the use of digital methods of communication, but electronic documents should now be recognised as fulfilling this requirement. Indeed, Art. 7 (Option 1) of the Model Law makes this clear: according to Art. 7(4), the requirement for an arbitration requirement to be in writing is met by an electronic communication (such as e-mail) "if the information contained therein is

---

16 T.E. Carbonneau, "The exercise of contract freedom in the making of arbitration agreements" (2003) 36 *Vanderbilt Journal of Transnational Law* 1190.

17 Cf. Art. 34(2)(iii) of the Model Law.

18 Art. 36(i)(a)(iii) of the Model Law, and Art. V(1)(c) of the New York Convention.

19 Art. II(1) New York Convention; Art. 7 (Option 1 – definition and form of arbitration agreement) Model Law. Note that Option 2 for Art. 7 does not contain any form requirements.

accessible so as to be useable for subsequent reference".[20] Digital forms of arbitration agreements should therefore meet the requirement that they are in writing.

Secondly, under the New York Convention[21] there may be a need for a signature of the parties, particularly in respect of a separate arbitration agreement[22] but also potentially of the arbitration clause in the commercial contract. The drafting of Art. II(2) of the New York Convention is not entirely clear. It states that the "term 'agreement in writing' shall include an arbitral clause in a contract or an arbitration agreement, signed by the parties or contained in an exchange of letters or telegrams". It is plausible that the requirement that there is a signature only relates to a separate arbitration agreement, but it could also apply to an arbitral clause in the parties' commercial contract. If this also applies to the arbitral clause, a related question is whether it would suffice for the contract as a whole to have been signed, or whether a separate signature against the arbitral clause would be required. In the case of electronic documents, a functional equivalent to a signature would be needed. In any case, a signature is not always required if the arbitration agreement (and possibly also the contract) is contained in an exchange of written communications. Art. II(2) refers to an "exchange of letters or telegrams", but an exchange of e-mails should suffice.

A further essential requirement, in additional to the formal requirements as to writing and (possibly) signature, is that there is a "defined legal relationship"[23] between the parties from which the dispute which is referred to arbitration may arise, or has arisen. A dispute arising from the parties' contractual relationship would satisfy this requirement, although it need not be based on a contractual relationship. Finally, the subject-matter of the dispute must be one that is capable of being settled by arbitration. This is known as the *arbitrability* of the issue(s) referred to arbitration.

4. The arbitration panel

It is important that care is taken in determining the composition of the arbitration panel, both with regard to the number of arbitrators and their expertise in respect of the subject-matter of the dispute. Unlike a court of law, an arbitration panel is not a permanent tribunal, but only established when the need arises. Where the arbitration is conducted under the auspices of an arbitration body or centre, there will be some external oversight of the panel. Should it become necessary, this will allow for an arbitrator to be replaced without great difficulty. However, in the case of an *ad hoc* arbitration largely arranged by the parties and not conducted through

---

20 This has become an established way of spelling out what the functional equivalent of "in writing" would be in the context of electronic communications. See Chapter 12 at 2.1.

21 No mention is made in the UNCITRAL Model Law for a signature requirement.

22 See, e.g., *Celio Moore v Seven Seas Cruises LLC and Voyager Vessel Co* (U.S. District Court, Southern District of Florida, case no 19–22085-CIV-MORENO) of 5 July 2019 (agreement initialled on each page and signed on final page).

23 Art. II(1) New York Convention.

an arbitration body, there will be less external oversight to ensure the proper conduct of the proceedings. If there are concerns over an arbitrator, it would only be possible to remove the arbitrator by a court and in accordance with the rules of the *lex arbitri*.[24]

Where the parties make their own arrangements for the appointment of the arbitration panel, care must be taken to ensure that the integrity of process is maintained and there is no risk of any conflicts of interest or bias. The parties should make sure that the arbitrator(s) they intend to appoint have the appropriate qualifications, experience of the parties' trade, and any expertise that may be relevant to the issues to be arbitrated in order to maximise the chances of a speedy and accurate resolution of their dispute. This is particularly important because there will usually be no possibility of appeal or review of the arbitration award on the merits but only on procedural grounds.[25] So it is important to choose the right panel to minimise the risk that the arbitrators will make a serious error about the content or application of the relevant law. Relevant knowledge or experience of the trade or industry will be important. Moreover, if the dispute involves complex points of law, it would seem sensible to appoint a legal expert as one of the arbitrators. There will also be more practical factors, such as whether all the arbitrators and the parties share a common language in which to conduct the proceedings, the availability of the arbitrators to conduct the proceedings (especially where these are likely to be lengthy) and the reputation of the arbitrators. All of this will have inevitable cost implications, because arbitrators will charge for the time spent on the arbitration, and those with expertise and a high reputation are likely to be able to command higher-than-average fees.

Usually, arbitration panels consist either of a sole arbitrator or of a panel of three arbitrators, (with the latter being the default position under the Model Law[26]), although any number could be chosen. The parties should avoid an even number of arbitrators to avoid a possible deadlock of the panel if it cannot agree on the outcome.

Key advantages of choosing more than one arbitrator are that this facilitates more deliberation between the arbitrators of the issues raised, and also that this makes it easier to bring together complementary expertise from different areas. For example, one arbitrator might have expertise in the legal issue relevant to the arbitration, another might have relevant technical expertise related to the factual issues of the dispute, and a third might have experience in the parties' trade sector. The award reached by a multi-arbitrator panel might therefore have greater authority and be more readily accepted by the parties. Generally, it seems advisable to use a panel of three arbitrators where the dispute is likely to be complex and involve multiple issues, and where large sums of money are at stake.

Whilst there is the theoretical possibility to choose arbitrators primarily based on their expertise, there is also a likelihood that the parties are not able to agree on the

---

24 See Arts. 13(3) and 14(1) of the UNCITRAL Model Law.
25 Cf. Art. 34 UNCITRAL Model Law. Note that under section 69 of the UK's Arbitration Act 1996, there is a limited possibility of appealing to court on a point of law.
26 See Art. 10(2) UNCITRAL Model Law.

particular arbitrators to be appointed to the panel which will hear their dispute. In such circumstances, it the default approach is that each party appoints one arbitrator each, and the two appointees will select a third arbitrator who will also act as chair of the panel.[27]

The way in which the selection process will be conducted will depend on the type of arbitration. For *ad hoc* arbitrations, the parties have generally more freedom, but also greater responsibility, in choosing their arbitrators. In the case of an arbitration under institutional rules, the rules of the chosen institution may specify how the arbitrators should be selected. In particular, the parties might be invited to make their selection from a pre-determined list of arbitrators drawn up by the institution.

4.1 Independence and impartiality

One common feature of all arbitration panels is that they must adhere to the principles of *impartiality* and *independence*. Impartiality entails that an arbitrator must not be biased in respect of the issues before the arbitral panel nor against or in favour of any of the parties. An arbitrator's independence means that they should not have any link to one of the parties, nor should they have any financial interest in the outcome of the dispute. Accordingly, under Art. 12(1) of the UNCITRAL Model Law, an arbitrator is obliged from the moment he or she is approached for appointment to disclose any circumstances which might create "justifiable doubts" as to that arbitrator's impartiality or independence.[28] Moreover, a justifiable doubt as to an arbitrator's impartiality or independence can be a ground for challenging that arbitrator in accordance with Art. 12(2) Model Law.[29] Similarly, the IBA's *Guidelines on Conflicts of Interest* stress the absolute duty of an arbitrator to be impartial and independent of the parties.[30] The *Guidelines* focus, in particular, on possible instances of a conflict of interest between those of an arbitrator and those of the parties. Instances are divided between three "lists": a red list, orange list and green list. As might be expected, situations in the green list are deemed to involve no objective conflict of interest. The orange list sets out situations where there is a possibility of a conflict of interest which could undermine the arbitrator's impartiality and/or independence, and so the arbitrator is obliged to disclose this to the parties (under General Standard 3 of the *Guidelines*). The red list is divided into waivable and non-waivable situations. The non-waivable list covers situations where an arbitrator is also one of the parties, a legal representative or employee of one of the parties, has a significant financial interest in one of the parties or the outcome of the arbitration, or regularly advises one of the parties and gains

---

27 Art. 11(3)(a) UNCITRAL Model Law. Where the two arbitrators fail to agree on the third, the competent court under the *lex arbitri* will appoint the third arbitrator.

28 The ICC Arbitration Rules put this simply as an obligation on each arbitrator to be, and to remain, impartial and independent of the parties involved in the arbitration (Art. 11 (1) ICC Arbitration Rules).

29 Both aspects of the UNCITRAL Model Law are also reflected in Arts. 11 and 12 of the UNCITRAL Arbitration Rules.

30 General Standard 1 IBA *Guidelines*.

significant financial income from this. These are all such serious situations of conflict that they disqualify that person from serving as an arbitrator. Those in the waivable category of the red list are less serious and can be waived by the parties if they are fully aware of the nature of the conflict of interest and expressly state that they would be willing to have this person serve as an arbitrator.[31] The orange list details those situations where there might be doubt as to a person's impartiality or independence, and the arbitrator is obliged to disclose this to the parties.[32] Following disclosure, the parties have to decide whether to object to this person serving as arbitrator, but if they do not raise any concerns, the person can act as arbitrator. The disclosure itself does not mean that the person lacks the impartiality and independence required of an arbitrator.[33]

5. Conducting the proceedings

Once the arbitration panel has been appointed, proceedings can commence. The precise procedure that will be followed for the proceedings will depend on whether the arbitration is conducted on an institutional or *ad hoc* basis. In the former case, the procedural rules governing the arbitration will be those of the chosen institution. In the latter case, the *lex arbitri* will provide any rules applicable to the proceedings.[34]

Generally, there will be an initial meeting of the panel with the parties to discuss whatever preliminary matters might arise, and to confirm the procedure which will be followed for the arbitration. They may confirm the terms of reference and the issues which are to be resolved by the arbitration panel (bearing in mind that arbitration panels may only consider those issues which the parties have agreed to refer to arbitration). This might include a decision of whether it will be necessary to hold hearings for the parties to present their arguments, and supporting evidence, or whether it would be sufficient for the arbitrators to proceed on the basis of written submissions from the parties and documentary evidence.[35] Any documents either party intends to rely on must be disclosed to the opposite party. As far as witnesses are concerned, they will generally provide written statements, but the parties can agree to direct examination and cross-examination of witnesses.

5.1. Role of courts in arbitration

The general rule is that the courts of the jurisdiction where the arbitration is located will not generally have any role in the arbitral process. However, there may be some instances where assistance from the courts is required, even after the arbitration has commenced. The extent to which this happens varies between jurisdictions.

An initial need for recourse to a court will arise where it becomes necessary to enforce an agreement to arbitrate and therefore to stay or abandon proceedings

---

31 General Standard 4(c) IBA *Guidelines*.
32 General Standard 3(a) IBA *Guidelines*.
33 Explanation (c) to General Standard 3.
34 See Chapter V of the UNICTRAL Model Law.
35 Art. 24 UNCITRAL Model Law.

commenced by one of the parties, where the issues brought before a court should be taken to arbitration instead.[36] We have already noted that courts can also be asked to assist with the appointment, and also the removal, or arbitrators.

A court might be called upon where its coercive powers are required to ensure that the parties do not act in a way that would undermine the arbitral process, including orders necessary to conserve the parties' assets to ensure that they can meet any obligations arising from the final award.[37] Arbitration panels are able to make orders for interim measures and related orders,[38] but they will not have the enforcement powers which a court has in respect of any orders it has made and therefore courts can be asked to enforce any interim orders made by an arbitration panel.[39]

6. Rules of law applied by arbitration panel

To the extent that the dispute between the parties raises questions of law, the arbitration panel will have to apply the law to the issues raised in the dispute to determine what the outcome should be. The key question here is *which* law the arbitration panel should apply. Before a court of law, the answer to this would be simple: the dispute has to be resolved on the basis of the law which applies to the contract or the particular legal issues before the court (if they are non-contractual). To the extent that the parties have not chosen the applicable law, or if their choice is not effective, the rules of private international law applied by the court hearing the case will determine the applicable law.

The situation is not quite as simple as that in the context of international commercial arbitration, which, far from being a drawback, is one of the particular characteristics of arbitration compared to litigation. Article 28 of the UNCITRAL Model Law sets out how the applicable law should be determined in the context of international commercial arbitration.

First, Article 28 gives priority to "such rules of law as are chosen by the parties as applicable to the substance of the dispute".[40] There are two things to note: first, the overriding criterion is the choice made by the parties. This means that the parties can choose the substantive law to be applied in the arbitration afresh, and they are not bound by the law deemed to be the applicable law in their contract. They can also choose a law that would not be applicable through the application of private international rules. Secondly, the phrase "rules of law" does not restrict the parties' choice of the law of a particular jurisdiction. The parties could also choose relevant international conventions (or even model laws) which might not otherwise be applicable to their contract, as well as other rules agreed internationally such as the UNIDROIT

36 See Art. II(3) of the New York Convention and Art. 8(1) of the UNCITRAL Model Law.
37 Cf. Art. 17J UNCITRAL Model law.
38 See Arts. 17–17G UNCITRAL Model Law.
39 Arts. 17H–I UNCITRAL Model Law.
40 Art. 28(1) UNICTRAL Model Law. See also Art. 35(1) UNCITRAL Arbitration Rules and Art. 21(1) ICC Arbitration Rules.

Principles on International Commercial Contracts.[41] It might also be possible for the parties to ask the arbitrators to resolve their dispute on the basis of the *lex mercatoria*. Indeed, it has been argued that arbitrators might prefer this to the choice of a national law or even international convention in view of the large margin of this discretion it would give them in resolving the dispute.[42]

In the absence of an express choice made by the parties, the arbitration panel will have to make that choice instead. Under the UNCITRAL Model Law, the arbitration panel would be required to apply the substantive law "determined by the conflict of laws rules which it considers applicable".[43] This is not dissimilar to what would happen before a court of law, although the arbitrators are not bound by one particular private international law[44] regime and may, for instance, consider whether the private international law regimes of the jurisdictions where the parties have their respective places of business point to the same applicable law. By way of comparison, under both the UNCITRAL and ICC arbitration rules, the arbitration panel is empowered to apply the rules of law which the panel "determines to be appropriate".[45] This gives the panel greater discretion than it would have if the rules from the Model Law applied.

In addition to the greater flexibility with regard to the rules of law which the arbitration panel can be required to apply to resolve the substantive issues of the dispute, the parties can also choose to ask the arbitration panel to resolve the dispute without reference to *any* rules of law and instead use what it regards as fair and equitable as the relevant yardstick. Thus, Art. 28(3) of the UNCITRAL Model Law specifies that "The arbitral tribunal shall decide *ex aequo et bono* or as *amiable compositeur* only if the parties have expressly authorized it to do so."[46] It is crucial that the parties have given express authorisation to the panel for this. The panel cannot decide of its own accord that this would be the appropriate way of reaching a decision; moreover, it would also not seem possible for the arbitration panel to choose this approach if the parties had asked the arbitration panel to choose the most appropriate substantive rules itself, because this is unlikely to be sufficient to be regarded as express authorisation.

Irrespective of which basis is chosen by which the arbitration panel is required to resolve the dispute, the panel will always be required to reach its decision on the basis of the terms of the contract between the parties, and account should be taken of any applicable trade usages.[47]

---

41 There is little evidence that many parties make this choice, however: R. Michaels, "The UNIDROIT Principles as global background law" (2014) 19 *Uniform Law Review* 643.
42 G. Cuniberti, "Three theories of *lex mercatoria*" (2014) 52 *Columbia Journal of Transnational Law* 369.
43 Art. 28(2) UNCITRAL Model Law.
44 "Conflict of laws" and "private international law" are used interchangeably.
45 Art. 35(1) UNCITRAL Arbitration Rules; Art. 21(1) ICC Arbitration Rules.
46 See also Art. 35(2) UNCITRAL Arbitration Rules, and Art. 21(3) ICC Arbitration Rules.
47 Art. 28(4) Model Law; see also Art. 35(3) UNCITRAL Arbitration Rules and Art. 21(2) ICC Arbitration Rules.

7. The award

At the end of the process, the arbitration panel will make its final determination and issue its conclusions. This is the arbitration award. This is a final and binding decision setting the outcome of the dispute between the parties. Any formalities which need to be complied with will be determined by the *lex arbitri* and the relevant procedural rules under which the arbitration was conducted. Generally, the award has to be in writing and signed by the arbitrators.[48] The arbitrators must give the reasons for the award, unless the parties have dispensed with the requirement for reasons.[49] It is important that the parties have a written award in order for the award to be recognised and enforced in the Contracting States of the New York Convention.[50]

8. Challenging an award

8.1 No challenge to an award based on its merits

Once the award has been handed down, the parties may wish to challenge the decision which the arbitration panel has reached. However, there is no appeals process within international commercial arbitration, and, as a general rule, there is no possibility to appeal an award to a court of law. This is so even when the arbitration panel has made an error in applying the relevant rules of law to the substance of the dispute. However, whilst the UNCITRAL Model Law does not envisage a possibility for the parties to appeal to a court, the *lex arbitri* may provide for this.

8.1.1 Appeal on a question of law: the example of the UK's Arbitration Act 1996

In the UK, for example, s.69(1) of the Arbitration Act 1996 provides for a limited possibility for appeal to a court on a question of law. However, the parties may exclude this possibility by agreement, e.g., by inserting a term to that effect into their arbitration agreement. The possibility of an appeal under s.69 of the Arbitration Act 1996 is also precluded by the decision of the parties not to require the arbitration panel to give reasons for its award.[51]

A party seeking to appeal on a question of law under s.69 must give notice to the other parties to the arbitration, as well as the arbitral tribunal. In addition, all the parties to the arbitration must agree with the decision to appeal.[52] If they do not all agree, the court may still give leave to appeal in any case,[53] but it may only do so if the

---

48   Art. 31(1) UNCITRAL Model Law; Art. 34(2) UNCITRAL Arbitration Rules.
49   Art. 31(2) UNCITRAL Model Law; Art. 34(3) UNCITRAL Model Rules; Art. 32(2) ICC Arbitration Rules.
50   Art. IV New York Convention.
51   S.69(1), Arbitration Act 1996.
52   S.69(2)(a), Arbitration Act 1996.
53   S.69(2)(b), Arbitration Act 1996.

criteria in s.69(3) are met. Thus, leave may only be given where (i) determining the question of law raised will substantially affect the rights of one or more of the parties; (ii) the question of law was one which the tribunal had been asked to determine; (iii) on the basis of the findings of fact made by the tribunal, the decision of the tribunal on the question is either "obviously wrong"[54] or "at least open to serious doubt"[55] where the question of law is of general public importance; and (iv) it would be "just and proper in the circumstances"[56] for the court to resolve this question, despite the parties' decision to take their dispute to arbitration. The outcome of the appeal may lead to a judgment which either confirms or varies the award, remits the award back to the tribunal so it can reconsider its decision in light of the court's decision regarding the question of law which was the subject of the appeal, or sets aside the award in whole or in part.[57] The court may give leave to appeal its judgment to the Court of Appeal, but only where the question of law is of general importance, or if there is another special reason why it should be appealed.[58]

Section 69 of the Arbitration Act 1996 tries to strike a balance between the general position that, once the parties have decided to take their dispute to arbitration, the court should have no involvement in the resolution of the substance of the dispute, and the significance of particular types of dispute for the development of the common law. English commercial law is predominantly common law based, and as such relies for its development on cases concerning unresolved or novel questions of law to reach the courts. An example to anyone familiar with English contract law is the inconsistency caused by the Court of Appeal's decision in *Williams v Roffey Bros*[59] for the doctrine of consideration. Whilst the Supreme Court in *Rock Advertising v MWB Business Exchange Centres*[60] may be criticised for not discussing this issue when that case presented the first opportunity for the Court to consider it, it is perhaps more striking that it took almost 30 years for this opportunity to arise in the first place. As arbitration will mean that a lower number of cases will reach the court, one important aspect of s.69 of the Arbitration Act is that it provides at least an occasional door for important points of law to reach the courts, even where the dispute itself is resolved through arbitration. It is important to bear in mind that s.69 generally requires the agreement of the parties before a court can hear an appeal in any case, and if one of the parties to the arbitration wishes to rule out this possibility altogether, it would push for an appropriate term to be inserted into the arbitration agreement.

54 S.69(3)(c)(i), Arbitration Act 1996.
55 S.69(3)(c)(ii), Arbitration Act 1996.
56 S.69(4), Arbitration Act 1996.
57 S.69(7), Arbitration Act 1996. An award may only be set aside if the court is satisfied that it would not be appropriate to remit the matter back to the tribunal.
58 S.69(8), Arbitration Act 1996.
59 *Williams v Roffey Bros & Nicholls (Contractors) Ltd* [1989] EWCA Civ 5, [1991] 1 QB 1.
60 *Rock Advertising Ltd v MWB Business Exchange Centres Ltd* [2018] UKSC 24.

8.2 Permitted grounds for challenging an award

Whilst it is not generally possible to challenge an award on its merits, Article 34 of the UNIDROIT Model Law provides a limited number of grounds on the basis of which an arbitration award may be challenged. The types of challenge which may be brought are limited to jurisdictional and procedural matters. It will become apparent that the grounds for challenging an award are essentially the same as the grounds on which the enforcement of an award under Article V of the New York Convention may be refused. A challenge must be brought before the designated court[61] of the *lex arbitri* within three months from the date on which the party challenging the award had received it.[62]

The first ground is that the arbitration agreement is invalid under the law which the parties have chosen as the applicable law, or, in the absence of such choice, under the law of the country where the award was made.[63] A challenge is also possible if the parties lacked capacity under the law applicable to them.[64] In either case, the basis for the challenge is that the entire arbitration lacked a basis as the arbitration agreement is ineffective.

The second ground is that the party against whom the award is invoked was not given the proper notice of the appointment of the arbitrator or of the arbitration proceedings, or did not have the opportunity to present its case.[65]

A third ground is, in essence, that the arbitration panel exceeded its jurisdiction by including matters not contemplated by the parties, not falling within the terms of submission to arbitration, or it decides issues beyond the scope of what the parties had agreed to submit to arbitration.[66] If matters going beyond the arbitration panel's jurisdiction can be separated from matters which it considered properly, then the award is only open to challenge with respect of matters beyond the panel's jurisdiction.[67]

A fourth ground for challenging an award is that the composition of the arbitral tribunal or the arbitration proceedings was not in accordance with the agreement of the parties, except where parties' agreement was in conflict with a mandatory provision of the national law on which the Model Law is based.[68] If there was no agreement by the parties on these aspects, and if the composition of the arbitral tribunal or the arbitration proceedings was not in accordance with the national rules given effect to the Model Law, then the award can also be challenged.

A fifth reason when an award can be challenged is that the subject-matter of the dispute was such that it could not be taken to arbitration under the law of the State where the arbitration was located.[69]

---

61 See Art. 6 UNCITRAL Model Law.
62 Art. 34(3) UNCITRAL Model Law.
63 Art. 34(2)(a)(i) UNCITRAL Model Law.
64 *Ibid.*
65 Art. 34(2)(a)(ii) UNCITRAL Model Law.
66 Art. 34(2)(a)(iii) UNCITRAL Model Law.
67 *Ibid.*
68 Art. 34(2)(a)(iv) UNCITRAL Model Law.
69 Art. 34(2)(b)(i) UNCITRAL Model Law.

The final reason is that the award is in conflict with the public policy of the State where the arbitration was located.[70]

These are the only grounds on which it is possible to challenge an award before the courts of the *lex arbitri* envisaged under the UNCITRAL Model Law. There is, of course, nothing that would prevent a State from adding additional grounds of challenge in their national law. However, as international commercial arbitration is a type of business on which there is considerable competition between different arbitration centres, States are likely to be very cautious in making it easier to challenge an award than permitted under the UNCITRAL Model Law.

9. Enforcing the award

After the award has been handed down, the parties are expected to abide by it and to take whatever action they are required to in order to comply with the award. Thus, if the arbitration award provides for a payment of damages by one party, then that party should do so. However, this may not always happen, and so it may become necessary for one of the parties to take steps to enforce the arbitration award. In most instances, this will mean having to apply to a court for the recognition and enforcement of the award in the State where the party against whom enforcement is sought has its place of business, or where the assets which are the subject of the arbitration award are located.

The recognition and enforcement of arbitral awards is greatly facilitated by the New York Convention. Article III of the Convention requires every Contracting State to recognise arbitral awards as binding, and further that it should enforce arbitral awards on the basis of whichever procedure applies in the State where enforcement is sought.[71] The fact that the New York Convention has been widely ratified, with more than 160 Contracting States, effectively ensures the global recognition and enforcement of arbitral awards. However, there is a possibility for a Contracting State to declare,[72] at the time of ratification, that it will apply the Convention only (i) in respect of arbitral awards which were made in another Contracting State (and therefore not recognise and enforce, at least not on the basis of the Convention, arbitral awards made in non-Contracting States);[73] and that it will (ii) limit the recognition and enforcement to awards arising from legal relationships considered as "commercial" under the law of that State.[74] In view of the large number of ratifications, a declaration

---

70 Art. 34(2)(b)(ii) UNCITRAL Model Law.
71 The conditions, fees and charges in respect of the enforcement of an international award should not be "substantially more onerous" than those applicable in respect of domestic arbitral awards: Art. III New York Convention.
72 Art. I(3) New York Convention.
73 A total of 79 Contracting States have made a declaration in respect of (i), including the United Kingdom. See UNCITRAL, *Status: Convention on the Recognition and Enforcement of Foreign Arbitral Awards*, https://uncitral.un.org/en/texts/arbitration/conventions/for eign_arbitral_awards/status2 [accessed March 2021].
74 A declaration in respect of (ii) has been made by 47 States.

to limit the recognition and enforcement to those handed down in another Contracting State will be of increasingly limited practical significance.

There is a strong presumption under the New York Convention in favour of recognition and enforcement. Consequently, it is not necessary for a party seeking enforcement to advance any reasons for seeking enforcement in its application for this. The party seeking the recognition and enforcement of an arbitral award is only required to provide an authenticated original or certified copy of the arbitral award *and* of the arbitration agreement.[75]

However, there are instances when a court *may* refuse to recognise and/or enforce an arbitral award. This is possible where the party *against whom* enforcement is sought provides proof to the court or competent authority of the State where recognition and enforcement is sought of the fact that one or more of the grounds listed in Article V of the New York Convention exists. Most of the grounds in Article V are identical to those listed in Art. 34 of the UNCITRAL Model Law as grounds for challenging an award, so the first to fourth grounds mentioned above are also grounds for refusing the recognition and enforcement of an award.[76] A further ground on which recognition and enforcement may be refused is where the award has either not yet become binding on the parties, or where the award has already been set aside or suspended by a court or competent authority in the State where, or under the law of which, the award was made.[77]

Furthermore, it was seen above that an award may be challenged before the courts of the *lex arbitri* where the issues referred to arbitration are not capable of being arbitrated under the law of that State, or where they are contrary to the public policy of that State. In the same vein, recognition and an enforcement may be refused where the issues of the arbitration are not arbitrable in, or against the public policy of, the State where recognition and enforcement is sought.[78] The upshot of this is that there are only limited grounds on which a court or competent authority in the State where recognition or enforcement is sought may refuse to do so. Moreover, the court or competent authority has a discretion, rather than an obligation, to refuse recognition or enforcement on the basis of one of these grounds. This is evident from the use of the word "may" in the opening words of Art. V. In other words, a court may recognise and enforce an award even where the party against whom enforcement is sought can make out one or more of the grounds listed in Art. V of the New York Convention.

10. Conclusion

International commercial arbitration is an important and widely used method of dispute resolution for international commercial transactions. It has some important advantages over court-based dispute resolution, both in terms of the process itself

---

75   Art. IV(1) New York Convention. If necessary, a certified translation of the award and the agreement into the official language of the State where enforcement is sought must be provided by the party applying for enforcement: Art. IV(2).
76   See Art. V(1)(a)–(d) New York Convention.
77   Art. V(1)(e) New York Convention.
78   Art. V(2) New York Convention.

and the possibility of resolving the substantive issues of the dispute by applying rules of law other than the applicable law. It also has the benefit of near-global backing as a result of the extensive ratification of the New York Convention. This has made it possible to resolve many disputes arising from international commercial transactions away from national courts and the confines of the law applicable to the transaction. However, this does not mean that the role of the courts in international commercial dispute resolution has become entirely redundant. Some types of disputes may not be amenable to arbitration and will have to be resolved before the courts. Moreover, where arbitration proceedings involve the application of national law rules, courts may still be involved in reviewing the correct application of this where the *lex arbitri* so permits.

12

INTERNATIONAL COMMERCIAL LAW AND THE DIGITAL ECONOMY

1. Introduction: digital technology and e-commerce

Since the turn of the millennium, there has been an exponential increase in electronic commerce around the globe, facilitated by rapid advances in digital technology. The spread of digital technology has helped commercial activity to develop in several ways: first, the process of contracting has become increasingly digitalised, with physical documents replaced by digital equivalents. In the early phases, digital technology was used for improved communications, e.g., through the use of e-mail. Documents could be drafted and transmitted more rapidly in digital form than physical, paper-based communications and documents could. Secondly, the internet has enabled established businesses as well as new entrants to develop an online presence and to broaden their reach and attract more customers. Thirdly, digital technology has facilitated the development of several specifically digital business models, such as online platforms or 3D-printing businesses. Digital technology now facilitates a high degree of automation in the conclusion and, at least to some extent, the performance of commercial contracts. Increasingly, devices are able to exchange data via the internet with one another (the "internet of things", or IoT). Today, the digital world is an integral part of commercial life, and it can be difficult to understand that this transformation only really began around three decades ago.

Invariably, the wide-spread utilisation of digital technology and the emergence of novel ways of engaging in commercial activity in the digital environment have prompted concerns about the suitability of existing legal regimes for the digital economy. Most legal regimes were adopted decades ago and have hardly been amended. They had not been designed with digital technology in mind, and therefore some existing rules may be difficult to apply to the digital environment. Even today, many contract law students are taught about

DOI: 10.4324/9781315692807-12

the curious postal rule,[1] developed as an exception to the general requirement that an acceptance of an offer must be communicated. This is despite the fact that e-mail and other digital communication methods have displaced the use of the postal service considerably.

Compared to traditional, paper-based, methods of communication, there are three key features of digital means of communication. The first is that digital communication is usually near-instantaneous. An e-mail can reach its designated recipients in a few seconds. Secondly, because digital communications and digital documents (and, increasingly digital assets) are not physical or tangible, the *dematerialisation* of communications and documents can raise difficult questions about relying on existing legal regimes developed in the non-digital era. A third characteristic is *delocalisation*, i.e., the shift from needing fixed premises to conduct many activities to having virtual offices and the ability to conduct commercial negotiations from anywhere in the world.

Assessing the suitability of existing legal regimes for the digital economy is an on-going challenge. As new ways of conducting commercial activities in the digital environment emerge and are adopted, and new digital business models take hold, it will be necessary to test existing legal regimes for their ability to facilitate and guide these developments. In some instances, it may be that the revolutionary impact of a particular digital development on commercial practice is significant, but that existing legal regimes are still able to cover the legal issues associated with such a development, perhaps with the aid of interpretative guidance which clarifies how the law applies to the digital context. Where this is not possible, or where this provides an insufficient legal framework, existing regimes might need to be adapted. This could be achieved through minor reforms, such as re-wording existing provisions to make them more readily applicable in the digital context, providing additional provisions which set out how the requirements of existing legal regimes could be met by digital equivalents, or through the adoption of supplementary rules. Sometimes, however, more significant changes will be needed, such as the introduction of new measures to provide a new legal regime for digital business models. In some instances, these could be developed analogously to existing regimes, but in others, wholly new legal regimes might be needed. There is no easy way of identifying what sort of changes to the law, if any, will be required to respond to digital developments. However, most lawyers will instinctively tend to remain closely attached to existing legal regimes and will attempt to push these as far as possible before countenancing more radical changes to the law. Reliance on existing regimes has the benefit of familiarity, and it also promotes coherence and consistency in the way the law deals with digital developments. Provided that a sufficient degree of legal certainty can be assured, there would seem to be little reason for moving too far from existing legal regimes.

This chapter will primarily provide an overview of the extent to which initiatives in the field of International Commercial Law have been adopted in response to the rise of the digital economy, and to highlight where further challenges might arise in the

---

1   *Adam v Lindsell* [1818]) 106 ER 250. On its history, see S. Gardner, "Trashing with Trollope: a deconstruction of the postal rules" (1992) 12 *Oxford Journal of Legal Studies* 170.

near future. It will be seen that there is hitherto only a limited dimension to International Commercial Law in this regard.

2. UNCITRAL Model Laws

2.1 UNCITRAL Model Law on Electronic Commerce 1996

The UNCITRAL Model Law on Electronic Commerce ("E-Commerce Model Law") was adopted at a point in time when wide-spread e-commerce was only about to take off. At that time, few countries had legislation which addressed the then novel issues which electronic contracting and e-commerce raised. However, the genesis of the E-Commerce Model Law goes back some time. Work on legal issues regarding electronic data interchange and automated data processing, addressing what were much more rudimentary means of exchanging information between businesses by electronic means,[2] had started as far back as 1984. This had focused primarily on electronic communications and did not yet envisage more advanced uses of e-commerce such as online transactions conducted via websites, let alone the digital business models which have become established more recently. Despite this, the E-Commerce Model Law came at a crucial point in time, with the internet having just been made widely available.[3] The primary objective of the E-Commerce Model Law was to "assist States … in enhancing their legislation governing the use of alternatives to paper-based methods of communication and storage of information and in formulating such legislation where none currently exists".[4] It deals with the use of data messages, a neutral term, defined as "information generated, sent, received or stored by electrical, optical or similar means including, but not limited to, electronic data interchange (EDI), electronic mail, telegram, telex or telecopy".[5] To a reader in the third decade of the 21st century, this definition sounds almost quaint, but it reflects the fact that the E-Commerce Model Law was adopted when e-commerce was very much in its infancy. Despite its seemingly grand title, much of the E-Commerce Model Law is concerned with the use and recognition of "data message" in the context of national laws which are still framed in terms of paper-based communication methods.

However, the fact that the E-Commerce Model Law was adopted in the early days of the evolution of digital commercial activity does not make it any less important. It is a clear example of how International Commercial Law can be used in a forward-looking manner to suggest legislative solutions to novel legal

---

2   For an overview of key developments, see J.K. Winn, "The Cape Town Convention's International Registry: decoding the secrets of success in global electronic commerce" (2012) 1 *Cape Town Convention Journal* 25.

3   Somewhat amusingly, the *Legislative Guide for Enactment* drafted by UNCITRAL put the word "internet" in all capital letters.

4   Resolution 51/62 *Model Law on Electronic Commerce adopted by the United Nations Commission on International Trade Law*, recital 6.

5   Art. 2(a)
    E-Commerce Model Law. Electronic Data Interchange (EDI) is defined in Art. 2(b) as "the electronic transfer from computer to computer of information using an agreed standard to structure the information".

challenges for international commerce, particularly at a time when action at the national level was limited or non-existent. Furthermore, despite its narrow focus on the legal recognition of electronic means of communication, it adopted an approach which continues to be used today, and also introduced definitions which form the basis of definitions in much more recent measures.

The approach of the E-Commerce Model Law referred to here is "functional equivalence". In essence, functional equivalence is an approach which seeks to provide a means of converting concepts developed for the physical world into the digital environment.[6] This approach is used by taking an aspect of the paper-based world, such as the fact that a document must be in "writing" or have a "signature", and then seeks to determine the hallmarks of "writing" or "signature". Having thus distilled the essential features of these notions, a basic rule is put forward that a data message which has these essential features will fulfil any legal requirement that something must be in "writing". Thus, Art. 6(1) of the E-Commerce Model law provides that "Where the law requires information to be in writing, that requirement is met by a data message if the information contained therein is accessible so as to be usable for subsequent reference." As can be seen, the essential feature of something being "in writing" is that it ensures that information which has been written down can be accessed afterwards, and referred to again at some future point. If it is possible to have a data message where the information it contains can similarly be accessed afterwards and referred to in the future, then the data message would be "in writing".

It should be noted that there is no particular technological means prescribed in the E-Commerce Model Law which would satisfy this requirement. This reflects a second fundamental principle of International Commercial Law rules relevant to the digital world: "technological neutrality". With technology evolving rapidly, the drafters of the E-Commerce Model Law avoided restricting its rules to particular technologies prevalent at the time of drafting, thereby ensuring that its rules can apply as technology evolves. A third fundamental principle is reflected in Art. 5 of the E-Commerce Model Law, which provides that "information shall not be denied legal effect, validity or enforceability solely on the grounds that it is in the form of a data message". This is a "non-discrimination" principle, i.e., it should not be permitted to discriminate between non-electronic and electronic communication methods when it comes to questions of validity or enforceability. As such, it seeks to ensure parity between both methods of communication.

For the purposes of this chapter, it is not necessary to provide a detailed analysis of all the provisions of the E-Commerce Model Law, not least because many of its provisions were developed and included in the UN Convention on the Use of Electronic Communications in International Contracts 2005, discussed below. A broad outline of what the E-Commerce Model law dealt with therefore suffices. Chapter 1 contains a number of general provisions, in particular a short list of definitions, as well as an Article on the rules of interpretation which is an adaptation of the standard provision used in most International Commercial Law conventions for a Model Law. This adaptation removes references to international

---

6   For a critique, see D. Harvey, *Collisions in the Digital Paradigm* (Hart, 2017), pp.55–63.

trade and to private international law because a Model Law takes effect as primary national law.

Chapter 2 deals with the application of existing legal requirements to data messages. It covers the legal recognition of data messages (Art. 5 – see above), and, in addition to how to determine whether a data message is functionally equivalent to something that has to be "in writing", there are provisions on the functional equivalent of a signature (Art. 7) and of an "original" (Art. 8). The criteria for assessing whether a data message has been signed by a person requires that

> (a) a method is used to identify that person and to indicate that person's approval of the information contained in the data message; and (b) that method is as reliable as was appropriate for the purpose for which the data message was generated or communicated, in the light of all the circumstances, including any relevant agreement.[7]

The criteria by which functional equivalence is to be established are set out in (a), whereas (b) clarifies the required level of reliability of the method used.

Other provisions in this chapter deal with the admissibility of data messages in legal proceedings and the evidential weight of these, requiring that admissibility is not denied solely because of the fact that information is contained in a data message (Art. 9). Article 10 deals with the functionally equivalent requirements in respect of the retention of data messages. In 1998, a new provision was added to the E-Commerce Model Law to address an area of uncertainty, which is the incorporation of information by a reference in a data message. Article 5*bis* states that information cannot be denied a legal effect, validity or enforceability just because it is not contained in a data message, but the data message merely includes a reference to that information (which can be found and accessed elsewhere).[8]

Chapter 3 then deals with aspects regarding the communication of data messages. Article 11 confirms that data messages may be used in the process of contract formation, and a "declaration of will" cannot be denied legal effect purely because it is contained in a data message (Art. 12). Article 13 tackles the attribution of data messages to a particular person. Article 14 deals with the acknowledgment of receipt of a data message. Finally, Article 15 sets out how the time and place of both dispatch and receipt of a data message should be determined.[9]

It will be clear from this brief overview that the E-Commerce Model Law is primarily concerned with clearing the way for the use of electronic communication methods in the formation and performance of commercial contracts. Crucially, it does so on the basis of existing legal regimes developed for the non–electronic world and provides the rules deemed necessary to ensure that it is possible to do in the digital environment what can already be done in the physical world. It does not include any

---

7   Art. 7 E-Commerce Model Law.
8   The *Guide to Enactment* refers to URLs as a method of reference, in particular: see para. 46–4.
9   There is also a separate part dealing with particular concerns regarding the carriage of goods (Art. 16) and transport documents (Art. 17).

new legal rules which are specific to digital contracts. This suggests that the E-Commerce Model Law also set the fundamental direction for any future initiatives on e-commerce or the digital economy, which is to retain and apply existing legal regimes in the digital context with only essential modifications. As noted earlier, this has the benefit of maintaining coherence, familiarity and continuity in the law, although it also presupposes that the digital environment does not raise altogether novel issues which might require more substantive intervention.[10]

Over the years since its adoption, the Model Law has been widely utilised, with legislation adopting the Model Law, or at least taking it as a template for national legislation, adopted in 74 countries, and a total of 153 jurisdictions.[11] However, there are only a few EU countries among the many countries which have adopted legislation based on the Model Law, but the EU adopted its own Directive on E-Commerce in 2000,[12] which covers similar issues.

2.2 UNCITRAL Model Law on Electronic Signatures 2001

The E-signatures Model Law, adopted in 2001, focuses specifically on the use of electronic signatures for commercial activities. The E-Commerce Model Law (Art. 7) had already suggested how to determine the functional equivalent to a physical signature in the electronic environment. As specific technological means developed which sought to create a digital type of signature using new encryption technology, the E-signatures Model Law was adopted to provide a set of rules on the use of such signatures. The key objective of this Model Law is to reduce the uncertainty regarding the legal effectiveness of electronic authentication technologies which were being used increasingly more widely at the time of its adoption. It is designed to build on the essential requirements set out in Art. 7 of the E-Commerce Model Law, in particular by offering "practical standards against which the technical reliability of electronic signatures may be measured".[13] The E-signatures Model Law does not prefer any particular type of technology; indeed, it provides for the equal treatment of different technological means by which the requirements regarding electronic signatures can be satisfied.[14]

An electronic signature is defined as "data in electronic form, affixed to or logically associated with, a data message, which may be used to identify the signatory in relation to the data message and to indicate the signatory's approval of the information contained

10   These ideas are developed more fully in C. Twigg-Flesner, *The Future of International Commercial Law in the Digital Economy* (forthcoming).
11   UNCITRAL, *UNCITRAL Model Law on Electronic Commerce 1996 – Status*. Available at https://uncitral.un.org/en/texts/ecommerce/modellaw/electronic_commerce/status [accessed December 2020].
12   Directive (EC) 2000/31 on certain legal aspects of information society services, in particular electronic commerce, in the Internal Market (2000) OJ L178/1.
13   UNCITRAL, *Guide to Enactment of the UNCITRAL Model Law on Electronic Signatures*, para. 4.
14   Art. 3 E-signatures Model Law.

in the data message".[15] The basic requirement for functional equivalence was established in Art. 7 of the E-Commerce Model Law (see above), to which Art. 6(3) of the E-signatures Model Law adds criteria for establishing whether an electronic signature is sufficiently reliable. This requires that (a) the electronic signature ("signature creation data") can be linked exclusively to the signatory; (b) the signature was under the signatory's exclusive control at the time of signing; (c) any changes to the signature after the time of signing can be detected; and (d) where the signature is used to confirm the integrity of the related information, any changes to that information after the time of signing can also be detected.[16] Whether a particular technology used satisfies these requirements may be determined by a nominated public or private authority, in accordance with international standards.[17] This would provide a degree of independent verification and provide certainty that particular technological means satisfy the requirements in respect of the reliability of an electronic signature.

Other provisions of the E-signatures Model Law deal with the way the signatory needs to ensure the correct use of the electronic signature,[18] the obligations of a certification service provider in respect of electronic signatures,[19] in particular the use of trustworthy systems, procedures and human resources,[20] and the recognition of certificates and electronic signatures from outside the particular jurisdiction.[21]

The E-signatures Model Law has had a lower take-up rate compared to the E-Commerce Model Law. To date, 33 countries have adopted legislation which is based on, or has at least been influenced by, the E-signatures Model Law.[22] None of these is an EU country. The EU had adopted a directive on electronic signatures in 1999,[23] but this has since been replaced by the so-called *eIDAS* Regulation.[24] At the time of writing, UNCITRAL Working Group IV was working on *Draft Provisions on the Cross-border Recognition of Identity Management and Trust Services*, which would be a development of the legal framework on identity management services and similar for the context of commercial and trade activities.[25]

---

15   Art. 2(a) E-signatures Model Law.
16   Art. 6(3) E-signatures Model Law.
17   Art. 7 E-signatures Model Law.
18   Art. 8 E-signatures Model Law.
19   Art. 9 E-signatures Model Law.
20   Art. 10 E-signatures Model Law.
21   Art. 12 E-signatures Model Law.
22   UNCITRAL, *UNCITRAL Model law on Electronic Signatures (2001) – Status*. Available at https://uncitral.un.org/en/texts/ecommerce/modellaw/electronic_signatures/status [accessed December 2020].
23   Directive (EC) 1999/93 on a Community Framework for Electronic Signatures (1999) OJ L13/12.
24   Regulation (EU) 910/2014 on electronic identification and trust services for electronic transactions in the internal market (2014) OJ L257/73.
25   Documents of the working group can be accessed on the UNCITRAL website at: https://uncitral.un.org/en/working_groups/4/electronic_commerce [accessed December 2020].

3. UN Convention on the Use of Electronic Communications in International Contracts

Following the adoption of its two model laws, UNCITRAL then prepared a Convention on the Use of Electronic Communications in International Contracts (CUECIC). Like the E-Commerce Model Law, the Convention does not seek to create a separate legal framework for contracting by electronic means, but instead to provide provisions which will enable the application of existing rules from other conventions when using electronic communication methods.

Following its adoption in 2005, 18 countries signed the Convention, of which six also subsequently ratified the Convention.[26] A further nine non-signatory countries have ratified the Convention,[27] making for a total of 15 Contracting States at the time of writing.[28] There are no EU countries among the Contracting States, nor have other countries such as China, the USA or Japan ratified the Convention (although both China and individual States within the USA have adopted legislation based on the E-Commerce Model Law). Despite the apparent low number of ratifications, it has been noted that many national laws are already broadly aligned with the Convention,[29] particularly where national legislation based on the E-Commerce Model Law was already in place.

The CUECIC takes the same approach as the E-Commerce Model Law and is based on the principles of non-discrimination between electronic communications and non-electronic communications,[30] technological neutrality and the use of functional equivalence of electronic communication methods. In addition, there are a small number of provisions introducing new, substantive, rules which reflect particular requirements of the electronic environment.

3.1 Scope of application

The CUECIC only applies to the use of electronic communications for the formation or performance of a contract,[31] so its reach is rather limited. The definition of "electronic communication" in Art. 4 CUECIC is somewhat long-winded. The basic definition in Art. 4(b) CUECIC is that an electronic communication is any communication made by means of data messages. "Communication", in turn, is broadly defined to mean "any statement, declaration, demand, notice or request, including an

---

26 Those six are: Honduras, Montenegro, Paraguay, Russia, Singapore and Sri Lanka.
27 Azerbaijan, Bahrain, Benin, Cameroon, Congo, Dominican Republic, Fiji, Kiribati and Mongolia.
28 See UNCITRAL, *Status: United Nations Convention on the Use of Electronic Communications in International Contracts (New York, 2005)* at https://uncitral.un.org/en/texts/ecommerce/conventions/electronic_communications/status [accessed December 2020].
29 J.B. Lambert, "The UN Convention on Electronic Contracting: back from the dead?" (2017) 25 *Michigan State International Law Review* 31.
30 Art. 8 CUECIC stipulates that a communication or a contract should not be denied validity merely because they are in the form of an electronic communication.
31 Art. 1(1) CUECIC.

offer and the acceptance of an offer",[32] which the parties make for the formation or performance of a contract. The definition of "data message" has been adapted from the E-Commerce Model Law as "information generated, sent, received or stored by electronic, magnetic, optical or similar means, including, but not limited to, electronic data interchange, electronic mail, telegram, telex or telecopy".[33] The inclusion of the final three examples might surprise a reader, but these were still common methods of communication at the time the CUECIC was adopted. The definition is not concerned with the method of transmission of a data message, not does it require communication of the information it contains and therefore also includes electronically generated records.[34]

Furthermore, as an International Commercial Law Convention, it only applies where the parties have their respective places of business in different States, although these need not be CUECIC Contracting States.[35] The CUECIC excludes from its scope a number of financial and securities transactions,[36] as well as certain commercial documents (bills of exchange, promissory notes, consignment notes, bills of lading, warehouse receipts or any other transferable document).[37]

3.2 Location of the parties

The CUECIC applies where the parties have their respective places of business in different States. In the CUECIC, a place of business is defined as "any place where a party maintains a non-transitory establishment to pursue an economic activity",[38] although not a specific location where a party might temporarily provide goods or services.

In the digital context, it may not always be readily apparent where a party's place of business is actually located. This may be particularly difficult if a party does not operate from fixed premises. Article 6 CUECIC addresses the difficulty of identifying where the parties are located, although it does not provide a complete solution. The primary criterion for determining where a party has its place of business[39] is the "location indicated by the party".[40] In other words, a basic disclosure by a party about the

---

32 Art. 4(a) CUECIC.
33 Art. 4(c) CUECIC. The inclusion of "similar means" is intended to provide a degree of future-proofing to cover communication techniques which were not yet in use at the time the CUECIC was adopted: UNCITRAL, *Explanatory Note by the UNCIRAL Secretariat on the United Nations Convention on the Use of Electronic Communications in International Contracts* ["*CUECIC Explanatory Note*"] (New York, 2007), p.38.
34 *CUECIC Explanatory Note*, p.39.
35 Note that a Contracting State may declare that it will only apply the CUECIC where the parties both have their places of business in Contracting States (Art. 19(1)(a) CUECIC).
36 Art. 2(1)(b) CUECIC.
37 Art. 2(2) CUECIC. See, however, the UNCITRAL Model Law on Electronic Transferable Records 2017.
38 Art. 4(h) CUECIC.
39 In the case of a natural person which does not have a place of business as such, the alternative criterion to be used is that party's habitual residence.
40 Art. 6(1) CUECIC.

location of its place of business is accepted as the indication of the party's location. This is subject to evidence to the contrary being provided by another party.

There is no fall-back rule if a party has not indicated the location of its place of business. However, if a party which has not indicated the location of its place of business has more than one place of business, then the CUECIC defaults to the place of business with the closest connection to the contract in light of the circumstances known at the time of concluding the contract.[41] It seems strange that there is no general criterion regarding a party's place of business where it only has one place of business but has not indicated its location, but that there is one in respect of a party with multiple places of business.

There are, however, a number of exclusionary provisions which are not determinative of the location of a party's place of business. Thus, the location of the equipment and information system technology used for the formation of the contract, or the location where it can be accessed, does not of itself determine the location of a party's place of business.[42] Furthermore, the use of a domain name or e-mail address which indicates a connection to a particular country (e.g., a ".co.uk" domain name or e-mail address) also does not give rise to a presumption that a party's place of business is located in that country.[43]

3.3 Functional equivalence

The E-Commerce Model Law was the first UNCITRAL measure which developed criteria for the functional equivalence of key form requirements, i.e., a requirement that a communication had to be in writing, signed or available in an original form. The CUECIC re-enacts these requirements at the international level. Whilst Art. 9 CUECIC does not mandate particular form requirements for communications or contracts of itself,[44] it does provide rules to determine how form requirements found elsewhere would be met by an electronic communication.

3.3.1 Writing

First, where there is a requirement that a communication or contract should be in writing, or where there are legal consequences as a result of something not being in writing, then an electronic communication will meet this requirement if the "information contained therein is accessible so as to be usable for subsequent reference".[45] The requirement that the information must be "accessible" entails that the information should be readable and interpretable, and, as it will be necessary to use some kind of software to access the information in the electronic

41 Art. 6(2) CUECIC.
42 Art. 6(4) CUECIC.
43 Art. 6(5) CUECIC.
44 Art. 9(1) CUECIC.
45 Art. 9(2) CUECIC.

communication, the software that is required for this purpose needs to be retained.[46] Furthermore, "usable" refers to use by both computers and humans.[47]

3.3.2 Signature

Secondly, for an electronic communication to comply with a legal requirement that a communication or contract must be signed, it will be necessary that a "method is used to identify the party and to indicate that party's intention in respect of the information contained in the electronic communication".[48] This requirement reflects the essential features of a physical signature for which a functionally equivalent electronic method is required, but does not specify any particular technology so as to ensure that the CUECIC remains technologically neutral on this point.[49] It is further required that this method is "as reliable as appropriate for the purpose for which electronic communication was generated or communicated in light of all the circumstances, including any relevant agreement".[50] Alternatively, if it can be proven that the method used did in fact identify the party and indicate that party's intention, then the method suffices (possibly with further evidence).[51] The key point here is that the method used in a particular case needs to be sufficient in the particular context; therefore, it is not envisaged that only the latest high-security technology would suffice.[52]

3.3.3 Original

Finally, there is the rather more difficult issue of finding a functionally equivalent electronic method for meeting a legal requirement that there is an original of a communication or a contract. An original of a document may be needed because it contains important information, the integrity of which is important, but because of the nature of electronic communications, which are easily replicated and multiplied, it becomes more challenging to ensure that the information in an electronic communication has not, somehow, been altered.

The essential features of an original, which have to be met by an electronic communication, are such that "there exists a reliable assurance as to the integrity of the information [an electronic communication] contains from the time it was first generated in its final form".[53] In turn, the criteria for determining "integrity" are that the information contained in the electronic communication "has remained complete and

---

46 *CUECIC Explanatory Note*, p.51.
47 *Ibid.*
48 Art. 9(3)(a) CUECIC. Paragraph 162 of the *CUECIC Explanatory Note* contains a long list of legal, technical and commercial factors which might be relevant for determining whether a particular method fulfils the requirements of Art. 9(3)(a).
49 *CUECIC Explanatory Note*, p.53.
50 Art. 9(3)(b) CUECIC.
51 Art. 9(3)(c) CEUCIC.
52 *CUECIC Explanatory Note*, p.56.
53 Art. 9(4)(a) CUECIC.

unaltered, apart from the addition of any endorsement and any change that arises in the normal course of communication, storage, and display".[54] The exemption of "endorsement" covers not only endorsements, but also notarisations, certifications and similar matters.[55] The reference to changes in "the normal course of communication, storage and display" refers to the technical additions or alterations which are made by the software to an electronic communication, e.g., the meta-data added to the header of an e-mail message (which is usually hidden from view).[56]

Furthermore, for the assurance as to the integrity of the information contained in an electronic communication to be *reliable*, the CUECIC provides that the standard of liability required will depend on both the purpose for which the information in question was generated and all the relevant circumstances.[57]

In addition to the functional equivalence requirements, Art. 9(4)(b) provides that where there is a requirement that information contained in the original is made available, the information has to be "capable of being displayed to the person to whom it is to be made available".

3.4 Time and place of dispatch and receipt

In addition to defining the criteria to determine whether something in the electronic environment is functionally equivalent to a feature of physical contracting, the CUECIC further addresses the difficult question of when and where an electronic communication is dispatched and received. For example, in the formation of a contract by means of electronic communications, it will be necessary to determine whether and when the acceptance of an offer has been received by the offeror in order to establish whether a contract has been concluded.[58] So if an electronic communication is sent to accept an offer, the question arises when that acceptance will become effective so as to create a binding obligation. There are several possibilities:[59] first, an electronic communication could be deemed to have been received as soon as it has been sent. This would be akin to the infamous postal rule of the common law, according to which an acceptance by letter is effective at the time of posting the letter.[60] However, that rule is an exception[61] to the general requirement that an acceptance must be received, and it has already been held that it would not be appropriate to instantaneous methods of communication,[62] including e-mails.[63] Secondly, an electronic communication could be treated as having been received once it has been transmitted to a server on which it can be accessed by the recipient, such as an e-mail server. This

---

54   Art. 9(5)(a) CUECIC.
55   *CUECIC Explanatory Note*, p.58.
56   *Ibid.*
57   Art. 9(5)(b) CUECIC.
58   Cf. Art. 18(2) CISG; see Chapter 4.
59   See also *CUECIC Explanatory Note*, p.59.
60   See *Adams v Lindsell* [1818] 106 ER 250; *Henthorn v Fraser* [1892] 2 Ch 27.
61   *Byrne v Van Tienhoven* [1880] 5 CPD 344.
62   *Entores v Miles Far East Corporation* [1955] 2 QB 327.
63   *Thomas v BPE Solicitors (a firm)* [2010] EWHC 306.

would mean that the question of whether an electronic communication has been received would be determined on the basis of whether the recipient *could* have read it, rather than whether the recipient actually did. A third possibility is that, in order to have been received, the electronic communication must have been accessed by the recipient, e.g., by opening an e-mail. In this instance, actual receipt of the electronic communication would be determinative. Finally, as a middle ground between the second and third possibility, an electronic communication might be deemed to have been received after it was accessible to the recipient and the recipient could have been expected to have accessed it. Each of these approaches, apart from the first one, would be a plausible way of resolving the question of when an electronic communication might have been received, and there is not necessarily an ideal solution. From the perspective of International Commercial Law, the key factor is that it is important to identify one solution to increase legal certainty. This is what Article 10 CUECIC seeks to provide. This provision deals with both the time of dispatch and the time of receipt of an electronic communication, as well as the place at which an electronic communication is dispatched and received. On the latter point, Art. 10(3) CUECIC provides a straightforward solution to the question of *where* an electronic communication has been dispatched and received. In short, the place of dispatch is the originator's (i.e., the sender's)[64] place of business, established in the way explained above. In the same vein, the place of receipt is that place of business where the addressee[65] has its place of business.[66] It therefore does not matter where the electronic infrastructures used by the originator and addressee respectively are located. By not linking the place of dispatch or receipt to the technology utilised by the parties, the CUECIC avoids complex, and potentially irresolvable, arguments about the precise place where a message was dispatched or received.

3.4.1 Time of dispatch

According to Art. 10(1) CUECIC, the time of dispatch of an electronic communication is the time when it leaves an information system under the control of the originator, or of the party who sent it on behalf of the originator. An "information system" is defined by Art. 4(f) CUECIC as a "system for generating, sending, receiving or otherwise processing data messages". This is a broad notion, which could cover infrastructure (servers or communication networks) as well as an e-mail client or similar.[67] The crucial point in time is therefore the moment when an electronic communication has left the originator's sphere of control, such as the moment at which an electronic message has left the originator's email server and has entered the process of transmission to the recipient's email server.

---

64 "Originator" is defined in Art. 4(d) CUECIC as "a party by whom, or on whose behalf, the electronic communication has been sent or generated prior to storage [...]".
65 "Addressee" is defined in Art. 4(e) CUECIC as "a party who is intended by the originator to receive the electronic communication [...]".
66 Art. 10(3) CUECIC.
67 *CUECIC Explanatory Note*, p.40.

This assumes that the sender of the electronic communication and its recipient are operating with different information systems. In some instances, both parties may be using the same information system (for example, an online intermediary platform). For such a situation, the CUECIC provides that the time of dispatch is the time at which the electronic communication has been received,[68] i.e., dispatch and receipt are treated as simultaneous occurrences.

3.4.2 Time of receipt

As explained above, when it comes to determining the time of receipt, there are a number of options, most of which are working on the basis of deemed receipt rather than actual receipt. The advantage of a rule based on deemed receipt is that it provides greater certainty to the originator that an electronic communication has been received as a matter of law, particularly where the recipient has unduly delayed accessing the communication.

The approach taken in the CUECIC is one of deemed receipt. Thus, Art. 10(2) CUECIC provides that the time of receipt of an electronic communication is "the time when it becomes capable of being retrieved by the addressee at an electronic address designated by the addressee".[69] The crucial point is that the electronic communication is *capable* of being retrieved, rather than that it has actually been retrieved. The point at which an electronic communication is presumed to be capable of being retrieved is the moment when it reaches the addressee's electronic address. This means that an electronic communication is deemed to have been received without the need for the addressee to have received notification of this. Thus, an e-mail is treated as received as soon as it has reached the recipient's email address, rather than the moment at which the e-mail is listed in the recipient's inbox; indeed, it is not necessary that the recipient's e-mail client is active in order for an e-mail to be deemed to have been received.

The electronic address in question must have been designated by the addressee, i.e., it must be the electronic address at which the addressee expects to receive electronic communications. For example, an offer made by e-mail may require the offeree to reply to that e-mail in order to accept the offer, in which case the designated electronic address would be the offeror's e-mail address used for sending the offer. However, it is possible that an electronic communication may have been sent to an electronic address which is different from the designated address. Take the example of an offer made by e-mail again, but assume that the offer specifies a different e-mail address to which an acceptance should be sent. This may occur, e.g., where an offer is sent by one employee of a company, but replies are sent to a central e-mail address for processing. If the offeree replies to the offer, then the electronic communication is not sent to a designated e-mail address. In such a situation, the offeree's reply could simply be treated as ineffective, i.e., as not having been received at all. However, this might not

---

68 Art. 10(1) CUECIC, final sentence.
69 This is so irrespective of whether the technical infrastructure and the addressee's place of business are in the same or in different locations: Art. 10(4) CUECIC.

be in accordance with commercial expectations. The CUECIC takes a different approach, and treats an electronic communication which has been sent to a different electronic address of the addressee as having been received when it is both capable of being retrieved at that address and once the addressee has become aware that the electronic communication has been sent to that address.[70] Thus, rather than simply treating an electronic communication sent to an electronic address other than the designated electronic address as not having been received at all, the CUECIC deems such a communication as having been received on condition that the addressee has knowledge of the fact that the electronic communication was sent to a different address. It seems that *actual* awareness by the addressee is required in this case.[71]

3.5 Provisions specific to the electronic environment

The CUECIC contains a number of provisions which deal with specific issues arising in the electronic environment which do not have a direct equivalent in the physical world. These relate, in particular, to electronic interfaces and automation of electronic communications and the resulting impact on contracts.

3.5.1 Websites as invitations to make offers

Early in their studies, contract law students will learn to grapple with the distinction between an *offer* and an *invitation to make an offer* (invitation to treat) and consider common situations where this distinction matters. In the non-electronic environment, the distinction has been considered in the context of goods displayed on the shelves in a shop,[72] in shop windows[73] and in respect of advertisements.[74] These are all situations where there is no specific offer directed at an individual person, but rather where goods are made available to persons generally, whether that be customers in a shop or persons reading an advertisement.

In the electronic environment, it is equally common to come across electronic communications which are not addressed to a specific recipient, but which are generally accessible. The most obvious example is a website which can be accessed by a large number of people; another example would be an electronic trading platform facilitating the automatic arrangement of transactions. As the CUECIC does not treat the electronic environment as something distinct but rather seeks to facilitate the application of existing legal regimes in the electronic environment, Art. 11 CUEIC deals with the distinction between offers and invitation to make offers so as to provide clarity and a greater degree of certainty for those involved in international commercial contracts concluded electronically. The general rule in Art. 11 CUECIC is that a proposal to conclude a contract made through an electronic communication which is generally accessible to anyone using

70 Art. 10(2) CUECIC, second sentence.
71 *CUECIC Explanatory Note*, p.64.
72 Cf. *Pharmaceutical Soc v Boots* [1952] 2 QB 795; [1953] 1 QB 401.
73 Cf. *Fisher v Bell* [1961] 1 QB 394.
74 Cf. *Partridge v Crittenden* [1968] 2 All ER 421.

information systems is classified as an invitation to make an offer. This applies irrespective of whether the electronic communication is passive or whether the electronic communication utilises an interactive application which allows others to place orders through such an information system. Although Art. 11 CUECIC is expressed in technologically neutral language and not limited to websites as such, the example of a website offers a useful illustration of this rule. Thus, a website which provides information about products sold by a business, which requires a prospective buyer to place an order, e.g., by sending a separate electronic communication, is presumed to be simply an invitation to make an offer. Similarly, a website which provides interactive features which allow for an order to be placed on that website (as is the case with most e-commerce websites) is presumed to be an invitation to make an offer.

The rule in Art. 11 CUECIC is, however, a general rule which can be displaced if the circumstances in which a particular electronic communication which is generally accessible show that the originator, i.e., the party who has made the proposal, intends to be bound if another party seeks to accept the originator's proposal.[75] This is intended to acknowledge the fact that there are business models which are based on the assumption that a generally accessible proposal is an offer which can be accepted by anyone responding to that offer. Where stocks are limited, acceptances may be based on the order in which they were received and on condition that sufficient stock is available.[76] Whilst the CUECIC does not seek to undermine such business models, they are regarded as an exception to the general principle that proposals made in generally accessible electronic communications should be treated as invitations to make offers only.

3.5.2 Using automated message systems

A second provision which could potentially take on great significance as certain digital business models evolve is Art. 12 CUECIC, which deals with contracts which are concluded through the use of automated message systems. This somewhat clunky phrase is defined in Art. 4(g) CUECIC as "a computer program or an electronic or other automated means used to initiate an action or respond to data messages or performances in whole or in part, without review or intervention by a natural person each time an action is initiated or a response is generated by the system". This somewhat complex definition seeks to cover an electronic system which can be used for the automatic negotiation and conclusion of a contract without the involvement of a human being on at least one side of the transaction.[77] It applies whenever a digital mechanism, such as an order-processing algorithm on a website, replaces a human being in deciding whether to enter into a contract. Such electronic systems are sometimes referred to as "electronic agents" to denote the use of electronic systems to act on behalf of human parties.[78] The one-sided use of automated message systems is

---

75 Art. 11 CUECIC, final part.
76 *CUECIC Explanatory Note*, p.68.
77 *Ibid.*, p.40.
78 See, e.g., A.J. Bellia Jr., "Contracting with electronic agents" (2001) 50 *Emory Law Journal* 1047.

well established; indeed, e-commerce websites generally work on this basis, as do many other services, such as cash-machines, ticket machines, etc. Moreover, the use of automated message systems by both parties to a contract is also becoming common. The upshot is that transactions can be arranged with little, or no, human involvement in the process. This invariably prompts two connected questions: first, should such transactions still be treated as contracts; and secondly, do such contracts satisfy the legal requirements for the formation of a contract? It may be thought that the absence of human oversight on one or both sides to a transaction might mean that such transactions are not contracts in the legal sense. However, Art. 12 CUECIC assumes that the lack of human involvement does not of its own affect the classification of such transactions as contracts, and the purpose of Art. 12 is to ensure the fact that contracts are concluded through the use of automated message systems by one or both parties to a transaction does not affect the validity or enforceability of such a transaction as a contract on the sole ground that there was no review or intervention by a natural person during the stages of arranging the transaction. As such, Art. 12 CUECIC is simply an enabling provision. However, it does not resolve more difficult questions which the use of automated message systems might pose, such as the attribution of the actions of an automated message system to a specific natural or legal person[79] – a question likely to become more complex as artificial intelligence algorithms become more advanced and able to adjust the criteria used in deciding whether or not to enter into a particular transaction. As such, Art. 12 CUECIC is essentially an instance of the general non-discrimination approach regarding the use of electronic technology in negotiating, concluding and performing contracts which treats transactions arranged through the use of automated message systems as no different from traditional contracts negotiated and concluded between natural persons.

3.5.3 Correction of input errors (Art. 14)

A provision related to the one-sided use of automated message systems, i.e., instances where only one party uses such a system for concluding a contract, is Art. 14 CUECIC on the correction of input errors. This may occur where a person ordering goods through a website inadvertently adds a greater quantity than required, or makes some other error when placing an order. In the context of contracts entered into as a result of negotiations conducted by natural persons, an error made by one person which has not been noticed before a contract has been concluded will usually mean that the contract is binding nonetheless, except to the extent that national doctrines regarding unilateral mistakes might operate.[80] If a party has a made a mistake during such negotiations, but the other party had no knowledge of the first party's real intent, then an objective assessment of the situation[81] will lead to the conclusion that the contract between the parties has been concluded despite the error made by one party.

---

79 *CUECIC Explanatory Note*, pp.69–70.
80 Cf. *Hartog v Colin and Shields* [1939] 3 ALL ER 566; *Chwee Kin Keong v Digilandmall.com Pte Ltd* [2005] 1 SLR 502.
81 Cf. Art. 8 CISG. See Chapter 4.

However, in the electronic environment, the likelihood of human error when placing an order, particularly when dealing with an automated message system, is higher.[82] For this reason, it was regarded as appropriate to introduce a specific rule for instances when a natural person exchanges an electronic communication with an automated message system, and the natural person makes an input error during this process. The scope of Art. 14 CUECIC is narrow: as well as only applying to input errors made by a natural person dealing with an automated message system, a further requirement is that the automated message system does not provide an opportunity to the natural person with an opportunity for correcting an input error. Thus, if the automated message system, having received the electronic communication from the natural person, displays the information contained in the communication and asks the natural person to confirm its accuracy or to make changes, then this would be an opportunity for correcting any input errors and so Art. 14 CUECIC would not apply. If the natural person fails to correct any input errors, having been given the opportunity to do so, then the person will be bound by the contract, subject to any rules of the applicable national law on mistake.[83]

Instead, Art. 14 CUECIC addresses a situation where the natural person communicating with an automated message system is not given the opportunity to correct any input errors. In such circumstances, the natural person, or the party on whose behalf the natural person was acting, can "withdraw the portion of the electronic communication in which the input error was made".[84] This is not the same as a full withdrawal of the electronic communication, although withdrawal of the erroneous element might well have the effect of rendering the entire electronic communication meaningless. Surprisingly, there is no scope for correcting the error; the only recourse for the natural person is to withdraw the element of the electronic communication containing the error. The *CUECIC Explanatory Note* states that this was a deliberate decision by UNCITRAL so as to avoid the creation of a specific rule for the electronic environment for which there was no parallel in the non-electronic environment; moreover, it might also be too costly for the provider of an automated message system to enable the correction of an input error after an electronic communication has been received, and also cause practical difficulties.[85] These might have been arguments which were persuasive at the time when the CUECIC was adopted but there are problems with these. First, Art. 14 CUECIC is based on the premise that the natural person does not have an opportunity to correct an input error, which means that the Article will not apply where such an opportunity exists. Therefore, the possibility for correcting an electronic communication was recognised in any case, so not requiring that such an opportunity exists and ruling out the possibility for subsequent correction where it does not seems difficult to justify. Secondly, the fact that UNCITRAL sought to avoid the introduction of a specific rule for the electronic environment at all

---

82 *CUECIC Explanatory Note*, p.73.
83 Art. 14(2) CUECIC makes it clear that national rules governing the consequences of any errors made by a party continue to apply.
84 Art. 14(1) CUECIC.
85 See *CUECIC Explanatory Note*, p.77.

costs fails to recognise that the electronic environment is not always just an equivalent means of what can be done in the physical world. Therefore, specific rules might be justified for some aspects of electronic contracting, and a right to correct an input error might have been the better solution here.

The case for a right to correct an input error, rather than merely withdrawing the erroneous aspect of an electronic communication, is further strengthened by the fact that Art. 14 CUECIC itself imposes strict conditions on the availability of the narrow right to withdraw the erroneous aspect. Thus, the person who has made the error, or the party on whose behalf that person was acting, has to notify the other party "as soon as possible after having learned of the error".[86] This means that prompt action is required once the error has been spotted, and the party who has made the error cannot raise this some time after the event. Furthermore, the right to withdraw the erroneous part of the electronic communication subject to the fact that the party who made the error, or on whose behalf it was made, has not received any "material benefit or value from the goods or services".[87] Consequently, once such a benefit or value has been received, the possibility of withdrawal is also lost.

Article 14 CUECIC is a difficult provision. It is a difficult balancing act between acknowledging that the electronic environment can have features with no immediate equivalent in the physical world and stopping short of developing specific substantive rules for the electronic environment. Perhaps it would have been preferable to accept that there are some features of the electronic environment which merit a different approach and to develop a more targeted solution.

3.6 Relationship with information duties and availability of contract terms

In addition to the various provisions discussed above, there are two provisions in the CUECIC which serve to clarify the relationship of the CUECIC with other rules of law, in case of an overlap between both. Thus, where a rule of law requires that a party has to disclose its identity, places of business or any other information, then the CUECIC does not affect the application of such rules. The same applies in respect of a rule of law which relieves a party which has made inaccurate, incomplete or false statements on such information from any legal consequences.[88] This approach, which defers to national law and other substantive conventions in respect of the existence of possible disclosure duties and consequences for non-compliance, was preferred to the introduction of a duty to disclose a party's place of business and related information in the CUECIC itself.[89]

A further instance relates to a situation where the contract was negotiated through the exchange of electronic communications and a rule of law requires that

---

86 Art. 14(1)(a) CUECIC.
87 Art. 14(1)(b) CUECIC.
88 Art. 7 CUECIC.
89 *CUECIC Explanatory Note*, p.45.

the electronic communications containing the terms of the contract have to be made available by one party to the other party of the contract. Article 13 CUECIC confirms that the Convention does not affect the application of such a rule, where it exists.

3.7 Concluding comments on the CUECIC

As the preceding discussion has shown, the CUECIC contains several provisions which seek to facilitate the use of electronic technology in the context of international commercial contracts. Its general approach is to supplement existing legal regimes with provisions which largely clarify the application of such existing regimes in the electronic environment, rather than to provide distinct rules applicable to the use of electronic communications in international commercial contracts. Indeed, the CUECIC is intended to be applied in connection with the formation or performance of contracts which fall within the scope of other existing conventions, such as the CISG, which are listed in Art. 20 CUECIC. The objective here is to ensure that electronic contracting is accommodated within the existing International Commercial Law regime without the need to modify earlier conventions. However, as seen, some CUECIC provisions are rather vague, and the interaction between the CUECIC and other conventions will not always be straightforward.

The CUECIC is significant in laying the foundations for the application of International Commercial Law rules in the digital environment. Relying on functional equivalence, technological neutrality and non-discrimination between electronic and non-electronic means of communication facilitates extending the reach of existing International Commercial Law conventions into the digital realm. This will provide greater legal certainty for commercial parties utilising digital technology for international commercial transactions, at least in the short term. However, as the digital economy evolves and distinct digital business models emerge, international commerce will increasingly move beyond doing physical things in an alternative digital manner. Existing legal regimes, developed for a different era and for different business models, may therefore increasingly be insufficiently suited to the digital economy. As a result, the approach underpinning the CUECIC may soon reach its limits, and new, targeted International Commercial Law rules may be required.

4. UNCITRAL Model Law on Electronic Transferable Records 2017

A more recent addition to UNCITRAL's texts on the digital economy is the Model Law on Electronic Transferable Records 2017 ("ETR Model Law"). This seeks to provide a legal regime specifically on electronic versions of common transferable documents used in commercial activity. A transferable document or instrument is defined in Art. 2 of the ETR Model Law as

a document or instrument issued on paper that entitles the holder to claim the performance of the obligation indicated in the document or instrument and to transfer the right to performance of the obligation indicated in the document or instrument through the transfer of that document or instrument.

The key feature of a transferable document/instrument is that such a document/instrument has certain rights attached to it which can be exercised by the person who has the document/instrument in their possession. Such a document/instrument is transferable, and whoever has the document/instrument in their possession at any particular point in time is the only person entitled to exercise the rights attached to the document/instrument. There are certain types of commercial documents which are recognised as transferable documents/instruments, such as "bills of exchange; cheques; promissory notes; consignment notes; bills of lading; warehouse receipts; insurance certificates; and air waybills".[90] The recognition of the documents/instruments as transferable documents, and therefore the transferability of the attached rights through the transfer of the document/instrument itself, is a matter for national law.

The commercial utility of transferable documents/instruments results from the fact that the rights attached to the document/instrument transfer with the document/instrument itself, and therefore no separate act of assignment or similar is required to effect the transfer: the mere fact that a person has the document/instrument in their possession suffices. As such documents/instruments have traditionally been paper based, the transfer of the paper document sufficed to transfer the attached rights.

However, with commercial activity increasingly taking full advantage of digital technology, a shift towards paperless transferable records may be desirable. That raises an immediate difficult: a paper-based transferable document/instrument will usually exist only as one original version, whereas an electronic document can easily be replicated. This makes it more difficult to establish whether an electronic document is an original. Moreover, in the case of transferable records, the fact that a person is in possession of the document/instrument, i.e., has physical custody of the same, is crucial. The translation of these features into the electronic context therefore poses particular challenges. The ETR Model Law seeks to offer a possible solution to facilitate the use of electronic versions of transferable documents/instruments in international commerce, although whether there will be a wide-spread shift towards the use of electronic transferable records will depend on the extent to which commercial parties can be confident that the electronic equivalents will fulfil the functions of the paper-based transferable document/instrument.[91]

4.1 Recognition of electronic transferable records

In the same way as the CUECIC, the ETR Model Law applies the principles of non-discrimination between electronic and paper documents,[92] functional

---

90 UNCITRAL, *Explanatory Note to the UNCITRAL Model Law on Electronic Transferable Records* ("*ETR Explanatory Note*"), p.21, referring to the exclusions from the CUECIC listed in Art. 2(2) CUECIC.

91 Cf. H.D. Gabriel, "The UNCITRAL Model Law on Electronic Transferable Records" (2019) 24 *Uniform Law Review* 261.

92 See Art. 7(1) ETR Model Law.

equivalence and technological neutrality in providing a regime for the utilisation of electronic transferable records. As well as following the template for functional equivalence in respect of "writing" and "signature" established in earlier UNCITRAL texts, the ETR Model Law additionally deals with the criteria for establishing whether an electronic record is functionally equivalent to a paper-based transferable document/instrument. Thus, Art. 10 ETR Model Law sets out two elements which have to be met by an electronic record in order to be treated as functionally equivalent to a paper-based transferable document/instrument. The first is that the electronic record contains the information which is required to be contained in a transferable document/instrument.[93] The second requirement is that a reliable method is used for the following purposes: first, to identify the electronic record as the electronic *transferable* record. Secondly, the reliable method must be used to make the electronic record "capable of being subject to control"[94] from the moment it is created until it ceases to have effect. Finally, the integrity of the electronic record must be maintained. Integrity is determined on the basis of whether the information contained in the electronic transferable record has remained complete and has not been altered.[95]

In addition to establishing how an electronic record can be functionally equivalent to a paper-based document/instrument, the ETR Model Law addresses the functional equivalent to "possession", which is a crucial feature of paper-based transferable documents/instruments. The notion of possession does not translate directly into the electronic environment. Instead, the ETR Model Law uses the notion of "control" over the electronic record as the functional equivalent to possession. Thus, Art. 11 ETR Model Law provides that a legal requirement as to possession of a transferable record/document is met by an electronic transferable record if a reliable method is used to establish that a person has exclusive control over the electronic transferable record, and that the person can be identified as the person which has control. Although "control" has not been defined further in the ETR Model Law, it seeks to reflect the fact that, just as a person in physical possession of a document/instrument can, in a practical sense, control what happens to that document/instrument, so a person in control of an electronic transferable record can determine what to do with that record. The "reliable method" required by Art. 11 ETR Model Law has to both allow a person to determine what happens to the electronic transferable record and allow for the identification of the person which is in control of that record. This means that another person who might have an electronic copy of the electronic transferable record, will not be in control (and therefore not be in possession) of the electronic transferable record and therefore unable to exercise the rights attached to the electronic transferable record.

A further feature of a transferable instrument/record is its transferability, which is effected by handing over the document/record to another person in the case of the

---

93 Art. 10(1)(a) ETR Model Law.
94 Art. 10(1)(b)(ii) ETR Model Law.
95 Art. 10(2) ETR Model Law. This does not affect the changes to the digital information used for communication, storage and display.

paper-based version. In the case of an electronic transferable record, this is achieved by transferring control over the electronic transferable record.[96]

4.2 Reliable method

The criteria for functional equivalence include the requirement that a "reliable method" is used. This requirement is also found in several other provisions of the ETR Model Law dealing with the indication of the time or place in relation to a transferable document/instrument,[97] amendments[98] and the replacement of a paper-based transferable document/instrument with an electronic transferable record or *vice versa*.[99] Article 12 ETR Model Law provides that the reliable method used must be as reliable as is appropriate in order to perform the function for which it is used. This is a rather vague notion, which is a consequence of the desire to keep the text of the ETR Model Law technologically neutral. However, Art. 12(a) ETR Model Law contains a list of relevant circumstances which may be taken into account in determining whether the method used is sufficiently reliable. Alternatively, the method used can be proven in fact to have performed that function, either by itself or together with additional evidence. In many instances, the criteria in Art. 12(a) will be of more relevance in determining whether a particular technical solution is sufficiently reliable. The circumstances listed in that provision are:

(i) Any operational rules relevant to the assessment of reliability;
(ii) The assurance of data integrity;
(iii) The ability to prevent unauthorized access to and use of the system;
(iv) The security of hardware and software;
(v) The regularity and extent of audit by an independent body;
(vi) The existence of a declaration by a supervisory body, an accreditation body or a voluntary scheme regarding the reliability of the method;
(vii) Any applicable industry standard.[100]

This is still fairly vague, but this is an invariable consequence of technological neutrality. However, there is recognition in this list that external validation, whether through a supervisor body or industry technical standards, will be relevant in fulfilling the requirement as to reliability for the purposes of the Model Law. The explicit inclusion of such criteria in the text of the Model Law is significant in that it recognises how legal requirements can interact with industry schemes and technical standards. In its *ETR Explanatory Note*, UNCITRAL states that such industry standards should ideally be internationally recognised, and that, moreover, the use

---

96   Art. 11(2) ETR Model Law.
97   Art. 13 ETR Model Law.
98   Art. 16 ETR Model Law
99   Arts. 17 and 18 ETR Model Law.
100 Art. 12(a) ETR Model Law.

of such standards could lead to the development of a common understanding of reliability.[101]

5. Future developments in International Commercial Law

This chapter shows that International Commercial Law is only gradually adjusting to the rise of the digital economy. Its primary concern has been to ensure that commercial parties are able to use electronic technology to do things they would otherwise do on the basis of physical documents, and most initiatives are confined to dealing with questions of functional equivalence so as to ensure the continued application of existing legal regimes, developed mostly for non-electronic contexts, in the digital realm. As an initial response to the digital economy, this is a sensible approach, but it is important that matters do not end there. Novel digital business models will increasingly fall outside the scope of existing legal regimes, unless these are stretched well beyond their intended scope of application. In due course, it will become necessary to consider which of the many new digital business models raise legal issues of specific concern from the perspective of International Commercial Law, and therefore require some sort of action at the international level. Thus far, the approach appears to be cautious, with few concrete initiatives on the agenda. Indeed, the only notable contribution by UNCITRAL has been the adoption of its *Notes on the Main Issues of Cloud Computing Contracts*.[102] These are notes directed at business parties, rather than national legislators, to guide them in negotiating contracts for cloud computing services by identifying many of the main issues which the parties should consider before entering into a contract for a cloud computing service. The *Notes* are essentially guidance notes to make the parties aware of the various issues they should address in a cloud computing contract. They are neither intended to provide guidance to legislators as to the legal issues of cloud computing, nor do the *Notes* contain model clauses or principles of cloud computing. They are therefore a very soft instrument, which will primarily enable business to approach cloud computing contracts more fully aware of the kinds of issues they need to consider.

However, at the time of writing, preparatory work is underway both at UNCITRAL and UNIDROIT for projects on aspects of the digital economy. UNCITRAL has identified a number of key areas for further exploration, including distributed ledger technology (blockchain), the use of algorithms in contracting (often referred to as "smart contracts", although not preferred by UNCITRAL), artificial intelligence and data transactions.[103] UNIDROIT has started work on digital assets and private law towards a guidance document, or principles, on digital assets.[104] Furthermore, the American Law Institute and the European Law Institute

---

101 *ETR Explanatory Note*, p.41.
102 UNICTRAL, *Notes on the Main Issues of Cloud Computing Contracts* (New York, 2019).
103 UNCITRAL, *Legal Issues Related to the Digital Economy – Note by the Secretariat*, A/CN.9/1012, 8 May 2020.
104 See https://www.unidroit.org/work-in-progress/digital-assets-and-private-law [accessed December 2020].

are collaborating on developing *Principles for a Data Economy*,[105] which, whilst not specifically designed for international commercial transactions, would undoubtedly have some impact in this context. Further developments are therefore on the horizon. It will be interesting to see whether, and how, these developments might change International Commercial Law, whether with regard to its substantive rules, in terms of the process of making International Commercial Law, or in respect of the types of instruments that will be utilised.

105 See https://www.europeanlawinstitute.eu/projects-publications/current-projects-feasibility-studies-and-other-activities/current-projects/data-economy/ [accessed December 2020].

INDEX

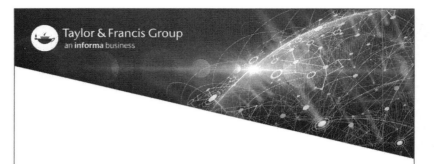

Made in the USA
Middletown, DE
04 May 2022

65264621R00163